The City of Ye in the Chinese Literary Landscape

Sinica Leidensia

Edited by

Barend J. ter Haar
Maghiel van Crevel

In co-operation with

P.K. Bol, D.R. Knechtges, E.S. Rawski,
W.L. Idema, H.T. Zurndorfer

VOLUME 145

The titles published in this series are listed at *brill.com/sinl*

The City of Ye in the Chinese Literary Landscape

By

Joanne Tsao

BRILL

LEIDEN | BOSTON

Cover illustration: Calligraphy by Timothy Wai Keung Chan 陳偉強.

The Library of Congress Cataloging-in-Publication Data is available online at http://catalog.loc.gov
LC record available at http://lccn.loc.gov/2019953029

Typeface for the Latin, Greek, and Cyrillic scripts: "Brill". See and download: brill.com/brill-typeface.

ISSN 0169-9563
ISBN 978-90-04-42013-7 (hardback)
ISBN 978-90-04-42014-4 (e-book)

Copyright 2020 by Koninklijke Brill NV, Leiden, The Netherlands.
Koninklijke Brill NV incorporates the imprints Brill, Brill Hes & De Graaf, Brill Nijhoff, Brill Rodopi, Brill
Sense, Hotei Publishing, mentis Verlag, Verlag Ferdinand Schöningh and Wilhelm Fink Verlag.
All rights reserved. No part of this publication may be reproduced, translated, stored in a retrieval system,
or transmitted in any form or by any means, electronic, mechanical, photocopying, recording or otherwise,
without prior written permission from the publisher.
Authorization to photocopy items for internal or personal use is granted by Koninklijke Brill NV provided
that the appropriate fees are paid directly to The Copyright Clearance Center, 222 Rosewood Drive,
Suite 910, Danvers, MA 01923, USA. Fees are subject to change.

This book is printed on acid-free paper and produced in a sustainable manner.

Contents

Acknowledgments VII
List of Table and of Figures VIII
A Note on Convention IX

Introduction 1

1 **The Construction and Development of Ye** 7
   1   Archeological Finds and Cultural Relics 7
   2   The City of Ye Prior to Cao Cao 11
   3   Cao Cao's City Plan and Built Environment 16
   4   The Post-Cao City of Ye 26

2 **Ye in Jian'an Literature** 45
   1   The Three Terraces of Ye as an Enduring Motif 45
   2   Ye's Gardens as a Motif of Ephemerality 57

3 **Ye the Dynastic Capital** 78
   1   The Representation of Ye by Jin Literati 79
   2   The Transformation of Ye in the Southern and Northern
       Dynasties 100

4 **Ye in the Mind of Poets from the Seventh Century and Beyond** 117
   1   Continuation of the Bronze Bird Trope 120
   2   The Tiles of Ye as Material Synecdoche 130

Conclusion 156

Postscript: Beyond the Song-Yuan Era 159

Works Cited 179
Index 201

Acknowledgments

This book is the fruit of my training in reading premodern Chinese poetry. I here express my deepest gratitude to Professor Robert Joe Cutter, who kindled my interest in the Early Medieval period in a graduate seminar on "Death" in 2010 and continued with his patient, critical, instruction on how to read Jian'an poetry. I am particularly indebted to Professor Paul W. Kroll, who read a preliminary manuscript and offered remarkable insights and suggestions. Many changes in my readings, mostly unnoted, reflect his discerning judgements about the language of medieval poetry. I sincerely appreciate the profundity of and the passion for literature that were expressed in Professor Kroll's detailed notes, as well as his support in finalizing the manuscript.

I owe a deep debt of gratitude to Professors Stephen Bokenkamp, Wilt Idema, Oh Young Kyun, and Wendy Swartz who, at various stages of writing and rewriting, all provided specific suggestions for preparing the manuscript. Professor Liu Yuan-ju also read and commented on my work at the outset. Two anonymous reviewers suggested additions and changes that are in the main incorporated. I would like to especially thank Dr. Liu Qian for locating hard-to-obtain materials from overseas. To Patricia Radder of Brill, I express my warm thanks for shepherding the book through to completion.

Finally, to Stephen H. West—partner, friend, mentor, and a light in both my personal and scholarly lives—thank you.

Table and Figures

Table

1   Poems on Bronze Bird Terrace in *Quan Tang shi*   123

Figures

1   Plan of Ye in *Shuijing zhu tu*   18
2   Ye as Constructed by Cao Cao   20
3   Wangcheng   22
4   Plan of Ye of the Eastern Wei and Northern Qi   40
5   The Ruins of Ye in Their Modern Setting   41
6   Print of a Bronze Bird tile inkstone, recto   131
7   Print of a Bronze Bird tile inkstone, verso   131

A Note on Convention

I follow standard accepted translations for architectural terms and, except for terms already popular in English like the Yellow River 黃河 and Bronze Bird Terrace 銅雀臺, I have chosen to leave all proper names in their original form, for example Wenchang Hall for *wenchang dian* 文昌殿, literally, "the Hall of Literary Brilliance." I also choose to leave Chinese measure words, article titles, and book titles in *pinyin* romanization. All translations are my own unless otherwise specified. Official titles are rendered according to Charles Hucker (Taipei: SMC Publishing Inc., 1995).

Introduction

The ancient city of Ye 鄴, located near modern day Linzhang 臨漳 county in Hebei 河北, is best known for two things: being the birthplace of the early third century Jian'an Literature (Jian'an *wenxue* 建安文學) and the powerbase of the military strongman and political figure Cao Cao 曹操 (155–220), who could handle both brush and sword.[1] Later, in the fourth century, Ye became the capital city of Shi Hu 石虎 (r. 334–349) of the Later Zhao 後趙 (319–349) and of Murong Jun 慕容儁 (349–360) of the Former Yan 前燕 (337–370). And, more than one hundred and fifty years later, Gao Huan 高歡 (496–547) placed Yuan Shanjian 元善見 (r. 534–550) on the throne in the capital city of Ye and established the Eastern Wei 東魏 (534–550). During the Eastern Wei, Ye was enlarged by an addition that was built against the southern city wall. The larger city continued on as the capital of the Northern Qi 北齊 (550–577), but the physical city met its end in 580 when the founding ruler of the Sui 隋 (581–619), Yang Jian 楊堅 (541–604), burned Ye to the ground.

As the birthplace of Jian'an literature and as the creation of Cao Cao, Ye has an important position in early medieval Chinese literature and history, demonstrated for instance in David Knechtges' expansive note on Ye in his translation of Zuo Si's 左思 (250–305) "Wei Capital Rhapsody" 魏都賦.[2] But Ye itself tends to be the focus of scholarship primarily in studies of city planning and society.[3] In addition, others have also looked at Ye in terms of its political or economic

---

1 The term Linzhang—"overlooking the Zhang"—first appeared in "*Fu* on Ascending the Terrace" (*Dengtai fu* 登台賦) attributed to Cao Zhi 曹植 (192–232). In it the poet voices, "I overlook the Zhang River's long course, / Gaze after at the burgeoning splendor of untold fruits" (臨漳水之長流兮，望園果之滋榮). See Robert Joe Cutter, "Cao Zhi's (192–232) Symposium Poems," *Chinese Literature: Essays, Articles, Reviews* (CLEAR) 6, no. 1/2 (1984): 2. The name of Ye was first changed to Linzhang in order to avoid a taboo on Emperor Min's 愍帝 name, Sima Ye 司馬鄴, on the *guihai* 癸亥 day of the eighth month in the second year of Jianxing 建興 reign [September 27, 313]. Fang Xuanling 房玄齡 (579–648) et al., *Jin shu* 晉書 (Beijing: Zhonghua shuju, 1974), 5.127.

2 See David R. Knechtges, trans., *Wen xuan, Or Selections of Refined Literature*, vol. 1, *Rhapsodies on Metropolises and Capitals* (Princeton: Princeton University Press, 1996), 1: 429–431. Scholars mentioned in this chapter are examples. Other scholars and their relative works will be listed in the following chapters.

3 On construction and planning, see Nancy Shatzman Steinhardt, *Chinese Imperial City Planning* (Honolulu: University of Hawai'i Press, 1990), 80–89 and Zhang Qinnan 張欽楠, *Zhongguo gudai jianzhu shi* 中國古代建築師 (Beijing: Sanlian shudian, 2008), 61–62; on social environment, see Zhan Zongyou 詹宗祐, "Wei Jin Nan Bei chao shiqi de Yecheng" 魏晉南北朝時期的鄴城 (MA thesis, Zhongguo wenhua daxue, 1990).

impact,[4] or discussed the ecology of the city and prospects for sustainability of the ancient site.[5] In addition to social science studies, others have assembled extant stories and anecdotes about Ye,[6] provided chronological accounts of historical incidents about the city,[7] or collated extant records on Ye.[8]

One of the underdeveloped, even neglected, aspects of the city is its place as a site of literary production, particularly after the Jian'an era. Ye is no less a victim to the processes—the vicissitudes of nature (floods), time (erosion), and human activity (war fires, etc.)—that have conspired to erase even the grandest cities of China. It has become a symbolic and literary site where "all temporal and mortal vanities inexorably wane and decline into inevitable desolation."[9] That being said, if one steps back a bit and looks at Ye from a wider point of view, it is clear that this city did not leave behind the obvious historical and cultural markers that other ancient capitals have, for example, Luoyang 洛陽, Chang'an 長安, or Kaifeng 開封. Ye differed from other major cities and capitals in medieval China not just because of its physical layout, but because of the way that it appeared in later historical and literary texts. As the birthplace of Jian'an literature, the city's early literary glory flourished and died with the Cao family. As a political site, it went through the hands of invaders from the steppes, and despite its claim to political significance, it was never associated with individual writers of the same quality that marked those of the South in the sixth century, being far eclipsed in the North by Luoyang. Still, Ye firmly secured its place in Chinese literature and, throughout history, it remained a productive site, generating writing about its former glory. The decaying palaces and ruined terraces, in particular the Bronze Bird Terrace, became an imagined space where one could ruminate on the rise and fall of greatness,

---

4 Liu Xinchang 劉心長 and Ma Zhongli 馬忠理, eds., *Yecheng ji Beichao shi yanjiu* 鄴城暨北朝史研究 (Shijiazhuang, Hebei: Hebei renmin chuban she, 1991); Chen Jinquan 陳金全, "Wei Jin Nan Bei chao shiqi Yecheng de diwei jiqi yingxiang yinsu yanjiu" 魏晉南北朝時期鄴城的地位及其影響因素研究 (MA thesis, Lanzhou daxue, 2011).

5 Liu Jia 劉佳, "Wei Jin Nan Bei chao shiqi Yecheng chengshi jianshe yu gengxin fazhan gouchen" 魏晉南北朝時期鄴城城市建設與更新發展鈎沈 (MA thesis, Hebei gongye daxue, 2007); Timothy R. Sedo, "Linzhang County and the Culturally Central Periphery in Mid-Ming China" (PhD diss., The University of British Columbia, 2010); Shi Changyou 史昌友, *Yecheng-Ye wenhua-Cao Cao* 鄴城－鄴文化－曹操 (Zhengzhou: Zhongzhou guji chuban she, 2012).

6 Hou Yansheng 侯延生, *Yecheng lishi gushi* 鄴城歷史故事 (Beijing: Guoji wenhua chuban gongsi, 1996).

7 Deng Zhongtang 鄧中堂, *Yedu chunqiu* 鄴都春秋 (Beijing: Zhongguo wenshi chuban she, 1999).

8 Xu Zuomin 許作民, *Yedu yizhi ji jiaozhu* 鄴都佚志輯校注 (Zhengzhou: Zhongzhou guji chuban she, 1996).

9 John Marney, "Cities in Chinese Literature," *Michigan Academician* 10, no. 2 (Fall 1977): 227–228.

INTRODUCTION

the brevity of human life, and the sadness of abandonment. While other major capitals had a number of literary and historical constellations, Cao Cao remained the lone star of Ye, outshining the other rulers who had taken up residence and had left their own traces within the city. To this very day, Cao Cao still "occupies" the real and imagined ruins of the Three Terraces and city. This singular intertwining of person and place has a force that cannot be matched by other cities. They may have had more luminaries or have been politically more important and culturally advanced; but none of them are tied in quite the same way to one person and personality. This is what set Ye apart from other cities and makes the memories and imagined scenes of Ye so monumental.

I intend to examine Ye as a site of literary production and ask how the city is represented through time. Cities, like humans, have a lifespan; and like humans, different parts of their lives are subject to different pressures from the environment at different times. Place can be considered as a localized part of a point at any moment in time, where it holds meaning in a certain way for the writer and can be used as a metaphor for comment on the writer's contemporary environment. This is especially true for China, where historical and cultural allusions are used for political criticism or for making generalized or universal comments on the human condition. Political criticism is woven into a larger fabric of aesthetics; indeed, part of the value of a work is how well it uses aesthetic circumlocution to make a point pertinent to the political world. This is best exemplified by the phrase "to point at the mulberry tree and curse the sophora" (*zhi sang ma huai* 指桑罵槐). Likewise, allusions that are employed to set scenes (such as the terrace-scape discussed in chapter three) can also be used as a linguistic trope or as an image to evoke a condition that can have universal application. In each of these historical layers of then-contemporary usage, the city passes its life through history, changing over time as it is evoked or discussed by whoever uses it as a metaphorical space. But like human lives, the lives of cities are cumulative as well. As the trope of Ye moves through time it accumulates ever more complex dimensions of representation.

I consider the best way to examine the city of Ye as an evolving and sustaining literary motif is through the lens of Chinese polite literature, particularly poetry. Ho Cheung Wing 何祥榮 explains:

> In the Jian'an era, the city of Ye concentrated a group of literati who composed poetry and prose that helped bring Jian'an literature to its flourishing height. Afterwards, from the Western Jin to the Southern and Northern Dynasties, there were always poets who composed works related to the city of Ye. All these works could be called "poems and rhapsodies of Ye."

The producing of these texts continued until the Qing Dynasty. This long-lasting cultural phenomenon is worthy of study.

在建安時期，鄴城凝聚了一群文人賦詩寫文，促成建安文學的繁盛。此後自西晉至南北朝，不斷有詩人創作以鄴都為題，或與鄴都相關的詩賦，均可稱為鄴都詩賦。鄴都詩賦的創作一直綿延至清代，歷久不衰，是值得研究的文化現象.[10]

As Ho illustrates, the composition of poetry related to Ye continued well into the Qing (1616–1911). I have discovered more than two hundred poems (these include *shi*-poems 詩, *ci*-poems 詞, and *fu* 賦) related to the city of Ye, composed by poets of different tastes and abilities from the third to the early twentieth century. In the interest of space and cohesion, I have chosen to end at the point at which the literary tropes are set for Ye and become standardized forms in the literary repertoire. This also coincides with a burgeoning discourse about the last physical remnants of the city: the tiles from Bronze Bird Terrace that were shaped into inkstones from the late Tang onward. I use a deductive methodology, picking a certain number of poems from the literary corpus that are more pertinent to what I perceive as the major issues over time and more relevant in defining the ritualized tropes, and then letting them speak as the voice of the city. I provide a translation and more or less close reading of these pieces. This method hopefully demonstrates that the city of Ye remained alive far beyond its physical existence. It lived on as an imagined place that metaphorically reproduced and represented the significant acts that took place within its spaces.

I first look at the known physical space of the city of Ye as it is revealed through archeology and at the development of its history as represented in texts. This step provides a visual and textual background for the poetic works read in the remaining chapters. Thus, chapter one traces the historical background of Ye. It first introduces the archeological finds and cultural relics recovered from the physical cities (northern and southern) of Ye. It examines the city before Cao Cao's time, Cao Cao's creation of a new "imperial" capital city, and the fate of Ye after his death in 220. Chapter two examines poetic works that use Ye as a space of celebration. This chapter selects poems about the terraces and gardens of Ye that demonstrate how these places represent human accomplishments or are celebrated as sites that bring both pleasure and anxiety. During the Jian'an period, Cao Cao and his sons Cao Pi 曹丕 (187–226) and

---

10   Ho Cheung Wing, *Han Wei Liuchao Yedu shifu xilun* 漢魏六朝鄴都詩賦析論 (Hong Kong: The Jao Tsung-I Petite Ecole, 2009), 1.

INTRODUCTION

Cao Zhi 曹植 (192–232) led a group of literati in Ye. Their symposium poems celebrate both the natural beauty of Ye and, contrasted with that, the idea of *carpe diem*. Poems produced in this era, particularly those of the Cao brothers about their excursion with their father to the Bronze Bird Terrace, as well as about roaming with their friends in the city's parks and gardens, provide modern-day readers a vivid picture of the city's popular spots and illustrate a culture of the city of Ye at its zenith. Chapter three focuses on poems that show how the celebratory trope turned into lament after Cao Cao's death and the fall of Cao Wei 曹魏 (220–265). When Shi Hu took over Ye and made it his capital, some Jin literati still saw the city as a ruin. This chapter first examines two verses about ascending the Ye terrace by Lu Chen 盧諶 (285–351) and Lu Yun 陸雲 (262–303). Differing from the terrace verses written by the Cao family, Lu Chen's and Lu Yun's works reveal a dramatic sense of loss and disappointment with the past. The poems from this period, demonstrate that Cao Cao and the physical environment that he had constructed remained the topical focus— even though the city of Ye had a new owner and was rebuilt. Still, some writers, like Lu Yun, saw the ruins as a magnificent testament to failed power. The Bronze Bird Terrace also began to take on a different meaning. It is believed that Cao Cao, on his deathbed, made female performers offer sacrifices to him and play music toward his grave tumulus. Poems began to be written about the sorrow implicit in this dramatic moment. Not only could one question Cao's arrogance and disregard for the lives of these entertainers, the site itself morphed into an allusion of place that could be used to describe the sorrowful voice of any abandoned woman. The poems written use such uniform language and images that I have coined the term "terrace-scape" to refer to this potent allusion. Chapter four explores the "poetic traces" of Ye: how texts generated after the destruction of Ye by Yang Jian in 580 were influenced not by Ye itself, but by earlier writing about the city. While the sorrow represented by the terrace-scape in the Bronze Bird poems (many of these works are titled "Bronze Bird Performers" or "Bronze Bird Terrace") continued, poets from this time onward also took up a protracted controversy over the meaning of Cao Cao and his city. This chapter first examines verses on the theme of the Bronze Bird Terrace. Next, it switches to poems by poets about the last physical remnants of the city and the terrace: its roof tiles. While these roof tiles and the inkstones could be seen as objects over which one could poeticize (*yongwu* 詠物) in a retrospective contemplation of the past, for some writers they connected directly to the pain and destruction caused by Cao Cao. (One writer remarked that Cao should have been ripped apart by four chariots so that his shoulders and ankles would wind up in separate places.) Some have pointed out that the collection of these artifacts by dilettantes (*haoshi zhe* 好事者) was mere conspicuous consumption, while others have problematized the obsession with these roof tiles. Such a contrast bespeaks a continuing ambiguity about the historical judgement of Cao Cao while keeping his name closely tied to that place in that space of time.

The allusions, images, and metaphors of the imagined spaces of Ye had become near clichés by the end of the Yuan, yet, as I demonstrate in the Postscript, poems on Ye continued to be written well into the late Qing. This is good evidence to show that while the city was physically present for fewer than four hundred years, it had a continuing influence on the literature and literary life of China for the past two millennia.

CHAPTER 1

The Construction and Development of Ye

To adequately treat the literary tradition of the city of Ye, it is necessary to first investigate the physical history of the city based on textual remains and material artifacts. By first examining the archeological finds and cultural relics of Ye, it is possible to probe the development of Ye from the beginning to the early third century, to Cao Cao's 曹操 (155–220) role in designing and building the city, and examine the history of Ye until its extinction as a capital at the end of the sixth century.

1   Archeological Finds and Cultural Relics

In 1957, Chinese archeologists began their initial research at the site of ancient Ye and in 1988 the Ye area became recognized as a major historical and cultural site, one to be protected at the national level and opened to public. A decade later, in April of 1998, while working his land a farmer from Anyang 安陽, Xu Yuchao 徐玉超,[1] unearthed a grave-epitaph (a stone buried on top of the grave itself) of a certain Lu Qian 魯潛 (271–345).[2] Unlike most epitaphs that sketch the life of the deceased and recount their achievements, this particular stone says very little about the life of the person buried beneath it, but it does give a detailed record of the location of Lu's grave in respect to that of Cao Cao. The epitaph reads:

> The day *dingmao*, the first day of the eleventh month of the year of Jupiter's transit, *yisi*, the eleventh year of the Jianwu reign of the Zhao dynasty [December 12, 345]. The late Chief Minister of the Court of the Imperial Stud and Commandant-Escort to the Consorts of Imperial Princesses, Lu Qian of Zhao'an County of Bohai, whose byname was Shifu

---

1   "Xi gaoxue cun cunmin Xu Yuchao: Lu Qian muzhi shi wo juan de" 西高穴村村民徐玉超: 魯潛墓志是我捐的, *Xinhua Daily Telegraph* 新華每日電訊, September 3, 2010, sec. 4. <http://news.xinhuanet.com/mrdx/2010-09/03/content_14121770.htm> (accessed September 18, 2014).

2   There are few records of Lu Qian. An account in the *Jin shu* 晉書 records a Lu Qian, then Commandant of Jin, who rebelled and surrendered Xuchang 許昌 to Shi Le 石勒 (274–333), founder of Later Zhao 後趙 (319–351). See Fang Xuanling 房玄齡 (579–648) comp., *Jin shu* (Beijing: Zhonghua shuju, 1974), 105.2742.

© KONINKLIJKE BRILL NV, LEIDEN, 2020 | DOI:10.1163/9789004420144_003

and who was seventy-five years of age, died on the *wuzi* day—twenty-first of the ninth month [November 3, 345]. He was buried on the *guiyou* day, the seventh day [December 18, 345]. The tomb is located 1,420 double paces[3] westward from the Gaojue bridge path and then 170 double paces south of that path, then 43 double paces westward from the northwest corner of the mausoleum of the former Emperor Wu of Wei, then 250 double paces back north to the sacrificial terrace in front of the grave. [The tomb] was sited by Xie Jian of Shangdang, byname Zifeng [or Zitai]. The tomb goes down four *zhang* deep and the spirit path [that leads to the tomb] faces southward.

趙建武十一年。太歲在乙巳，十一月丁卯朔。故大仆卿附馬都尉，勃海趙安縣魯潛，年七十五，字世甫。以其年九月二十一戊子卒。七日癸酉葬。墓在高決橋陌西行一千四百二十步，南下去陌一百七十步，故魏武帝陵西北角，西行四十三步，北回至墓明堂二百五十步。上黨解建，字子奉（泰）所安。墓入四丈，神道南向.[4]

The exact location of Cao's tomb had always been a part of common lore, particularly to readers of Chinese fiction and drama, where the popular legend of Cao constructing seventy-two decoy tumuli (*qishier yizhong* 七十二疑塚) was a standard theme.[5] Even though some voiced reservations about the authenticity of this new find, the uncovering of Lu Qian's epitaph generated new excitement about the possibility of identifying Cao Cao's final resting place. Such a discovery had a direct bearing on Ye since the city has always been tightly connected to Cao Cao. In addition, as Liu Qingzhu 劉慶柱 points out in his discussion of Cao Cao's tomb, Gaoling 高陵,[6] "In ancient times 'tombs were

---

3   The Chinese *bu* is a double-pace (equal to approximately five feet).

4   The discovery and the authenticity of the epitaph itself are still at issue. See for example Li Min's 李旻 article, "Lu Qian muzhi de lishi jiedu: jian bo zaowei lun" 魯潛墓誌的歷史解讀: 兼駁造偽論, Fudan daxue chutu wenxian yu guwenzi yanjiu zhongxin 復旦大學出土文獻與古文字研究中心, August 30, 2010. <http://www.gwz.fudan.edu.cn/SrcShow.asp?Src_ID=1246>, (accessed September 18, 2014).

5   For recent discussions of this curiosity and fascination with Cao Cao's gravesites, see for example, Xu Zuosheng 徐作生, "Jianxiong sihou yi qiren: Cao Cao qishier yizhong tafang" 奸雄死後亦欺人: 曹操七十二疑塚踏訪, in *Zhongwai zhongda lishi zhi mi tukao* 中外重大歷史之謎圖考 (Beijing: Zhongguo shehui kexue chuban she, 2006), 191–239; He Yun'ao 賀雲翱 and Shan Weihua 單衛華, comps., *Cao Cao mu shijian quan jilu* 曹操墓事件全記錄 (Jinan, Shandong: Shandong huabao chuban she, 2010); and Henan sheng wenwu kaogu yanjiu suo 河南省文物考古研究所, comp., *Cao Cao gaoling kaogu faxian yu yanjiu* 曹操高陵考古發現與研究 (Beijing: Wenwu chuban she, 2010).

6   Cao Cao was buried at Gaoling, according to *San guo zhi* 三國志. See Chen Shou 陳壽 (233–297), *San guo zhi* (Beijing: Zhonghua shuju, 1959), 1.53.

THE CONSTRUCTION AND DEVELOPMENT OF YE

built like cities.' The recent discovery of Cao Cao's purported tomb has generated a great fervor that has also spilled over into archeological works on the city of Ye."[7] Over the years, archeological investigations at Ye have had two major foci: urban planning and material culture of the area.

In 2004, Xu Guangji 徐光冀 presented a report on the archeological findings at Ye that concluded that the site consisted only of the ruins of some broken city walls, parts of the Golden Tiger Terrace (Jinhu *tai* 金虎臺) and the southeast corner of the Bronze Bird Terrace (Tongque *tai* 銅雀臺). The Ice Well Terrace (Bingjing *tai* 冰井臺) and the rest of the city were all destroyed and inundated by sand and mud from the Zhang River 漳水. Xu Guangji also stated that he believes that the ancient city of Ye that was built by Duke Huan of Qi 齊桓公 (716–643 BCE) and governed by Ximen Bao 西門豹 (fl. 445–396 BCE) is not the site identified as Ye today. Rather, the ancient city should be near a town now called Jiangwu City 講武城, which is about five kilometers outside of Ye.[8] Other scholars, however, have complete faith not only that the currently designated site of Ye is the one that was begun by Duke Huan and Ximen Bao but also that Ye has been in the same location since earliest times.[9] Although this seems debatable if Ye followed the pattern of other major cities that were often rebuilt at different times.

The archeological discoveries at Ye have indeed provided a significant number of material objects for the study of religion, agriculture, economics, and daily life of the area—not only during the time of Cao Cao but also for the period up to the ninth century. On March 19, 2013, the Institute of Archeology of the Chinese Academy of Social Sciences and the Institute of Cultural Relics in Hebei jointly announced that the Ye archeological research team had unearthed nearly three thousand pieces of Buddhist sculpture in an area three kilometers east of the eastern ancient Ye city wall.[10] Zhu Yanshi 朱岩石, who heads the Ye site team, points out that this finding provides a great resource not only for scholars who study cultural exchange between central Asia and

---

7 He and Shan, *Cao Cao mu shijian quan jilu*, 350.

8 See Chen Jian 陳劍, "Ye cheng yizhi de kantan fajue yu yanjiu: Xu Guangji yanjiu yuan xueshu baogao hui jiyao" 鄴城遺址的勘探發掘與研究: 徐光冀研究員學術報告會紀要, *Sichuan wenwu* 四川文物, no. 1 (2005): 87–89.

9 See for example, Niu Runzhen 牛潤珍, "Qin Han Ye cheng gouchen" 秦漢鄴城鈎沈, *Jinyang xuekan* 晉陽學刊, no. 6 (2011): 111–15; and Hou Tingsheng 侯廷生, "Meiyou weizhi de gudu: Ye cheng de lishi yu wenhua diwei kaocha" 沒有位置的古都: 鄴城的歷史與文化地位考察, *Handan zhiye jishu xueyuan xuebao* 邯鄲職業技術學院學報, 16, no. 4 (2003): 12–16.

10 Yang Yang 楊陽, "Ye cheng chutu foxiang yi shi miefo yundong suo mai" 鄴城出土佛像疑是滅佛運動所埋, *Zhongguo shehui kexue bao* 中國社會科學報, March 21, 2012. <http://news.sina.com.cn/c/2012-03-21/163924152099.shtml>, (accessed October 3, 2019).

China but also for the religious history of the area and for the study of the development of material culture from the third to ninth centuries.[11]

In addition to huge numbers of Buddhist sculptures, archeologists have also excavated many burial sites around ancient Ye that date back to the Northern Dynasties 北朝 (ca. 439–589). Many of them are in the northwestern outskirts of the city. Li Meitian 李梅田 explains that the Ye area, like that of Luoyang 洛陽, holds a preponderance of Northern Dynasty burial tombs. More importantly perhaps than the actual number of artifacts are the high quality structures and paintings of the tombs that wonderfully reflect changes in social and institutional culture through history.[12] Lei Jianhong 雷建紅 concludes that the "Ye archeological project" is so important because the city holds a key to understanding the historical significance and actual form of ancient city planning, the patterns of traffic and communication, the use of water and irrigation systems, and the shape of military defense.[13]

In addition to urban design, other scholars also focus on the material culture found at Ye. In 1957, Yu Weichao 俞偉超 conducted a five-day research visit to the site and published his report in *Kaogu* in 1963. His report was the first to point out that a very large number of bricks and tiles still surround the Three Terraces. Some of them display the familiar rope pattern of bricks and tiles dating from the Warring States, Western Han, and Northern dynasties.[14] Also, Ye Xiaojun 葉驍軍 notes that Ye apparently was the first city to have used

---

11   Zhu Yanshi 朱岩石 and others, "Hebei Linzhang xian Ye cheng yizhi Bei Wuzhuang fojiao zaoxiang maicang keng de faxian yu fajue" 河北臨漳縣鄴城遺址北吳莊佛教造像埋藏坑的發現與發掘, *Kaogu* 考古, no. 4 (2012): 3–6.

12   Li Meitian 李梅田, "Cong Luoyang dao Ye cheng: Beichao mushi huaxiang ji xiangzheng yiyi de zhuanbian" 從洛陽到鄴城: 北朝墓室畫像及象徵意義的轉變, *Kaogu yu wenwu* 考古與文物, no. 2 (2006): 65–72. Also see Li's "Bei Qi muzang wenhua yinsu fenxi: yi Ye cheng, Jinyang wei zhongxin" 北齊墓葬文化因素分析: 以鄴城、晉陽為中心, *Zhongyuan wenwu* 中原文物, no. 4 (2004): 59–65; and Zhuang Chengheng 莊程恆, "Bei Qi Jinyang: Ye cheng diqu mushi bihua de sangzang zhuti jiqi kongjian yingjian: yi Bei Qi Xu Xianxiu mu wei zhongxin" 北齊晉陽: 鄴城地區墓室壁畫的喪葬主體及其空間營建: 以北齊徐顯秀墓為中心, *Meishu xuebao* 美術學報, no. 2 (2011): 23–32.

13   Lei Jianhong 雷建紅 comp., "Wei Jin Bei chao kaogu zongshu" 魏晉北朝考古綜述, in *Hebei kaogu zhongyao faxian* 河北考古重要發現 (1949–2009), ed. Hebei sheng wenwu yanjiu suo 河北省文物研究所 (Beijing: Kexue chuban she, 2009), 209. Also, in recent years, the archeological team at Ye has shared its findings in *Kaogu* 考古; see for example, "Hebei Linzhang xian Yecheng yizhi Dong Wei Bei Qi fosi taji de faxian yu fajue" 河北臨漳縣鄴城遺址東魏北齊佛寺塔基的發現與發掘, *Kaogu*, no. 10 (2003): 3–6; and "Hebei Linzhang xian Ye cheng yizhi Zhaopeng cheng Beichao fosi yizhi de kantan yu fajue" 河北臨漳縣鄴城遺址趙彭城北朝佛寺遺址的勘探與發掘, *Kaogu*, no. 7 (2010): 31–42,102–105.

14   Yu Weichao 俞偉超, "Ye cheng diaocha ji" 鄴城調查記, *Kaogu* 考古, no. 1 (1963): 15–25.

THE CONSTRUCTION AND DEVELOPMENT OF YE

bricks to build city walls, and Jiao Zhiqin 焦智勤 points out the tiles used in Ye are significant in revealing the historical periods of the city's development.[15]

The bricks and tiles found in Ye are known to history as "Ye *wa*" 鄴瓦 and are said to be extremely durable and thus very valuable. This was noted as early as the Song. Su Shi 蘇軾 (1037–1101) once wrote a poem in response to his brother Su Che's 蘇轍 (1039–1112) celebrating a new inkstone. Su Shi opens his poem with the couplet, "All the world competes to extol the durability of Ye tiles, / A single piece cannot be exchanged for a distribution of a hundred in gold" (舉世 爭誇鄴瓦堅, 一枚不換百金頒).[16]

2   The City of Ye Prior to Cao Cao

The early history of Ye is not well documented. Duke Huan of Qi is conventionally given credit for establishing Ye. In the "Xiaokuang" 小匡 section of the *Guanzi* 管子, it states:

> [Duke Huan] built Wulu [near modern day Puyang 濮陽, Henan], Zhongmou [near modern day Zhengzhou 鄭州, Henan], Ye, Ge [perhaps near modern day Runan 汝南, Henan or Yishui 沂水, Shandong 山東], and Muqiu [near modern day Renping 茌平, Shandong] in order to protect all the lands of Xia. It was how he demonstrated persuasive [power] to the central states.
>
> 築五鹿、中牟、鄴、蓋、與牡丘,以衛諸夏之地。所以示勸於中 國也.[17]

Since historical records of Ye only became substantial enough to provide information around the Warring States 戰國 period (ca. 475–221 BCE), our

---

15   Ye Xiaojun 葉驍軍, *Zhongguo ducheng fazhan shi* 中國都城發展史 (Xi'an: Shanxi Remin chuban she, 1988), 129; and Jiao Zhiqin 焦智勤, "Ye cheng wadang fenqi yanjiu" 鄴城 瓦當分期研究, *Yindu xuekan* 殷都學刊, no. 2 (2007): 43–54.

16   See Su Shi's poem, "Matching in Order the Rhymes of Ziyou's [Original Poem] on Wanting to Obtain a Piece of Chengni Ink-stone from Mount Li" ("Ciyun he Ziyou yude Lishan chengni yan" 次韻和子由欲得驪山澄泥硯) in Zeng Zaozhuang 曾棗莊 comp., *Su shi huiping* 蘇詩彙評 (Chengdu: Sichuan wenyi chuban she, 2000), 107; Wang Wengao 王文 誥 (b. 1764), ed., *Su Dongpo shiji* 蘇東坡詩集, proofread by Tang Yunzhi 唐云志 (Beijing: Zhuhai chubanshe, 1996), 185–186; and Wang Wengao, ed., *Su Shi shiji* 蘇軾詩集, proofread by Kong Fanli 孔凡禮 (Beijing: Zhonghua shuju, 1982), 5. 211–212.

17   Yin Zhizhang 尹知章 (ca. 669–718), ed., *Guanzi jiaozheng ershisi juan* 管子校正二十四 卷, in Xinbian Zhuzi jicheng 新編諸子集成 vol. 5 (Taipei: Shijie shuju, 1978), 8.128.

12   CHAPTER 1

knowledge about the conditions in the area of Ye at that time or any details of
the city Duke Huan built are scant. During the Warring States, Ye was part of
the territory of one of the so-called "seven major states," Wei 魏. Marquis Wen
of Wei 魏文侯 (r. 446–396 BCE) "appointed Ximen Bao to protect Ye, and the
Henei [area] came to be known for its good government" (任西門豹守鄴而河
內稱治).[18] As a local official, Ximen Bao faced a major problem in that the
same rivers that brought benefits to Ye also constantly flooded. The Zhang
River, in particular, was problematic since it often changed course. The famous
fable about how Ximen Bao dealt with the folk tradition of annually sacrificing
a young girl to the river god (*Hebo quqi* 河伯娶妻) was very possibly related to
his hydrological efforts to control the Zhang and the Yellow Rivers, the changing courses of which caused severe floods in the Ye area.[19]

It is believed that Ximen Bao excavated twelve ditches or canals along the
Zhang River to control the flood and provide for irrigation.[20] These twelve
ditches were later called the Twelve Ditches to Guide the Zhang (*Yin* Zhang
shier qu 引漳十二渠) or the Ditches of Ximen (Ximen *qu* 西門渠). Since each
ditch had its own weir to control the water flow, they were also called the
Twelve Weirs (*Shier yan* 十二堰). After Ximen Bao, another magistrate of Ye
during the Warring States period, Shi Qi 史起 (fl. ca. 300 BCE), continued to
improve the irrigation and regulate flooding. During the reign of king Xiang of
Wei 魏襄王 (r. 318–296 BCE), Shi Qi expanded the earlier hydraulic construction of Ximen Bao and brought more water from the Zhang River into the farm
fields.[21] A fragmentary early description of Ye, one of the "extremely rare sources for the material culture of early medieval China," provides invaluable information on Ye.[22] This is the *Yezhong ji* 鄴中記, a description of Ye attributed to
Lu Hui 陸翽 (fl. 317). The surviving text is a description of the city during the

---

18   Sima Qian 司馬遷 (145–ca. 86 BCE), *Shiji* 史記 (Beijing: Zhonghua shuju, 1959), 44.1839.

19   See the story of Ximen Bao and the river god in Sima, *Shiji*, 126.3211–3213. See also, for
        example, Whalen Lai, "Looking for Mr. Ho Po: Unmasking the River God of Ancient
        China," *History of Religions* 29, no. 4 (May 1990): 335–350; Alvin P. Cohen, "Coercing the
        Rain Deities in Ancient China," *History of Religions* 17, no. 3/4 (May 1978): 244–265; David
        Schaberg, "Travel, Geography, and the Imperial Imagination in Fifth-Century Athens
        and Han China," *Comparative Literature*, 51, no. 2 (Spring 1999): 173–175; Song Yanpeng
        宋燕鵬, "Ximen Bao xinyang: Zhonggu Yexia jumin de yige shenghuo neirong" 西門豹信
        仰: 中古鄴下居民的一個生活內容, *Handan zhiye jishu xueyuan xuebao* 邯鄲職業技
        術學院學報, 20, no. 4 (December, 2007): 7–11; and Timothy R. Sedo, "Linzhang County
        and the Culturally Central Periphery in Mid-Ming China" (PhD diss., University of British
        Columbia, 2010), 102–187.

20   Sima, *Shiji*, 29.1048 and 126.3211–13.

21   Sima, *Shiji*, 126.3213.

22   See Shing Müller, "Yezhong ji," in *Early Medieval Chinese Texts: A Bibliographical Guide*, ed.
        Cynthia Chennault and others (Berkeley: Institute of East Asian Studies, 2015), 442.

THE CONSTRUCTION AND DEVELOPMENT OF YE

Later Zhao 後趙 dynasty (319–351), particularly the reign of the notorious Shi Hu 石虎 (295–349), who was emperor for the last fifteen years of his life. An appendix to the text, by an unknown author, appears in early fifteenth century editions. In this appendix we find the following:

> During the time of marquis Wen of Wei, Ximen Bao was the magistrate of Ye. By a system of weirs, he drew in water from the Zhang River to irrigate Ye and thereby enriched the Henei area of Wei. Later, Shi Qi became the magistrate of Ye. [He used] the Twelve Ditches to Guide the Zhang to irrigate hundreds of *qing* of farmland in Wei. And Wei became richer and more substantial. Later, [people] stopped using the weir system, and the farmlands lay in waste. [Later Cao Cao] once more repaired [the irrigation system and named it] the Weirs of Heaven's Well. [He] channeled a small stream from the Zhang River, eighteen *li* west [of the city] in a small offshoot through the center [of the city] that flowed eastward and into southern part of Ye. [He] built twenty weirs within twenty *li*.[23]

> 當魏文侯時，西門豹為鄴令。堰引漳水溉鄴以富魏之河內。後史起為鄴令，引漳水十二渠。灌溉魏田數百頃。魏益豐實。後廢堰田荒。更修天井堰，引鄴城西面漳水十八里，中細流東注鄴城南。二十里中作二十堰.[24]

And Zuo Si 左思 (ca. 250–305) writes, "Ximen irrigated the area first; / Shi Qi watered it next" (西門溉其前, 史起灌其後).[25] By all accounts, then, Ximen Bao and Shi Qi laid a solid foundation for the development of the city of Ye. The

---

23 The two lines before the last are very ambiguous: they could also be read as "[He] led the Zhang River from west of the walls of Ye, and eighteen *li* of middling and smaller flows funneled to the south of the Ye city walls" (引鄴城西面漳水, 十八里中細流東注鄴城南). Also, since the passages that are incorporated into the appendix of the *Yezhong ji* are very fragmentary, clearly the last eight characters of the text seem to be taken from another source. There is some possibility that these lines may stem from the relevant passage in the *Shuijing zhu* 水經注, where it reads "[He] built twelve drainage ways within twenty *li*" (二十里中作二十墱). Li Daoyuan 酈道元 (d. 527), *Shuijing zhu*, ed. Chen Qiaoyi 陳橋驛 (Shanghai: Shanghai guji chuban she, 1990), 10.212.

24 The base text of the *Yezhong ji* is found in (*SKQS* ed.), 1a–13b. There is an older translation (which does not include the appendix) of the *Yezhong ji* in Edward H. Schafer, "The *Yeh Chung Chi*," *T'oung Pao* 76 (1990): 147–207; and a more precise one in Shing Müller, *Yezhong ji: Eine Quelle zur materiellen Kulture in der Stadt Ye im 4. Jahrhundert* (Stuttgart: Steiner, 1993). Müller's work is a superior translation and has a plethora of notes and illustrations pertinent to medieval grave culture and art history.

25 David R. Knechtges, trans., *Wen xuan, Or Selections of Refined Literature*, vol. 1, *Rhapsodies on Metropolises and Capitals* (Princeton: Princeton University Press, 1996), 1: 449; see Xiao

14   CHAPTER 1

hydraulic system not only regulated the floods and provided irrigation for farming, but more importantly it also improved the soil conditions of the Ye area. Studies show that the land around Ye had saline-alkaline soil (*yanjian tu* 鹽鹼土). Part of the irrigation practice known as "silting the fields" (*yutian* 淤田) helped improve the soil quality. Mud was drawn from rivers into farm fields to cover the salty soil. The hydraulic system diluted the salt content in the soil and as a result, people were able to grow lowland paddy rice (*shuidao* 水稻) in the Ye area.[26] A song dating from pre-Qin 秦 (221–207 BCE) times demonstrates the joy of the commoners of Ye at the agricultural productivity of the land.

"Song of the Locals of Ye" ("Yemin ge" 鄴民歌)

	鄴有賢令兮	Ye has a worthy magistrate—,
2	為史公	He is the noble Shi.
	決漳水兮	He breached the Zhang River—,
4	灌鄴旁	To irrigate the surroundings of Ye.
	終古舃鹵兮	Ended the old salty soil—
6	生稻梁	To produce rice and millet.[27]

At the fall of the Eastern Zhou 東周 (770–256 BCE), Ye became a township or a conventionally named county (*xian* 縣). During the battle between the states of Qin and Zhao 趙, the army of the future First Emperor of Qin 秦始皇 (r. 246–210 BCE), led by Wang Jian 王翦 (fl. 236 BCE), Huan Yi 桓齮 (d. 227 BCE), and Yang Duan 楊端 (fl. 236 BCE), joined forces to begin a campaign that would eventually take over Ye and nine other towns by the eleventh year of the emperor's reign (236 BCE).[28] Few contemporary scholars pay much attention to Ye of the Qin era, but Niu Runzhen 牛潤珍 has argued that Ye was an instrumental site in Qin's defeat of Zhao and eventual unification of China. Niu believes that in order to annex Zhao, Qin's army used the Zhang River as a route along which to advance. The Qin troops first moved along the river's south bank and

---

  Tong 蕭統 (501–31), *Wen xuan* 文選, comm. Li Shan 李善 (d. 689) (Beijing: Zhonghua shuju, 1977), 6.13b.

26 Yang Wenheng 楊文衡, "Turang dili" 土壤地理, in *Zhongguo gudai dili xue shi* 中國古代地理學史, ed. Zhongguo kexue yuan ziran kexue shi yanjiu suo dixueshi zu (Beijing: Kexue chuban she, 1984), 225–27.

27 The text of this song is in Lu Qinli's 逯欽立, ed., *Xian Qin Han Wei Jin Nanbeichao shi* 先秦漢魏晉南北朝詩 (Beijing: Zhonghua shuju chuban she, 1983), 1:18–19. Lu also indicates that in *Shi ji* 詩紀, Feng Weina 馮惟訥 (1513–1572) states that this work is also entitled "Song on the Henei Region of Wei" (Wei *henei ge* 魏河内歌) or "Song on the Zhang River" (Zhang *shui ge* 漳水歌).

28 Sima, *Shi ji*, 6.231.

THE CONSTRUCTION AND DEVELOPMENT OF YE

took over Ye. After settling Ye and occupying it as a military base, they continued to defeat other places on the south side and then moved to the north bank. The fact that the First Emperor was able to successfully take over Handan 邯鄲 (in the southwestern part of modern day Handan city in Hebei) in the fifteenth year of his reign (232 BCE) was, according to Niu, attributable to the unique location of his base at Ye.[29]

In the early Han 漢 (206 BCE–220 CE), Ye remained a county and was attached to the Wei Commandery 魏郡.[30] But by the end of Western Han 西漢 (206 BCE–9 CE), it had been elevated to be the chief prefectural city (*zhou* 州) and was headed by a regional governor. Ye escaped destruction when Dong Zhuo 董卓 (d. 192) moved Emperor Xian of Han 漢獻帝 (r. 189–220) to Chang'an 長安 (modern day Xi'an 西安) and razed the eastern capital Luoyang in the first year of the Chuping 初平 reign (190) in the last years of Eastern Han 東漢 (25–220).[31] Two years later, Dong Zhuo was killed and Li Jue 李傕 (d. 198) and Guo Si 郭汜 (d. 197) took over Chang'an, destroying most of what was left.[32] A well-known poem by Wang Can 王粲 (177–217) vividly describes the disorderly and chaotic times he witnessed in the capital city:

"Seven-fold Sorrows" ("Qi ai shi" 七哀詩)
(excerpt)

	西京亂無象	The Western Capital was in unparalleled turmoil,
2	豺虎方遘患	jackals and tigers were wreaking havoc.
	復棄中國去	So I abandoned the heartland and went away,
4	遠身適荊蠻	going to Jingman to be far off.[33]
	親戚對我悲	My kin faced me in sadness,
6	朋友相追攀	my friends went after me clinging.
	出門無所見	Going out of the gate, I saw nothing,
8	白骨蔽平原	just white bones covering the plain.[34]

---

29 Niu, "Qin Han Ye cheng gouchen," 111–115.

30 Ban Gu 班固 (32–92), *Han shu* 漢書 (Beijing: Zhonghua shuju, 1962), 28.1573.

31 See Chen, *San guo zhi*, 6.176.

32 Chen, *San guo zhi*, 6.179–81.

33 The character *man* in Jingman exhibits a slightly pejorative tone of "uncultured" for the Jing prefecture (Jing *zhou* 荊州) in the south, around the area of modern day Xiangyang 襄陽 of Hubei 湖北, where a long-standing friend of the Wang family—Liu Biao 劉表 (142–208)—was its governor at the time.

34 Lu, *Xian Qin Han Wei Jin Nan Bei chao shi*, 1:365. The English translation is from Stephen Owen, *The Making of Early Chinese Classical Poetry* (Cambridge, MA: Harvard University Asia Center, 2006), 35.

What the reader does not see in Wang Can's description is that, while the eastern and western capital cities—Luoyang and Chang'an—were burned down and destroyed, Ye simultaneously grew into an important city.

Ye had been the administrative center of Ji Prefecture (Jizhou 冀州, in modern day Hebei) from the fourth year of Zhongping 中平 (187) of Emperor Ling of Han 漢靈帝 (r. 168–189). In the second year of Chuping (191), Yuan Shao 袁紹 (d. 202) took Jizhou and occupied Ye, subsequently replacing Han Fu 韓馥 (141–191) as the local administrator. Yuan Shao died ten years later. Then, two of his sons, Yuan Tan 袁譚 (d. 205) and Yuan Shang 袁尚 (d. 207), fought over their father's territory. Eventually, in the ninth year of Jian'an 建安 reign (204), Cao Cao defeated both Yuan sons and captured Ye.[35]

3 Cao Cao's City Plan and Built Environment

Even though Ye did not suffer the same devastation and chaos at the end of the Eastern Han as Luoyang and Chang'an did, by the time Cao Cao took over Ye, the inner city had been destroyed—"within the city walls, all had completely collapsed" (chengzhong bengju 城中崩沮).[36] Cao Cao immediately began to rebuild Ye. Although he never actually proclaimed himself an emperor, he constructed this monumental city in the mold of an imperial capital. Cao Cao also recreated the hydraulic system, built the famous Three Terraces and palace complex, and designed a brand-new plan for the entire city.

After settling in, Cao first built the Xuanwu Reservoir (Xuanwu chi 玄武池) in the northwest of the city (see Figure 1) in the first month of the thirteenth year of Jian'an (208) to conduct naval exercises.[37] In 213, he began to repair the hydraulic system that had been sporadically used since the end of the Zhou. He reconstructed the Twelve Weirs and renamed them the Weirs of Heaven's Well (Tianjing yan 天井堰).[38] He also opened up waterways (gou 溝) near the

---

35 Regarding the battles involving Ye during the fall of the Eastern Han, see Chen, San guo zhi, 6.193–94, 202–06. See also the armed conflicts between Cao Cao and the Yuan Shao in chapters five to seven of Carl Leban, "Ts'ao Ts'ao and the Rise of Wei: The Early Years" (PhD diss., Columbia University, 1971), 187–381.

36 See Chen, San guo zhi, 1.25.

37 Chen, San guo zhi, 1.30. The reservoir was located in a park bearing the same name, the Xuanwu Park 玄武苑. Like many other constructions in Ye, Xuanwu reservoir was multifunctional. In addition to naval exercises, the reservoir was also used for boating and other activities: there were fishing bridges, fishing docks, groves of bamboos and bushes. See Li, Shuijing zhu, 9.205.

38 Then in the second year of the Tianping 天平 reign of Eastern Wei 東魏 [February 20, 535–February 9, 536], the Weirs of Heaven's Well were combined, rebuilt, and renamed as

THE CONSTRUCTION AND DEVELOPMENT OF YE

17

terraces at the northwest side of the city to draw water from the Zhang River into the city and then channel it to flow into to the Huan 洹 and Yellow Rivers that flowed to the south (see Figure 1).[39] In the *Shuijing zhu*, Li Daoyuan sums up the hydraulic systems that had been built in the area:

> Long ago, Marquis Wen of Wei made Ximen Bao the magistrate of Ye. [Ximen] guided the Zhang to irrigate and the locals of Ye relied on it. After that, King Xiang of Wei made Shi Qi the magistrate of Ye. Again, [Shi Qi] made weirs in the Zhang in order to irrigate the farm fields in Ye and they all became fertile soil. Locals praised this in songs. King Wu of Wei again dammed up the Zhang and made it windingly flow into the east and called it 'Weirs of Heaven's Well.' [He] built twelve drainage ways within twenty *li*. These drainage ways were three hundred double paces apart. He made them irrigate in conjunction and one source became twelve separate flows, and each had a sluice gate.

> 昔魏文侯以西門豹鄴令也。引漳以溉， 鄴民賴其用。其後至魏襄王以史起為鄴令，又堰漳水以灌鄴田。咸成沃壤，百姓歌之。魏武王又竭漳水。迴流東注，號天井堰。二十里中作十二墱，墱相去三百步。令互相灌注，一源分為十二流，皆懸水門.[40]

After Cao Cao solved the major issue—water—in Ye, in 210 he built the first of his iconic Three Terraces—the Bronze Bird Terrace.[41]

When Cao Cao became the Duke of Wei (Wei *gong* 魏公) in the eighteenth year of Jian'an (213),[42] he established a local court, which was "validated" by the Han court and allowed him to administer Ye and perform rituals there. In the winter of the same year, Cao Cao set up the Imperial Secretariat (*shangshu* 尚書), Palace Attendants (*shizhong* 侍中), and the Six Ministers (*liuqing* 六卿) for his court. In the city, he built the Wei ancestral temple and a second terrace, the Golden Tiger. Cao Cao did not build Ye primarily as a traditional ritual site to demonstrate imperial power. Rather, he seemed to construct it rationally to be a self-functioning city. It provided a secure control base that offered great

---

the Tianping Weirs 天平堰.

39 "In the ninth month [of the eighteenth year of Jian'an, October 3–31, 213] [Cao Cao] built the Golden Tiger Terrace and opened up trenches. [He] guided the Zhang into the White Waterway to connect to the Yellow River" (九月，作金虎臺。鑿渠引漳水入白溝以通河). Chen, *San guo zhi*, 1.42.

40 Li, *Shuijing zhu*, 10.211–212.

41 Chen, *San guo zhi*, 1.32.

42 Chen, *San guo zhi*, 1.37.

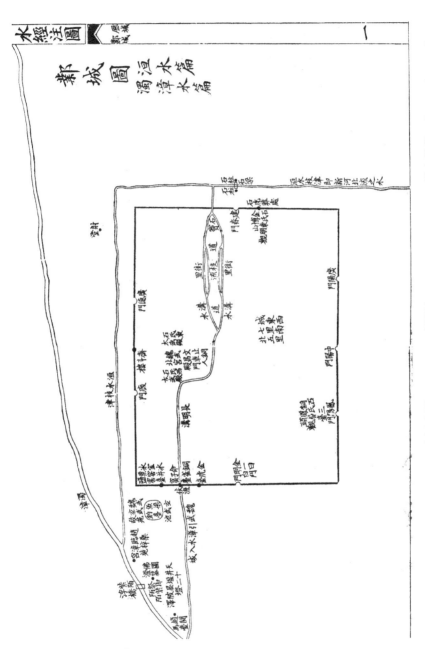

FIGURE 1 Plan of Ye in *Shuijing zhu tu* 水經注圖. Xie Chengren 謝承仁, comp., *Yang Shoujing ji* 楊守敬集, vol. 5. (Wuhan: Hubei renmin chuban she, 1988), 332.

THE CONSTRUCTION AND DEVELOPMENT OF YE

protection for his household and a place to store arms and provisions for warfare. There were military posts at the corners of the southern wards of Ye. Along both sides of the vertical main street from the palace complex that ran south to a central gate, he sited government offices and buildings. Also, the Three Terraces were high towers built on the northwest section of the city wall.[43] Extant texts describe them as "raised towering-like aloft, their height like mountains" (巍然崇舉, 其高若山),[44] they "standing in a row, rise rugged and tall" (列峙以崢嶸).[45] From a number of literary works in the chapters that will follow, a reader of today would be led to imagine that Cao Cao built them solely for the purpose of pursuing an extravagant lifestyle, characterized in part by luxurious banquets and the presence of beautiful women. But they were, in fact, also constructed for military and storage purposes and were well connected to other sections of the city by streets. Wang Shihan 汪師韓 (b. 1707) notes in the *Wenxuan lixue quanyu* 文選理學權輿 that the Three Terraces and ritual halls each had raised walkways that connected one to another (三臺與法殿皆閣道相通).[46] Archeological digs have also shown that there are cellars, vaults, and wells that appear to have been used as storage facilities for grain, water, salt, and fuel located nearby, as were armories and horse stables.[47]

Although Cao Cao only had the title of a duke at the time (213), he actually held power over other enfeoffed princes and kings. Emperor Xian engaged three of Cao Cao's daughters as honorable ladies (*guiren* 貴人), and he granted Cao Cao possession of a gold imperial seal of state (*jinxi* 金璽).[48] Also, the emperor accorded Cao Cao special treatment when Cao had an audience with him: there was no need for court officials to announce his name; Cao did not need to hurry forth when he approached the throne, and he could enter the hall carrying his sword and wearing his shoes (天子命公贊拜不名, 入朝不趨,

---

43   Even though it is said in *Yezhong ji* that both the Golden Tiger and Ice Well Terraces were built in the eighteenth year of Jian'an (Cf. Schafer, "The Yeh Chung Chi," 175.), the construction of Ice Well Terrace lacks any record of its date of construction. It is possible that ice wells were so common and such a functional space that the historical scribes or officials (*shiguan* 史官) simply made no record of it.

44   Li, *Shuijing zhu*, 10.212.

45   Knechtges, *Wen xuan*, 1:445. The text of the line is in Xiao, *Wen xuan*, 6.10b.

46   Cited in Ho Cheung Wing 何祥榮, *Han Wei Liuchao Yedu shifu xilun* 漢魏六朝鄴都詩賦析論 (Hong Kong: The Jao Tsung-I Petite Ecole, 2009), 12.

47   See for example, Ye, *Zhongguo ducheng fazhan shi*, 129; and Shen Youshun 申有順, "Ye cheng—woguo gudai chengshi fazhan shi shang de licheng bei" 鄴城: 我國古代城市發展史上的里程碑, *Handan zhiye jishu xueyuan xuebao* 邯鄲職業技術學院學報, 20, no. 2 (2007): 4–9.

48   Chen, *San guo zhi*, 1.42–43.

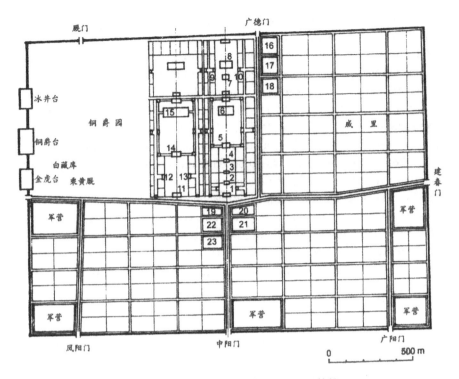

FIGURE 2   Ye as constructed by Cao Cao. From Zhang Qinnan 張欽楠, *Zhongguo gudai jianzhu shi* 中國古代建築師 (Beijing: Shenghuo, dushu, xinzhi Sanlian shudian, 2008), 62. Zhang Qinnan does not specify the numbered locations in this plan. In his book, *Zhongguo ducheng fazhan shi* 中國都城發展史 (Xi'an: Shanxi Renmin chuban she, 1988), 130, Ye Xiaojun 葉驍軍 has a similar figure of the plan of Ye that has some of the these locations marked. The figure shows #8 and #7 are the rear palace (*hougong* 後宮), #6 and #5 are Tingzheng Hall 聽政殿, #15 and #14 are Wenchang Hall 文昌殿, #12 is the drum tower (*gulou* 鼓樓), and #13 is the bell tower (*zhonglou* 鐘樓). The locations from #19 to #23 are not listed in Ye Xiaojun's figure, however, on the sides of the vertical street from the palace-city to Guangyang Gate, there are parallel locations marked as government offices (*yashu* 衙署).

劍履上殿).[49] The influence and prestige of Cao Cao were much higher than his official titles indicated. His plan for Ye surely reflected both this status and his desire to establish his own base of power.

As part of this display of power, Cao Cao constructed a palace complex in north central Ye (See Figure 2). Some, like Nancy Steinhardt, believe that in his

---

49   Chen, *San guo zhi*, 1.36.

THE CONSTRUCTION AND DEVELOPMENT OF YE

21

mind Cao Cao saw himself as the legitimate successor to the throne; since the palace complex he built in Ye "corresponded to the location of the palace area of Jiang in Eastern Zhou times."[50] Before Cao Cao's Ye, most capital cities were built in a shape similar to the character *huí* 回. They had single or double palace complexes near the center area demarcated by a wall, which in turn was in the center of the space defined by the city walls. As described in the *Kaogong ji* 考工記 in the case of the royal city of the Zhou period, the palace complex should be in the exact center of the nine-square gridded city—looking almost like the character *tóng* 囲 if the left vertical stroke were straight within the enclosure. The Son of Heaven would sit with his back to the north and face south, with "the ancestral temple on his left and the temple of the gods land and grain on his right, the market being in the northern part of the city while the court was in the south" (左祖右社面朝後市).[51] (See Figure 3)

As a departure from the standard 回-shaped city, Ye was the first urban administrative site to build the palace complex *against* the northern city wall, with a north-south axial street connecting it to the south gate.[52] The palace complex with the south-running main street thus looks more like the character *xiá* 囲. This north-south main street that connects the palace and the south gate became the prototype of the "imperial street" (*yujie* 御街)—a feature that marks all imperial cities after Ye.[53]

Historians of urban archeology also recognize that in Cao Cao's design there is a street connecting the Jinming Gate 金明門 to the west and the Jianchun Gate 建春門 to the east. This east-west axial road separated administrative space to the north from the commoners' space in the southern half of the city.[54] This design again is different from that specified in the *Kaogong ji*, in which the

---

50 Nancy Shatzman Steinhardt, *Chinese Imperial City Planning* (Honolulu: University of Hawai'i Press, 1990), 81.

51 Zheng Xuan 鄭玄 (127–200) and Jia Gongyan 賈公彥 (ca. 7–8 century), comm. and ann., *Zhouli zhushu* 周禮注疏, in *Shisan jing zhushu fu jiaokan ji* 十三經注疏附校勘記, ed. Ruan Yuan 阮元 (1764–1849), 8 vols., (Taipei: Yiwen yingshu guan, 1982), 3: 41.24b–25a.

52 Archeologists have detected several north-south axial streets connecting to an east-west main street just inside what would have been the south city wall. Their findings confirm that the widest street (seventeen meters) that goes to the central gate of the southern wall was the equivalent of the imperial street of a capital. See Cheng Yi 程義, "Shilun Ye beicheng de sheji sixiang, buju yu yingxiang" 試論鄴北城的設計思想、佈局與影響, *Xibei daxue xuebao* 西北大學學報 31, no. 1 (2001): 106–111.

53 For more information on the layout of the palace-city and official offices of Ye, see Guo Jiqiao 郭濟橋, "Cao Wei Ye cheng zhongyang guanshu buju chushi" 曹魏鄴城中央官署佈局初釋, *Yindu xuekan* 殷都學刊, no. 2 (2002): 34–38.

54 This street (still buried underground) has been test-probed by the archeologists and found to be twenty-one hundred meters long. See Cheng Yi, "Shilun Ye beicheng de sheji sixiang, buju yu yingsiang," 106–111.

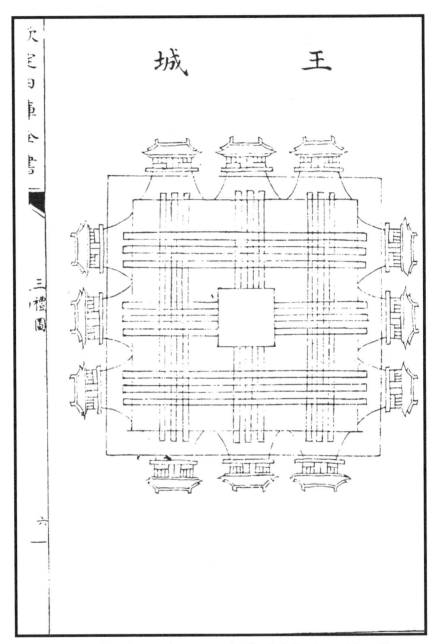

FIGURE 3 Wangcheng [*Henan zhi* as preserved in *Yongle dadian, juan* 9561], see Nancy Shatzman Steinhardt, *Chinese Imperial City Planning*, 34.

THE CONSTRUCTION AND DEVELOPMENT OF YE

commoner markets should be located in the northern part of (behind) the city [so the Son of Heaven could]: "Face the court, and (have his) back to the market; / Both market and court are one *fu*" (面朝後市, 市朝一夫).[55]

The imperial street ran from the city gate on the southern wall, Zhongyang Gate 中陽門, to the southern gate of the palace complex, made a bend to the east, and then proceeded north again along the eastern side of the palace wall, exiting through Guangde Gate 廣德門 in the northern wall (see Figure 2). When it made its eastern bend, it followed a short segment of the horizontal street that separated the administrative space from the commoners' space. This division also created another special feature of Cao Cao's Ye—it was the first major city in Chinese urban history to be neatly organized into four quadrants.[56] The northeastern quarter was called "relative's ward" (*qili* 戚里) and was the residential area for the Cao clan. The northwestern quadrant was "Bronze Bird Park" (*Tongque yuan* 銅雀園). Since it was located on the west side of the main palace hall, Wenchang Hall 文昌殿, it was also referred to as the Western Park (*Xi yuan* 西園).[57] It is here that the Cao family had held many banquets and produced the courtly feast poetry or "poetry for the lord's feast" (*Gongyan shi* 公燕詩).[58]

---

55   *Fu* 夫 is a square of one hundred *bu* 步 (double paces) to each side. Zheng, *Zhouli zhushu*, 41.25a.

56   Archeologists have detected several vertical streets connecting the horizontal main street to the south wall. In their findings, the one that goes to the center south gate is the widest, at about seventeen meters. See Cheng Yi, "Shilun Ye beicheng de sheji sixiang, buju yu yingxiang," 106–111.

57   In the Ming 明 (1368–1644) dynasty gazetteer, *Zhangde fu zhi* 彰德府志, Cui Xian 崔銑 (1478–1541) also lists other parks that Cao Cao built such as Fanglin 芳林 and Lingzhi 靈芝 (which once housed a cockfighting terrace). Cited in Ho, *On the Poems and Fu from the Han-Wei-Six Dynasties Related to the Capital Ye*, 15–16. This is an issue that will be addressed further in the following chapter.

58   This type of poem usually shares the same topic and was composed by literati who feasted together. As David Knechtges tells us:
   Gong yan is a type of poem composed for court feasts. These pieces were usually written by groups of poets for the host who was usually a ruler or a member of the ruling family. The earliest grouping of poems under this rubric is in the *Wen xuan*. The occasions for which such pieces were written include formal court banquets, excursion feasts (or picnics), and banquets held for the *shidian* 釋奠 or "school sacrifice" ceremony. Although scholars have traced the origins of *gong yan* poetry to the *Shi jing*, the form does not emerge until the late Han when members of the Cao family hosted banquets and outings at which participants composed poems in honor of the feast and the host. Scholars have included in the *gong yan* category poems composed for seasonal festivals such as the third day of the third month and the ninth day of the ninth month as well as certain group compositions of *yongwu* poems.
   See David R. Knechtges and Chang Taiping, *Ancient and Early Medieval Chinese Literature:*

Other than the physical construction of the city, Cao Cao also increased Ye's population and created an environment that became an intellectual and literary space. We know many literati and scholars came to join the Cao family in Ye, but Cao Cao also sought other worthy and talented people and brought them to his city and his government. Prior to building the Bronze Bird Terrace in the winter of 210, Cao Cao issued a decree in the spring. In it he said:

> From antiquity, has it ever been that a sovereign in receipt of the Mandate and in a time of restoration did not gain worthy and princely men together with whom to set the empire in order? And in gaining the worthy, how is a Prime Minister to be met with if one never goes out the village gate or alleyways? For the superior man does not seek the office.
>
> Today, when the empire has not yet been made secure, is an especially pressing time to seek the worthy. "To be a Venerable for Chao and Wei, Meng Kung-ch'o is more than capable, but he cannot be employed as a Great Officer for T'eng and Hsüeh," said the Sage. But if one can only put a gentleman to use after making certain of his probity, how could Huan of Ch'i have become Overlord of his age? Can it be that the empire today is without those who, though clad in homespun, hold a jade in their bosom, angling on the banks of the Wei? May there not be some who, while they debauch their sister-in-law or take bribes, have yet to meet with a Wu-chih?
>
> My several men! Assist me in bringing to light and raising up the unorthodox and the lowly. As long as a man be talented, he is to be recommended. Upon gaining him, I shall put him to use.[59]

自古受命及中興之君, 曷嘗不得賢人君子與之共治天下者乎! 及其得賢也, 曾不出閭巷, 豈幸相遇哉? 上之人不求之耳。今天下尚未定, 此特求賢之急時也。『孟公綽為趙、魏老則優, 不可以為滕、薛大夫』。若必廉士而後可用, 則齊桓其何以霸世! 今天下得無有被褐懷玉而釣于渭濱者乎? 又得無盜嫂受金而未遇無知者乎? 二三子其佐我明揚仄陋, 唯才是舉, 吾得而用之.[60]

A Reference Guide, Part I (Leiden: Brill, 2010), 275. See also, Robert Joe Cutter, "Cao Zhi's (192–232) Symposium Poems" *Essays, Articles, Reviews* (*CLEAR*) 6, no. 1/2 (1984), 1–32. Other scholars' works on this subject are mentioned in the following chapter.

59 The translation is from Paul W. Kroll, "Portraits of Ts'ao Ts'ao: Literary Studies on the Man and the Myth" (PhD diss., University of Michigan, 1976), 17–18.

60 Chen, *San guo zhi*, 1.32.

THE CONSTRUCTION AND DEVELOPMENT OF YE 25

Not only did Cao Cao's appreciation for true talent attract many worthies to him, but he also relocated a massive number of commoners to Ye.[61] Historical accounts show that many times, under Cao Cao's influence, important families relocated to Ye. For example, after Tian Chou 田疇 (169–214) moved all his family members and relatives of the Tian clan, about three hundred households, to Ye, Cao Cao bestowed upon them carriages, horses, grains, and silk.[62] Cao Cao also praised one of his commanders, Li Dian 李典 (fl. 210), who volunteered to move his army and clan—more than thirteen thousand people—to live in Ye.[63] And Cao Cao's Commandant-escort (*fuma duwei* 駙馬都尉) Du Xi 杜襲 (fl. 216) successfully convinced more than eighty thousand people to move from Hanzhong 漢中 (in modern day Shaanxi 陝西) to Luoyang and Ye.[64]

From historical accounts, literary texts, and archeological finds, one can identify parts of the city with some accuracy, although literary and historical texts tend to deal in hyperbolic numbers. Records show that by the end of the Eastern Han, Ye had a city wall that was roughly forty *li* in circumference. One of the accounts in the *San guo zhi* describing Cao Cao's battles with the Yuan brothers in Ye states that he surrounded the city and dug a moat that was two *zhang* deep and wide around the city wall. According to this account, the length of the moat was forty *li*.[65] This measurement is different in the *Shuijing zhu*. Li Daoyuan describes the city walls of Ye: "The city wall from east to west is seven *li* and south to north is five *li*. The surface is decorated with bricks. There is a storied building every hundred double paces" (其城東西七里南北五里, 飾表以塼, 百步一樓).[66] The size of Ye described here is countered by archeological reports that Ye is about twenty-four to twenty-five hundred meters wide (east-west) and seventeen hundred meters long (north-south), that is ±8400 meters. The archeological data, however, seems to represent only the latest form of the city.[67]

---

61   Liu Zhiling 劉志玲, "Zonglun Wei Jin Bei chao Ye cheng de zhongxin diwei" 縱論魏晉北朝鄴城的中心地位, *Handan xueyuan xuebao* 邯鄲學院學報 18, no. 4 (2008): 27–32.

62   Chen, *San guo zhi*, 11.343.

63   Chen, *San guo zhi*, 18.534.

64   Chen, *San guo zhi*, 23.666.

65   Chen, *San guo zhi*, 6.202.

66   Li, *Shuijing zhu*, 10.213.

67   See Cheng Yi, "Shilun Ye beicheng de sheji sixiang, buju yu yingxiang," 106–11. Also see Shen, "Ye cheng—woguo gudai chengshi fazhan shi shang de licheng bei," 4–9. For further summaries of Cao Cao's design and construction of Ye, see Guo Shengqiang 郭勝強 and Xu Hu 許滸, "Cao Wei Ye du de yingjian ji yingxiang" 曹魏鄴都的營建及影響, *Sanmenxia zhiye jishu xueyuan xuebao* 三門峽職業技術學院學報, 10, no. 2 (June, 2011): 34–37; and Cheng Sen 程森 and Li Junfeng 李俊鋒, "Lun Cao Wei Ye cheng ji qi zhoubian

26 CHAPTER 1

This section has looked at Cao Cao's major design and building of Ye from its general configuration—the hydraulic system, the terraces, the palace complex, and the quadrant organization of the city—and from reading the description of Ye in the *Shuijing zhu* and the map of Ye (shown in figure 1); from these accounts, one can see that Cao Cao wove the hydraulic system, the terraces, and the entire city together into an organic whole:

> Taking what was already in place, [Emperor Wu of Wei] led the Zhang to flow eastward from west of the city wall. It directly went by the base of the Bronze Bird Terrace and entered the city underground. As it flowed eastwards it was called Changming waterway. The trench of water then continued on southwards underneath the Zhiche Gate.[68] [Emperor] Wu of Wei had been enfeoffed in Ye, where he built the northern palace. The palace [complex] housed the Wenchang Hall. The waterway flowed on both sides of the street on the north and south. Branch waterways were led to irrigate, and they completely irrigated everything. [The Changming] waterway then went out underneath Shidou [weir] and flowed into the Huang River.

> 魏武又以郡國之舊，引漳流自城西東入，逕銅雀臺下，伏流入城。東注，謂之長明溝也。渠水又南逕止車門下。魏武封於鄴為北宮，宮有文昌殿。溝水南北夾道，枝流引灌，所在通溉。東出石竇（堰）下，注之湟水.[69]

4 The Post-Cao City of Ye

Ye remained a seat of power until 220 when Cao Pi 曹丕 (187–226) took the throne (r. 220–226) after his father's death and established his own capital in Luoyang.[70] Nevertheless, along with Chang'an, Qiao 譙, Xuchang 許昌, and

---

ziran jingguan he wenhua jingguan" 論曹魏鄴城及其周邊自然景觀和文化景觀, *Sanmenxia zhiye jishu xueyuan xuebao* , 7, no. 3 (2008): 42–45.

68 *Zhiche* 止車 gates were usually placed outside of palace complexes where officials had to alight from their transportation and proceed on foot.

69 Li, *Shuijing zhu*, 10.212.

70 There is no record of the specific date that Cao Pi formally moved his capital to Luoyang from Ye. We only know that in the twelfth month of the first year of Huangchu 黃初 (January 11–February 9, 221) he initiated the construction of Luoyang Palace (Luoyang *gong* 洛陽宮) and he visited it on the day of Wuwu 戊午 (January 27, 221). Chen, *San guo zhi*, 2.76.

THE CONSTRUCTION AND DEVELOPMENT OF YE

Luoyang, Ye continued to be one of the major cities of that time.[71] After the Cao Wei, the Later Zhao 後趙 (319–351), Former Yan 前燕 (337–370), Ran Wei 冉魏 (350–352), Eastern Wei 東魏 (534–550), and Northern Qi 北齊 (550–577) also located their capitals at Ye. The Eastern Wei added a southern addition (Ye *nancheng* 鄴南城) to the city.[72]

---

71 See commentary quoting the *Wei lue* 魏略 in Chen, *San guo zhi*, 2.77. Also, Jiang Shaohua 蔣少華, "Cao Wei wudu kaolun" 曹魏五都考論, *Xiangfan xueyuan xuebao* 襄樊學院學報, 31, no. 12 (December, 2010): 5–10. The five *du*-cities 五都 here should be remarked since *du* means cities that house ancestral temples and thus have a heightened importance. As the *Shuijing zhu* explains, "Wei took its example from the Han dynasty and restored its capital at Luoyang, and took Qiao (modern day Bozhou 亳州 Anhui 安徽) as the original fief of ancestors. Xuchang was where the Han resided. Chang'an was the historical ruin of the western capital, and Ye was the original foundation of Wei's establishment. Therefore they are called the five *du*-cities" (魏因漢祚復都洛陽, 以譙為先人本國, 許昌為漢之所居, 長安為西京之遺跡, 鄴為王業之本基, 故號五都也). See Li, *Shuijing zhu*, 10.213–214. Also see the relationship between capital cities and ancestor rituals in, for example, Wang Lin 王琳, "Zhongguo gudai zaoqi wangdu de jiben tezheng" 中國古代早期王都的基本特徵, *Zhongyuan wenwu*, no, 4 (2006): 22–28; and Chang Kwang-chih, "Towns and Cities in Ancient China," in *Early Chinese Civilization: Anthropological Perspectives* (Cambridge, MA: Harvard University Press, 1976), 61–71.

72 Some believe that the southern city of Ye (Ye *nancheng* 鄴南城) was the first city in China to have had both *li* 里 and *fang* 坊 districts (i.e., wards). See for example, Ye Xiaojun, *Zhongguo ducheng fazhan shi*, 132; Niu Runzhen, "Dong Wei Bei Qi Yejing lifang zhidu kao" 東魏北齊鄴京里坊制度考, *Jinyang xuekan* 晉陽學刊, no. 6 (2009): 81–85; and Guo Jiqiao, "Beichao shiqi Ye nancheng buju chutan" 北朝時期鄴南城佈局初探, *Wenwu chunqiu* 文物春秋, no. 2 (2002): 16–26. *Li* and *fang* were, throughout Chinese dynasties, territorial administrative districts or wards of residential grouping of various numbers of households; for instance, "each 100-household group in the neighborhood was organized as a Village (*li* 里)," as Hucker states in his introduction to the territorial administration of the Qin dynasty. See Charles O. Hucker, *A Dictionary of Official Titles in Imperial China* (Taipei: Nantian shuju, 1995), 9. Heng Chye Kiang 王才強 argues that *li* and *fang* were part of the social and functional segregation of the wards at the capitals, especially *li,* which was a Legalist aristocratic social and economic organization. Heng states that, "By then, [i.e. the Sui] the system of enclosed wards and curfew had been in practice in China for more than 800 years, at least since the Qin period (221–207 BC), although the wards were then known as *li.* The *li* system, which was already in place during the tyranny of Qin Shi Huang 秦始皇, was even more oppressive than the later *fang* system. Only one gate was allowed in each walled ward." See his *Cities of Aristocrats and Bureaucrats: The Development of Medieval Chinese Cityscapes* (Honolulu: University of Hawai'i Press, 1999), 47. For a more detailed discussion of *li* and *fang*, see Liu Mingwei 劉銘緯 and Lai Guangbang 賴光邦, "Zhongguo gudai chengguo dushi xingtai jianlun: Fangshi geming yiqian Huaxia ducheng xingtai de juhe, fenhua yu qi zhidu hua chengxu" 中國古代城郭都市形態簡論: 坊市革命以前華夏都市型態的聚合、分化與其制度化程序, *Guoli Taiwan daxue jianzhu yu chengxiang yanjiu xuebao* 國立臺灣大學建築與城鄉研究學報, no. 16 (December, 2010): 79–119; also Miyazaki Ichisada 宮崎市定, "Kandai no risei to Tōdai no bōsei" 漢代の里制と唐代の坊制, in *Miyazaki Ichisada*

28   CHAPTER 1

In the era of the Sixteen States 五胡十六國 (304–420 or 439), which ran contemporaneously with most of the Jin 晉 (265–420), Shi Le 石勒 (274–333) of the Jie 羯 people founded the Later Zhao dynasty.[73] After the death of Shi Le, his second son Shi Hong 石弘 (314–335), the crown prince who had once been posted in Ye, was forced out and later killed by his cousin Shi Hu 石虎 (295–349). Shi Hu then personally claimed to be the Heavenly King of the Great Zhao (*Da Zhao tianwang* 大趙天王) in the third year of Xiankang 咸康 [February 18, 337–February 6, 338]. He moved the capital of the Later Zhao from Xiangguo 襄國 (modern day Xingtai 邢台, Hebei) to Ye, where he had previously been the Governor of Wei Commandery (Wei *jun taishou* 魏郡太守) and had guarded the Three Terraces.[74] In the *Jin shu*, the Shi family is portrayed as violent, lustful, and greedy; but of course, no standard history of China was free of a subjective or political viewpoint, and this portrayal may be as much about ethical bias or moral didacticism as about political or social reality.

Shi Hu, according to the *Jin shu*, was not a kind ruler, and he spent most of his resources and efforts on constructing palaces and indulging in pleasure. The only court matters he cared to deal with personally were warfare and court judgments and punishments (*zhengfa xingduan* 征伐刑斷).[75] Shi Hu was known for his lavish and extravagant lifestyle. He decided to relocate the capital to Ye right after he dethroned Shi Hong in the first year of Xiankang (335). Once he decided to move back to Ye, he intended to remake the city according to his own desires.

Shi Hu expended a lot of capital and labor to reconstruct some buildings and erect others in all major cities under his control, but especially in Ye. His biography in the *Jin shu* states: "[Shi Hu] at the same time lavishly constructed major buildings in Ye. He erected more than forty terraces and watchtowers. He also planned and constructed palaces in Chang'an and Luoyang. The numbers of workers on these projects were more than four hundred thousand" (兼盛興宮室於鄴，起臺觀四十餘所。營長安洛陽二宮。作者四十餘萬人).[76] The account does not specify which buildings, but the *Zhangde fu zhi* points out that these included such watchtowers and buildings as Xiaoyao Tower

---

　　zenshū 宮崎市定全集, vol. 7 (Tokyo: Iwanami Shoten, 1962), 87–115; and "Les villes en Chine à l'époque des Han," *T'oung Pao* 通報 48, no. 4–5 (1960): 376–392.

73　According to the *Wei shu* 魏書, the Jie people were descendants of the northern Xiongnu 匈奴 and resided in Jieshi 羯室 in the Shangdang 上黨 area (modern Yushe 榆社 Shanxi). Wei Shou 魏收 (507–572) comp., *Wei Shu* (Beijing: Zhonghua shuju, 1974), 95.2047.

74　Fang, *Jin shu*, 106.2762 and 2765.

75　Fang, *Jin shu*, 106.2762.

76　Fang, *Jin shu*, 106.2772.

THE CONSTRUCTION AND DEVELOPMENT OF YE

逍遙樓, Xuanwu Watchtower 宣武觀, Lingxiao Watchtower 陵霄觀, and Ruyi Watchtower 如意觀; Kunhua Hall 琨華殿, Huihua Hall 暉華殿, and Jinhua Hall 金華殿; Changhe Gate 閶闔門 and Western Zhonghua Gate 西中華門, Lingfeng Terrace 靈風臺 and Zhong Terrace 中臺. And it also states that, "these halls, gates, terraces, and watchtowers here listed after Kunhua are seen in records, but no one knows where they were. They probably were erected by Shi Hu. Within and without the palace area, halls great and small, along with nine terraces and watchtowers, amounted to more than forty sites. As for the palaces of Cao Wei, they were renovated and changed a lot" (自琨華以下殿門臺觀, 雖見於傳記而莫知所在。蓋石虎所起。內外大小殿九臺觀, 四十於所。其於曹魏宮室, 改易多矣).[77]

Among the buildings that Shi Hu supposedly built, the records of Taiwu Hall 太武殿 are the most intriguing. The *Shuijing zhu* notes that Shi Hu built the east Taiwu Hall and west Taiwu Hall on the location of the former Wenchang Hall (石氏于文昌故殿處, 造東西太武二殿).[78] This account conflicts with the one in the *Jin shu*, which remarks that [Shi Hu] erected Taiwu Hall in the state of Xiang, and built the east and west palaces in Ye (於襄國起太武殿, 於鄴造東西宮).[79] But then Taiwu appears again in the second part of Shi Hu's biography in *Jin shu* when it describes the chaos in the capital after Shi Hu passed away:

> Violent winds uprooted trees, thunder shook; hail rained down as big as bowls and cups. The Taiwu Hall and Huihua Hall were obliterated. All gates, watchtowers, and chambers were destroyed, and most of the chariots and clothing were burned. The fire lit up the sky, even metal and stones were totally gone. The fire lasted for more than a month before it was out. It rained blood all around the city of Ye.

> 暴風拔樹, 震雷, 雨雹大如盂升。太武、暉華殿災, 諸門觀閣蕩然, 其乘輿服御燒者大半。光焰照天, 金石皆盡。火月餘乃滅。雨血周遍鄴城。[80]

In addition to the *Shuijing zhu* and the *Jin shu*, the *Yezhong ji* shows that Taiwu was in Ye, but not at the site of the former Wenchang Hall as the *Shuijing zhu*

---

77 Cited in Ho, *On the Poems and Fu from the Han-Wei-Six Dynasties Related to the Capital Ye*, 20.

78 Li, *Shuijing zhu*, 10.212.

79 Fang, *Jin shu*, 106.2765.

80 Fang, *Jin shu*, 107.2789. This passage is clearly a fictional hyperbole used by the authors of the *Jin shu* to demonstrate Heaven's displeasure with the continuation of the Shi clan as rulers, who began a series of usurpations and assassinations even before Shi Hu was buried.

states. Instead, it mentions that it was at one of the terraces that Cao Cao built: "Shi Hu erected Taiwu Hall at [one of] Wei Wu's former terraces. The windows and doors were contoured and painted as a cloudy haze to imitate the Ebang palace of Qin and the Lingguang Hall of Lu" (石虎於魏武故臺立太武殿, 牕戶 宛轉畫作雲氣, 擬秦之阿房魯之靈光).[81]

In addition to the Taiwu and the other buildings listed above, Shi Hu also added features to conspicuously display his own success and power. He was clearly in competition with the memory of Cao Cao's magnificent architectural achievements. For example, he built the Dongming Watchtower 東明觀 on the east city wall and an unusually high-rising Qidou Tower 齊斗樓 on the north city wall of Ye. In the *Shuijing zhu*, it is described as:

On top of the east city wall, Shi erected the Dongming Watchtower. On top of it, [he] added a gold Boshan incense burner and called it "Clanging Heaven." On top of the north wall, there was the Qidou Tower that rose above all other buildings on the terrace. Uniquely tall, it stood prominently.

東城上石氏立東明觀, 觀上加金博山, 謂之鏘天。北城上有齊斗樓, 超出 群榭, 孤高特立.[82]

As for Cao Cao's iconic structure—the Bronze Bird Terrace—according to the *Shuijing zhu*:

Shi Hu increased its height by two *zhang* and erected a room, linking ridgepole to ridgepole, and connecting rafter to rafter. [He] completely covered the top of it and separated into [concentric?] circular partitions. It was named "Teaching Offspring Den." Also, on top of the room [Shi Hu] built a five-storied tower that was fifteen *zhang* high, which was twenty-seven *zhang* above ground level. Then [he] built a bronze bird on the very top of the tower, spreading its wings as though flying.

石虎更增二丈, 立一屋, 連棟接榱。彌覆其上, 盤迴隔之。名曰命子窟。 又於屋上起五層樓, 高十五丈, 去地二十七丈。又作銅雀於樓顛, 舒翼若 飛.[83]

---

81 Lu, *Yezhong ji*, 1b.
82 Li, *Shuijing zhu*, 10.213. *Qidou* probably means "a height equal to the Dipper."
83 Ibid.

THE CONSTRUCTION AND DEVELOPMENT OF YE

The *Yezhong ji* also remarks that Shi Hu made the Three Terraces more adorned and embellished than they were at the beginning of the Wei (更加崇飾, 甚於魏初). According to the *Yezhong ji*, however, the "Teaching Offspring Den" was not on top of a high tower, but rather an underground construction: "Two wells were dug at the Bronze Bird Terrace, and there was an underground path with an iron bridge constructed to join the two wells. This was called the Teaching Offspring Den" (於銅雀臺穿二井。作鐵梁地道以通井。號曰命子窟).[84]

Shi Hu seemed to have an overwhelming passion for construction. He sent a military officer, Zhang Mi 張彌 (n.d.), to move several large objects from Luoyang to his new capital. These included musical bell racks (*zhongju* 鍾簴) and sculptures such as the nine dragons (*jiulong* 九龍), stone guardians (*wengzhong* 翁仲),[85] bronze camels (*tongtuo* 銅駝), and the legendary bird *feilian* 飛廉.[86] In order to transport these items, it was necessary to build a huge vessel and a two-*chi*-long and four-*chi*-wide four-wheel cart wound about with netting. In the process of this move, one of the bells fell into the Yellow River. A team of three hundred divers tied to bamboo ropes and one hundred oxen attached to pulleys were used to retrieve the object.[87] It is also believed that Shi Hu once adopted Xie Fei's 解飛 (n.d.) idea of depositing stones into the Yellow

---

84 Lu, *Yezhong ji*, 3b.

85 These are life-sized stone guardians often seen next to palace gates or imperial gravesites. In his commentary to the *Shi ji*, Sima Zhen 司馬貞 (679–732) states that "in the twenty-sixth year [since the First Emperor became the king of the Qin state] (220 BCE), a tall man appeared in Lintao 臨洮 [near modern day Dingxi 定西 Gansu 甘肅]. [The emperor ordered] melting weapons down to cast [a statue] to reflect his image" (二十六年, 有長人見于臨洮, 故銷兵器, 鑄而象之). Sima Zhen also quotes from Xie Cheng's 謝承 (182–254) now lost *Hou Han shu* 後漢書, which further adds, "The bronze human [statue] is called Wengzhong. Wengzhong is his name" (銅人, 翁仲。翁仲其名也。), along with the statement from the *Sanfu jiushi* 三輔舊事: "twelve bronze human statues were made and each weighed three hundred forty thousand *jin*, and they were placed in front of the main gate of Changle Hall during the Han dynasty" (銅人十二, 各重三十四萬斤。漢代在長樂宮門前). Sima Zhen describes that Dong Zhuo destroyed ten of these statues for cash, Shi Jilong 石季龍 moved the remaining two to Ye, and later Fu Jian 符堅 (337–385) again moved and melted them down in Chang'an. Zhang Shoujie's 張守節 commentary also quotes from the "Wuxing zhi" 五行志 of the *Han shu* stating that, "in the twenty-sixth year, there were huge men who appeared in Lintao. They were five *zhang* tall and wearing six *chi* size shoes. Each of them was dressed in the clothing of Yi and Di [non-Han Chinese apparel]. There were twelve in total appeared in Lintao. Therefore, [the emperor ordered] melting weapons down to cast [statues] to reflect their images" (二十六年, 有大人長五丈, 足履六尺, 皆夷狄服, 凡十二人, 見于臨洮, 故銷兵器, 鑄而象之). See Sima, *Shi ji*, 6.240n6.

86 Cf. Knechtges, *Wen xuan*, 1: 136, note to line 330.

87 Fang, *Jin shu*, 106.2764.

River directly south of Ye in an attempt to build a flyover bridge (*feiqiao* 飛橋). The labor and material costs were exorbitant, and the bridge just could not be built. Shi Hu consequently called off the project.[88]

Shi Hu resorted to repugnant methods to finance his projects. Both Shi Le and Shi Hu were described as greedy and immoral (*tan er wuli* 貪而無禮), unsatisfied even though they ruled a large territory and possessed gold, silk, pearls, jade, and rare exotic objects in numbers too great to count. They excavated the tombs of the former emperors, kings, and former worthies to steal their burial treasure. Shi Hu is even reported to have opened the tomb of the First Emperor of Qin and melted down its bronze columns to cast other objects.[89]

From these various sources, we can see that Shi Hu, like Cao Cao a hundred years before him, put in much effort in renovating and new construction in the city of Ye. Cui Xian gives a very sharp summary of the contributions of these two main figures, who controlled Ye in the third and fourth centuries:

> From the time Cao Cao constructed the foundation, a host of officials like Liang Xi (d. 230) and others only relied on the labor of the people of Ji Prefecture and took materials from the forested mountains of Shangdang. The scale of it was magnificent, as demonstrated in the Wenchang and Tingzheng Halls, the Terraces of the Golden Tiger and Bronze Bird, and the Palaces of Minghe and Qiuzi. Before his excessiveness and indulgence came to its natural end, in short order he suffered usurpation. Shi Hu belonged to the different category of the [foreign] Yi and Di. He relied on [Shi] Le's powerful enterprise to grasp and keep the imperial regalia [of emperorship]. [Shi Hu's] ambitions overflowed, and his manner was arrogant. He excessively raised edifices with silver columns and gold pillars, pearl curtains and jade walls. His extravagant heart unsatisfied, so he ordered bell racks, the nine dragons, the bronze camels, and the *feilian* moved from Luoyang to his palace halls and courtyards [in Ye]. He built a ten-thousand-*hu*[90] vessel to ferry them across and transported them by a four-wheel cart wound with netting .... Father, sons, brothers all slaughtered each other like making mincemeat. Dead bodies floated onto the Zhang riverbanks and there were no living beings in the households. [Shi

---

88   Fang, *Jin shu*, 106.2764.

89   Fang, *Jin shu*, 107.2781–2782.

90   The word *hu* is a measure word for volume. One *hu* was about ten *dou* 斗 and one *dou* was about ten *sheng* 升, which conventionally converts into one liter today. Thus, one *hu* might have been close to one hundred liters. Here the term "ten-thousand *hu*" 萬斛 indicates a great amount.

THE CONSTRUCTION AND DEVELOPMENT OF YE

Hu] accumulated evil nonstop, [so] how appropriate it was [when he was] abolished and exterminated!

自曹操基構, 群臣梁習等, 止用冀州民力, 取上黨山林之材。制度壯麗, 見於文昌、聽政等殿, 金虎、銅雀之臺, 鳴鶴、楸梓之宮, 奢淫未終旋遭篡奪。石虎夷狄異類。藉勒威業, 攘神器而有之。志溢氣驕。盛興宮室, 銀楹金柱, 珠簾玉壁。侈心不足, 復命徙洛陽鐘虞、九龍、銅駝、飛廉置諸殿庭。造萬斛舟以渡之, 載以四輪纏輞車。…… 父子兄弟更相屠繪, 尸浮漳濱, 家無噍類。積惡不已, 舍滅亡何適哉?[91]

After Shi Hu's death in 349, his ten-year-old son Shi Shi 石世 (339–349) succeeded to the throne only to be immediately killed by his older brother, Shi Zun 石遵 (d. 349). During the chaos of this fratricidal incident in the capital, Ran Min 冉閔 (ca. 322–352), an ethnic Han who worked under Shi Hu, took the throne and changed the dynasty name to Wei (known in history as the Ran Wei); this regime lasted for two years (350–352) and is conventionally counted as one of the dynasties that located their capitals in Ye. Ran Min occupied Ye for two years and was later captured by the Murong family of the Xianbei 鮮卑. When Murong Ping 慕容評 (fl. 339–352) surrounded Ye in 352, the city was in dire straits: "[People] of Ye were starving, and they ate each other. Almost all of the ladies who had been in the palace in Shi Hu's time were eaten." (鄴中饑, 人相食。季龍時宮人被食略盡).[92] The battle for power and control of Ye continued, and the devastating conditions in the capital city worsened. Murong Jun 慕容儁 (319–360) killed Ran Min and, in 350, he established the capital of the Former Yan in Ji 薊 (modern Jixian 薊縣, between Tianjin 天津 and Beijing). Seven years later, however, he moved the capital back to Ye, granting a pardon to all within its boundary, repairing and renovating its buildings, and restoring the Bronze Bird Terrace (儁自薊城遷于鄴。赦其境內, 繕修宮殿, 復銅雀臺).[93]

Murong Jun now settled into his new capital, but the ghost of Ye past still troubled the new ruler. An anecdote illustrates that one night, Murong Jun dreamed that Shi Hu bit his arm. He was so disgusted by the dream that he ordered Shi Hu's grave exhumed, split his coffin open and brought out the corpse. He then trampled on the corpse and cursed it, "[you] dead barbarian, how dare you appear in a dream to the living Son of Heaven!" Then Murong Jun

---

91　*Zhangde fuzhi*, 8.482, cited in Ho, *On the Poems and Fu from the Han-Wei-Six Dynasties Related to the Capital Ye*, 25–26.

92　Fang, *Jin shu*, 107.2797.

93　Fang, *Jin shu*, 110.2838.

had his Palace Commandant of Censors, Yang Yue 陽約 (n.d.), whip Shi Hu's body according to the numbers of Shi Hu's wrongdoings and crimes and then dump the body in the Zhang River (儁夜夢石季龍齧其臂, 寐而惡之。命發其墓, 剖棺出尸, 蹋而罵之曰, 死胡敢夢生天子！遣其御史中尉陽約數其殘酷之罪鞭之, 棄于漳水).[94] The Murong family's Former Yan dynasty eventually ended when Fu Jian 苻堅 (338–385), the ruler of the Former Qin 前秦 (350–394), chased Emperor You 幽帝, Murong Wei 慕容暐 (350–384), out of Ye in 370.

To recap, from the time Cao Cao began his construction in 204 to his death in 220, the city of Ye was the Cao family's power base. As a result, it is intimately connected in people's minds with the great poets of the period and thought of as the place that nourished the rise of Jian'an literature. The city receded into the background when Cao Pi established the Cao Wei capital in Luoyang, but one hundred years later, in 335, Shi Hu began to renovate Ye and moved the capital of the Later Zhao there from Xiangguo. Even though the Shi family was violent, and the succeeding Ran and Murong clans induced chaos in their struggle for power, the city of Ye once again came into the spotlight during those years.

Still, human chaos had terribly damaged the city. By the fourth century— unlike the city of Cao Wei that was filled with literati and poetry composed in abundant banquets—Ye had become a place of horror in the hands of those who grasped for power. The *Jin shu* hyperbolically describes Shi Hu's rule as follows:

> Blood flowed from between the rocks of the mountains west of Ye. The flow was more than ten double paces long and two *chi* wide. All of the ancient sages painted [on the walls] in the Taiwu Hall turned into barbarians. After ten days and more, their heads were all sucked into their shoulders.

> 鄴西山石間血流出，長十餘步，廣二尺餘。太武殿畫古賢悉變為胡。旬餘，頭悉縮入肩中.[95]

94　Fang, *Jin shu*, 110.2841. The *Zizhi tongjian* 資治通鑑 expands on this story:
　　Jun dreamt that the King of Zhao, Hu, took a bite of his shoulder, so he opened Hu's tomb, looked for the corpse but could not find it. He put out a reward of a hundred gold. A young woman of Ye, Li Tu, knew where it was and informed him. He found the corpse underneath Dongming Daoist monastery, and it was in rigor but had not decayed. Jun trampled it and cursed him saying, "You dead barbarian! How dare you frighten a living Son of Heaven!" He enumerated his crimes of violence and whipped [the corpse], then threw it into the Zhang River, but it caught on a pillar of a bridge and did not float away.
　　See Sima Guang 司馬光, *Zizhi tongjian* (Beijing: Guji chubanshe, 1956) 100.3174.

95　Fang, *Jin shu*, 106.2773.

THE CONSTRUCTION AND DEVELOPMENT OF YE

Though this may only be an anecdote given to emphasize Shi Hu's inhumanity, it conveys how later people viewed Shi Hu and his capital. The sages represented in the painting, certainly Han Chinese at that time, all turned into northern barbarians because the Shi family, of a non-Han tribe, now ruled. The transformation of the cultural heroes of the Han mimicked the transformation of the landscape, which had transformed from a peaceful agrarian world into one besotted with blood. But even the Hu could not bear to watch the destruction wrought by Shi Hu and they sucked their heads into their shoulders. Similar hyperbole also occurs in other places in Shi Hu's Biography in the *Jin Shu*. One passage remarks, "From the time [Shi Hu] first set out for Ye, those who were widowed and then seized and sent to their death by hanging numbered more than three thousand" (自初發至鄴, 諸殺其夫及奪而遣之縊死者三千餘 人).[96] In another section, it describes the numbers of people who perished during his renovations. For instance, Shi Hu's desire to pierce through the northern city wall in order to draw water into the Hualin Park caused the collapse of a wall that buried more than a hundred people alive" (鑿北城引水於 華林園。城崩壓死者百餘人).[97]

After Shi Hu died, the fate of Ye did not improve. There is no extant record that solely focuses on the damage to the city during this time, but from accounts of battles for power, we can get a rough idea. In 350 when Ran Min fought with Shi Jian 石鑒 (d. 350) for the throne, Ran attacked the city with a force of several thousand men who entered Ye by breaking through the Jinming Gate 金明門 [the main gate on the western city wall, see Figure 2]. As a result, "From Fengyang Gate [the west gate on the southern city wall, see Figure 2] to Kunhua Hall, corpses were piled one atop another, and the blood flowed until it turned into runnels" (自鳳陽至琨華, 橫尸相枕, 流血成渠).[98] After Ran Min broke into the capital, he slaughtered the Jie and all other non-Han people. He made an announcement that anyone who would bring a non-Han person's head to the Fengyang Gate would be advanced three levels as a civil official or would be appointed a position of *yamen* 牙門 as a military officer (文官進位三等, 武職悉拜牙門).[99] As a result, several tens of thousands of people were beheaded in a single day. And,

no matter whether noble or humble, male or female, young or old, [they] were all decapitated. The ones who died were more than two hundred

---

96　Fang, *Jin shu*, 106.2777.
97　Fang, *Jin shu*, 107.2782.
98　Fang, *Jin shu*, 107.2791.
99　Fang, *Jin shu*, 107.2791–2792.

thousand. The dead bodies outside of the city wall were all eaten by wild dogs, jackals, and wolves. During this period of time, of those who were killed after receiving Ran Min's announcement, more than half were ones with high noses and much facial hair.

無貴賤男女少長皆斬之。死者二十餘萬。尸諸城外悉為野犬豺狼所食。所在承閏書誅之，于時，高鼻多鬚至有濫死者半.[100]

More than a hundred and fifty years later, Ye was occupied by the Eastern Wei, which located its capital there in 534. This short-lived dynasty had only a single ruler, Emperor Xiaojing 孝靜帝 who, in actuality, was controlled by his Chancellor (*chengxiang* 丞相), Gao Huan 高歡 (496–547). After Gao Huan's death in 547, Emperor Xiaojing was quickly usurped by Gao Huan's son, Gao Yang 高洋 (526–559), who established the last dynasty to call Ye its capital, the Northern Qi, and is known to history as Emperor Wenxuan 文宣帝 (r. 550–559). The founding of the Northern Qi was unique in the sense that Gao Huan was ethnically a Han but culturally a Xianbei. This dynasty also shares similarities with the Cao Wei. Gao Huan, like Cao Cao, never took the throne even though he held a position as Chancellor and controlled tremendous political and military power. His title—Emperor Xianwu 獻武帝 (later changed to be Emperor Shenwu 神武帝)—was bestowed on him only after his son, Gao Yang, took the throne and established this new dynasty—just as Cao Pi had done. Also, like Cao Cao, Gao Huan recognized the significance of Ye as a capital city. Before the Eastern Wei had been established, Gao Huan had already suggested to the ruler of the Northern Wei 北魏 (386–534), Emperor Xiaowu 孝武帝 (r. 532–535), that he should relocate his seat of government to Ye. Gao Huan thought that, "Since Luoyang had suffered from death and disorder for so long, its kingly aura has declined and disappeared. Although it has [the strategic location that makes use of] the security of the mountains and rivers, its area is narrow and cramped. It is not as good as Ye" (洛陽久經喪亂，王氣衰盡。雖有山河之固，土地褊狹，不如鄴).[101] Nonetheless, Emperor Xiaowu rejected his suggestion. Because of ongoing conflict with Gao Huan, whose power he could not contain, Xiaowu fled the court in 534. Gao Huan then put one of the great-grandsons of Emperor Xiaowen 孝文帝 (r. 471–499) of the Northern Wei, Yuan Shanjian 元善見 (524–551), on the throne (known as Emperor Xiaojing) and established the Eastern Wei. Once again, Gao Huan suggested moving the

---

100   Ibid.

101   Li Baiyao 李百藥 (565–648), comp., *Bei Qi shu* 北齊書 (Beijing: Zhonghua shuju, 1972), 2.16.

THE CONSTRUCTION AND DEVELOPMENT OF YE

capital to Ye because of its location, which would allow him to control the plain above the Yellow River. He addressed the court, saying:

> Since Emperor Xiaowu has gone to the west [to Chang'an], I fear he may put pressure on the areas of Mount Yao [northwest of Luoyang] and Shan [i.e., Shaanxi]. Also, Luoyang is located beyond [i.e., south of] the Yellow River close to the borders of Liang [the area of modern Zhengzhou 鄭州]. If he moves toward Jinyang [the area of modern Taiyuan 太原], we will not be able to conjoin the benefits of the topography. Therefore, I suggest we transfer [our capital] to Ye.

> 孝武既西, 恐逼崤陝。洛陽復在河外, 接近梁境, 如向晉陽, 形勢不能相接, 乃議遷鄴.[102]

The ten-year-old emperor and his Capital Protector (*hujun* 護軍) gladly accepted Gao Huan's idea. Ten days after he was put on the throne, the young emperor sent down a decree saying:

> "To find security in what makes one secure, but still be able to move"[103] is a clear precedent from ancient times; to have the place you reside as unfixed is the set rule of the past. This is why that the Yin moved through eight cities,[104] and the Zhou made geomantic prognostication in three places.[105] Good and ill luck have their destinies, rise and fall has no

---

102   Li, *Bei Qi shu*, 2.18. Also, see the geographic parallel between Jinyang and Ye in, for example, Su Xiaohua 蘇小華, "Dong Wei Bei Qi zhongbei qingnan de yuanyin ji qi yingxiang" 東魏、北齊重北輕南的原因及其影響, *Shehui kexue pinglun* 社會科學評論, no. 4 (2009): 80–87; and Cui Yanhua 崔彥華, "Ye—Jinyang: Liangdu tizhi yu Dong Wei Bei Qi zhengzhi" 鄴—晉陽: 兩都體制與東魏、北齊政治, *Shehui kexue zhanxian* 社會科學戰線, no. 7 (2010): 242–245.

103   This is from "Quli" 曲禮 of the *Liji* 禮記. It states: "One who is worthy can be close to others but still respect them; can be in awe but still favor them; can be partial to others but still understand their moral repugnance; can dislike others but still understand their moral goodness; they can accumulate [things] but still are able to distribute them; they are able to find security in what makes one secure, but still are able to move" (賢者狎而敬之, 畏而愛之。愛而知其惡, 憎而知其善。積而能散, 安安而能遷). See Zheng Xuan 鄭玄 (127–200) and Kong Yingda 孔穎達 (574–648), comm. and ann., *Liji zhengyi* 禮記正義, in *Shisan jing zhushu fu jiaokan ji* 十三經注疏附校勘記, ed. Ruan Yuan 阮元 (1764–1849), 8 vols., (Taipei: Yiwen yingshu guan, 1982), 5: 1.6a–b.

104   It is said that from its ancestor Zi Xie 子契 (ca. 2100 BCE) to its dynasty founder Zi Lü 子履 (ca. 1600 BCE), the Shang 商 tribe had moved its "capital city" eight times.

105   These three places could include the fief of Jiang Shang 姜尚 (ca. 1156–1071 BCE), Yingqiu 營丘 (modern day Linzi 臨淄) and the two capitals, Haojing 鎬京 (inside of modern day

constancy. Matters derive from change or continuity, and principles come from necessity. The exalted progenitor Emperor Xiaowen respectfully observed astronomical phenomena, bent over to compromise with other's plans, set out from Wu Prefecture to come to reside in Song County.[106] Although Wei was an old state, its destiny was renewed. At the end of the Zhengguang era, the fate of our state was critical.[107] Death and disorder never ceased, bandits and traitors struck one after another. It pressed upon our people and there was no way to stop it. Now, from the distant past I honor old precedents as I deeply test the affairs of our time. I investigated tortoise [shells for divination] and got a propitious sign to move our dwelling to Zhang [River] and Fu [River]. I sincerely hope that we can once more make the grand enterprise burgeon, and for a second make the imperial destiny shine like a crystal.

「安安能遷」，自古之明典；所居靡定,往昔之成規。是以殷遷八城,周卜三地。吉凶有數, 隆替無恆。事由於變通, 理出於不得已故也。高祖孝文皇帝式觀乾象, 俯協人謀, 發自武州, 來幸嵩縣, 魏雖舊國, 其命惟新。及正光之季, 國步孔棘, 喪亂不已, 寇賊交侵, 俾我生民, 無所措手。今遠遵古式, 深驗實事, 考龜襲吉, 遷宅漳滏。庶克隆洪基, 再昌寶曆.[108]

On November 20, 534, only four days after this decree was released, "the imperial carriages were sent out at once, and four hundred thousand households set out onto the road in disarray" (車駕便發, 戶四十萬狼狽就道).[109] The fact that these words are most probably those of Gao Huan instead of the young emperor is clear and was so understood at that time. This relationship is well described in a children's ditty (*tongyao* 童謠) that was current at the time:

| 可憐青雀子 | The pitiful wax-bill sparrow chick,[110] |
| 飛來鄴城裡 | Flew to the city walls of Ye. |

Xi'an 西安 city limit) and Luoyi 雒邑 (inside of modern day Luoyang city limit).

106   Songxian is in modern day Luoyang. Emperor Xiaowen moved the Northern Wei capital from Pingcheng to Luoyang in 494.

107   Zhengguang [August 20, 520–July 16, 525] era, was the third reign title of Emperor Xiaoming 孝明帝 (r. 515–528).

108   Wei, *Wei shu*, 12.297–298.

109   Li, *Bei Qi shu*, 2.18.

110   The term *qingque* 青雀 (*Eophona migratoria*) refers to the wax-bill sparrow, which is also known as the black tailed wax-bill sparrow 黑尾蠟嘴雀 or *sanghu* 桑扈. See Gao Mingqian 高明乾, Tong Yuhua 佟玉華, and Liu Qun 劉坤, *Shijing dongwu shigu* 詩經動物釋詁 (Beijing: Zhonghua shuju, 2005), 250–252.

| 羽翩垂欲成 | His feathered wings drooped, were about to fledge, |
| 4 化作鸚鵡子 | But he transformed into the chick of a parrot.[111] |

Although Gao Huan never took the throne himself, he clearly held absolute power in his hands during the Eastern Wei after it and its counterpart, the Western Wei 西魏 (535–557), split from the Northern Wei.

By the time the Eastern Wei established its court in Ye, the city had been greatly destroyed by the years of warfare. And without preparation, the "[young] emperor arrived in Ye on *gengyin* day [December 4, 534] [without even a proper palace in which to dwell], so he stayed at the Xiang prefectural offices in the northern city. In the autumn of the second year [of Tianping] on the *jiawu* day of the eighth month [October 4, 535], the court commissioned seventy-six thousand people to build a new palace" (庚寅, 車駕至鄴, 居北城相州之廨。二年秋八月甲午發眾七萬六千人營新宮).[112]

This brief passage is all that we know now about the addition of a southern section to the city of Ye (called in historical sources, "the southern city of Ye" 鄴南城 or "the southern city of the capital Ye" 鄴都南城). Thus, Ye became a double city, as the new area was developed, using the old southern wall of Ye as the new district's northern perimeter (see Figure 4). The construction of the southern city was led by Xin Shu 辛術 (500–559) and his contemporary Gao Longzhi 高隆之 (494–554). Xin Shu was known as having a logical perspective and being accomplished in all of the crafts (術有思理, 百工克濟).[113]

Gao Longzhi was the Chief Administrator (*puye* 僕射) at the time. He was

> ... the major leader of planning and construction, and in the making of the capital everything stemmed from him. [He] added on the southern city, the wall was twenty-five *li* in circumference. Because the Zhang River was close to the capital, [he] erected a long dyke to prevent the calamity of flood. [He] also dug canals to draw water from the Zhang to flow around the outer city walls; he [also] built water-powered mills and both of these were beneficial to the age.

> 領營構大將, 京邑製造, 莫不由之。增築南城, 周迴二十五里。 以漳水近於帝城, 起長堤以防溢之患。 又鑿渠引漳水周流城郭, 造治水碾磑, 並有利於時.[114]

---

111   That is repeating what Gao Huan says. Li, *Bei Qi shu*, 2.18.

112   Wei, *Wei shu*, 12.298–299.

113   Li, *Bei Qi shu*, 38.501.

114   Li, *Bei Qi shu*, 18.236.

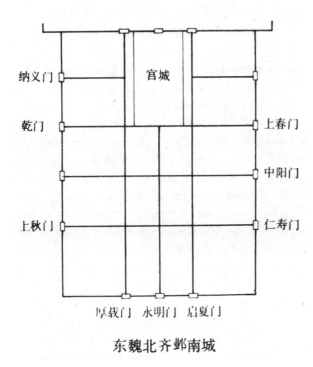

FIGURE 4
Plan of Ye of the Eastern Wei (534–550) and Northern Qi (536–577), showing Wei kingdom Ye directly north. [Murata, *Chūgoku no teito*, p. 227; published with permission of Sōgeisha Press], Nancy Shatzman Steinhardt, *Chinese Imperial City Planning*, 89.

The construction of the new palace and southern city of Ye took nearly five years.[115] The new city had fourteen city gates—the three on the northern wall were the gates of the southern wall of the original city which, from that time on, was called the northern city of Ye (Ye *beicheng* 鄴北城). Compared to the northern city that was still active as part of the capital at this time, the southern city of Ye is vertically longer and had two round city-wall corners on the south side (see Figure 5).[116] There were four gates on each east and west city

---

115   The new city was completed on the *guihai* 癸亥 day of the eleventh month of the first year of Xinghe 興和 (December 11, 539) and the court moved into the new palace on the *dingchou* 丁丑 day of the first month of the following year (February 23, 540). See Wei, *Wei shu*, 12.303–304.

116   These two round corners are something of a mystery since most ancient Chinese cities constructed straight walls with square corners unless the city was built alongside a mountain or river and it had to curve. Zhu Yanshi does mention that the newly built city walls were not straight and have slight curves. The southeastern and southwestern corners were round, and the shape and form were new and strange. See Zhu's "Ye cheng yizhi" 鄴城遺址, in *Hebei kaogu zhongyao faxian* 河北考古重要發現 (1949–2009), ed. Hebei sheng wenwu yanjiu suo 河北省文物研究所 (Beijing: Kexue chuban she, 2009), 214. I have not yet found a scientific reason behind rounding the corners in the southern city of Ye; nonetheless, there is a story that indicates the curved corners to the vertical rectangle were

THE CONSTRUCTION AND DEVELOPMENT OF YE 41

图一 赵彭城北朝佛寺遗址位置图

FIGURE 5 The ruins of Ye in their modern setting. See Zhu Yanshi and others, "Hebei Linzhang xian Yecheng yizhi Zhaopengcheng Bei chao fosi yizhi de kantan yu fajue" 河北臨漳縣鄴城遺址趙彭城北朝佛寺遺址勘探與發掘, *Kaogu* 考古, no. 7 (2010): 32.

meant to represent the shape of the tortoise shell. The appendix of the *Yezhong ji* quoting the *Record of Visiting Ancient sites on the North Banks of the Yellow River* (*Heshuo fanggu ji* 河朔訪古記), a partially extant work attributed to Naixian 乃賢 (ca. 1309–1363) of the Qarluq 葛邏祿, states: In Ye, the southern city was six *li* from east to west and eight *li* plus sixty double paces from north to south. Because Gao Huan felt that the northern city was narrow and cramped, he ordered his Chief Administrator Gao Longzhi to rebuild the [southern] city. [In the process, they] dug up a divine tortoise that was bigger than one *zhang* square. The shape of the city's walls and battlements all took the image of the

42   CHAPTER 1

wall, and the south wall had three.[117] In addition to the city walls, the southern city also had a moat around the city and horse-face bastions (*mamian* 馬面) on both the eastern and western outer city walls. Nancy Steinhardt points out that materials for building the southern city of Ye came from dismantled buildings of Luoyang that had been burned in 534. She further indicates that the appearance of the southern city of Ye and the use of old building materials suggest that "Luoyang was its model—and perhaps, therefore, that the plan of Luoyang had its palace complex in the north center also."[118]

The city of Ye had a fairly peaceful time as the capital of the Northern Qi prior to its final moment. Even though it never reached the zenith of the Jian'an era as a cultural site, the city was a center for Buddhism and the production of Buddhist arts and crafts.[119]

A piece of court text from the succeeding ruler tells us what the city of Ye in the sixth century might have been like and what happened to it when the political power shifted. On the *xinchou* 辛丑 day of the first month of the sixth year of the Jiande 建德 reign [March 2, 577], after he wiped out the Northern Qi, Emperor Wu 武帝 (r. 560–578) of the Northern Zhou issued an imperial edict, "Edict to Destroy Gardens and Terraces of the State of Qi" ("Huiche Qi guo yuantai zhao" 毀撤齊國園臺詔), in which he announces:

> The bogus Qi was ruthless and domineering, and falsely occupied the Zhang River banks. For generations, they indulged in their wanton customs, and in activities, they exhausted every possible carving and decoration. Whether digging reservoirs or transporting rocks to make mountains and imitate oceans, whether piling up terraces or constructing multiple layers in order to soar to the sun and reach the clouds, they went to the limit of waste and extravagance by their violent and chaotic hearts. 'No one who possesses one among these [faults listed above] has never not come to his end [because of it].'[120] I 'eat simply and dress

---

   tortoise found there. 鄴中南城, 東西六里, 南北八里六十步。高歡以北城窄隘, 故令僕射高隆之更築此城。掘得神龜, 大踰方丈。其堵堞之狀, 咸以龜象焉. See Lu, *Yezhong ji*, 12b.

117 These gates were: (from the northeast of the city) Zhaode 昭德, Shangchun 上春, Zhongyang 中陽, Renshou 仁壽, Qixia 啟夏, Zhuming 朱明, Houzai 厚載, Shangqiu 上秋, Xihua 西華, Qian 乾, and Nayi 納義 (at the northwest of the city).

118 Steinhardt, *Chinese Imperial City Planning*, 88.

119 Regarding Buddhist tradition in the Ye area during the Northern Dynasties, see for example, Ma Aimin 馬愛民, "Yexia foxue zhisheng he Beichao, Sui Tang de Anyang fosi wuseng wuyi" 鄴下佛學之盛和北朝、隋、唐的安陽佛寺武僧武藝, *Anyang shifan xueyuan xuebao* 安陽師範學院學報, no. 5 (2009): 22–29.

120 This is a near quote from the second piece of the "Songs of the Five Sons" (*Wuzi zhi ge* 五子之歌) in the *Xia shu* 夏書 of *Shang shu* 尚書. The song reads "The instruction has

THE CONSTRUCTION AND DEVELOPMENT OF YE

humbly'[121] in order to spread 'teaching by moral example.'[122] I recollect the cost to people and also think about the toil of corvée labor. I shall change this corrupt custom and lead people back to restraint and frugality. Its eastern mountains, southern gardens, and the Three Terraces can all be torn down together. As for the materials like the tiles and wood that can be reused, give them all to the lesser people. As for the fields of these mountains and gardens, return each piece to its original owner.

偽齊叛渙, 竊有漳濱, 世縱淫風, 事窮雕飾。或穿池運石, 為山學海；或層臺累構, 棨日凌雲。以暴亂之心, 極奢侈之事。有一於此, 未或弗亡。朕菲食薄衣, 以弘風教, 追念生民之費, 尚想力役之勞。方當易茲弊俗, 率歸節儉。其東山、南園及三臺可並毀撤。瓦木諸物, 凡入用者, 盡賜下民。山園之田, 各還本主.[123]

In this text, Emperor Wu of the Northern Zhou desires to emphasize his own virtue by exaggerating the wastefulness of the Northern Qi. Nonetheless, his description of Ye corresponds with the archeological findings and other records of the city that have been noted above. Simultaneously, this text demonstrates that any excavation of Ye cannot paint a complete picture of the city as it was under the Cao Wei, or even when it was the capital city of the Northern Qi or the Eastern Wei. For instance, this imperial edict of Emperor Wu of the Northern Zhou, as well as other historical accounts (which will appear in discussions in following chapters), demonstrates that the Three Terraces constructed by Cao Cao in the third century—which have long stood as

---

this: He who wallows in lust indoors and indulges in hunting outdoors, is fascinated with drinking or obsesses with music, or dwells under lofty roofs and within decorated carving walls; there has never been one of these that did not (come to his) end" (訓有之, 內作色荒外作禽荒, 甘酒嗜音峻宇彫牆。有一于此未或不亡). See Kong Anguo 孔安國 (ca. 156–74 BCE) and Kong Yingda 孔穎達 (574–648), comm. and ann., *Shang shu zhengyi* 尚書正義, in *Shisan jing zhushu fu jiaokan ji* 十三經注疏附校勘記, ed. Ruan Yuan 阮元 (1764–1849) 8 vols. (Taipei: Yiwen yingshu guan, 1982), 1: 7.6b.

121   This term is first seen in the account of the Biography of Emperor Wu of Liang (r. 502–549) 梁武帝. See Yao Silian 姚思廉 (557–637), comp., *Liang shu* 梁書 (Beijing: Zhonghua shuju, 1973), 1.15.

122   On "wind and teaching" (*feng jiao* 風教) see, for example, the "Little Preface" 小序 to "Odes of Zhou and the South" 周南 in the *Shijing* 詩經: "For Lessons of manners the term *wind* is used, denoting the influence of instruction. Wind moves [things], and instruction transforms the people" (風風也, 教也。風以動之, 教以化之). The English translation is from James Legge, trans., *The Chinese Classics with a Translation, Critical and Exegetical Notes, Prolegomena, and Copious Indexes: The She King or The Book of Poetry*, 2nd ed., (Taipei: Wenshizhe chuban she, 1971), 37.

123   Linghu Defen 令狐德棻 (583–666), comp., *Zhou shu* 周書 (Beijing: Zhonghua shuju, 1971), 6.101.

metonymical symbols of the city and its greatness—had actually been added to or torn down over a period of three hundred years by various occupants of the city. But, unlike any other capitals, such as Chang'an, that became symbols of successive dynasties, Ye is always remembered as the city of Cao Cao. This disparity between actuality and cultural memory should be kept in mind when reading historical or literary writings on the city of Ye.

Ye met its final demise at the hands of Yang Jian 楊堅 (541–604) in the second year of the Daxiang 大象 reign (580). Yang had been the military might behind the throne of Emperor Xuan 宣帝 (559–580) of the Northern Zhou, who occupied the throne for only a year, during which time Yang flexed his military force and brought the Northern Zhou to an end, founding the Sui 隋 (581–618). During his coup, Yang Jian defeated Yuchi Jiong 尉遲迥 (d. 580) at Ye. Yuchi killed himself on the city wall to avoid being captured, Yang Jian then entered and burned down the city. Even though Ye was a short-lived city compared to many other capital cities throughout Chinese history, some modern scholars believe that Ye played an influential role in the development of several major cities in neighboring countries. In many of his articles, Niu Runzhen points out that many cities, like Kaesong 開城, old Pyongyang 古平壤城, and Gongju 公州 in North Korea and South Korea and Fujiwara-kyō 藤原京 and Heijō-kyō 平城京 in Japan, are all modeled after Ye.[124]

The burned remains of Ye were all that was left after the ravages of nature (floods), time (erosion), and human activity (war, fires, etc.) conspired to erase one of the grandest cities of China. Yet, while the physical remains of Ye have disappeared, its memory is kept alive through writing. In close readings of selected literary works throughout dynastic history examined in the following chapters, the reader will find that Ye represents not only the celebration of the victories and achievements of larger than life heroes but also a lamentation for their defeats and failures. Although its physical existence had been erased, the city of Ye would continue as a powerful symbol of the vicissitudes of human life and history.

124　See for example, Niu Runzhen, "Hou Zhao Ye ducheng zhi jianzhu kao: Zhong shiji dong-ya ducheng zhidu tanyuan zhi er" 後趙鄴都城制建築考: 中世紀東亞都城制度探源之二, *Hebei xuekan* 河北學刊 28, no. 3 (2008): 84–90; "Ye yu zhongshiji dongya ducheng chengzhi xitong" 鄴與中世紀東亞都城城制系統, *Hebei xuekan* 26, no. 5 (2006): 105–14; "Ye cheng chengzhi dui gudai Chaoxian, Riben ducheng zhidu de yingxiang" 鄴城城制對古代朝鮮、日本都城制度的影響, in *Hanguo yanjiu luncong (Di shiwu ji)* 韓國研究論叢 (第十五輯), edited by Shi Yuanhua 石源華, (Beijing: Shijie zhishi chuban she, 2007), 271–289; and "Ye cheng: Zhongguo, yazhou yu shijie chengshi shi yanjiu zhong de yige mi" 鄴城: 中國、亞洲與世界城市史研究中的一個迷, *Shilin* 史林, no. 3 (2009): 12–20.

CHAPTER 2

Ye in Jian'an Literature

As the preceding chapter demonstrates, Ye was an important city in the political and military history of early China, and it remains today a repository of material artifacts. It has exercised an influence on the development of city design and planning, but as an actual site, it suffered the inevitable fate of many other ancient cities in premodern China and was destroyed by natural and human disasters. Still, the archeological artifacts and material remains give us an outline of what the physical city might have been like. Beyond its actual presence, though, Ye also lived on to the present as a theme in Chinese literature—for nearly two thousand years. I would like now to consider how Ye develops as a trope, a part of the imaginary world of literature, as a celebrated site of contemporary political power and prestige and as a symbol of the transience of power and nostalgia for the past. In the present chapter, I choose the two most significant sites of Ye in literature—the terraces and gardens—as a case study of the city of Ye in literature of the Jian'an 建安 (196–220) period.[1]

1 The Three Terraces of Ye as an Enduring Motif

At the font of the legacy of Ye stand Cao Cao and two of his sons, Cao Pi 曹丕 (187–226), the later Emperor Wen of Wei 魏文帝 (r. 220–226), and Cao Zhi 曹植 (192–232), known for their passion for and talents in letters. For them, the bond between the political and literary was tight; as Cao Pi said in his famous "On Literature" in his *Standard Treatises* (*Dianlun lunwen* 典論·論文):

> Writing is the grand enterprise that orders the state and the prosperous matter that does not decay. The years granted to one have a specified time

---

1   Many scholars have worked or are presently working on Jian'an literature and literati. I will not focus on the whole of that literature but will turn directly to the works related to the city of Ye itself. Jian'an literature is well covered, for example, in the works of (listed alphabetically by surname) Robert Joe Cutter, Jean-Pierre Diény, Hans H. Frankel, Gong Kechang 龔克昌, Howard L. Goodman, Donald Holzman, Huang Jie 黃節, Itō Masafumi 伊藤正文, David R. Knechtges, Paul W. Kroll, Li Baojun 李寶均, Li Wenlu 李文祿, Liao Guodong 廖國棟, Mei Chia-ling 梅家玲, Ronald C. Miao, Pan Xiaolong 潘嘯龍, Shih Hsiang-lin, Suzuki Shûji 鈴木修次, Wang Mei 王玫, Wang Pengting 王鵬廷, Wang Wei 王巍, Wu Fusheng 吳伏生, Xu Gongchi 徐公持, Yu Guanying 余冠英, Yu Shaochu 俞紹初, Yu Xianhao 郁賢皓, Zhang Caimin 張采民, Zhang Keli 張可禮, Zhao Jianjun 趙建軍, Zhao Youwen 趙幼文, and others.

© KONINKLIJKE BRILL NV, LEIDEN, 2020 | DOI:10.1163/9789004420144_004

they will end; glory and pleasure end with one's physical body. Both are a constant appointment that must be kept, and neither can be compared to the infinity of writing.

文章經國之大業，不朽之盛事。年壽有時而盡，榮樂止乎其身。二者必至之常期，未若文章之無窮.[2]

The most iconic image of Ye is that of the Three Terraces that Cao Cao constructed and which "became a favorite poetic topic starting in the fifth century."[3] Particularly prominent is the Bronze Bird Terrace and the story about Cao's concubines residing on the terrace after his death. After the construction of the Bronze Bird Terrace was completed, Cao Cao toured the terrace in the company of his sons and commanded them to compose poems to commemorate the occasion.[4] Cao Pi's preface describes the event that led to the poem's composition as follows:

In the spring of the seventeenth year of Jian'an [ca. May, 212], [we] visited West Garden and ascended Bronze Bird Terrace. [Father] ordered us, we brothers, all to compose. Its text reads:

建安十七年春，遊西園，登銅雀臺。命余兄弟竝作。其詞曰：

登高臺以騁望　　We ascend the high terrace and release our gaze into the distance,

---

2   See the complete text in Xiao Tong 蕭統 (501–31), *Wen xuan* 文選, comm. Li Shan 李善 (d. 689) (Beijing: Zhonghua shuju, 1977), 52.6a–52.8a. For English translations, see for example, Tian Xiaofei, "Cao Pi, 'A Discourse on Literature,'" in *Hawai'i Reader in Traditional Chinese Culture*, ed. Victor H. Mair and others (Honolulu: University of Hawai'i Press, 2004), 231–233; David Pollard, "*Ch'i* in Chinese Literary Theory," in *Chinese Approaches to Literature from Confucius to Liang Ch'i-ch'ao*, ed. Adele Rickett (Princeton: Princeton University Press, 1978), 43–66; Donald Holzman, "Literary Criticism in China in the Early Third Century AD," *Asiatische studien* 28.2 (1974): 113–149; Ronald C. Miao, "Literary Criticism at the End of the Eastern Han," *Literature East and West* 16 (1972): 1016–1026; Stephen Owen, "A Discourse on Literature," in *Readings in Chinese Literary Thought* (Cambridge: Council on East Asian Studies Harvard University, 1992), 57–72; and E. R. Hughes, *The Art of Letters: Lu Chi's "Wen fu" AD 302* (New York: Pantheon Books, 1951), 231–234.
3   Tian Xiaofei, "A Preliminary Comparison of the Two Recensions of 'Jinpingmei,'" *Harvard Journal of Asiatic Studies* 62, no. 2 (2002): 353.
4   In the *Shuijing zhu* 水經注, a statement reads, "Therefore, the Martial Emperor's [Cao Cao] 'Fu on Ascending the Terrace' says that 'We led the Changming to irrigate streets and *li*-districts,' it refers specifically to this canal" (故魏武登臺賦曰引長明灌街里，謂此渠也). Li Daoyuan 酈道元 (d. 527), *Shuijing zhu*, ed. Chen Qiaoyi 陳橋驛 (Shanghai: Shanghai guji chuban she, 1990), 10.212. But no extant "*Fu on Ascending the Terrace*" that is attributed to Cao Cao can be found.

YE IN JIAN'AN LITERATURE

47

2	好靈雀之麗嫻	And delight in the beautiful refinement of this noumenal bird.[5]
	飛閣崛其特起	The flying galleries jut up, rising uncontested,
4	層樓儼以承天	And storied buildings are majestic enough to uphold heaven.
	步逍遙以容與	Pacing at ease we are free and easy,
6	聊遊目于西山	And for a time let our eyes roam over the western mountains.
	溪谷紆以交錯	Creeks and valleys twine and intersect,
8	草木鬱其相連	Plants and trees are luxuriant and continuous,
	風飄飄而吹衣	Wind gusts and blows my clothes,
10	鳥飛鳴而過前	Birds, flying and singing, pass before me.
	申躊躇以周覽	I prolong my slow pace to take in the surrounding view,
12	臨城隅之通川	And look out over the flowing stream at the corner of the city wall.[6]

This piece is clearly only a fragment. In the first two couplets, Cao Pi describes the location—the terrace—in detail. Then the poet begins to describe what the brothers saw from their view atop of the terrace. In contrast to the majestic terrace that "juts up" and "suddenly appears," the "free and easy" roamers enjoy surroundings that offer a horizontal sight filled with creeks and valleys, plants and trees; the softness and tenderness of which—in contrast to the hard man-made structures—softly and tenderly "twine and intersect" in a "luxuriant and continuous" manner. In lines nine and ten as the gusting wind brings the reader's gaze back to the clothes of the poet, the poet begins to describe his physical response to the scene, slowing his pace to take in the wondrous view. Unfortunately, this outward, then inward, then outward again movement between poet and landscape is left undone, as we will never know what the rest of the piece says.

Luckily, Cao Zhi also wrote a piece. (It is in a similar prosodic form as that of his brother's piece above—in the *San guo zhi* edition—however, the empty word *xi* 兮 at the end of odd numbered lines is still attached as in standard *sao*-style; see notes below.) This piece has survived in its entirety—conventionally titled as the "*Fu* on Ascending the Terrace" ("Deng tai fu" 登臺賦). It "describes the view from the terrace and pays tribute to the achievements of his father."[7] The poem reads:

---

5 The noumenal bird (*lingque* 靈雀) here probably refers to the Bronze Bird Terrace.
6 Shih Hsiang-Lin has also translated this preface. See her "Jian'an Literature Revisited: Poetic Dialogues in the Last Three Decades of the Han Dynasty" (PhD diss., University of Washington, 2013), 99. The text of this poem is in *Quan San guo wen* 全三國文, 4.5a, in *Quan shanggu sandai Qin Han San guo Liu chao wen* 全上古三代秦漢三國六朝文, comp. Yan Kejun 嚴可均 (1762–1843) (Beijing: Zhonghua shuju, 1991).
7 David R. Knechtges, ed., *Ancient and Early Medieval Chinese Literature: A Reference Guide, Part I* (Leiden: Brill, 2010), 91.

	從明后之嬉遊兮	We followed the enlightened lord and happily wandered,[8]
2	聊登臺以娛情	For a time we ascended the terrace to give joy to our emotions.
	見天府之廣開兮	I saw the broadness and openness of the storehouse of Heaven,[9]
4	觀聖德之所營	And gazed upon that which sagely virtue had built.[10]
	建高殿之嵯峨兮	Constructing the craggy heights of the lofty palace hall,[11]
6	浮雙闕乎太清	They floated twin pylons in the great clarity.[12]

8   The text of this poem in the Tang 唐 (618–907) commonplace book, *Yiwen leiju* 藝文類聚, does not include the character *xi* 兮. See Ouyang Xun 歐陽詢 (557–641) and others comps., *Yiwen leiju* (rpt. Taipei: Wenguang chuban she, 1974), 62.1120.

9   Some read *tianfu* 天府 as *taifu* 太府 or *dafu* 大府, the Grand Storehouse, following the version found in Chen Shou 陳壽 (233–297), *San guo zhi* 三國志 (Beijing: Zhonghua shuju, 1959), 35.912; and Yan, *Quan Sanguo wen*, 13.10a. Gong Kechang 龔克昌, Su Jui-lung 蘇瑞隆, and Zhou Guanghuang 周廣璜 understand the term to refer to a government building, which makes it a specific reference to the physical construction. See their note, "*Taifu* is an official title. There is a *dafu* in "Tianguan" of the *Zhouli*, it handles official storage and state finance accounts. Here it indicates its official bureau" (太府：官名。《周禮・天官》有大府，掌府藏會計。這裏指其官署) in *Quan Sanguo fu pingzhu* 全三國賦評註 (Ji'nan: Qi Lu chuban she, 2013), 403n3.

10   An indirect reference to Cao Cao.

11   The text in *San guo zhi* and *Quan shanggu sandai Qin Han Sanguo Liuchao wen* read *gaodian* as *gaomen* 高門, the "lofty gate." This reading also carries the idea of a prestigious or noble family, as in "saw the eminence then of our prestigious family." The metaphorical meaning of "noble family" first occurs in this sense in the *Zhuangzi* 莊子, particularly in the Tang commentary of Cheng Xuanying 成玄英 (ca. 601–690). In the section entitled, "Full Understanding of Life" (*Dasheng* 達生) describing, "There was one named Zhang Yi, he who at his lofty gates hung a doubled blind. Everyone rushed to [visit] him" (有張毅者，高門縣薄，無不走也). Cheng Xuanying's 成玄英 sub-commentary states, "The lofty gates are the rich and noble families" (高門富貴之家也). See Guo Qingfan 郭慶藩 (1844–1896), ed., *Zhuangzi ji shi* 莊子集釋 (Beijing: Zhonghua shuju, 1961), 7a.646. The term was in current use in this meaning, as shown in the biography of Jia Xu 賈詡 (147–223) in *San guo zhi* which describes how Jia cut himself off from high society to keep Cao Cao from becoming suspicious of his loyalty. He "shut the door and kept to himself. He withdrew and had no private interactions with others. When boys or girls were married off, they avoided tying the knot with 'lofty gates'" (闔門自守，退無私交。男女嫁娶，不結高門). See Chen, *San guo zhi*, 10.331.

12   Cao Zhi also mentions these paired pylons (*shuangque* 雙闕) in his work, "For Xu Gan" (*Zeng* Xu Gan 贈徐幹), where he writes, "For the moment I go on an outing at night, / I roam between those pair of pylons" (聊且夜行游，游彼雙闕間). Zhao Youwen 趙幼文 points out that, according to the description from "*Fu* on the Wei Capital" (Wei *du fu* 魏都賦), the pylons are outside of Wenchang Hall (Wenchang *dian* 文昌殿) on either side of the main south gate (*duan men* 端門). See Zhao, *Cao Zhi ji jiaozhu* 曹植集校注 (Beijing: Renmin wenxue chubanshe, 1984), 42. Great clarity refers to sky or heaven. The term appears earliest in alchemical texts. For further discussion on the term see, for example, Fabrizio Pregadio, *Great Clarity: Daoism and Alchemy in Early Medieval China* (Stanford: Stanford University Press, 2005).

YE IN JIAN'AN LITERATURE   49

	立沖天之華觀兮	And erected ornate lookouts that charge into heavens,[13]
8	連飛閣乎西城	That linked flying pavilions to the western wall.
	臨漳川之長流兮	Looking down on the constant flow of the Zhang River,
10	望眾果之滋榮	I gazed at the succulent splendor of all fruits,[14]
	仰春風之和穆兮	Lifting my head to the peaceful harmony of spring breezes,
12	聽百鳥之悲鳴	I heard the sad cries of a hundred birds.
	天功恒其既立兮	Heavenly merits eternalize what he has accomplished,[15]
14	家願得而獲呈	What our family would attain is procured and displayed.
	揚仁化於宇內兮	He spreads humane transformation within the cosmos,
16	盡肅恭於上京	And receives all solemn respect in the capital.
	雖桓文之為盛兮	Although we take Huan and Wen's time to be the most prosperous,[16]
18	豈足方乎聖明	How can that be sufficient to match this sagely brilliance?
	休矣美矣	Striking! Beautiful!
20	惠澤遠揚	His benevolent fecundity spreads afar.
	翼佐我皇家兮	To assist our royal household,
22	寧彼四方	He pacifies those four directions.
	同天地之矩量兮	Matching the rules and capacity of heaven and earth,
24	齊日月之輝光	He is equal to the radiant light of the sun and moon.
	永貴尊而無極兮	May his nobility and honor last forever without limit,[17]
26	等年壽於東王	And his years be as long as the Eastern King.[18]

---

13 There is a variant of *chongtian* in *San guo zhi* and *Quan shanggu sandai Qin Han Sanguo Liuchao wen*, which introduce *zhongtian* 中天 as to "be in the center of heaven."

14 *Zhongguo* 眾果 is read as *yuanguo* 園果 in *San guo zhi*. It can be understood as "the fruits of the Bronze Bird Park."

15 The text in *San guo zhi* and *Quan shanggu sandai Qin Han Sanguo Liuchao wen* read this line as "Heavenly clouds walled around that which had been erected" (天功垣其既立). The *Chuxue ji* 初學記, however, erroneously states this line is "Heavenly merits feared for that which had been erected" (天功怛其既立), which does not make as much sense. See *Chuxue ji*, ed. Xu Jian 徐堅 (659–729) vol. 2 (Taipei: Dingwen shuju, 1972), 24.576.

16 Duke Huan of Qi 齊桓公 (r. 685–643 BCE) and Duke Wen of Jin 晉文公 (r. 636–628 BCE) were the two best known rulers of the Five Hegemons of the Spring and Autumn period (*chunqiu wuba* 春秋五霸). The other three are: Duke Xiang of Song 宋襄公 (r. 650–637 BCE), Duke Mu of Qin 秦穆公 (r. 659–621 BCE), and King Zhuang of Chu 楚莊王 (r. 613–591 BCE).

17 The last couplet (lines twenty-five and twenty-six) is not shown in the text of *Yiwen leiju*. See Ouyang, *Yiwen leiju*, 62.1120.

18 Here the Eastern King refers to the King Father of the East (*Dong wang fu* 東王父), known as the counterpart of the transcendent Queen Mother of the West (*Xi wang mu* 西王母). The text of this poem is found in the commentary to Cao Zhi's biography in Chen, *San guo zhi*, 19.558; and Yan, *Quan Sanguo wen*, 13.10a. See Robert Joe Cutter's translation and reading of this poem in his, "Cao Zhi (192–232) and His Poetry" (PhD diss., University of Washington, 1983), 67–69; and "Cao Zhi's (192–232) Symposium Poems," *Essays, Articles, Reviews* (*CLEAR*) 6, no. 1/2 (1984): 1–32. I am using the text that is found in Zhao, *Cao Zhi ji jiaozhu*, 44–45.

Certainly, the importance of these two *fu*-poems composed by the gifted Cao brothers could very much be one reason why the terraces of Ye became such a popular topic in the polite and popular traditions. And while the poems are a product of the direct perception of the poets and can give us an idea of size, shape, and meaning of the terraces in their own time, they are also verses that "sing praise of merit and eulogize virtue" (*gegong songde* 歌功頌德); that is, they are outwardly directed to please a powerful audience and, therefore, eulogize the lord's merit and virtue. Even though these are technically in the tradition of *fu*, they are good examples of "poems written at imperial command" (*yingzhao shi* 應詔詩) in spite of the fact that the one who commanded their composition was not officially "imperial" at the time. In his article on Wang Can 王粲 (177–217), Wu Fusheng 吳伏生 suggests that all eulogy poems (*songshi* 頌詩) have an intended readership, are more direct and urgent than normal, and were done under the gaze of the intended reader or audience.[19] The composition by Cao Zhi clearly has his father as the intended reader,[20] and he utilized the completion of Bronze Bird Terrace as an opportunity to praise Cao Cao's achievements and merits.[21]

Cao Zhi's famous *fu* has been extensively discussed by Robert Joe Cutter and the reader is directed there for a full analysis of the poem.[22] Still, it is necessary to emphasize that these terraces, especially Bronze Bird, were used as powerful symbols of what later ages took to be Cao Cao's success, ambition, or desires. This is a tradition that is passed on in both the polite and popular traditions, two traditions that often come together in the literati writing of later times. To understand the importance of this "terrace theme" in the totality of Chinese literature, it is useful to examine it as represented in the popular tradition, in two fictional tales about the Three Kingdoms 三國 (220–280) period from the late thirteenth to the late fifteenth century: *Sanguo pinghua* 三國平話 and *Sanguo yanyi* 三國演義. The *Sanguo yanyi*, ascribed to Luo Guanzhong 羅貫中 (ca. 1330–1400), states that after Cao Cao took control of the area east of the Liao River (Liaodong 遼東), he wished to build Bronze Bird Terrace in order to amuse himself in his golden years. At this time, according to the *Sanguo yanyi*, Cao Zhi suggested to his father, "If you're going to build storied terraces, you must build three. Name the middle one Bronze Bird, on the left make the Jade Dragon, and on the right, Golden Phoenix. Then, build two flying bridges rising

---

19   Wu Fusheng 吳伏生, "Wang Can 'Congjun shi' xilun: Jiantan gudai de songshi 王粲《從軍詩》析論—兼談古代的誦詩," *Zhongguo shixue* 中國詩學, no. 10 (2004): 75–81.

20   Ibid.

21   See Cutter, "Cao Zhi's (192–232) Symposium Poems," 2–3.

22   Cutter, "Cao Zhi (192–232) and His Poetry," 67–69; and "Cao Zhi's (192–232) Symposium Poems," 1–32.

YE IN JIAN'AN LITERATURE   51

across the void between them, only then will it be a magnificent sight" (若建層臺必立三座。中間名銅雀，左為玉龍右為金鳳。更作兩條飛橋，橫空而上乃為壯觀). Cao Cao was pleased with the idea and posted his sons Pi and Zhi to Ye in order to oversee the construction of the terraces.[23]

To add to the drama and mystery of the iconic structures and create a more intriguing characterization of Cao Cao, the popular materials link the terraces to beautiful women. In the colloquial tradition, Liu Bei 劉備 (161–223), a distant descendant of the Han and ruler of Shu 蜀, seeks to ally himself with the ruler of Wu 吳, Sun Quan 孫權 (182–252), in order to defeat Cao Cao. Liu Bei sends his field marshal, Zhuge Liang 諸葛亮 (181–234), to persuade Sun Quan's lead general, Zhou Yu 周瑜 (175–210) to join the fight. Zhou Yu is married to one of the two beautiful Qiao sisters, who are cast as the impetus for Cao Cao's construction of the terrace. In the *Sanguo pinghua*, the site of the terraces is transferred to Chang'an 長安, but its instrumental use is made clear when Zhuge Liang persuades Zhou Yu to take up arms against Cao Cao:

> Let's talk for the moment about Zhuge. He was nine feet two inches tall and had just reached thirty. His beard was raven-black and his nails were three inches long. He was as handsome as could be! After Zhou Yu had treated Zhuge to wine, the servants presented oranges in a golden bowl. Zhuge pushed back his sleeves, held an orange in his left hand, and with his right hand raised a knife. Lu Su said, "Martial Marquis, you offend against propriety." But Zhou Yu said with a smile, "I've been told that Zhuge is from a lowly background. He's just a peasant and simply not used to this." He then divided his orange into three equal parts. Kongming[24] divided his into three parts of different sizes: one large, one small, and one even smaller, and placed them on a silver tray.
>
> Zhou Yu asked, "Field marshal, what do you mean by this?" Zhuge explained, "The big one is Minister Cao; the smaller one is Caitiff-Suppressing Sun; and the smallest one is my lord, the lonely and desperate Liu Bei. Cao Cao's military might is like a mountain and there is no one who can oppose him. Sun Zhongmou[25] can offer only a bit of resistance. Alas, my lord has a limited number of troops and few officers, so we request aid from the land of Wu. But you, Grand Marshal, claim to be too sick." When Zhou Yu remained silent, Kongming shouted with intimidating force, "If

---

23   Cf. Luo Guanzhong, *Three Kingdoms: A Historical Novel*, trans. Moss Roberts (Beijing: Foreign Languages Press and Berkeley: University of California Press, 1994), 34.405.

24   Zhuge Liang.

25   Sun Quan.

Cao Cao now has set his army in motion to come from afar to conquer the lands of the River and of Wu, it is not because of some fault of the Imperial Uncle. And, you must also know that Cao Cao has built his Bronze Bird Palace in Chang'an and is scouring the empire for beautiful women. If Cao Cao would take the lands of the River and of Wu and make the two daughters of Lord Qiao his captives, Grand Marshal, wouldn't that defile your fine reputation?" Zhou Yu pushed back his sleeves and rose to his feet and ordered his wife to return to the rear chambers [as he said,] "I am a real man, I will never be shamed. I will visit the Caitiff-Suppressing General and be appointed grand marshal. I will kill Lord Cao."[26]

When this story is adapted into the *Sanguo yanyi* and the terraces are once again located in Ye, the author adds a fictitious version of Cao Zhi's "*Fu on Ascending the Terrace*," which is entitled "*Fu on the Bronze Bird Terrace*" ("Tongque tai fu" 銅雀臺賦). This *fu* is similar to Cao Zhi's piece found in the commentary of the *San guo zhi*, but with two additional stanzas. Between lines ten and eleven of Cao Zhi's purported original piece, the Zhuge Liang version inserts eight extra lines. These lines read:

	立雙臺于左右兮	He raises twin terraces to the left and right—,
2	有玉龍與金鳳	And there are the Jade Dragon and the Gold Phoenix.
	攬二喬於東南兮	Taking the two Qiao girls of the southeastern land—,
4	樂朝夕之與共	He delights to be with them morning and night.
	俯皇都之宏麗兮	He looks down upon the grand beauty of the royal city—,
6	瞰雲霞之浮動	And takes a bird's eye view of the floating movement of the rosy clouds.
	欣群才之來萃兮	He is happy that the gathering of his group of talents—,
8	協飛熊之吉夢	Will aid the auspicious dream of the flying bear.[27]

And a final addition occurs at the end of the verse:

| | 御龍旗以遨遊兮 | Driving the dragon flag to roam about at pleasure—, |
| 2 | 回鸞駕而周章 | Turning the *luan*-bird carriage to travel around.[28] |

---

26 Translation by Wilt L. Idema and Stephen H. West, from *Records of the Three Kingdoms in Plain Language* (Indianapolis: Hackett Publishing Company, 2016), 90–92.

27 The dream of a flying bear in this line refers to a story about King Wen of Zhou 周文王 (r. ca. 1099–1061 BCE), who once dreamed that a bear with wings came to his court. Duke Zhou 周公 explained the dream as a sign of someone worthy coming to aid the king. Later, King Wen found Jiang Shang 姜尚 (1156–1017 BCE) to assist him to defeat King Zhou of Shang 商紂王 (r. ca. 1076–1046 BCE) and hence established the Zhou dynasty.

28 Both terms, "dragon flag" and "*luan*-bird carriage," in this couplet indicate the appearance

YE IN JIAN'AN LITERATURE

	恩化及乎四海兮	His grace and transformative power extends to the four seas—,[29]
4	嘉物阜而民康	We praise that things are plentiful and people are at peace.
	願斯臺之永固兮	We pray this terrace be ever solid—,
6	樂終古而未央	And that this happiness will be everlasting and never end.[30]

The result of Zhuge's visit to Sun Quan and Zhou Yu is a combined force that defeats Cao Cao at the famous Battle of the Red Cliffs (Chibi *zhi zhan* 赤壁之戰), which not only thwarted Cao Cao's plans for full conquest, but also created the three way split (the Three Kingdoms) at the end of the Eastern Han. Of course, the more reliable historical account of the battle only states that Liu Bei sent Zhuge Liang to visit Sun Quan, and that the battle occurred at the Red Cliffs, where Cao Cao was defeated and withdrew north of the Yangzi River.[31] From the preface of Cao Pi's poem we also know the Cao brothers' verses on the terrace were probably composed in the year 212, some two years after Zhou Yu's death. Nonetheless, the story of the Bronze Bird Terrace and the Qiao sisters in the popular tradition aroused people's imagination for countless generations.

While the Bronze Bird Terrace inspired many literary works, it perhaps also held much personal meaning for Cao Cao. In his "Lamenting the Death of Emperor Wu of Wei" ("Diao Wei Wudi wen" 弔魏武帝文), Lu Ji 陸機 (261–303)

---

  of the royal entourage. The *luan* is a mythical bird. Here *luanjia* 鸞駕 means the carriage has bells shaped like the bird as the usage seen in lines, "When gentlemen reached to a stop, the bell sounds were loud and clear" (君子至止，鸞聲將將), in the "Tingliao" 庭燎 of the *Shijing* 詩經. *Mao shi* 182. Also see David Knechtges' note on the *luan*-bells in his *Wen xuan, Or Selections of Refined Literature*, vol. 1, *Rhapsodies on Metropolises and Capitals* (Princeton: Princeton University Press, 1996), 1:140, L. 397n.

29 As for the four seas, there are various readings. One is that in ancient belief China was surrounded by seas in four directions. Another definition of the four seas is the neighboring areas around the Han people. "The nine Yi tribes [in the east], eight Di tribes [in the north], seven Rong tribes [in the west], and six Man tribes [in the south] are called the four seas" (九夷八狄七戎六蠻謂之四海). See Guo Pu 郭璞 (276–324) and Xing Bing 邢昺 (932–1010), comm. and ann., *Erya zhushu* 爾雅註疏, in *Shisan jing zhushu fu jiaokan ji* 十三經注疏附校勘記, ed. Ruan Yuan 阮元 (1764–1849), 8 vols., (Taipei: Yiwen yingshu guan, 1982), 8: 7.8b.

30 The "happiness" that is "everlasting" in this line reminds us of the contrasting feeling of not being able to enduringly bear certain emotions and is an allusion to a couplet from the famous poem, "Encountering Sorrow" 離騷, of the *Chuci* 楚辭, which reads, "To carry these feelings in my bosom and not express them, / How could I bear this with me for eternity?" (懷朕情而不發兮，余焉能忍而與此終古). See Hong Xingzu 洪興祖 (1090–1155), *Chuci buzhu* 楚辭補注, ed. Bai Huawen 白化文 and others (Beijing: Zhonghua shuju, 1983), 35. It also is reflected in the common saying, "Sorrow is born at the height of happiness" (*le ji bei sheng* 樂極悲生).

31 Chen, *San guo zhi*, 54.1262.

begins by saying that he had read Cao Cao's "Testamentary Command" ("Yi-ling" 遺令) when he was working in the imperial archives in the eighth year of Yuankang 元康 reign [January 29, 298–February 16, 299]. In that testament, the once virile hero, now near death, gave his last words and wishes to his sons. Filled with pitiable grief he entrusted his young children and precious belongings to his adult sons. In this part of his testament, he not only mentioned loved ones whom he was leaving behind and the possessions for which he had worked so hard, but also the rituals he desired held as sacrificial remembrance. He commanded that these take place on top of Bronze Bird Terrace, where his wives and sons could think about him and gaze afar at his eternal resting place. On his deathbed, Cao Cao said:

> "Bring all my concubines and performers on to Bronze Bird Terrace. In the hall on top of the terrace, place an eight-*chi* long bed and hang there a soft-hemp mourning tent. At the time of *chao* and *bu*,[32] present food like jerked meat and dried grain. On the first and fifteenth days of each month, then have the [entertainers] perform, facing the [mourning] tent of fine silk. You [my sons] should from time to time ascend Bronze Bird Terrace and gaze upon my western tumulus in the burial grounds." And [Cao Cao] also said, "the leftover incense can be split among my ladies. If they have nothing to do in their chambers, they can learn to make decorative lacings for shoes and sell them. The silk cords that I've earned from the years of being an official,[33] in each and every case shall be stored away. My leftover summer clothes and winter furs can be stored away separately. The ones that cannot be so arranged, you brothers may split equally."

> 吾婕好妓人，皆著銅爵臺。於臺堂上施八尺床，繐帳，朝晡上脯糒之
> 屬。月朝十五，輒向帳作妓。汝等時時登銅爵臺，望吾西陵墓田。」
> 又云：「餘香可分與諸夫人。諸舍中無所為，學作履組賣也。吾歷官
> 所得綬，皆著藏中。吾餘衣裘，可別為一藏。不能者兄弟可共分之.[34]

This sentimental portrayal of Cao Cao's thrift is moving, but we should remember that it is a final moment of self-fashioning that is rendered ironic by the tradition that begins soon after Cao's death, which sees Bronze Bird Terrace

---

32   *Zhao* and *bu* 朝晡, also known as *chen* 辰 and *shen* 申, are time periods from seven to nine in the morning and from three to five in the afternoon. These were the time when people had their two meals of the day.

33   These are ties used to attach to seals of office, jade belt pendants, and official seals.

34   Xiao, *Wen xuan,* 60.17b–18a. Tian Xiaofei also translated this passage in her "Fan Writing: Lu Ji, Lu Yun and the Cultural Transactions between North and South," in *Southern Identity and Southern Estrangement in Medieval Chinese Poetry,* edited by Ping Wang and Nicholas Morrow Williams, 43–78 (Hong Kong: Hong Kong University Press, 2015), 50.

YE IN JIAN'AN LITERATURE

primarily as a symbol of his rapaciousness and lust. This popular tradition ties the terrace to the two daughters of Duke Qiao 橋 (or 喬) 公, so-called "state beauties" (*guose* 國色) who became the wives of Sun Ce 孫策 (175–200) and Zhou Yu, two of Cao Cao's rivals. The *San guo zhi* simply reports that Sun Ce and Zhou Yu "attacked the state of Wan and took it. At that time, they obtained the two daughters of Duke Qiao, both 'state beauties.' Sun Ce himself took in the elder Qiao girl and Zhou Yu took the younger Qiao" (攻皖, 拔之。時得橋公兩女, 皆國色也。策自納大橋, 瑜納小橋).[35] In Yu Fu's 虞溥 (fl. 265) *Jiangbiao zhuan* 江表傳, cited by Pei Songzhi 裴松之 (372–451) in his commentary to the *San guo zhi*, we read: "Sun Ce casually joked with Zhou Yu, 'Even though Duke Qiao's two daughters were displaced by the chaos, he got the two of us as sons-in-law, and that should be enough to make him happy.'"[36] In the unofficial tradition, as we have seen, the two women become the object of Cao Cao's lust and his rationale for constructing Bronze Bird Terrace. Note that by the Tang dynasty, this apocryphal story had become part of accepted lore about Cao Cao. These two traditions merge in literati writing, for instance, in the following quatrain (*jueju* 絕句) by the Tang poet Du Mu 杜牧 (803–852), entitled "The Red Cliff" ("Chibi" 赤壁).

折戟沈沙鐵未銷	A snapped halberd sunk in the sand, its iron not yet disintegrated,
2 自將磨洗認前朝	I took it to polish and clean and recognized the former dynasty.
東風不與周郎便	If the east wind had not worked in lord Zhou's favor,
4 銅雀春深鎖二喬	Then in deep spring in Bronze Bird they would have locked away the Qiao sisters.[37]

---

35 Chen, *San guo zhi*, 54.1260.

36 Chen, *San guo zhi*, 54.1260, n2.

37 This poem is also attributed to Li Shangyin 李商隱 (813–ca. 858). See *Quan Tang shi* 全唐詩, 541.6254; and Zhu Biliang 朱碧蓮, *Du Mu xuanji* 杜牧選集 (Shanghai: Shanghai Guji chuban she, 1995), 98. Others have also translated this poem, see for example, Stephen Owen, *Remembrances: The Experience of the Past in Classical Chinese Literature* (Cambridge, MA: Harvard University Press, 1986), 51–52, his *The Late Tang: Chinese Poetry of the Mid-Ninth Century* (827–860) (Cambridge, MA: Harvard University Asia Center, 2006), 292; and Charles Egan, "Recent-Style Shi Poetry: Quatrains (*Jueju*)," in *How to Read Chinese Poetry: A Guided Anthology*, ed. Zong-Qi Cai (New York: Columbia University Press, 2008), 217–218. In addition to translating and reading Du Mu's "The Red Cliff," Stephen Owen also points out that "... a tradition of interpretation begun in the Sung by Hsü Yen-chou [Xu Yi 許顗], that Tu Mu's poem is a 'veiled' criticism of Ts'ao Ts'ao; he peels away the veiling surface of the text and reveals Tu Mu's true intention, to expose Ts'ao's greater interest in taking the two Ch'iao sisters than in his more serious duty of reunifying China. Later critics bared the moral lesson even more nakedly, adding that Ts'ao Ts'ao military failure was the inevitable consequence of his impure motives." Owen, *Remembrances*, 53–54.

Reading Du Mu's piece, one cannot help but think about another Tang poet, Li He 李賀 (791–817), and his famous "An Arrowhead from the Battlefield of Changping" ("Changping jiantou ge" 長平箭頭歌).[38] These two verses are similar in that both poets use a small but tangible object found on a historical battlefield to introduce the poet's thoughts on the historical event that transpired at the location. What makes Du Mu's poem perhaps even more interesting is the way the poem begins with the inanimate—a snapped halberd—and ends it with the once-living, the Qiao sisters. The movement from the lifeless sharp metal objects to the sentimentalized beauties not only enhances the various contrasts of the poem—animate versus inanimate and material remains versus imaginary remains—but the last line and evocation of "spring" makes Cao Cao's magnificent terrace simply a marker of a life that comes and goes like the seasons—an ephemeral moment marked not as the height of power but as a site of lust and desire.

Even though it is a very short poem, the poet captures the highlight of the battle. The biography of Zhou Yu in the *San guo zhi* describes that at the time of the battle, Cao Cao and the armies of Liu Bei and Sun Quan were on either side of the Yangtze. One of Zhou Yu's divisional commanders, Huang Gai 黃蓋 (n.d.), noticed that Cao Cao had chained up all his battle ships from prow to stern. Huang thereupon prepared several dozens of "attack-ships" (*mengchong doujian* 蒙衝鬥艦) by filling them up with dry reeds and oil. Earlier, Huang had sent a letter to Cao in which he had pretended to surrender and deliver fodder to Cao's army. Thinking that these boats were Huang's defecting division, they allowed him to approach. But Huang Gai set his ships free and set them afire, letting a gust of strong wind carry them into Cao's chained up fleet and into his base on the bank as well.[39]

The Three Terraces are surely the most iconic and enduring objects that Cao Cao built in his power base Ye. They became a symbol of the hero and his accomplishments, but they also became a locus of his rapacious desire, overreaching ambition, and finally his pitiful end. And, after the city was destroyed by war and floods, the ruins of the terraces became a site over which either to eulogize Cao Cao's accomplishments or to lament his fall and all that led to it; or, in a more general way, as will be explored in the following chapters, as a place that evokes the futility of human endeavor against the ravages of history and time.

---

38   *Quan Tang shi*, 393.4432.
39   Chen, *San guo zhi*, 54.1262–1263.

YE IN JIAN'AN LITERATURE   57

2   Ye's Gardens as a Motif of Ephemerality

The other space in Ye that gained an enduring place in literature is its gardens. In contrast to the long-lasting terraces (partial foundations are still standing today), the gardens of Ye did not survive repeated wars and floods. Also, unlike the Three Terraces, the numbers of and histories of the gardens of Ye are not as clearly recorded. Yet, a modern-day reader can still "see" some of the gardens in extant literary works.

From literary works and a few historical entries, we know at least two parks that existed in Ye were named Xuanwu 玄武苑 and Bronze Bird 銅雀園 (also known as West Garden 西園).[40] The site of Xuanwu Park is perhaps indicated by accounts of the reservoir bearing the same name, which was located in the northwestern part of Ye (see Figure 1). According to the *San guo zhi*, "in the spring, the first month of the thirteenth year [of Jian'an] [February 4–March 4, 208], Cao Cao returned to Ye and constructed the Xuanwu reservoir for conducting naval exercises" (十三年春正月，公還鄴，作玄武池以肄舟師).[41] As for Bronze Bird Park, The *San guo zhi* states that in the winter of the fifteenth year [of Jian'an], which would fall between late 210 and early 211, Cao Cao built Bronze Bird Terrace (十五年 ... ... 冬，作銅雀臺).[42] Since neither garden is specifically mentioned in the historical records, these minimalist accounts about construction work must be the bases on which we make calculated guesses about their creation. Unlike Xuanwu Park, which is only briefly mentioned, Bronze Bird Park is better represented in the extant literary corpus.

Many writers on the history of gardens say that Cao Cao built Xuanwu, Bronze Bird, Fanglin/Hualin Park 芳林園 / 華林園, and Lingzhi Park 靈芝園in Ye.[43] There is, however, no tangible evidence in the standard historical sources

---

40 Huang Shoucheng 黃守誠, however, believes that West Garden is the Xuanwu Park. He states, "The so called 'West Garden' is actually the pond and park [area] next to the Xuanwu Reservoir" (所謂「西園」，乃玄武池邊之池苑也). See his *Cao Zijian xintan* 曹子建新探 (Taipei: Zhi shufang chuban jituan, 1998), 187.

41 Chen, *San guo zhi*, 1.30.

42 Chen, *San guo zhi*, 1.32.

43 For example, Ho Cheung Wing 何祥榮, *Han Wei Liuchao Yedu shifu xilun* 漢魏六朝鄴都詩賦析論 (Hong Kong: The Jao Tsung-I Petite Ecole, 2009), 15–16; and Ōji Oka 岡大路, *Zhongguo gongyuan yuanlin shi kao* 中國宮苑園林史考, trans. Chang Yingsheng 常瀛生 (Beijing: Xueyuan chuban she, 2008), 39. Ōji Oka states that Cao Cao built four gardens in Ye. These include the Lingzhi, Yuanwu Park 元武苑, Fanglin Park, and the Bronze Bird Park. Yuanwu is a taboo name for Xuanwu. Others have simply named the parks in their works but fail to further investigate. For example, Zheng Hui 鄭輝 and others, "Cao Wei shiqi Ye cheng yuanlin wenhua yanjiu" 曹魏時期鄴城園林文化研究, *Beijing linye daxue xuebao* 北京林業大學學報, 11, no. 2 (June, 2012): 39–43. In this article, the authors only mention the name Hualin yuan 華林苑 without stating its location or builder. Also

indicating that Cao Cao was the one who built the Fanglin and Lingzhi Parks. The conclusion that Cao Cao built these two parks is probably drawn from the following passage in the sixteenth century gazetteer *Zhangde fu zhi* 漳德府志: "*Tu jing* [probably *Luoyang tu jing*] cites *Wei zhi* and says, when the Great Progenitor [Cao Cao] was enfeoffed in Ye, he placed Fanglin Park in the east and Lingzhi Park in the west. And in the second year of the Huangchu reign [February 10, 221–January 29, 222], sweet dew descended into the parks" (圖經載魏志云太祖受封於鄴，東置芳林園，西置靈芝園。黃初二年，甘露降於園中).[44]

Without verification we cannot say definitively that Cao Cao constructed these gardens. In fact, the one brief mention of these sites in the *San guo zhi* simply says that Emperor Wen, Cao Cao's son Cao Pi, constructed a Lingzhi Reservoir 靈芝池 in (probably the last month of) the third year of Huangchu 黃初 [January 1–29, 222].[45] It is reasonable to assume a connection between Lingzhi reservoir and Lingzhi Park. The earliest record of Fanglin Park in the *San guo zhi* is in a commentary to the annals of Cao Pi. Wang Chen's 王沈 (d. ca. 265) *Wei shu* 魏書 records, "on the *bingyin* day of the twelfth month [in the fourth year of Huangchu reign] [January 20, 224], [Emperor Wen] granted the wife of the Duke of Shanyang[46] a fief to supply taxes for bathing equipment,[47] and the Duke's daughter, [Liu] Man, was made the princess of Changle

---

      see, Li Wencai 李文才, "Wei Jin Nanbei chao shiqi de Hualin yuan: Yi Luoyang, Jiankang liangdi wei zhongxin lunshu" 魏晉南北朝時期的華林園：以洛陽、建康兩地為中心論述, in *Wei Jin Nanbei chao Sui Tang zhengzhi yu wenhua lungao* 魏晉南北朝隋唐政治與文化論稿 (Beijing: Shijie zhishi chuban she, 2006), 126–166.

44   Cui Xian 崔銑 (1478–1541), comp., *Jiajing Zhangde fu zhi* 嘉靖彰德府志 (rpt. Shanghai: Guji shudian, 1964), 8.9b.

45   Chen, *San guo zhi*, 2.82.

46   This is one of Cao Cao's daughters, Cao Jie 曹節 (d. 260). Her biography in *Hou Han shu* 後漢書 reads:

      In the eighteenth year of Jian'an [February 8, 213–January 28, 214] Cao Cao presented his three daughters, Xian, Jie, and Hua to be [Emperor Xian's] concubines. [The emperor] gave fifty thousand *pi* of bound silk and black and red fabric as betrothal gifts. The youngest remained home until she was age appropriate. In the year she became nineteen [January 29, 214–February 16, 215], the emperor engaged them as honorable ladies. In the following year, upon the time when Empress Consort Fu was killed, [the emperor] crowned Jie his empress consort.

      建安十八年，操進三女憲，節，華為夫人，聘以束帛玄纁五萬匹，小者待年於國。十九年並拜為貴人。及伏皇后被弒，明年，立節為皇后。

      After he deposed the last Han dynasty in 220, Cao Pi demoted Emperor Xian of Eastern Han 漢獻帝 (r. 189–220), also known in history as Liu Xie 劉協 (181–234), to be Duke of Shanyang 山陽公. See Cao Jie's biography in Fan Ye 范曄 (398–445) comp. *Hou Han shu*, Li Xian 李賢 (654–684), ed. (Beijing: Zhonghua shuju, 1965), 10b.455.

47   This term is mentioned in the *Han shu* 漢書, where the commentator, Yan Shigu 顏師古 (581–645), remarks, "A 'hot water for bathing' district is one in which taxes are used to

YE IN JIAN'AN LITERATURE

Commandery. They each received taxation income from five hundred households. This winter, sweet dew fell in the Fanglin Park" (十二月丙寅，賜山陽公夫人湯沐邑，公女曼為長樂郡公主，食邑各五百戶。是冬，甘露降芳林園). Pei Songzhi explains that the "Fanglin is now Hualin Park which was renamed Hualin when the Prince of Qi 齊王, Cao Fang 曹芳 (r. 239–254), took the throne" (芳林園即今華林園，齊王芳即位，改為華林).[48] Cao Pi had established his capital in Luoyang after his father's passing in 220, and this entry is dated after an entry that says "on the day *jiachen* of the ninth month [November 4, 222], [the emperor] made a visit to Xuchang Palace" (九月甲辰，行幸許昌宮).[49] In light of this, we cannot say for sure that Fanglin Park was even in Ye—let alone whether or not Cao Cao had constructed it. And in the preface attached to his "Inscription of the Dew-Catching Plate" ("Chenglu pan ming" 承露盤銘), Cao Zhi states that the emperor built a dew-catching plate in Fanglin Park. The preface to this work reads:

> Among all forms that can be seen, none is better than height; of objects that cannot decay, none is better than metal; the purest of all *qi* is the dew; and the most secure of all containers is the plate. Therefore, the emperor commanded those with authority to cast bronze in order to make a dew-catching plate in Fanglin Park. Its stem is twelve *zhang* long and ten double-arm widths wide. The upper plate is four *chi* and nine *cun* in diameter, the lower one is five *chi* in diameter. A bronze dragon wraps around its root. The dragon is one *zhang* long and carries two babies on its back. Ever since it was set up in Fanglin Park, sweet dew indeed has been falling. [The emperor] ordered me to compose a eulogistic inscription.

> 夫形能見者莫如高，物不朽者莫如金。氣之清者莫如露，盛之安者莫如盤。皇帝乃詔有司鑄銅建承露盤在芳林園中。莖長十二丈，大十圍。上盤逕四尺九寸，下盤逕五尺，銅龍遶其根。龍身長一丈，背負兩子。自立於芳林園，甘露乃降。使臣為頌銘.[50]

---

supply bathing implements.'" (These were for the use of the royal family only). See Ban Gu 班固 (32–92), *Han shu* (Beijing: Zhonghua shuju, 1962), 1b.74 and 1b.75n8.

48   See Chen, *San guo zhi*, 2.84n3. The change in name was to avoid the taboo of Cao Fang's name.

49   Chen, *San guo zhi*, 2.83. The palace is located in modern Xuchang in Hebei.

50   I follow the text of this preface and the inscription in Zhao, *Cao Zhi ji jiaozhu*, 476–477. The text, with interchangeable characters *jing* 徑 for 逕 and *rao* 繞 for 遶, is also in Yan, *Quan Sanguo wen*, 19.2a–b.

60 CHAPTER 2

Cao Zhi does not say which emperor, but he passed away in 232. Therefore, it could not be Cao Fang to whom he refers, since Cao Fang was not installed on the throne until 239. Cao Zhi may be referring to Emperor Ming 明帝 (r. 226–239), Cao Rui 曹叡, who was Cao Pi's son and Cao Fang's adoptive father. This would be consistent with Pei Songzhi's note that the park was still named Fanglin in Cao Zhi's lifetime.

To further muddy the waters—even though we are confident that a garden called Fanglin Park changed its name to Hualin 華林 to avoid the taboo name of Cao Fang as Pei Songzhi states—Hualin was also the name of one of the Han gardens in Luoyang where both the Eastern Han and Cao Wei had located their capitals.[51] Moreover, the Hualin Park that is listed in the fourteenth century *Zhangde fu zhi* possibly, or even probably, refers not to the one that was renamed because of the taboo, but one that was either built or rebuilt later in Ye by Shi Hu 石虎. In the gazetteer, the section on Fanglin Park reads:

> The *Yezhong ji* says [Fanglin Park] was built by Cao Cao, and later changed its name to Hualin in order to avoid the taboo name of the Prince of Qin.[52] Shi Hu of the Later Zhao renovated the park in the fourteenth year of the Jianwu reign [February 17, 348–February 4, 349]. But, the *Jin shu* states that Shi Hu followed the advice of a monk and utilized six hundred thousand men and women to construct [a new] Hualin Park. We are still unclear about the truth of the matter.

> 鄴中記曰魏武所築，後避秦王諱，改名華林。後趙石虎建武十四年重修。然晉書載記言虎用沙門之言，起男女六十萬人築華林苑。未詳其實.[53]

The *Jin shu* passage that this gazetteer mentions is in the account listed under the third year of the Yonghe 永和 reign [January 29, 347–February 16, 348]:

> At the time, a monk named Wu Jin proposed to Jilong [Shi Hu], "The prominent cycle of Hu is about to decline, and the Jin shall be restored. It is better to harshly labor the Jin people to suppress their *qi*." Jilong,

---

51 In his "*Fu* on the East Capital" (*Dongjing fu* 東京賦) Zhang Heng 張衡 (78–139) writes: "In Sleek Dragon, Fragrant Grove, / Nine Valleys, Eight Streams" (濯龍芳林，九谷八溪). This is David Knechtges' translation, and he notes that while Fanglin 芳林 was another garden we know very little about, Zhuolong 濯龍 was a pond in the eastern part of the Northern Palace and this park had a large garden where the emperor went for outings and banquets. The Jiugu 九谷 and Baxi 八溪 are fish-cultivating ponds. Knechtges, *Wen xuan*, 1:258 and 259. See the text of Zhang Heng's *fu* in Xiao, *Wen xuan*, 3.9b.

52 This is perhaps a scribal error for Prince of Qi 齊王.

53 See Cui, *Jiajing Zhangde fu zhi*, 8.9a–b.

YE IN JIAN'AN LITERATURE

61

thereupon, ordered his imperial secretary, Zhang Qun, to send out a hundred sixty thousand men and women from neighboring commanderies, along with a hundred thousand carriages, to transport soil to build Hualin Park and a long wall in the north of Ye. The breadth and width were several tens of *li*.

時沙門吳進言于季龍曰：「胡運將衰，晉當復興，宜苦役晉人以厭其氣。」季龍於是使尚書張群發近郡男女十六萬，車十萬乘，運土築華林苑及長牆于鄴北，廣長數十里.[54]

As mentioned in the previous chapter, Shi Hu's biography in the *Jin shu* also states that, "At the same time [he] lavishly constructed major buildings in Ye. He erected more than forty towers and buildings. He also planned and constructed palaces in Chang'an and Luoyang. The numbers of workers on these projects were more than four hundred thousand" (兼盛興宮室於鄴，起臺觀四十餘所。營長安洛陽二宮。作者四十餘萬人).[55] From these anecdotes, we know that Shi Hu spent lavishly on materials and labor to build significant sites that would showcase his power. Thus, the number of laborers enlisted to build Hualin Park noted in the *Jin shu* may well lie within the realm of the possible.[56]

While long gone, the Xuanwu and Bronze Bird Parks of Ye still appear in their beauty in the writing of literati, who wax fulsome about what the space and experience of the gardens meant to them. Three hundred years after Cao Cao's death, in the *Shuijing zhu*, Li Daoyuan spoke about the multi-functional uses of the Xuanwu Park in his section on the Huan River (Huan *shui* 洹水), "the park used to have Xuanwu Reservoir to practice boats and oars. There were fishing bridges, fishing docks, and groves of bamboos and bushes. [But] now the reservoir and the woods have all disappeared and not even a trace is left of them" (苑舊有玄武池，以肄舟楫。有魚梁，釣臺，竹木，灌叢。今池林絕滅，略無遺跡矣).[57] Zuo Si 左思 (ca. 250–305) provides a more poetic description of the park:

54　Fang Xuanling 房玄齡 (579–648) and others, comp., *Jin shu* 晉書 (Beijing: Zhonghua shuju, 1974), 107.2782.

55　Fang, *Jin shu*, 106.2772.

56　Zhou Weiquan 周維權 lists Hualin park as one of the parks in Shi Hu's massive constructions and supports his finding with the entry from the *Jin shu* quoted above. See his *Zhongguo gudian yuanlin shi* 中國古典園林史 (Beijing: Qinghua daxue chuban she, 1999), 89. Pauline Lin is another scholar who works on the physical and social spaces of Chinese gardens. Lin presented "From Utilitarian to Aesthetic: Fragrant Grove Park and a Changing Garden Aesthetic in Third century Luoyang" in 2011 Association for Asian Studies conference in Honolulu. See the abstract of her presentation on <http://aas2.asian-studies.org/absts/2011abst/abstract.asp?Session_ID=150&year=2011&Category_ID=2&area=China+and+Inner+Asia&Meeting_ID=20> (accessed October 3, 2019).

57　Li, *Shuijing zhu*, 9.205.

	苑以玄武	The garden was Xuanwu,
2	陪以幽林	Matched by secluded woods.
	繚垣開囿	Encircling walls opened on a hunting park,[58]
4	觀宇相臨	The eaves of watchtowers faced one another.
	碩果灌叢	Large fruit (trees) grew in the irrigated groves,
6	圍木竦尋	Thick trees rose tall.[59]
	篁篠懷風	Bamboos embraced the wind,
8	蒲陶結陰	Grapes knotted together in the shade.
	回淵漼	The whirling pool was yawning,
10	積水深	The standing water was deep.
	蒹葭贙	Reeds and bulrushes were *xuan*-like,[60]
12	藿蒻森	Rushes and cattails grew like forests.
	丹藕凌波而的皪	Cinnabar lotuses lay across the waves and shone in beauty,
14	綠芰泛濤而浸潭	Green water caltrops floated in the billows and invaded the ponds.[61]

Zuo Si's description of Xuanwu Park is more literary than Li Daoyuan's simple list of what one could have been found therein. But as Zhou Yiliang 周一良 (1913–2001) states, "Even though it is Zuo Si the literatus who composed the *fu*, which is full of rhetorical elaborations, he could not have written it without any basis at all" (即使左太沖文人作賦，頗有鋪陳，也不能全無依據).[62] Zuo Si's description still provides a very good impression of what the park might

---

58 *You* 囿 is a fenced area where rulers kept animals. A famous one was the hunting park of King Wen (ca. 1100 BCE) 文王之囿 in *Mencius*, I.B.2.

59 One *xun* 尋 is a measure of length in about eight *chi* 尺. It is used to indicate a length object.

60 A *xuan* 贙, according to *Erya* 爾雅, is a powerful beast. It is said that a *xuan* looks like a dog, has a lot of strength and is vicious. See the entry and its commentary in Guo, *Erya zhushu*, 10.17b. In this line, the term is used to describe how the reeds and bulrushes grew aggressively to compete with each other, like beasts that fought against (*duizheng* 對爭) with one another.

61 See Zuo Si's "Wei Capital Rhapsody" (*Wei du fu* 魏都賦) in Xiao, *Wen xuan*, 6.12b. Cf. Knechtges, *Wen xuan*, 1:429–477. For further discussion on Zuo Si and his "Rhapsody on the Three Capitals" ("San du fu" 三都賦), see for example, Gao Guihui 高桂惠, "Zuo Si shengping jiqi Sandu fu zhi yanjiu" 左思生平及其三都賦之研究 (MA thesis, Guoli Zhengzhi daxue), 1981; John Marney, "Cities in Chinese Literature," *Michigan Academician* 10, no. 2 (Fall 1977): 225–238; and Wang Dehua 王德華, "Zuo Si 'Sandu fu' Yedu de xuanze yu miaoxie: Jianlun 'Luoyang zhigui' de lishi yu zhengzhi Beijing" 左思《三都賦》鄴都的選擇與描寫—兼論「洛陽紙貴」的歷史與政治背景, *Zhejiang daxue xuebao* 浙江大學學報 43, no. 4 (July 2013): 146–156.

62 Zhou Yiliang 周一良, "Du *Yezhong ji*" 讀《鄴中記》, in *Wei Jin Nan Bei chao shilun* 魏晉南北朝史論, 585–606 (Shenyang, Liaoning: Liaoning jiaoyu chuban she, 1998), 589.

YE IN JIAN'AN LITERATURE

have felt like, even though the vocabulary and terminology are overly generalized. It indicates categories of experience that people who frequented the garden would understand and acknowledge as a literary equivalent of a more scientific description. The garden would have been immediately recognizable as a certain kind of space: secluded, walled-off, full of ornamental and fruit-bearing trees, dotted with lotus ponds surrounded by cattails and reeds, with water caltrops infringing on the open surface. This was a general category of garden, filled with plants that have immediate cultural affinities: the lotus with purity, the water caltrop as food, the secluded place that allows for meditation or perhaps sharing intimate space with friends at a literary outing, exchanging poetry as they feasted.

Another work that also allows us this imaginary insight into the Xuanwu Park but with more emotional appeal that can be related to a specific subject is Cao Pi's "Poem Composed on the Xuanwu Bank" ("Yu Xuanwu bei zuo shi" 於玄武陂作詩).

	兄弟共行遊	We brothers traveled and roamed together,[63]
2	驅車出西城	Driving our carts out through the western city wall.
	野田寬開闊	The fallow fields broadly opened wide,
4	川渠互相經	Rivers and canals crisscrossed one another.
	黍稷何鬱鬱	The broomcorn and millet, how luxuriant they are!
6	流波激悲聲	Their flowing waves stir up a sad sound.[64]
	菱芡覆綠水	Water chestnuts and foxnut cover the green water,
8	芙蓉發丹榮	Lotuses send forth their cinnabar glory.
	柳垂重蔭綠	Willows droop and double the shady green,
10	向我池邊生	Facing me, they grow by the edge of the pond.
	垂渚望長州	We approach the islet in the water and gaze at the long island,
12	群鳥讙讙鳴	Flocks of birds chirp loudly.
	萍藻泛濫浮	Duckweed floats all around,

---

63   It is not clear which brother or brothers accompanied Cao Pi to the park here. It is believed that Cao Cao fathered more than two dozen sons. See a table listed "wives, sons, and grandchildren of Cao Cao" in Robert Joe Cutter and William Gordon Crowell, *Empresses and Consorts: Selections from Chen Shou's Records of the Three States with Pei Songzhi's Commentary* (Honolulu: University of Hawai'i Press, 1999), 145–146.

64   The "sad sound" (*beisheng* 悲聲) can also be understood as "a sound solemn and stirring" (*beizhuang zhi sheng* 悲壯之聲). For example, "The sound and rhythm are solemn and stirring, of the ones who listened to it, none did not feel vehement and fervent" (聲節悲壯，聽者莫不慷慨). See Fan, *Hou Han shu*, 80b.2655. In his *Wei Wendi ji quanyi* 魏文帝集全譯, Yi Jianxian 易健賢 reads *beisheng* 悲聲 as "the sound delighted one's ear" (悅耳的聲音) for "Silk [string instruments] sound is sad" (絲聲哀) in the *Liji* 禮記. See Yi, *Wei Wendi ji quanyi* (Guiyang: Guizhou renmin chuban she, 2008), 355n3.

14	澹澹隨風傾	Undulatingly bending with the wind.
	忘憂共容與	Forgetting our worries, together we are carefree and at leisure,
16	暢此千秋情	Giving free rein to this sentiment of a thousand autumns.[65]

At first glance, this piece seems similar to Zuo Si's description of the scenery of Xuanwu; but the poet of this verse actually uses the scenery to reflect layers of emotions portrayed by interweaving descriptions of the vegetation, birds, colors, and sounds that the brothers experienced in the park. In the opening couplet, the poet expresses the persona's intention—together the brothers drive (*quche* 驅車) out of the closed space and into the wide-open fields. And then in the following lines, we see the abundant grains, water chestnut and foxnut, lotuses and willows, and chirping birds. The visual imagery of the vegetation and birds in or near the pond, along with the sounds (lines six and twelve) and colors (lines seven, eight, and nine) describe the scene fully and engage the readers' senses. The poet divides the verse into three elements: the first two couplets identify the persona's movement through space, the middle six couplets are about the "natural" scene, and the final two couplets express the speaker's inner feelings generated by his experience of the outing. A word stands out in the middle of this poem. In lines three and four, the wide-open fields the poet saw right after leaving the city are described, but this expansiveness seems to be "regulated" by the crisscrossing rivers and canals that imprint the open space with patterns of order and regulations. The poet's choice of using the verb *jing* 經 to describe the way that the waterways interlaced or crisscrossed in the open fields is worth noting, because this word always carries the idea of consistency and regular order.[66] One might take this sense of regulation and the worries (*you* 憂) in line fifteen to be a reflection of the conflict between the poet's political ambition and obligation and his inner desire, but these are also expressions of genuine human feelings when one immerses

---

65   See Lu Qinli 逯欽立, ed., *Xian Qin Han Wei Jin Nanbeichao shi* 先秦漢魏晉南北朝詩 (Beijing: Zhonghua shuju chuban she, 1983), 1:400. A complete English translation of the piece is also in Lois Fusek, "The Poetry of Ts'ao Pi (187–226)" (PhD diss., Yale University, 1975), 243. In her translation, Fusek translates the word *bei* 陂 "edge" while Yi Jianxian reads it as "lake or pond" (*huchi* 湖池). See Yi's *Wei Wendi ji quanyi*, 354.

66   *Jing* originally means the vertical silk thread of weaving. According to Duan Yucai's 段玉裁 (1735–1815) commentary to this character in the *Shuowen jiezi* 說文解字, "To weave [fabric], the vertical silk is called *jing*. It is a must to have the vertical silk first and then have the horizontal one. This is why the Three Principles, Five Consistencies, and Six Skills are called the constant *jing* of the heaven and earth (織之從絲謂之經。必先有經而後有緯。是故三綱五常六藝謂之天地之常經). See Xu Shen 許慎 (ca. 58–147), ed.; Duan Yucai, comm., *Shuowen jiezi zhu* 說文解字注, Qing edition 1873 photo-reprinted, (Shanghai: Shanghai guji chuban she, 1981), 13a.2b.

YE IN JIAN'AN LITERATURE   65

oneself in nature. In the following lines, the poet uses the loud chirping of
birds and the full bloom of the summer plants to indicate that he was aware
that the harvest (i.e., something regularly accomplished in good times) was
coming but that reaping that harvest also signaled the approach of winter and
the end of things. At the end of the poem, the poet notes that he observed the
singing flocks of birds by the shore of the island and their contrast, the quiet
and reserved duckweed that floated on the water, passively moved by the wind.
In this moment between activity (*dong* 動) and quietness (*jing* 靜), he expresses a desire to enjoy the eternity this single moment of stasis offers and to forget
about all else.[67] With his brothers, the poet enjoys this very moment of both
physical and emotional freedom and sentiment. This piece well portrays Xuanwu Park as a social and sentimental space that is set apart from the bustle of
the city.

Bronze Bird Park 銅雀園, as mentioned earlier, is also known as the West
Garden (*Xiyuan* 西園) because it was located west of the Wenchang Hall 文昌
殿. It is particularly well known to us as a site of symposia and poetic excur-
sions during that time. Located between the iconic Three Terraces and the palace complex in the northwestern quarter of Ye, it served not only as a garden
for the royal family, but also an entertainment space for the Caos and their literati guests to spend time to escape the pressures of daily life and amid seren-
ity. This particular park became the representative site of the so-called Lord's
Feast poems (*Gongyan shi* 公燕詩) that describe the pleasant times writers and
others shared in the West Garden during the Cao family era.[68] The literati

---

67   This *carpe diem* mentality is discussed in Cutter, "Cao Zhi's (192–232) Symposium Poems,"
      6.
68   Being one of the most popular subjects in the early medieval Chinese literary tradition, it
      has been well treated by scholars. In addition to the list of names on scholars whose
      works include Jian'an literature and its literati noted above, there are also some other ex-
      ample works on feast poems (listed alphabetically by surname): Christopher Leigh Con-
      nery, *Empire of the Text: Writing and Authority in Early Imperial China* (New York: Rowman
      & Littlefield Publishers, Inc., 1996), and Connery's "Jian'an Poetic Discourse" (PhD. Diss.,
      Princeton University, 1991); Deng Fushun 鄧福舜 and Li Decheng 李德成, "Yexia wenren
      jihui yu Yexia shifeng" 鄴下文人集會與鄴下詩風, *Daqing gaodeng zhuanke xuexiao
      xuebao* 大慶高等專科學校學報 16, no. 3 (1996): 30–34; Liu Huairong 劉懷榮, "Lun
      Yexia houqi yanji huodong dui Jian'an shige de yingxiang" 論鄴下後期宴集活動對建
      安詩歌的影響 in *Zhongguo zhonggu wenxue yanjiu* 中國中古文學研究, ed. Zhao Min-
      li 趙敏俐 and Satō Toshiyuki 佐藤利行 (Beijing: Xueyuan chuban she, 2005), 511–520;
      Fang Dai, "Drinking, Thinking, and Writing: Ruan Ji and the Culture of his Era" (PhD diss.,
      University of Michigan), 1994; He Hongyan 何紅艷, "Lun Jian'an gongyan shi de jiazhi
      xuanze" 論建安公宴詩的價值選擇, *Nei Menggu shehui kexue* 內蒙古社會科學 24, no.
      6 (2003): 77–80; Huang Yazhuo 黃亞卓, *Han Wei Liuchao gongyan shi yanjiu* 漢魏六朝公
      宴詩研究 (Shanghai: Huadong shifan daxue chubanshe, 2007) and "Lun Jian'an gongyan

66   CHAPTER 2

gatherings at the West Garden (*Xiyuan zhi hui* 西園之會) are also recognized as one of the earlier models for such literary gatherings.[69] Later, many followed in the Jian'an footsteps and created other similar events: the gathering at the Golden Valley Garden (*Jingu zhi hui* 金谷之會) of the Western Jin 西晉 (265–316), the gathering at the Lanting (*Lanting zhi hui* 蘭亭之會) in 353, and the fifth-century gathering of the Xie 謝 clan on the Wuyi Lane (*Wuyi zhi you* 烏衣之游).[70]

---

shi jiqi dianfan yiyi" 論建安公宴詩及其典範意義, *Guangxi shifan xueyuan xuebao* 廣西師範學院學報 23, no. 2 (2002): 59–63; Thomas Lavallee, "Formality and the Pursuit of Pleasure in Early Medieval Chinese Banquet Poetry" (PhD. Diss., Washington University, Saint Louis, Mo.), 2004; Wei Hongcan 魏宏燦, "Caoshi fuzi yu Yexia wenshi de wenxue jiaoyou" 曹氏父子與鄴下文士的文學交游, *Fuyang shifan xueyuan xuebao* 阜陽師範學院學報 100, no. 4 (2004): 39–42; Zhang Zhenlong 張振龍, "Yexia wenren jituan neibu huodong dui wenren guannian de yingxiang" 鄴下文人集團內部活動對文人觀念的影響, *Nanyang shifan xueyuan xuebao* 南陽師範學院學報 4, no. 5 (2005): 71–77 and "Yexia wenxue jituan jiaoji huodong de wenxue tezheng" 鄴下文學集團交際活動的文學特徵, *Xi'an wenli xueyuan xuebao* 西安文理學院學報 8, no. 3 (2005): 5–8; Zheng Liang-shu 鄭良樹, "Chuti fengzuo: Cao Wei jituan de fuzuo huodong" 出題奉作—曹魏集團的賦作活動 in *Wei Jin Nanbeichao wenxue lunji* 魏晉南北朝文學論集, ed., Hong Kong Zhongwen daxue Zhongguo yuyan xenxue xi (Taipei: Wenshizhe chubanshe, 1994), 181–209; and Zheng Yu-yu 鄭毓瑜, "Shilun gongyan shi zhiyu Yexia wenren jituan de xiangzheng yiyi" 試論公讌詩之於鄴下文人集團的象徵意義 in *Liuchao qingjing meixue zonglun* 六朝情境美學綜論 (Taipei: Taiwan Xuesheng shuju, 1996), 171–218.

69   This statement does not include the gatherings of Prince of Huainan 淮南王, Liu An 劉安 (179–122 BCE) nor the Rabbit Garden 兔園 (also known as the East Park 東苑) of the Western Han. The garden is known in history for its large size (described to be seventy *li* bigger than the city of Suiyang 睢陽 [near modern day Shangqiu 商丘 Henan] in the *Han shu*) while Prince Xiao of Liang's 梁孝王 daily bird shooting and fishing with his palace entourage and guests, are described in the *Xijing zaji* 西京雜記; there is no record of any literary events that occurred at this park. See the description of Liu An and his guests in Ban, *Han shu*, 44.2145. As for the Rabbit Garden, see Ban, *Han shu*, 47.2208. Also see Liu Xujie's description of the Rabbit Garden in Nancy Steinhardt and Fu Xinian, *Chinese Architecture* (New Haven: Yale University Press, 2002), 46; and another description in Sun Lian 孫煉, "Dazhe zhao tiandi zhi biao xizhe ru haoqian zhi nei: Han dai yuanlin shi yanjiu" 大者罩天地之表細者入毫紆之內：漢代園林史研究 (MA thesis, Tianjin daxue 天津大學, 2003), 104–107. Duncan Campbell states that "From the Han [206 BCE–221 CE] and Wei [221–265] dynasties onwards, however, stately tours of the Western Garden became all the rage as constituting the very grandest of affairs." The Western Garden Campbell mentioned here includes the Imperial Forest Park (Shanglin yuan 上林苑) in Luoyang described in Zhang Heng's 張衡 (78–139) "Eastern Metropolis Rhapsody" ("Dongdu fu" 東都賦). See his "Transplanted Peculiarity: The Garden of the Master of the Fishing Nets," *New Zealand Journal of Asian Studies* 9, no. 1 (June, 2007): 19n31.

70   See further discussion in David R. Knechtges, "Jingu and Lanting: Two (or Three?) Jin Dynasty Gardens," in *Studies in Chinese Language and Culture: Festschrift in Honor of Christoph Harbsmeier on the Occasion of His 60th Birthday* (Oslo: Hermes Academic Publishing, 2006), 399–403; Wendy Swartz, "Revisiting the Scene of the Party: A Study of the Lanting Collection," *Journal of the American Oriental Society* 132, no. 2 (2012): 275–300; and Wan

YE IN JIAN'AN LITERATURE

Cao Pi's "Poem Composed on the Furong Pond" ("Furong chi zuo shi" 芙蓉池作詩) is not a feast poem, but it describes an evening stroll in the West Garden where Furong Pond was located. In particular, the first three couplets describe how their carriage tops were stroked by the tree branches during their nighttime roaming.[71] This is a common motif in Lord's Feast poems.

	乘輦夜行游	[We] mounted *nian*-carriages to roam in the night,[72]
2	逍遙步西園	And wandering freely we paced the West Garden.
	雙渠相溉灌	Double ditches fed into one another,
4	嘉木繞通川	And beautiful trees curled around circulating streams.
	卑枝拂羽蓋	Low branches stroked the feathered [carriage] roof,
6	脩條摩蒼天	Long boughs rubbed the grayish-blue sky.
	驚風扶輪轂	Violent winds pushed against the wheel hubs,
8	飛鳥翔我前	Flying birds soared in front of me.
	丹霞夾明月	Cinnabar clouds bracketed the bright moon,
10	華星出雲間	Resplendent stars appeared between the clouds.
	上天垂光彩	Heaven above draped down gleaming radiance,
12	五色一何鮮	The five colors so fresh and new.[73]
	壽命非松喬	Our allotted life span is not that of Red Pine and Prince Qiao,
14	誰能得神仙	Who is capable of becoming a divine transcendent?
	遨遊快心意	Let us roam in pleasure to please our minds and intentions,
16	保己終百年	And preserve our "own-ness" to live out our hundred years.[74]

Shengnan 萬繩楠, *Wei Jin Nanbei chao wenhua shi* 魏晉南北朝文化史 (Taipei: Zhishu-fang chuban jituan, 1995), 128–140.

71   We also see similar wording in line five of Cao Pi's poem in Sima Xiangru's 司馬相如 (ca.179–118 BCE) "*Fu* of Sir Vacuous" ("Zi Xu fu" 子虛賦): "Grazing thoroughwort and basil below, / Brushing feathered canopies above" (下靡蘭惠，上拂羽蓋). See David R. Knechtges, trans, *Wen xuan, Or Selections of Refined Literature*, vol. 2, *Rhapsodies on Sacrifices, Hunting, Travel, Sightseeing, Palaces and Halls, Rivers and Seas* (Princeton: Princeton University Press, 1996), 2:65; Xiao, *Wen xuan*, 7.21b.

72   The *nian* 輦 is a kind of hand-carriage—drawn by men instead of animals—that was used by royal family members.

73   The five colors usually mean blue, yellow, red, white, and black; here it is used as a metonymy, for all colors and for the reality (*shense* 神色) of the scene. One might suppose, however, that the poet is describing the *aurora borealis*.

74   The text of this work is in Lu, *Xian Qin Han Wei Jin Nanbeichao shi*, 1:400; also in, Xiao, *Wen xuan*, 22.5b–7a. For other English translations of this poem, see Wu Fusheng, "I Rambled and Roamed Together with You: Liu Zhen's (d. 217) Four Poems to Cao Pi" *Journal of the American Oriental Society* 129, no. 4 (Oct.–Dec. 2009): 624; and Ronald Miao's translation in Liu Wu-chi and Irving Yucheng Lo, eds., *Sunflower Splendor: Three Thousand Years of Chinese Poetry* (New York: Anchor Press, 1975), 45.

The poem begins on the move, as we follow the speaker into the park, from a space that is most likely dominated by formal behavior to one that expands horizontally as his vision moves across the landscape of water and vegetation. Like the poem presented above, one can read these lines as containing an emotional parallel to the movement of the physical body: the persona moves from a constrained space to one that allows his feelings to expand as he travels. Lines five and six change the direction of movement from horizontal to vertical, with the low branches of the beautiful trees touching the carriage top, a mediating action that leads the eye to the long boughs that rise upward into the sky. Within this three-dimensional framing of the space of the garden, activity and color are introduced by the soaring birds and the colors of the night, sparkling stars and the radiance of the reddish clouds. The culmination of these acts of perception is captured in line twelve, in the recognition of the overwhelming and self-renewing power of nature to present a constantly new and fresh face. This strong declaration, couched in the traditional form of a rhetorical question, shifts the tenor of the poem to preoccupation as the poet contrasts man's limited life with nature's eternal renewal and generates the ultimate human question in the poet's mind as he concludes the poem. Confronted here by an awareness of the limited duration of his being, the poet first laments that he cannot live to the legendary spans of Red Pine or Prince Qiao, yet he can still protect himself by living in the moment of travel and what it provides to the mind and feelings of the subject (*kuai xinyi* 快心意). While this act of keenly feeling the moment cannot offset the eventual destruction of body, it can give meaning to the subject, whose mind is witness to the physical process of decline. This is accomplished in the poem by the three different projecting directions of moving the line of sight outward, upward, and then back to the subjective self.

This poem is also interesting in its use of Red Pine and Prince Qiao as models since the reader does not always get the sense that Cao Pi necessarily believes in the search for immortality. In his poem, "Snapping the Willow" ("Zhe yangliu xing" 折楊柳行) Cao Pi writes, "Prince Qiao lied with vacuous words, / Red Pine left behind empty words" (王喬假虛辭, 亦松垂空言) and "The hundred schools [of thought] are mostly off the mark and strange, / The *dao* of the sages is that which I observe" (百家多迂怪, 聖道我所觀).[75] This poem may also direct us to a slightly altered reading of Cao Pi's "Furong Pond." Cao Pi was aware that none of us could live to the lifespan of either immortal—even if they existed—but we still need access to the sages, whether Confucian or Daoist, to provide us models for action. His use of the term preserving what is our "own-ness" (*baoji* 保己) stems from the "Zeyang" 則陽 chapter of the *Zhuangzi*

---

75   For other translations and readings of this poem, see Jack W. Chen, "The Writing of Imperial Poetry in Medieval China." *Harvard Journal of Asiatic Studies*, vol. 65, no. 1 (June, 2005): 68–70; and Owen, *The Making of Early Chinese Classical Poetry*, 147–149.

YE IN JIAN'AN LITERATURE   69

莊子, in which the sage is described as one who "in his relationship to things, is happy to be with them; in relationship to men, he delights in his communing with others and in preserving his 'own-ness' therein" (聖人 ... ... 其於物也, 與之為娛矣; 其於人也, 樂物之通而保己焉). Guo Xiang's 郭象 (ca. 252–312) notes to the first part of the passage read, "He does not embitter himself because of other things" (不以為物自苦), and Cheng Xuanying's 成玄英 (fl. 631) subcommentary expands, "He is one with the world and engaging with things, he has no partiality toward any thing, and wherever he goes it is appropriate; therefore he is never unhappy" (同塵涉事, 與物無私; 所造皆適, 故未嘗不樂也). The respective note and subcommentary to the second part read, "He communes with others but does not lose his selfhood" (通彼不喪我), and "He mixes his traces among men but is neither stilled nor stifled, and although he frequently communes with other things, he does not lose the selfhood, in action he is not harmed by loneliness and constantly abides in the true realization" (混迹人間而無滯塞, 雖復通物而不喪我, 動不傷寂而常守於其真).[76] We have no way of knowing how Cao Pi himself understood this term, although Guo Xiang's commentary would represent a near contemporary interpretation. Cheng Xuanying's subcommentary helps elucidate Guo Xiang's comments, but are anachronistic to Cao Pi. Yet, we can understand the overall context of the term: to find happiness as an individual in an ephemeral world, engaged with the Way but secure enough in one's own self to find pleasure in the short span of life.

The poem thus may be seen as carrying out the mandate of *Zhuangzi*: the persona views all other things and delights in them, and he realizes that in that moment there is a free-roaming through the universe of things that allows him to share in a fellowship of the *Dao*, becoming a part of all things without losing that which is unique to the individual. And it is this moment of transcendence that compensates for and consoles the individual whose corporal body must perish.

Another piece attributed to Cao Zhi also has the title "Poem on Furong Pond" ("Furong chi shi" 芙蓉池詩). But, only a fragment of two couplets survives, "Wandering about at leisure at the Furong pond, / We lightly frolic in small boats. / In the poplar in the south, a pair of swans perch, / In the willow in the north, there are cooing doves" (逍遙芙蓉池, 翩翩戲輕舟。南陽 [楊] 棲雙鵠, 北柳有鳴鳩).[77] Notwithstanding the fact that only these four lines remain, they still vividly represent the speaker sporting on the water in his skiff and, as the birds congregating in the trees may suggest, surrounded by his friends.

---

76   Guo, *Zhuangzi ji shi*, 8b.878 and 879n3, 4.

77   Here I adopt the reading of the plant poplar (*yang* 楊) because of the parallel "willow" in the following line. See the text of this fragment in Lu, *Xian Qin Han Wei Jin Nanbeichao shi*, 1:462.

70 CHAPTER 2

I will not go on to discuss the Lord's Feast poems; but a ballad attributed to Cao Pi entitled "Marvelous!" ("Shanzai xing" 善哉行) or "Poem on the Bronze Bird Park" ("Tongque yuan shi" 銅雀園詩) describes the gathering in the garden and is an excellent example that demonstrates that the guests and performers at the feasts and banquets in Ye were not limited to ones who resided in the city. The poem reads:

	朝遊高臺觀	In the morning we roamed the tall terrace's tower,
2	夕宴華池陰	In the evening, we feasted on the south side of the flowery pond.[78]
	大酋奉甘醪	The *daqiu* offered sweet ale,[79]
4	狩人獻嘉禽	And the *shouren* presented delicious birds.[80]
	齊倡發東舞	Dancers from Qi started the eastern dance,
6	秦箏奏西音	And the zither from Qin played a western sound.[81]
	有客從南來	There were guests who came from south
8	為我彈清琴	And played their elegant lutes for us.
	五音紛繁會	All five tones met in complicated profusion,[82]

---

78 The term "flowery pond" (*huachi* 華池) is not specified in this poem. It can mean an ornate body of water, as in "Chickens and ducks filled up palace-halls, / Water-frogs swam in flowery ponds" (雞鶩滿堂壇兮，鼃黽游乎華池) from Dongfang Shuo's 東方朔 (ca. 161–93 BCE) "False Admonition" ("Miu jian" 謬諫) of his "Seven Admonitions" ("Qi jian" 七諫). See Hong, *Chuci buzhu*, 257. But, scholars often equate this term with the legendary pond in Mount Kunlun 崑崙山. See, for example, Chen, "The Writing of Imperial Poetry in Medieval China," 70n35.

79 The word *qiu* 酋, according to Zheng Xuan's 鄭玄 note in the *Liji* 禮記, means the ale is ready for consumption (酒熟曰酋) and *daqiu* 大酋 is the title of the position of the head of the alcohol office. See Zheng Xuan 鄭玄 (127–200) and Kong Yingda 孔穎達 (574–648), comm. and ann., *Liji zhengyi* 禮記正義, in *Shisan jing zhushu fu jiaokan ji* 十三經注疏附校勘記, ed. Ruan Yuan 阮元 (1764–1849), 8 vols., (Taipei: Yiwen yingshu guan, 1982), 5: 17.18a.

80 *Shouren* is the title of the official position of one who was in charge of the "fishing nets" (*gu* 罟), "farm field" (*tian* 田), and "animals" (*shou* 獸). *Shouren* were also responsible for supplying the imperial meals. For example, they offered wolves in winter and deer in summer. See Zheng Xuan 鄭玄 (127–200) and Jia Gongyan 賈公彥 (fl. 618–907), comm. and ann., *Zhouli zhengyi* 周禮正義, in *Shisan jing zhushu fu jiaokan ji* 十三經注疏附校勘記, ed. Ruan Yuan 阮元 (1764–1849), 8 vols., (Taipei: Yiwen yingshu guan, 1982), 3: 1.10a.

81 This couplet reminds the reader the lines in Cao Zhi's "In Attendance on the Heir Apparent" ("Shi taizi zuo" 侍太子坐): "Qi people paid tribute with rare music, / Singers came out from Qin in the west" (齊人進奇樂，歌者出西秦). See this poem in Lu, *Xian Qin Han Wei Jin Nanbeichao shi*, 1:450. Cf. Owen, *The Making of Early Chinese Classical Poetry*, 209.

82 The five tones of the ancient Chinese five-tone scale were *gong* 宮, *shang* 商, *jue* 角, *zhi* 徵, and *yu* 羽. After the Tang, the names of these notes were also called: *he* 合, *si* 四, *yi* 乙, *chi* 尺, and *gong* 工. Also, this line is similar to one in a couplet, "Five tones variously—orchestrated together, / The [Eastern] lord pleased—joy and pleasant" (五音紛兮繁會，君欣欣兮樂康), in *Chuci*, see for example, Hong, *Chuci buzhu*, 57.

YE IN JIAN'AN LITERATURE

71

10	拊者激微吟	As the drummers rousingly but softly hummed.
	淫魚乘波聽	*Yin*-fish rode on the waves to listen,[83]
12	踴躍自浮沈	Jumping and rising, they bobbed up and down.
	飛鳥翻翔舞	Flying birds, tumbled and soared as they danced
14	悲鳴集北林	And called mournfully as they gathered in the northern woods.[84]
	樂極哀情來	When *happiness* reaches its extreme, sad sentiment comes,[85]
16	寮亮摧肝心	Loud and clear, it wrenched my gut and heart.
	清角豈不妙	The clear-sound *jue*, how was it not wonderful,[86]
18	德薄所不任	It was something one deficient in virtue could not do.
	大哉子野言	So great! Ziye's words,[87]
20	弭弦且自禁	Loosen the strings and restrain the self.[88]

---

83 *Yin*-fish 淫魚 are said to be members of the sturgeon family (*xun* 鱘 [鱣]). This line is possibly an allusion to the description of the famous musician Huba 瓠巴 in the *Huainanzi* 淮南子. When he strummed the *se*-lute; *yin*-fish would come out to listen to him (瓠巴鼓瑟而淫魚出聽). See the translation of this line, in John S. Major and others, *The Huainanzi: A Guide to the Theory and Practice of Government in Early Han China*, trans. (New York: Columbia University Press, 2010), 626.

84 Cao Zhi has a couplet in one of his "Random Poems" ("Zashi" 雜詩) that reads, "On the tall terrace, much sad wind, / The morning sun shines on the north woods" (高臺多悲風，朝日照北林). See Lu, *Xian Qin Han Wei Jin Nanbeichao shi*, 1:456.

85 This line adopts the line "Happiness and music are extreme—, / Sad sentiments are many" (歡樂極兮哀情多) from the "Lyrics on the Autumn Wind" ("Qiufeng ci" 秋風辭) attributed to Emperor Wu of Han 漢武帝 (r. 141–87 BCE). See this poem in Lu, *Xian Qin Han Wei Jin Nanbeichao shi*, 1:94–95. Many read the character 樂 as happiness, which is often associated with music, and the two meanings were often interchangeable in many pre-modern texts, but we should also take into consideration that in the "Record of Music" ("Yueji" 樂記) of the *Liji*, it states that "when the music reaches to its extreme, then it is worrisome; when the rites are coarse, then they are off-center" (樂極則憂，禮粗則偏矣). In his sub-annotation, Kong Yingda 孔穎達 explains that "As for [the line] 'when the music reaches to its extremeness, then it is worrisome:' music is that which people favor, but the harm is in being excessive and clumsy. If it reaches to the extreme and is not stopped, it will then arrive during worrying and straitening [circumstances]" (樂極則憂者，樂，人之所好，害在淫佚。若極而不止，則必至憂蹙也). See Zheng, *Liji zhengyi*, 37.17a–18a.

86 The clear-sound *jue* (*qingjue* 清角) is the name of a music tone. See note on the five tones above.

87 Ziye 子野 is the blind musician Master Kuang 師曠 (fl. ca. 557–532 BCE).

88 The text of this work is in Lu, *Xian Qin Han Wei Jin Nanbeichao shi*, 1:393; and as "Poem on the Bronze Bird Park" (with variants, see below) in Ouyang, *Yiwen leiju*, 28:500. Cf. Chen, "The Writing of Imperial Poetry in Medieval China," 70–73. While this poem is credited to Cao Pi in both Lu Qinli's *Xian Qin Han Wei Jin Nanbeichao shi* and Ouyang Xun's *Yiwen leiju*, they have different versions. The version in Lu Qinli's collection has twenty lines, but only ten remain in Ouyang Xun's, where lines seven to twelve and lines seventeen to twenty are omitted. This is not surprising, since *Yiwen leiju* often abridges its entries. Lu Qinli noted that the poem as retained in the *Yiwen leiju* uses five rhyme words: *yin* 陰, *qin* 禽, *yin* 音, *lin* 林, and *xin* 心. These characters are the endings of lines two, four, six, fourteen, and sixteen. The other major difference is that the word *liaoliang* 寮亮 in line sixteen is

The last two couplets (lines seventeen to twenty) are a direct reference to the fourth of the "Ten Faults" ("Shi guo" 十過) related in the *Hanfeizi* 韓非子. The story goes that, in a banquet for honoring the visit of Duke Ling of Wei 魏靈公 (r. 534–493 BCE), the host, Duke Ping of Jin 晉平公 (r. 557–532 BCE), asked Master Kuang to perform music. But when Duke Ping requested to hear the clear-sound *jue* mode, Master Kuang refused to play it and said the following:

> No! In ancient times, the Yellow Emperor gathered the spirits and divinities on the top of Mount Tai. Riding in an elephant-carriage drawn by six flood-dragons, Bifang kept up by his side while Chiyou was stationed before him. The wind-god swept the way and the rain-master sprinkled the road. Tigers and wolves in the vanguard, spirits and divinities followed. Writhing serpents were on the ground below and phoenixes soaring above, he called the spirits and divinities to a great assembly and created the music of the clear-sound *jue* mode. But now, you, my lord, are deficient in virtue, therefore not worthy to hear it. If you were to hear it, I fear something bad would come about!

> 不可。昔者黃帝合鬼神於西泰山之上。駕象車而六蛟龍。畢方並鎋，蚩尤居前。風伯進掃，雨師灑道。虎狼在前，鬼神在後。騰蛇伏地，鳳皇覆上。大合鬼神，作為清角。今主君德薄，不足聽之。聽之將恐有敗.[89]

Despite the musician's warning, the duke begged to hear it anyway. As Master Kuang played the clear-sound *jue* mode, dark clouds formed and violent wind swept through, tearing down banners and curtains, overturning drinking cups and bowls, and shaking down the terrace roof. From that night on, the state of Jin suffered a great drought for three years and Duke Ping broke out in sores all over his body.

The couplets come at the end of a staged dramatic scene that begins in leisure and happiness—morning roaming and evening feast (*zhaoyou xiyan* 朝遊夕宴)—and ends in a moment of self-control or self-restrain (*zijin* 自禁), moving from joy to a moral caveat. The issue of assembly is paramount in the beginning: the garden stands as a focal point on which musicians, roamers,

---

replaced by *liaohen* 憭恨 in Ouyang Xun's *Yiwen leiju*. In the *Song Shu* 宋書, this poem contains all twenty lines with a variation of *liaoliang* 憭亮 in line sixteen. Shen Yue 沈約 (441–513), comp., *Song shu* (Beijing: Zhonghua shuju, 1974), 21.614.

89   Wang Xianshen 王先慎 (fl. ca. 1897), comp., "Han Fei zi jijie 韓非子集解," in *Xinbian zhuzi jicheng* 新編諸子集成, vol. 5, 1–368 (Taipei: Shijie shuju, 1979), 3.44. Cf. translation in Burton Watson, trans., *Han Fei Tzu: Basic Writings* (New York: Columbia University Press, 1964), 55.

YE IN JIAN'AN LITERATURE   73

and even birds and fish converge. This at once livens up the scene with music, guests, fine ale, and hearty food. In one respect, it also represents the power, prestige, and wealth of the Cao family to gather these guests from all different regions and make this assembly happen. This reach of power outward to bring these people and things together in harmony is inherent in the metaphor of a tone that is profuse and complicated but still in harmony, as suggested by the line, "Five tones variously—orchestrated together" (五音紛繁會). But just as the birds that tumbled and rolled in the sky roosted with mournful cries, the happiness turned immediately to sorrow. This cyclical nature of joy and sorrow also seems to be a slight but ironic comment on the exercise of power that had brought everyone together in the first place.

A final piece, the "*Fu* on Regulating Roaming" ("Jieyou fu" 節遊賦), attributed to Cao Zhi,[90] unites monumentality, transience, friendship, and sorrow. By beginning the poem with a description of the palace complex, the terraces, and the garden, the poet celebrates the grandness of Ye and the achievement of its architect. But, by metaphorically posing the end of a day of drinking and feasting with friends as the conclusion of a full life, he asks if historical memory and enduring materiality are enough to compensate for the brevity of one's existence.

	覽宮宇之顯麗	Surveying the manifest beauty of palaces,
2	實大人之攸居	It is truly a residence for a Great Man.
	建三臺于前處	He built the Three Terraces in the front,
4	飄飛陛以凌虛	And set aloft the flying steps to drift up and soar into the void.[91]
	連雲閣以遠徑	He connected the cloud-high galleries to extend the walkways,
6	營觀榭于城隅	And constructed watchtowers and kiosks at the corners of the city.[92]
	亢高軒以回眺	They braved the tall windowed-corridor to look down and around,

---

90   Zhao Youwen suggests that for its lamenting tone, this piece was probably written after the epidemic of twenty-second year of Jian'an [January 25, 217–February 12, 218]. Zhao, *Cao Zhi ji jiaozhu*, 186. Gong Kechang and his fellow editors also date this piece to 217. They base this on the fact that Yang Xiu 楊修 (175–219) also wrote a poem having the same title; this piece was a poem of "response" (*changhe zhi zuo* 唱和之作). But, other men like Wang Can and Xu Gan 徐幹 (170–217) did not leave any work with this same title. Therefore, it is possible that this piece was done in 217, after the epidemic. See Gong and others, *Quan Sanguo fu pingzhu*, 431.

91   In his "Seven Inducements" (Qi qi 七啟), Cao Zhi also says "The flowering buildings [reach] to the edge of clouds, / The flying steps soar into the void" (華閣緣雲, 飛陛凌虛). See the text in Xiao, *Wen xuan*, 34.13b–25a. *Lingxu* 凌虛 here means soaring to the sky or heaven. And the steps (*bi* 陛) are the ones that lead to a throne.

92   *Guan* 觀 are observatory buildings and *xie* 榭 are structures added on terraces.

74 CHAPTER 2

8	緣雲霓而結疏	And traced the cloudy rainbow to connect the windows.
	仰西岳之崧岑	Looking up at the jagged-steep hills of the mountain in the west,[93]
10	臨漳滏之清渠	And overlooking the clear conduits of the Zhang and Fu Rivers.
	觀靡靡而無終	The view is refined, beautiful, and has no ending,[94]
12	何眇眇而難殊	How faraway it is and hard to surpass!
	亮靈后之所處	A dwelling place of the bright noumenal sovereign,
14	非吾人之所廬	Is not a place for people like you and me to reside.[95]
	于是	Thereupon,
	仲春之月	The second month of the spring,
16	百卉叢生	Hundreds of flowers bloom together.
	萋萋藹藹	Luxuriant and in full prime,
18	翠葉朱莖	With kingfisher-green leaves and vermillion stems.
	竹林青蔥	The bamboo forests are verdant,
20	珍果含榮	The precious fruits are about to burst into glory.
	凱風發而時鳥讙	A gentle breeze stirs and seasonal birds chirrup,[96]
22	微波動而水蟲鳴	Slight waves move and water creatures sound.
	感氣運之和潤	I feel the warm moisture of the seasonal transition,
24	樂時澤之有成	And delight in what seasonal fecundity brings to full form.
	遂乃	Then,
	浮素蓋	I set afloat the plain-silk awnings [of carriages],
26	御驊騮	And drive the Hualiu-horses,[97]

---

93 Mount Taihang 太行山.

94 This line reminds the reader of the one that reads "For a moment, I lingered in the eastern chamber—, / The view, oh well, is refined, beautiful and has no limit" (間徙倚於東廂兮，觀夫靡靡而無窮) in Sima Xiangru's 司馬相如 (ca. 179–118 BCE) "Rhapsody on the Tall Gate Palace" ("Changmen fu" 長門賦), see Xiao, *Wen xuan*, 16.9b–10a; also rendered in David R. Knechtges, trans, *Wen xuan, Or Selections of Refined Literature*, vol. 3, *Rhapsodies on Natural Phenomena, Birds and Animals, Aspirations and Feelings, Sorrowful Laments, Literature, Music, and Passions* (Princeton: Princeton University Press, 1996), 3:163.

95 Cf. Ban Gu's "Western Capital Rhapsody" ("Xijing fu" 西京賦): "It is truly a lodging place for the immortals, / Not a place where we humans are at ease" (實列仙之攸館，非吾人之所寧). See Knechtges, *Wen xuan*, 1:135.

96 *Kaifeng* 凱風 is the warm gentle breeze from the south. "The gentle breeze from the south, / Blew on the heart of those sour jujube bushes" (凱風自南，吹彼棘心). *Mao shi* 32.

97 *Hualiu* 驊騮 is the name of a legendary fine horse. It is said in the *Shi ji* 史記 that "Zaofu was favored by King Miu of Zhou for his driving skills. [Once] he drove the king on a four-in-hand with Deji, Wenli, Hualiu, and Luer [four horses] for a hunting trip in the west. [The king] had such a good time and he forgot to return" (造父以善御幸於周繆王。得驥、溫驪、驊騮、騄耳之駟，西巡狩，樂而忘歸). In his *Shi ji* commentary, Pei Yin 裴駰 (fl. 430) quoted Guo Pu 郭璞 (276–324) and said that the color of *hualiu* is red like

YE IN JIAN'AN LITERATURE

	命友生	I call out friends,
28	攜同儔	And bring along companions.
	誦風人之所歎	Praising that over which poets have sighed,[98]
30	遂駕言而出遊	We consequently take our carriages and go out to roam.[99]
	步北園而馳騖	Pacing the north garden and galloping swiftly,[100]
32	庶翱翔以解憂	Hoping to soar on spread wings to relieve our worries.
	望洪池之滉漾	Gazing over the vast broadness of the grand pond,[101]
34	遂降集乎輕舟	We go down to cluster in light boats.
	沈浮蟻于金罍	And sinking the "floating-ants" in the golden wine jars,[102]
36	行觴爵于好仇	We circulate the flagons and cups among good friends.
	絲竹發而響厲	Strings and woodwinds issue forth and their echo is harsh,
38	悲風激于中流	Sad winds stir in mid-stream.
	且容與以盡觀	Momentarily carefree and relaxed to exhaust the view,
10	聊永日以忘愁	We temporarily prolong the day to forget our melancholy.
	嗟羲和之奮策	We sigh over Xihe plying his whip,[103]

---

flowers (色如華而赤). See Sima Qian 司馬遷 (145–ca. 86 BCE), *Shi ji* (Beijing: Zhonghua shuju, 1959), 5.175 and 176.

98 The word *fengren* 風人 possibly used to refer to those who supposedly collected songs seen in the "Guofeng" 國風 of the *Shijing*, *Mao shi* 1–160, and later it became a term for poets.

99 See the couplet, "Took a carriage and went to roam, / To dispel my worries" (駕言出游，以寫我憂), in the "Quanshui" 泉水 of the *Shijing*. *Mao shi* 39.

100 Zhao Youwen states that the north garden probably is Xuanwu Park but Gong Kechang and his fellow editors think it is wrong since Xuanwu Park was located to the west of the city. See Zhao, *Cao Zhi ji jiaozhu*, 185n26; and Gong and others, *Quan Sanguo fu pingzhu*, 430n20.

101 Following his reading of line thirty-one, Zhao Youwen states that this is Xuanwu reservoir. See his note twenty-eight in Zhao, *Cao Zhi ji jiaozhu*, 185.

102 "Floating ants" (*fuyi* 浮蟻) is a term used to describe the dregs of grain floating on the surface of alcohol before its distillation process. In his "Rhapsody on the Southern Capital" ("Nandu fu" 南都賦), Zhang Heng 張衡 (78–139) writes: "The wines include: The sweet spirits of Nine Fermentations, / The doubly clear Ten Weeks wine, / Unstrained spirits covered with inch-thick sediment, / With "floating ants" like duckweed. / Their taste does not injure the palate, / And one may drink his fill and never feel the effects" (酒則九醞甘醴，十旬兼清。醪敷徑寸，浮蟻若萍。其甘不爽，醉而不醒). See Knechtges, *Wen xuan*, 1:325; and Xiao, *Wen xuan*, 4.6b–7a.

103 Xihe 羲和 refers to the sun, derived from the stories of the sun god or the one who drives the chariot of the sun, or the mother of the sun(s). The humanized story in "Annals of the Five Emperors" (*Wudi benji* 五帝本紀) of the *Shi ji* states that Yao 堯 ordered Xi 羲 and He 和 to "show respect and obedience to heaven" (*jingshun haotian* 敬順昊天) and sent two Xi brothers (Xizhong 羲仲 and Xishu 羲叔) and two He brothers (Hezhong 和仲 and Heshu 和叔) to the four directions so that they could observe the astronomical phenomena and create a calendar accordingly. Pei Yin quoted Kong Anguo 孔安國 (fl. 156–74 BCE) that Xi and He were the descendants of Chong 重 and Li 黎, and the Xi and He clans were the officials in charge of heaven and earth for generations. (孔安國曰重黎之後，

42	怨曜靈之無光	And resent the absence of rays from that glorious numen.[104]
	念人生之不永	Ponder on the transience of human life—,
44	若春日之微霜	It is like a light frost in a spring sun.
	諒遺名之可紀	I understand that a name left behind can be recorded,[105]
46	信天命之無常	And believe the inconstancy in one's heaven-ordained fate.[106]
	愈志蕩以淫遊	[Wanting] all the more to stir my ambitions to roam in excess,
48	非經國之大綱	Is not the "main hawser" that can order the state.[107]
	罷曲宴而旋服	We ended the music and feast and quickly drove [back],
50	遂言歸乎舊房	And so went back to our old rooms.[108]

While the theme of the poem is "roaming" (*you* 遊), some fourteen lines pass before it is introduced. The early lines are about place making, situating the Three Terraces in the surroundings of their physical environment of mountains and rivers. The roaming occurs from line fifteen to line thirty-six. Having situated the act of roaming within a physical space, the poet moves on to time. Time has two aspects. The first is that roaming itself is an activity that must by its nature take place through time. But, also the blooming of the vegetation, the sounds of birds, and the development of color all parallel the growing excitement and activity of the group of friends, who move from carriages to boats to probe the pleasures of spring. Spring is the best season of all, the beginning of life and hope, but is also one that the poet knows cannot last. This message is brought home in lines thirty-seven and on. As opposed to spring, which will

---

義氏、和氏世掌天地之官). See the story and Pei Yin's note in Sima, *Shi ji*, 1.16–17. Sarah Allan has a comprehensive paper on the mythical roles regarding Xihe from texts such as "Encountering Sorrow" (Lisao 離騷) of the *Chuci* and the *Shan hai jing*. See her "Sons of Suns: Myth and Totemism in Early China," *Bulletin of the School of Oriental and African Studies, University of London*, vol. 44, no. 2 (1981): 290–326.

104   The "glorious numen" is the sun.

105   In his "Seven Inducements," Cao Zhi writes that the "Master Mirrors the Minute" (Jingji zi 鏡機子) said to the "Master Profound Subtlety" (Xuanwei zi 玄微子): "I heard that a gentleman does not escape from the common custom of leaving behind his name, and a wise man does not turn his back on the generation and destroy merits" (予聞君子不遁 俗而遺名，智士不背世而滅勛). See the text in Xiao, *Wen xuan*, 34.13b–25a.

106   Heavenly fate indicates one's destiny, the happenings, or natural span of life. In the beginning of the Zhongyong 中庸 account in the *Liji*, it states, "The heavenly fate is called nature. To follow nature is called the way, and to cultivate the way is called teaching" (天命 之謂性，率性之謂道，修道之謂教). And Zheng Xuan's 鄭玄 commentary reads that "Heaven-ordained fate: this means that by which heaven ordains in giving people life. It is called the fate of human nature" (天命，謂天所命生人者也，是謂性命). See Zheng, *Liji zhengyi*, 52.1a.

107   The "main hawser" here indicates the major principle laws that regulate the state.

108   Cf. "[I] announced to return" (言告言歸) in "Getan" 葛覃 of the *Shijing*. *Mao shi* 2. The text of this poem is in Yan, *Quan Sanguo wen*, 13.5b–6a.

return in eternal renewal, the friends struggle to make this one day an eternity (*liao yong ri* 聊永日), knowing all the time that it is just a momentary cessation of the anxieties of a life that is all too short. The realization that the pursuit of leisure runs counter to perpetuation of the political order (*fei gang* 非綱) closes off the possibility of the desire to extend their fun forever; they return then to their "old rooms," the familiar environment that surrounds them with duty and responsibility. The focus of the poem shifts to the second aspect: on the one hand, there is the awareness that their own lives are as short as frost in the warm sun, but there is also an acknowledgment at the end that they can be part of a greater enterprise of culture that will endure beyond a single lifetime. Like the poem above, which touches on the possibility of immortality through history, this implies an existence that lives beyond the self. This explains, to some degree, their choice to "quickly return" (*xuanfu* 旋服), to go back to their ordinary lives. Roaming may give individual pleasure, but it cannot assure the perpetuation of either name or the cultural entity.

We can never know what the intention of these Jian'an poets was: if the poet was simply lamenting shortness of life as he noticed how quickly time passed, or if, as assumed by modern readers, that the sudden wholesale death of friends spurred these thoughts. The reader, nevertheless, can see the foundational development of Ye as an enduring symbol in literature. Its grand monumental image, particularly the Three Terraces and gardens, made an impact on poets' minds. But while the city demonstrated the accomplishments of human power, at the same time these structures dotted a literary landscape that contrasted those accomplishments with the impermanence of human life. The few poems discussed in this chapter show the rich layers of emotions brought out by the grand man-made structures and the beautiful views of the natural world they afforded. But this moment of looking from a structure—a terrace, a garden, a wall—inevitably allowed a look into the eternity of nature and its seemingly never-ending scale. In some sense, it was the structures themselves that generated the thinking about how short human life really was by situating place against space and that moment of human history against the flow of time. But the poems leave the reader with an unmarked ending, like a movie that does not tell the viewer what happened after a character's moment of epiphany. It stops with the realization itself, leaving later action a puzzle for the viewer and the reader.

CHAPTER 3

Ye the Dynastic Capital

The air and style of Ye was abundant in the Jin,
And heroic capacity still appeared in the "Song of the Chipped Pot."
As for "winds and clouds"—should one resent Zhang Hua's lack,
Then what of the new voices of Wen [Tingyun] and Li [Shangyin]?
YUAN HAOWEN, "Thirty Poems on Poetry"

鄴下風流在晉多
壯懷猶見缺壺歌
風雲若恨張華少
溫李新聲奈若何
元好問《論詩三十首》

∵

During the late Eastern Han 東漢 (25–220) and Three Kingdoms 三國 (220–280) period, Ye had reached a material and cultural apex. Even though it never became the capital of the Cao Wei 曹魏 (220–265), Ye remained a major city after Cao Pi 曹丕 (187–226) had established his capital at Luoyang 洛陽. After the fall of the Cao Wei, Ye continued to be a major metropolis in north China and finally reached its status as a dynastic capital during some reigns and short-lived dynasties: first under Shi Hu 石虎 (r. 334–349) of the Later Zhao 後趙 (319–349), then under Murong Jun 慕容儁 (r. 349–360) of the Former Yan 前燕 (337–370). In 534, the high official Gao Huan 高歡 (496–547) installed Emperor Xiaojing 孝敬帝 (r. 534–550) on the throne of the Eastern Wei 東魏 (534–550), and Gao Huan's son Gao Yang 高洋 (526–559) went on to found the Northern Qi 北齊 (550–577) dynasty. Both sited their capital at Ye.[1] The celebratory motif associated with the Cao Wei ruling family largely disappeared after the Jian'an 建安 (196–220) era, and instead, Ye came to be used as a site that evoked the memory of Cao Cao's brief glory and, subsequently, a general trope for loss and the brevity of human life.

---

1 Ye was briefly renamed Linzhang 臨漳 to avoid the taboo name of Emperor Min of Jin 晉愍帝 (r. 313–316), Sima Ye 司馬鄴, on September twenty-seventh the year 313. See Fang Xuanling 房玄齡 (579–648) and others, *Jin shu* 晉書 (Beijing: Zhonghua shuju, 1974), 5.127.

YE THE DYNASTIC CAPITAL

1 The Representation of Ye by Jin Literati

The city of Ye under Shi Hu was best captured in Lu Hui's 陸翽 (fl. 317) *Yezhong ji* 鄴中記. As mentioned in chapter one, this is mainly an account of affairs at the capital city of the Later Zhao dynasty during Shi Hu's rule.[2] The bibliographical treatise of the *Sui shu* 隋書 lists it as "the *Yezhong ji*, two fascicles, composed by Lu Hui, instructor in the national academy of Jin" (鄴中記二卷。晉國子助教陸翽撰).[3] It is recorded as "Lu Hui, *Yezhong ji*, two fascicles" (陸翽鄴中記二卷) in the *Xin Tang shu* 新唐書.[4] The *Yezhong ji*, however, has survived only in fragments that are contradictory and redundant; nevertheless, modern scholars still value these extant segments as rare geographical and historical documentation of the capital of Ye and the life of Shi Hu.[5] Rather than rehash what has already been done on the *Yezhong ji*, I would like to offer here, instead, a poem that appears to summarize in verse many key elements of the *Yezhong ji* and also demonstrates the impression Shi Hu and his capital Ye left on one particular Tang poet's imagination. The following is "A Song of Cherry Zheng" ("Zheng Yingtao ge" 鄭櫻桃歌) attributed to Li Qi 李頎 (690–751):

	石季龍	Shi Jilong
2	潛天祿	Misappropriated Heaven's beneficence,
	擅雄豪	And arrogated to himself heroic power.
4	美人姓鄭名櫻桃	There was a beauty named Cherry Zheng.
	櫻桃美顏香且澤	Cherry's beautiful face was fragrant and dewy,
6	娥娥侍寢專宮掖	A fairylike beauty serving his bedchamber, she monopolized the consort chambers.

---

2 For a brief description of Ye in the Southern and Northern Dynasties period, see Miyakawa, *Rikuchō shi kenkyū*, pp. 537–546.

3 Wei Zheng 魏徵 (580–643) comp., *Sui shu* 隋書 (Beijing: Zhonghua shuju, 1973), 33.983.

4 Ouyang Xiu 歐陽修 (1007–1072) and Song Qi 宋祁 (998–1061) comps., *Xin Tang shu* 新唐書 (Beijing: Zhonghua shuju, 1975), 58.1504.

5 Those include, for example, Bao Yuanhang 鮑遠航, "Jin Lu Hui *Yezhong ji* kaolun: 'Shuijing zhu' zhengyin wenxian kao zhi yi" 晉陸翽《鄴中記》考論—《水經注》徵引文獻考之一, *Huabei shuili shuidian daxue xuebao* 華北水利水電大學學報 30. 3 (June 2014): 1–4; and the "Palace Buildings of the Capital Ye" (*Yedu gongshi* 鄴都宮室) entry in Cui Xian 崔銑 (1478–1541), comp., *Jiajing Zhangde fu zhi* 嘉靖彰德府志 (rpt. Shanghai: Guji shudian, 1982), 8.1a–8.44b. Also see Feng Junshi 馮君實, "*Yezhong ji* jibu"《鄴中記》輯補, *Guji zhengli yanjiu xuekan* 古籍整理研究學刊, no. 2 (1985): 5–13 and 17; and Huang Huixian 黃惠賢, "Jijiao *Yezhong ji*" 輯校《鄴中記》in *Yecheng ji Beichao shi yanjiu* 鄴城暨北朝史研究, ed. Liu Xinchang 劉心長 and Ma Zhongli 馬忠理 (Shijia zhuang, Hebei: Hebei Renmin chuban she, 1991), 368–377. There are two modern translations and studies in Western languages: Edward Schafer and Shing Müller, see Ch. 1.

	後庭卷衣三萬人	[Although] "rolled robes" in the rear garden were thirty-thousand strong,[6]
8	翠眉清鏡不得親	Those kingfisher-green brows in the clear mirror could not draw near [him].[7]
	宮軍女騎一千匹	A palace army of female riders—a thousand head of horses,
10	繁花照耀漳河春	Luxuriant flowers shining radiantly—a Zhang River spring.
	織成花映紅綸巾	Woven flowers glint on their red ribboned-scarves,[8]
12	紅旗挐曳滷簿新	Red flags tow the retinue that was renewed.
	鳴鼙走馬接飛鳥	Sounding handheld drums and racing their horses, they "catch the flying birds."[9]

---

6   The term, "rolled robes" (*juanyi* 卷衣), refers to women who had been favored by the emperors. A verse titled "Qin Prince Rolls Robes" ("Qin wang juanyi" 秦王卷衣) credited to the Southern Liang 梁 (502–557) poet Wu Jun 吳均 (469–520) reads:

	咸陽春草芳	The spring grass of Xianyang is fragrant,
2	秦帝卷衣裳	The Qin ruler rolls up his garment.
	玉檢茱萸匣	A jade missive in an ailanthus box,
4	金泥蘇合香	Golden paste and sweetgum perfume,
	初芳薰複帳	The first [puff] of these fragrances infuses the double-curtain,
6	餘輝耀玉牀	And the remaining light will shine on the jade bed.
	當須晏朝罷	He must wait until the evening court ends,
8	持此贈華陽	To take these gifts to Lady Huayang.

See the text of this verse in Lu Qinli 逯欽立, ed., *Xian Qin Han Wei Jin Nanbeichao shi*先秦漢魏晉南北朝詩 (Beijing: Zhonghua shuju chuban she, 1983), 2:1724.

Lady Huayang 華陽夫人 (d. 230 BCE) was the beloved of Ying Zhu 嬴柱 (302–250 BCE), the Qin prince—who later became King of Xiaowen 孝文王 but died after three days on the throne (r. November 12, 250–November 14, 250 BCE). When her adopted son, Ying Zichu 嬴子楚 (281–247 BCE), took the throne after his father King of Xiaowen and became King of Zhuangxiang 莊襄王 (r. 250–247 BCE), Lady Huayang became Empress Dowager Huayang (alongside the king's birth mother Empress Dowager Xia 夏).

7   Kingfisher-green eyebrows were colored with greenish black kohl (*qingdai* 青黛). Here it is a metaphor for the court ladies who were all made up and waiting in vain for the emperor to summon them.

8   In *Yezhong ji* a statement describes that Jilong [Shi Hu] also once used one thousand female performers as his formal retinue. Each of them wore purple ribboned-scarves (季龍又嘗以女伎一千人爲鹵簿，皆著紫綸巾). Lu, *Yezhong ji*, 4b. See below.

9   It is believed that Ji Qingji 姬慶忌 (fl. 500 BCE), King Wu of the Wu state 吳國武王 (r. 526–514 BCE)—Ji Liao's 姬僚 (d. 515 BCE) son, was brave and bold, and he could chase after beasts on foot and catch flying birds by hand. An anecdote states that after Ji Guang 姬光, better known as Helü 闔閭 (d. 496 BCE), killed his uncle and took the throne, he plotted to kill his cousin Qingji as well. Helü told Yaoli 要離 (fl. 500 BCE), whom he recruited for the mission, that:

The braveness of Qingji has been heard by the whole world. [His] physical faculty is courageous and forceful, and ten thousand men cannot block [him]. [He] can run on foot to chase after running beasts and catch flying birds with [his] hands. [His] bones leap and his flesh fly. Just tapping on [his] knees, [then he] could go for several hundred *li*. I once

YE THE DYNASTIC CAPITAL

14	銅駝琴瑟隨去塵	The bronze camels *patinate* and go the way of dust.[10]
	鳳陽重門如意館	[In] the Ruyi Hall by the double-doored Fengyang Gate,[11]
16	百尺金梯倚銀漢	A hundred *chi* golden ladder leaned on the Silver Han.[12]
	自言富貴不可量	[She] said herself that her wealth and nobility were unmeasurable,
18	女為公主男為王	[Her] daughters became princesses and her sons, princes.
	赤花雙簟珊瑚床	Paired reed-mats of red flowers on the coral bed,
20	盤龍斗帳琥珀光	A canopy curtain with coiled dragons shone with amber.[13]

---

chased him to the Yangtze, [my] galloping four-in-hand could not catch up to him. [I] shot him [with an arrow], but [he] caught it; no arrows could hit him. Now your strength is not up to him.

慶忌之勇世所聞也。筋骨果勁，萬人莫當。走追奔獸，手接飛鳥。骨騰肉飛，拊膝數百里。吾嘗追之於江，駟馬馳不及。射之闇接，矢不可中。今子之力不如也。

See Huang Rensheng 黃仁生, ed., *Xinyi Wu Yue chunqiu* 新譯吳越春秋 (Taipei: Sanmin shuju, 1996), 81–82.

10 Reading *sese* 瑟瑟 instead of *qinse* 琴瑟. On the bronze camels, see Ch. 1.

11 The term double-door (*chongmen* 重門) often refers to gates of palaces or places that were important and required extra security. The Fengyang was the west gate on the southern wall of Ye. In the *Yezhong ji* it is described as follows:

The Ye palace had three gates on the south face. The western one was the Fengyang Gate. It was twenty-five *zhang* tall. There were six storeys on top and its upward eaves faced the sun. Two gates opened below. There was also a large bronze phoenix installed on its top. [The phoenix's] head was raised one *zhang* and six *chi* high. [There were] ... red pillars with white walls. One could see this gate in the distance while still seven or eight *li* away from the city. (See Lu, *Yezhong ji*, 1a.)

鄴宮南面三門，西鳳陽門。高二十五丈，上六層，反宇向陽。下開二門，又安大銅鳳于其巔，舉頭一丈六尺。... ... 朱柱白壁。未到鄴城七八里，遙望此門。

And another entry provides more information about the phoenix:

Fengyang gate was a five-storey tower that rose thirty *zhang* from the ground. [They] installed a pair of golden phoenixes. When Shi Hu was on the verge of going into decline, one flew into the Zhang River. On sunny days it appeared on the water. For the other, they secured its feet with iron nails. It is still there. (See Lu, *Yezhong ji*, 1b.)

鳳陽門五層樓，去地三十丈，安金鳳凰二頭。石虎將衰，一頭飛入漳河。會晴日見于水上。一頭以鐵釘釘足。今存。

12 The "golden ladder" occurs in texts from the Southern Dynasties in connection with the dwelling places of lovelies, anticipating its much more extensive use in the Tang era. Fei Chang 費昶 [fl. 510] wrote: "In the morning, I climbed the golden ladder up to [your] Phoenix chamber, / In the evening, I took off the jade-decorated hook and rested in [your] palace-hall" (朝逾金梯上鳳樓，暮下瓊鈎息鸞殿). Here, in Li Qi's poem, it probably refers to the beautiful but neglected consorts who cannot reach the stellar heights of Cherry Zheng. The Silver Han is the Milky Way. See the full text of Fei Chang's poem, "Travelling is Hard" ("Xinglu nan" 行路難), in Guo Maoqian 郭茂倩 (1041–1099), comp., *Yuefu shiji* 樂府詩集 (Beijing: Zhonghua shuju, 1979), 3:70.1003.

13 Lu, *Yezhong ji*, 7a, has a description of the double-curtain and incense infusion of Shi Hu's bedding. It reads:

| | 82 | CHAPTER 3 |

淫昏偽位神所惡　　A licentious muddlehead usurping the throne is what the
　　　　　　　　　　spirits hate,

22　滅石者陵終不誤　　"The one who destroys the Shi is Ling—," in the end this was
　　　　　　　　　　not wrong.[14]

鄴城蒼蒼白露微　　On walls of Ye now dark and somber, white dew faintly forms,

24　世事翻覆黃雲飛　　Where worldly affairs tumbled and changed, yellow clouds
　　　　　　　　　　fly.[15]

In the winter months, [they] set up fine brocade canopy curtain with tassels. At its four corners [they] placed pure-gold dragons, and the heads held in their mouths the five-colored tassels. Some of them were made of green thick silk with shiny brocade, some were made of red thick silk with polychrome *denggao* brocade,* and some were made of purple thick silk with large and small brocade. The threads were made of cotton from Fangzi (near modern day Lincheng 臨城, Hebei) and one hundred and twenty *jin* of white thin silk lining. This was called a double-curtain. At the corners of the curtain opening were placed pure gold or silver mirrors and inlaid incense burners to burn graphite together with famous incense. On the top of the curtain, [they] placed a golden lotus blossom. In the middle of the flower hung gold leaves woven into a curtain sachet. It could hold three *sheng* and was used to hold incense. On all four sides of the curtain, there were twelve incense sachets, their patterns and colors were also the same.

冬月施熟錦流蘇斗帳，四角安純金龍，頭銜五色流蘇。或用青綈光錦，或用緋綈登高文錦，或紫用大小錦。絲以房子綿，百二十斤白縑裏，名曰複帳。帳門角安純金銀鑒鏤香爐，以石墨燒集和名香。帳頂上安金蓮花，花中懸金箔織成綩囊。囊受三升以盛香。帳之四面上十二香囊，采色亦同。

*Zhao Feng 趙豐 explains that,

According to *Yezhong ji*, the Later Zhao (319–351) had a brocade weaving bureau, which was a place specializing in producing brocades. Among its products, there were "large *denggao*" and "small *denggao*." In fact, [these] are *denggao* brocades with patterns in various sizes. *Denggao* is just climbing mountains, so perhaps the cloud-patterns in these *denggao* brocades were that of mountains. They are continuous with no gaps and are also called "mountain shaped clouds."

據《鄴中記》載，東晉十六國時期的後趙有織錦署，就是專門生產織錦的機構，其中生產的產品有「大登高」和「小登高」，其實就是圖案大小規格不同的「登高」錦。「登高」就是爬山，所以這些登高錦中的雲紋，可能就是山的描繪，它是連續和不間斷的，又稱「山狀雲」。

See Zhao Feng, *Jincheng—Zhongguo sichou yu sichou zhi lu* 錦程：中國絲綢與絲綢之路 (Hong Kong: City University of Hong Kong Press, 2012), 75.

14　This refers to the prophetic remark regarding the destruction of the Shi family by Ran Min 冉閔 (d. 352) [also known as Shi Min 石閔; some believe he is the son of Shi Hu's adopted son, Ran Zhan 冉瞻 (d.328)]. In Shi Hu's biography there is an account that states, "In the beginning, a prophecy had said "A tumulus [*ling*] will be what destroys the stone [*shi*]." Shortly after that, Shi Min's fief title was changed to be Duke of Lanling. Jilong [Shi Hu] hated it and changed the prefect name from Lanling to Wuxing. But when it came to this, [the Shi family] was in the end wiped out by Min" (初，讖言滅石者陵，尋而石閔徙封蘭陵公，季龍惡之，改蘭陵為武興郡，至是終為閔所滅). See Fang, *Jin shu*, 107.2792.

15　The text of this poem is in the *Quan Tang shi* 全唐詩, 29.421. Cf. Schafer, "The Yeh Chung Chi," 160–162. My reading of lines differs from his. In the *Yangzhou huafang lu* 揚州畫

YE THE DYNASTIC CAPITAL

This poem begins by illustrating the most potent weapons that any woman in early medieval China could deploy—her beauty and the intimate relationship with her patron that it granted. The use of the single character "to monopolize" (*zhuan* 專) in line six portrays how much Cherry was favored by Shi Hu, leaving no room for any other court ladies to spend the night alone with the emperor. Cherry Zheng (d. 349) was an entertainer before becoming one of Shi Hu's first three wives. After eliminating Shi Hu's two other wives, Ladies Guo 郭夫人 (n.d.) and Cui 崔夫人 (n.d.), and giving birth to two sons—Shi Sui 石邃 (ca. 310–337) and Shi Zun 石遵 (d. 349)—Cherry Zheng became Shi Hu's sole favorite and later his empress when he took power in a coup in 334.[16]

Following the introduction of Cherry's personal qualities, the poet then describes Cherry's public display and floods the poem with vivid colors of red as the poem describes the colorful female cavalry that formed the royal couple's imperial retinue. (These include the repeating appearances of the name Cherry in lines four and five, the red ribboned-scarves in line eleven, the red flags in line twelve, the red flowers and coral [often red] in line nineteen.) The *Yezhong ji* describes this unit thusly: "Jilong also once used one thousand female performers as his formal retinue. Each of them wore purple ribboned-scarves, fine brocade pants, a gold and silver inlaid belt, and boots that were woven with five patterns as they roamed on the terraces" (季龍又嘗以女伎一千人為滷簿，皆著紫綸巾，熟錦袴，金銀鏤帶，五文織成鞾，遊臺上).[17] And when his empress went out, she was accompanied by "a thousand-female cavalry as her retinue. In winter, each of them dressed in purple upper vestments and kerchiefs, with riding tops and pants made of brocade tapestry from Sichuan" (女騎一千為滷簿。冬天皆著紫衣巾，蜀錦袴褶).[18] The bronze camels, in line fourteen, are described as being "... shaped like horses, one *zhang* long and one *zhang* tall. Their feet were [cloven] like an ox's and their tails were three *chi* long. Their spines were like horse saddles. Outside of Zhongyang Gate they faced each other on either side of the road" (二銅馳如馬形，長一丈，高一丈。足如牛，尾長三尺，脊如馬鞍。在中陽門外，夾道相向).[19] Zhongyang was the central main gate on the southern wall of Ye and the imperial street ran from this gate straight up to the palace complex. These bronze camels could

---

舫錄, this poem is attributed to Li Shun 李順, which is most certainly a vestige of a scribal error. See Li Dou 李斗 (fl. ca. 1770), *Yangzhou huafang lu*, ed. Wang Beiping 汪北平 and Tu Yugong 涂雨公 (Beijing: Zhonghua shuju, 1960), 342.

16 Shi Hu's biography in the *Jin shu* reads that, "Jilong killed Guo because [he] favored and was obsessed with a child entertainer, Cherry Zheng. Further [he] took in the daughter of the Cui family of Qinghe (near modern day Xingtai 邢台, Hebei), but Cherry again slandered her and had her killed as well" (季龍寵惑優僮鄭櫻桃而殺郭氏，更納清河崔氏女，櫻桃又譖而殺之). See Fang, *Jin shu*, 106.2761.

17 Lu, *Yezhong ji*, 4b.

18 Lu, *Yezhong ji*, 9b.

19 Lu, *Yezhong ji*, 5b.

84   CHAPTER 3

possibly have been part of the shipment of large objects that Shi Hu had transported to Ye from Luoyang, as discussed in the previous chapter.[20]

Red has a long association with the colors of high summer, the beauty of the female face, and with erotic pleasure. Here it is a fulgent display of beauty that can be read allegorically both temporally, as the full blossom of the dynasty, but also as a public display of Shi Hu's indulgence in women: they are allowed to replace a proper retinue that should be male, and the color red suggests a public display of color that should have been held within the private spaces of the palace. The patinating color of the camels replaces the brightness of flowers toward the end of spring and suddenly brings the flood of red to a halt. It is difficult not to read this section as direct criticism of the price one pays for indulging a favorite concubine, expending an excess of love and material wealth at the neglect of history's lessons that warn of the power of female attraction.

At the end of the poem, the poet draws attention back from public space to the intimacy of the bedchamber—Shi Hu's ostentatious coral bed in lines nineteen and twenty—where the lesson is completed. The vivid color of the animating spirit of life, red, that symbolized the heat of summer and passion, first yielded to decaying green, and now to white dew—an indication of autumn's onset and the rise of the dark power of *yin* that scatters away the yellow clouds, a symbol of rulership. Yellow, in the cycle of the Five Phases, marks the center; it is the point of harmony and balance, where it stands for the emperor, dressed in his yellow robes.[21] This poem represents the historical dynasty and its ruler, Shi Hu, caught in the power of nature's relentless revolution through the seasons. His indulgence in women (*yin*) to the neglect of his public duty (*yang*) hastens the circuit of time; in the end, his power as emperor (symbolized by yellow) flutters away into disaster and warfare. And yellow, while the imperial color, is also the color of loess dust raised by warhorses.

When reading this poem alongside the *Yezhong ji*, the reader finds it also provides a fragmentary imaginative space in Ye: one of splendor, indulgence in women, and quick dynastic succession. Perhaps, through Shi Hu's obsessions, the poem rereads Cao Cao's experience in Ye of power as indulgence and nostalgia. It does not specifically make claims about the role of the city itself. While seeing it primarily as a stage where action takes place, the sites of Ye are implicated in events. Li Qi's poem, with its emphasis on progression of the seasons through his use of color imagery, places events within the realm of nature rather than in history; at the same time, it seems to suggest that there is

---

20   Find details of these objects described in the previous chapter and in Fang, *Jin shu*, 106.2764.

21   The other four phases are: green is the color of east and spring, red is south and summer, white is west and autumn, and black is north and winter.

YE THE DYNASTIC CAPITAL

something in the place itself that is resistant to historical duration. The poet captures this beautifully in his use of the discarded camels, moved from capital to capital, only to wind up as mute witnesses, guardians of a stage where minor dynasties can play out their roles. Whether or not the events were true, they were embedded within the cultural tradition of Ye and they resurfaced over and over in history, taking on a certain amount of reliability as a repetitive philosophical truism rather than empirical truth. In the minds of later generations, Shi Hu's occupation of Ye was to be remembered primarily by his lavish construction projects that were meant as ostentatious displays of power and wealth.[22]

While Shi Hu was building Ye as a capital city, some poets of the Jin, a dynasty that viewed itself as the legitimate successor of Cao Wei, had a different perspective on Ye. Their view of the city did not reflect what we read in the *Yezhong ji*. Instead of the glories of the city, they describe a Ye in ruins. Lu Chen 盧諶 (285–351) wrote a "*Fu* on Ascending the Ye Terrace" ("Deng Yetai fu" 登鄴臺賦).[23] This short verse, surely a fragment, reads:

	顯陽隤其顛隧	Xianyang Gate collapsed and tumbled down,[24]
2	文昌鞠而為墟	Wenchang Hall fell forward to become ruins.
	銅爵隕於臺側	The bronze bird plummeted to the side of the terrace,
4	洪鍾寢於兩除	The large bell lay by the palace steps.
	奚帝王之靈宇	Why did the numinous eaves of the monarch,[25]
6	為狐兔之攸居	Become the dwelling place of foxes and hares?[26]

Lu Chen is primarily known through his exchanges with Liu Kun 劉琨 (270–318). He lived a turbulent life despite his family background. As the first line of his biography in the *Jin shu* 晉書 remarks: "He was clear-thinking, quick-witted and had a logical mind. He was fond of *Laozi* and *Zhuangzi* and excelled at

---

22 Some criticisms of Shi Hu are outlined in Schafer, "The *Yeh Chung Chi*," 160–165.

23 David Knechtges gives Lu Chen's date as 285–351, but he also points out that some, for example Xu Gongchi 徐公持, give 284–350. See David R. Knechtges, "Liu Kun, Lu Chen, and Their Writings in the Transition to the Eastern Jin," *Chinese Literature: Essays, Articles, Reviews* (*CLEAR*) 28 (Dec., 2006): 1n2.

24 See Xianyang Gate in Zuo Si's "Rhapsody on the Wei Capital" (*Wei du fu* 魏都賦) in Xiao Tong 蕭統 (501–31), *Wen xuan* 文選, comm. Li Shan 李善 (d. 689) (Beijing: Zhonghua shuju, 1977), 6.9a; and also in David R. Knechtges, trans., *Wen xuan, Or Selections of Refined Literature*, vol. 1, *Rhapsodies on Metropolises and Capitals* (Princeton: Princeton University Press, 1996), 1: 440, note to line 215 and 1: 441. Here reading 隧 as *zhui*.

25 The word "numinous eaves" (*lingyu* 靈宇) means memorial temples or the former abode of one who was deceased.

26 Ouyang Xun 歐陽詢 (557–641) and others comps., *Yiwen leiju* 藝文類聚 (rpt. Taipei: Wenguang chuban she, 1974), 62.1121.

writing."[27] Born into an elite scholarly family, Lu Chen's fifth-generation grandfather was the renowned Ruist scholar Lu Zhi 盧植 (d. 192). In its description of Lu Chen's granduncle, Lu Qin 盧欽 (d. 278), the *Jin shu* remarks, "For generations, [a family] notable for its Ruist occupation (世以儒業顯)."[28] Lu Chen's father, Lu Zhi 盧志 (d. 312), had once served as the prefect of Ye. When Sima Ying 司馬穎 (279–306), who had participated in the Disorder of the Eight Princes (*bawang zhi luan* 八王之亂),[29] established his command post at Ye, he put Lu Zhi 盧志 in charge of formulating strategy.[30] Lu Zhi 盧志 remained in Ye throughout the rebellion. When Sima Ying died, Lu Zhi 盧志 was the only official in the funeral cortège.[31] From the *Jin shu*, we can tell that not only was Lu Chen from an educated elite family, he also possessed loyalty and integrity.

But Lu Chen's family status and achievements counted for little during the transitional and tumultuous time of fourth-century China. After the so-called "Disorder of Yongjia" (Yongjia *zhi luan* 永嘉之亂) broke out in 311,[32] Lu Chen's father tried to lead the family to seek refuge with Liu Kun 劉琨 (270–318), but eventually Lu Chen's parents and siblings were all slain. Even earlier in life, Lu Chen had suffered some misfortune. He had been selected to marry a daughter of Emperor Wu of Jin 晉武帝 (r. 265–290), Princess Xingyang 滎陽公主 (n.d.), and therefore to receive the title of Commandant-escort (*fuma duwei* 駙馬都尉). But the princess died before the wedding took place. It was only after his entire family was wiped out that he was finally able to seek refuge with Liu Kun, who had previously married Lu Chen's maternal aunt. But this respite of peace did not last long. He was soon removed from Liu Kun's staff by Duan Pidi 段匹磾 (d. 322) after Liu Kun had taken up a position with Duan. Although Lu Chen worked for Duan Pidi for a while after the latter had slain Liu Kun, Lu Chen again had to flee, this time to Duan Mobo 段末波 (d. 325). Later Duan Mobo died and Lu Chen once more "fled disaster and was separated from old [generational] friends for nearly twenty years" (流離世故且二十載).[33]

27　Translation by David R. Knechtges, "Liu Kun, Lu Chen, and Their Writings in the Transition to the Eastern Jin," 26.

28　Fang, *Jin shu*, 44.1255.

29　The "Disorder of the Eight Princes" was a decade-long series of conflicts among the Jin imperial family beginning about 291. This chaos weakened the Jin and led to its collapse in 316. See, for example, Mark Edward Lewis, *China between Empires: The Northern and Southern Dynasties* (Cambridge, MA: Harvard University Press, 2009), 51.

30　Fang, *Jin shu*, 44.1256.

31　Fang, *Jin shu*, 44.1258.

32　This refers to a series of events involving non-Chinese forces invading the Jin capital, Luoyang, and committing a massacre during the Yongjia 永嘉 (307–313) reign period. See Lewis, *China Between Empires*, 51–53.

33　Fang, *Jin shu*, 44.1259.

YE THE DYNASTIC CAPITAL

The reader can see in the six lines of the poem above that the poet uses the conditions of the iconic places and structures of Ye metonymically to represent the final fate of the city. It may seem that these are rather straightforward lines. But the very starkness of the images leaves a haunting imprint on the mind of the reader. The first four lines are in the mode of "factual" reporting that describes the broken-down condition of these once magnificent structures. But, based on dominant early Chinese poetic theory that believes in a close relationship between interior states of the poet's mind and exterior political condition, the lines are probably meant to express a material and political parallel to the frustrated and failed ambitions of the poet. This is made clear in the last couplet, when the former abode of emperors becomes the dwelling place of "foxes and hares." One could read this last couplet as a simple description of how broken-down ruins, as symbols of human endeavor, return to a natural state to be inhabited by animals. But the term "foxes and hares" can also be used to describe self-seeking and crafty people. Perhaps it is a simple comment that all that remains of a dynasty of splendor are self-serving survivors, or it may even be a direct comment on the political relationships in his own life. In either reading, the contrast of the monarch and the animals (*diwang* 帝王 vs. *hutu* 狐兔) is stark and points outward to the physical ruins of Ye and perhaps inward to a sad and frustrated emotional state.

Lu Yun 陸雲 (262–303) was a few decades older than Lu Chen but died much younger and did not live to see Shi Hu's move to Ye. He also left a *fu*-poem titled "*Fu* on Ascending the Terrace" ("Dengtai fu" 登臺賦). Unlike Lu Chen's fragmentary work, Lu Yun's entire work survives, along with a preface that may give us an idea of the poet's inspiration for composing the piece. In the preface, the poet prepares the reader for the mood and emotions generated by his ascension of the terrace and discloses reason behind composing this piece, "when I ascended [the terraces], I was moved, and thus wrote a *fu*." The preface reads:

> In the middle of the Yongning [April 301–November 302] reign, [I took part in the assisting staff of the Chamberlain for the Palace Bursary in Ye. Due to some matters at that time], I went on for an inspection tour to the Ye palace complex and the Three Terraces. When I ascended the terraces, I was moved; [thereupon I used the experience to talk about rise and fall], and thus wrote a *fu*. It reads:

> 永寧中，（參大府之佐於鄴都，以時事）巡行鄴宮三臺。登高有感，（因以言崇替），迺作賦云：

	承后皇之嘉惠兮	Bearing the fine kindness of Heaven and Earth—,[34]
2	翼聖宰之威靈	Sheltered under the awesome prestige of the sage ruler.
	肅言而述業兮	I make my words conscientious to describe his enterprise—,
4	乃啟行乎北京	Now, I begin my journey at the northern capital.[35]
	巡華室以周流兮	Going forth to inspect the magnificent buildings as I tour around—,
6	登崇臺而上征	Ascending the tall terrace and marching upward.
	攀凌坻而遂隮兮	I scramble up the high hills and ascend—,
8	迄雲閣而少憩	Only after reaching the gallery in the clouds can I rest a bit.
	爾乃	There,
	佇眄瑤軒	I halt and gaze from the jade railing,
10	滿目綺寮	What fills my eyes are the traceried windows.
	中原方華	The central plain just flowering,[36]
12	綠葉振翹	Green leaves shaking and quivering.
	嘉生民之亹亹兮	Celebrating the diligent persistence of people—,
14	望天晷之苕苕	I gaze at the unending reach of heaven's sundial [sun].
	歷玉階而容與兮	Carefree and leisurely I pass over the jade steps—,
16	步蘭堂以逍遙	And tread in the orchid hall to roam at ease.
	蒙紫庭之芳塵兮	Covered by the fragrant dust of the purple courtyard—,[37]
18	駭洞房之迴飆	I am startled by a whirlwind from the grotto-rooms.[38]
	頹響逝而忤物兮	As its dying sound passes it affronts me—,
20	傾冠舉而凌霄	My tilted cap flies up and mounts to the clouds.
	曲房營而窈眇兮	The inner chambers twist about and are secluded—,
22	長廊邈而蕭條	The long walkway stretches on, empty and desolate.
	於是	Thereupon,
	迴路委夷	[I see] circling roads that are truly easy [to walk],
24	邃宇玄芒	Expansive buildings that are dark and dim.
	深堂百室	Interior halls with a hundred rooms behind them,
26	會臺千房	Gathered terraces with a thousand wing-rooms.
	闢南窗而蒙暑兮	I open up a south-facing window to receive the summer—,

---

34 *Hou* 后 and *huang* 皇 indicate earth and heaven. See Wang Yi's 王逸 (fl. 114–119) commentary in the "Nine Pieces" (*Jiuzhang* 九章) of the *Chuci* 楚辭. Hong Xingzu 洪興祖 (1090–1155), *Chuci buzhu* 楚辭補注, ed. Bai Huawen 白化文 and others (Beijing: Zhonghua shuju, 1983), 153.

35 Luoyang.

36 In this line I literally translate *zhongyuan* 中原 as central plain. It should be noted that this word also means in the middle of the plain, *yuanzhong* 原中. Cf. Zheng Xuan's 鄭玄 (127–200) commentary to *Mao shi* 196.

37 The purple courtyard refers to the imperial dwelling.

38 "Grotto-room" refers to the innermost chambers.

YE THE DYNASTIC CAPITAL   89

28	啟朔牖而履霜	And throw wide the leaves of the northern door to tread in the frost.[39]
	游陽堂而冬溫兮	I roam in the sunny hall and the winter warms—,
30	步陰房而夏涼	Pace in the shady room and the summer cools.
	萬禽委蛇於潛室兮	Ten thousand birds weave through hidden chambers—,
32	驚鳳矯翼而來翔	And a startled phoenix spreads its wings to come soaring.
	紛譎譎於有象兮	Confusing and slowly overflowing within are images—,[40]
34	邈攸忽而無方	Remote and faraway and without [fixed] directions.[41]

	於是	Thereupon,
	南征司火	I trudge southward, toward the controller of fire—,[42]
36	朱明鬱遂	Where the "vermillion brightness" is oppressive.[43]
	縣車式徐	As the hanging-chariot [of the sun] slackens—,
38	曜靈西墜	The radiant numen sinks into the west.
	暑乘陰而增炎兮	In the heat, I try to take advantage of the shade, but it grows hotter—,
40	景望淵而曖昧	In the shadows, I gaze hopefully into the depth, but it grows darker and dimmer.
	翫瓊宇而情厭兮	Enjoying myself under these jeweled eaves, I feel content—,
42	覽八方而思銳	Viewing in all directions, my thoughts sharpen.
	陋雨館之常規兮	I despise the daily routine of buildings in the rain—
44	鄙鳴鵠之蔽第	And detest the rundown mansion of the trumpeting swans.[44]

---

39   The *Liji* 禮記 states, "Once the frost and dew descend, gentlemen walked on them. They must have a melancholy heart but it is not because of the cold" (霜露既降，君子履之，必有悽愴之心，非其寒之謂也). See Zheng Xuan 鄭玄 (127–200) and Kong Ying-da 孔穎達 (574–648), comm. and ann., *Liji zhengyi* 禮記正義, in *Shisan jing zhushu fu jiaokan ji* 十三經注疏附校勘記, edited by Ruan Yuan 阮元 (1764–1849), 8 vols. (Taipei: Yiwen yingshu guan, 1982), 5: 47.1a.

40   The *Laozi* 老子 illustrates, "As for the features of the great *de*, they follow only the *dao*. As for *dao* becoming material things, it is unclear and uncertain. But within this unclearness and uncertainty, there are images; and within this unclearness and uncertainty, there are things" (孔德之容，惟道是從。道之為物，惟恍惟惚。惚兮恍兮，其中有象；恍兮惚兮，其中有物). See Chen Guying 陳鼓應, ed. and tran. *Laozi jinzhu jinyi ji pingjie* 老子今註今譯及評介 (Taipei: Taiwan shangwu yinshu guan, 1970), 104.

41   I take these two lines to mean something like, "In all that comes overwhelming in disorder there are images, / But they are far distant and vague and unbound to any direction."

42   The south is associated with fire.

43   In the *Chuci*, *zhuming* 朱明 is used to describe the radiance of the rising sun in the morning, as in "the vermillion brightness receives the night—, / Time is not standing still" (朱明承夜兮，時不可淹). See Ma Maoyuan 馬茂元 and others, *Chuci zhushi* 楚辭註釋 (Hubei: Renmin chuban she, 1985), 521 and 525n11.

44   The no-longer-extant collection *Names of the Palaces of the Jin* (*Jin gongque ming* 晉宮闕名) listed Minghu Park, Putao Park, and Hualin Park in Ye (鄴有鳴鵠園，蒲萄園，華林園). See Ouyang, *Yiwen leiju*, 65.1160.

	仰凌眄於天庭兮	I raise my head to gaze far away at the courtyard of heaven—
46	俛旁觀乎萬類	And lower it to observe the ten thousand categories of things.
	北溟浩以揚波兮	The Northern Abyss overflows and stirs its waves—,[45]
48	青林煥其興蔚	The green woods radiate with thriving luxuriance.[46]
	扶桑細於毫末兮	The legendary Fusang Tree is thinner than the tip of [autumn's] fine hair—,
50	崑崙卑乎覆簀	Mount Kunlun is lower than a turned-over bamboo basket.[47]
	於是	Thereupon,
	忽焉俛仰	In a split second between lowering and raising my head,
52	天地既閟	Heaven and earth have become blocked out.
	宇宙同區	And space-time occupies the same region,[48]
54	萬物為一	All objects become one.
	原千變之常鈞兮	They originate in the constant standard of a thousand changes—,
56	齊億載於今日	And equal a billion years on this day.
	彼區中之側陋兮	That narrow and simple little corner of this realm—,
58	非吾黨之一室	It is not an abode for my kind.[49]

---

45 The size of the Northern Abyss is described by the well-known quote about the fish that dwelled in it: "In the Northern Abyss there is a fish, its name is Kun. As for the size of Kun, no one knows how many thousands of *li* it is" (北冥有魚，其名為鯤。鯤之大，不知其幾千里也). See Guo Qingfan 郭慶藩 (1844–1896), ed., *Zhuangzi ji shi* 莊子集釋 (Beijing: Zhonghua shuju, 1961), 2.

46 The "green woods" (*qinglin* 青林) are also known as the constellation "Celestial Meadows" (*tianyuan* 天苑). See Li Shan's 李善 (630–689) commentary on Zhang Heng's 張衡 (78–139) "*Fu* on Pondering over the Abstruse" ("Sixuan fu" 思玄賦) in the *Wen xuan*. See Xiao, *Wen xuan*, 15.17a.

47 In this couplet, both "the tip of fine hair" (*haomo* 毫末) and "a turned-over bamboo basket" (*fukui* 覆簀) indicate objects of the smallest size. The *Laozi* states, "A two-arm thick tree grew from [the size] of the tip of fine hair; a nine-storey terrace is built from piling of earth. A thousand *li* journey beginnings from where under your feet" (合抱之樹生於毫末。九層之臺起於累土。千里之行始於足下). See Chen, *Laozi jinzhu jinyi ji pingjie*, 64.263. Also, in the *Analects* (*Lunyu* 論語) 9.19 Confucius once said, "For example, it is like building a mountain. If it needs to stop at one basket incomplete, I will stop. Again, it is like [building a mountain] from scratch. If it needs to proceed, even though it has only poured over one basket [of dirt on the ground], I will keep going" (譬如為山，未成一簣，止，吾止也。譬如平地，雖覆一簣，進，吾進往也). See Yang Bojun 楊伯峻, ed., *Lunyu yizhu* 論語譯注 (Beijing: Zhonghua shuju, 1958), 100.

48 "From furthest antiquity to the present days is called 'extension-in-time;' / The four directions [plus] up and down are called 'extension-in-space'" (往古來今謂之宙，四方上下謂之宇). See Liu An 劉安 (179–122 BCE), *The Huainanzi: A Guide to the Theory and Practice of Government in Early Han China*, trans. John S. Major and others (New York: Columbia University Press, 2010), 415.

49 Cf. Sima Xiangru's 司馬相如 (179–117 BCE) "*Fu* on the Great Man" ("Daren fu" 大人賦): "Forced by the narrowness and restriction of this realm—, / [I] stretched my [ambition

YE THE DYNASTIC CAPITAL

	本達觀於無形兮	Having already gained sight of the formlessness—,
60	今何求而有質	Why would I now seek for that which has substance?
	於是	Thereupon,
	聊樂近遊	Taking momentary joy in nearby roaming,
62	薄言儀佯	I rush to set myself adrift.
	朝登金虎	In the morning I ascend the Golden Tiger Terrace,
64	夕步文昌	In the evening, I paced Wenchang Hall.
	綺疏列於東序	The delicately carved windows are aligned in the eastern extension,
66	朱戶立乎西廂	Red doors stand in the western wing.
	經蕤暉以披藻兮	I pass through the radiant colors of flowers to cleave the dense growth—,
68	椒塗馥而遺芳	And the pepper plastered [walls] emit scents and leave behind a fragrance.[50]
	感舊物之咸存兮	I am affected by the presence of all the old things—,
70	悲昔人之云亡	And lament over the death of that one from long ago.[51]
	憑虛檻而遠想兮	Leaning on the empty guardrail I let my thoughts go afar—,
72	審歷命於斯堂	To examine all the past souls in this hall.[52]
	於是	Thereupon,
	精疲遊倦	My essence flags and roaming turns weary,
74	白日藏輝	As the white sun hides away its brilliance.
	鄙春登之有情兮	I detest that springtime ascents are full of feeling,
76	惡荊臺之忘歸	Hate that forgetting to return from the Bramble Terrace.[53]

---

and] moral principal out of the northern perimeter." (迫區中之陿陜兮，舒節出乎北垠。) See this *fu*-poem in *Quan Han wen* 全漢文, 21.7a–21.8a, in *Quan shanggu sandai Qin Han San guo Liu chao wen*, comp. Yan Kejun. Cf. Stephen Owen, ed. and trans., *An Anthology of Chinese Literature: Beginnings to 1911* (New York: W. W. Norton & Company, Inc., 1996), 182–184.

50　Traditionally, the empress's chambers would have the pepper-plastered walls. See Knechtges, *Wen xuan*, 1: 122, note to line 178.

51　This might mean Cao Cao, but also might refer to people of former days.

52　This line can also mean all of the mandates of heaven that had been held here.

53　The Bramble Terrace was in the state of Chu 楚 during the Eastern Zhou 東周 (770–256 BCE) period, in modern day Hubei 湖北, and Bramble (Jing 荊) was also the old name of the state. This line refers to the story that King Ling of Chu 楚靈王 (r. 540–529 BCE) once roamed the Yunmeng marsh 雲夢澤 area and took a break on the Bramble Terrace. The king gazed at the surroundings and then said, "Magnificent! This enjoyment can make me reject aging and forget about death" (盛哉斯樂，可以遺老而忘死也). Later Li Xian's 李賢 (654–684) commentary quotes Liu Xiang's 劉向 (77–6 BCE) *Shuoyuan* 說苑 saying that the young King Zhao of Chu 楚昭王 (r. 515–489 BCE) once wished to visit the Bramble Terrace, but the general, Sima Ziqi 司馬子綦 (n.d.), admonished against it. Sima's

	聊弭節而駕言兮	So I tentatively stop and go—,
78	恨將逝而徘徊	And am disappointed that it is about to end, as I pace back and forth.
	感崇替之靡常兮	Moved by the inconstancy of rise and replacement—,
80	悟廢興而永懷	I understand the eternal feelings over decline and prosperity.
	隆期啟而雲升	When the period of burgeoning opens, clouds arise,
82	逮運靡其如頹	And when the cycle of passing grows weak, it is like decay.
	長發惟祥	What is long sent out is precisely a good omen,[54]
84	天鑒在晉	And now heaven's mirror is turned toward the Jin.[55]
	肅有命而龍飛兮	They respectfully held this mandate and the dragon flew aloft—,[56]
86	跚重斯而肇建	And slowly pacing back and forth, valued this and began the establishment [of Jin].
	嘉有魏之欽若兮	Praise the Wei for its respect and yielding—,
88	鑒靈符而告禪	It scrutinized the noumenal tally and declared abdication.
	清文昌之離宮兮	They purified the detached palace of the Wenchang—,[57]
90	虛紫微而為獻	And vacated Purple Tenuity, making it tribute.[58]
	委普天之光宅兮	Handed over the most radiant residence in all of heaven—,

---

reason was that "the enjoyment [of the terrace] makes people reject aging and forget about death. All the lords of people who have visited there entirely lost their kingdoms for it. [I] wish you, my lord, do not go to visit there" (其樂使人遺老而忘死，人君游者盡以亡其國。願大王勿往游焉). See Fan Ye 范曄 (398–445) comp., *Hou Han shu* 後漢書, Li Xian 李賢 (654–684), ed. (Beijing: Zhonghua shuju, 1965), 80b.2640–2641.

54   Here, describing virtues of the king is essential to prolong the life of his kingdom. In the "Changfa" 長發 of the *Shijing,* it expresses that the vast virtue of the Shang that has long sent out its omens (濬哲維商，長發其祥). And Zheng Xuan noted that "deeply know that the virtue of the house of Shang, and long sent out to see its auspicious omen" (深知乎維商家之德也，久發見其禎祥矣). Cf. *Mao shi* 304.

55   As possessors of the mandate, they mirror heaven's mind.

56   Here indicates the rise of the Jin emperor.

57   The term *wenchang* refers to the palace-hall for ritual, i.e. a Wenchang Palace 文昌宮, also known as *daikuang* 戴筐, a six-star constellation dominated by the Big Dipper. It is described, in the "Treatise of Astronomy" (*Tianwen zhi* 天文志) in the *Jin shu*, "The *Wenchang* has six stars. It is in front of the bowl of the Big Dipper. It is the six government organs of the heaven and controls accumulating and calculating of the heavenly principles/orders" (文昌六星，在北斗魁前。天之六府也，主集計天道). See Fang, *Jin shu*, 11.291.

58   According to the "Treatise of Astronomy" (*Tianwen zhi* 天文志) in the *Jin shu*, the constellation *Zigong yuan* 紫宮垣 has fifteen stars. Seven [formed] a fence shape in the west [the Right Wall], and eight [formed] a fence shape in the east [the Left Wall]. It is to the north of the Big Dipper. One [of the names] is called *Ziwei*. It is the throne of the Heavenly Emperor, [therefore] is the common dwelling place of the Son of Heaven, and it controls fate and measurements of all beings (紫宮垣十五星，其西藩七，東藩八，在北斗北。一曰紫微，大帝之坐也，天子之常居也，主命主度也). See Fang, *Jin shu*, 11.290. For further discussion on this constellation and on the Dipper, see, for

YE THE DYNASTIC CAPITAL   93

92 質率土之黎彥   And pledged to the [Jin] all of the worthy men within the
                         boundaries.
    欽哉皇之承天   Respect this! Our emperor's receiving of the Way of Heaven,
94 集北顧於乃眷   Concentrate your northern gaze with solicitude.[59]
    誕洪祚之遠期兮   And extend the long destiny of prosperous fortune—,
96 則斯年於有萬   So will this year be only one of ten thousand![60]

Huang Kui 黃葵 points out that "Lu Yun's achievement in poetic texts is not
high. Some [of his] *fu* and prose pieces, however, carry the author's own feelings and experiences, although they do not have deep and profound content.
He has written them in a way that is quite refreshing and natural" (陸雲詩文創
作成就不高，但有一些賦和文，雖然內容並不深厚，但較有自己的感觸與
體會，寫得也還清新自然). Huang goes on to say "This shows that he fully
possesses seasoned skills in handling parallel style writing and is well versed in
language and lexicon" (這表現了他具有駕馭駢儷文章的熟練技巧，在語言
文字上有一定的素養).[61] This "*Fu* on Ascending the Terraces" is a concrete
demonstration of Lu Yun's ability to create imagery through words and is a fine
example of Huang Kui's remark. When the reader reads the entire piece in one
sitting, he is entirely drawn into the poet's emotions: Lu Yun's sincere excitement about his assignment, his fatigue from climbing, the stunning view that

---

      example, Edward H. Schafer, *Pacing the Void: T'ang Approaches to the Stars* (Berkeley: Uni-
      versity of California Press, 1977), particularly the chapter entitled "The Stars," 42–53.

59   See the indication of the kind regards bestowed from heaven in the couplet, "[He] then
      gazed towards the west with solicitude, / And there gave a dwelling place" (乃眷西顧，
      此維與宅) in "Huangyi" 皇矣 of the *Shijing*. Cf. *Mao shi* 241. Here, it might mean that
      now the emperor collects all with his northern regard into his mindful protection.

60   Wu Sujane dates this piece to 303. See her "Clarity, Brevity, and Naturalness: Lu Yun and
      his Works" (PhD diss., University of Wisconsin-Madison, 2001), 20–21. The text and pref-
      ace are in *Quan Jin wen* 全晉文, 100.4b–5a, in *Quan shanggu sandai Qin Han San guo Liu
      chao wen* 全斗古三代秦漢三國六朝文, comp. Yan Kejung 嚴可均 (1762–1843) (Bei-
      jing: Zhonghua shuju, 1991); and Lu Yun 陸雲 (262–303), *Lu Yun ji* 陸雲集, ed. Huang Kui
      黃葵 (Beijing: Zhonghua shuju, 1988), 15–16. I have also consulted the notes to the text in
      Han Geping 韓格平 et al., *Quan Wei Jin fu jiaozhu* 全魏晉賦校注 (Changchun: Jilin wen-
      shi chubanshe, 2008), 326–328. The text of the preface placed in brackets in English and
      parentheses in Chinese is not shown in *Yiwen leiju*, where the poem also does not include
      the character *xi* 兮, the first four couplets, lines thirteen and fourteen, lines seventeen to
      twenty, lines twenty-three to fifty-eight, lines sixty-three and sixty-four, lines sixty-seven
      and sixty-eight. The version of the poem in this commonplace book stops at line seventy-
      eight. See Ouyang Xun, *Yiwen leiju*, 62.1120–1121. Tian Xiaofei has translated lines sixty-
      nine and seventy and also the last four couplets of this poem in her "Fan Writing: Lu Ji, Lu
      Yun and the Cultural Transactions between North and South" in *Southern Identity and
      Southern Estrangement in Medieval Chinese Poetry*, ed. Ping Wang and Nicholas Morrow
      Williams, 43–78 (Hong Kong: Hong Kong University Press, 2015), 54.

61   Lu, *Lu Yun ji*, 3.

appears before his eyes from atop the terrace, his physical senses as they are stimulated by the surroundings, then the turmoil that arises from the contrast of one's own minute existence to the ultimate absolute of being; and finally at the end, the poet's pleading wish for his dynasty to last in a world of constant and indecipherable change.

In the opening two couplets of the poem, the poet speaks directly in a first-person voice about his motivations for the trip to Ye. He then shifts to a descriptive mode as he details his physical movements in ascending the terraces. Lines five through eight deliver a concrete sense of space that the poet traverses at the same time he tries to situate the reader alongside of him. As the poet reaches the cloud-high gallery (*yunge* 雲閣), the focus of the poem follows the shift of his own vision and expands horizontally to the limits of sight. Lines nine to forty-eight describe the persona's movement atop the terraces and in the high gallery, where the concreteness of the individual images dissolve into a haze as the cardinal directions of his view and movement are collapsed into something that is "far distant and vague, unbound to any direction."

He then introduces several mystical terms for the sun—heaven's sundial (*tiangui* 天晷), vermillion brightness (*zhuming* 朱明), hanging-chariot (*xuanche* 縣車), and radiant numen (*yaoling* 曜靈)—and mixes these astral images with the concrete description of the objects and buildings. The poem moves from the distant but still visible image of the sun to images beyond the sight and ken of humans. For example the imperial purple courtyard (*ziting* 紫庭) in line seventeen, the Fusang Tree 扶桑 in line forty-nine, and Mount Kunlun 崑崙 in line fifty, are all terms commonly associated with transcendents and their dwellings in heavenly abodes.

The poet's careful diction thus interlaces the physical movement of ascent and its physical perceptions with a mental space that expands his sight into the heavens, the juncture between the human and spiritual world, and then into the imagined abode of the immortals. But this tone of exultation about celestial phenomena, living creatures, seasons and vegetation, as well as his admiration for man-made monuments and buildings, shifts at line fifty-one. This line breaks the sense of unfettered vision (note he describes images he sees in heaven from below and those on earth from above) in the blink of an eye. In just that split second between lowering and raising his head, he becomes aware of the ephemerality of one's life as merely a brief moment in an eternal process of change. His distant views may have taken him into the universal and timeless, but this momentary shift of attention collapses everything into a oneness dominated by the paradox of eternity: the constant (*chang* 常), becoming one (*weiyi* 為一), and sameness (*tong* 同, *qi* 齊) contrasted with thousands of ceaseless changes (*qianbian* 千變). With a sudden awareness brought about by this glimpse into formlessness, he begins his ardent pursuit

YE THE DYNASTIC CAPITAL

of the pleasures of roaming, "rushing to set myself adrift" (*boyan changyang* 薄言儴佯). But this only brings him face to face with objects that remain as markers of history, and these trigger sorrowful meditations on historical process as a creation of humans doomed to failure. He is caught in the paradox of the constancy of process, the durability of the material objects, and the inevitable decline of people and power. Material things may remain as markers of historical moments, but they evoke in him only a sadness and melancholy for the people once attached to them: "I lean on the empty guard rail and let my thoughts go afar—, / I examine all the past souls in this hall" (憑虛檻而遠想兮, 審歷命於斯堂).

His sadness is coupled with a flash of insight (*wu feixing* 悟廢興) that the lives of dynasties (*tianming* 天命) are the same as those of people (*renming* 人命); the attention he paid to the sun in earlier lines re-emerges in the philosophical interests of the poem as it brings to the fore the relationship between a natural order of change—the basic metaphor of which is the solar and biological process of annual change and movement—and a world that is otherwise timeless. Against these two—the rebirth of the natural world and the rising of the sun every day stand both human life and endeavor—both have only a single cycle. People and dynasties will reappear like the sun and the spring, but in both cases, it will always be other people and other dynasties, stripped of the subjectivity that makes "this" person who he is and of the power that makes "this" dynasty what it is. At this point, the poet brings his mind back to his initial desire described in the first two couplets: he was going to make his words conscientious to describe the enterprise of his sage ruler (*suyan er shuye* 肅言而述業). The builder of the city of Ye and its terraces are in the past—just as everything is in a past that stretches for billions of years (*yizai* 億載). Heaven has now given that moment of life to the Jin. At the conclusion, the poet sends his respects to the emperor who now receives that mandate, expressing the wish that this present moment will be one of the ten thousand years that the Jin court will last.

In one of the letters he traded with his older brother, Lu Ji 陸機 (261–303), Lu Yun sent this piece to him and hoped he would edit it. In an extract from this letter, we find the same sincere thoughts and efforts that mark Lu Yun's effort in his poem. The part of the letter reads:

> Earlier, I ascended the city gate. I was full of emotions, so I composed "*Fu on Ascending the Terrace.*" I have exhausted [my ability] but was not able to complete it. Then Cui Junmiao [also] composed one.[62] I again tried in

---

62   While there is no birth or death dates of Cui Junmiao, in another letter to his brother, Lu Yun said that Cao Zhi 曹志 (d. 288), Cao Zhi's 曹植 second sun, is Cui Junmiao's father-in-law (曹志苗之婦公). See Lu Yun's "Yu xiong Pingyuan shu" 與兄平原書 in *Lu Yun ji,*

a desultory manner to complete my previous intention, but I still cannot make it good. After I wore myself out for days, still, I said it is better than the two *fu*-pieces I sent you earlier. I was wondering if you, my brother, would judge it and what you would say? I am hoping for a small editing, even if just one or two characters, I do not dare to wish for more. As for pronunciation, it is in the *Chu* sound; I hope you, my brother, can finalize it at your convenience.

前登城門，意有懷，作《登臺賦》。極未能成，而崔君苗作之。聊復成前意，不能今佳。而羸瘁累日，猶云愈前二賦，不審兄平之云何？願小有損益，一字兩字，不敢望多。音楚，願兄便定之.[63]

In another letter to his brother, Lu Yun enclosed Cui Junmiao's *fu* and again expressed his determination to write a better one of his own. He said, "Now, I am sending you Junmiao's *"Fu* on Ascending the Terrace." It is a well-written work. If I revise [mine] again, do you think it will be better than this? Do you know if I can surpass it or not" (今送君苗《登臺賦》，為佳手筆，云復更定，復勝此不？知能愈之不？).[64] Since Cui's piece has not survived, we cannot judge its merit. But from Lu Yun's words we can tell he tried hard to polish his work and his letters portray his own insecurity about his ability. Perhaps Lu Yun himself knew, as Huang Kui commented, that his "achievement in poetic texts is not high."

From this *fu*, we can see that Lu Yun appears to be loyal to the Jin court even though he was a native of Wu 吳 (modern day Suzhou 蘇州 area). The Lu brothers were the grandsons of the Chancellor (*chengxiang* 丞相) of the Wu state (222–280), Lu Xun 陸遜 (183–245); and their father, Lu Kang 陸抗 (226–274), was the Grand Minister of War (*da sima* 大司馬) of Wu. Even though coming from a politically illustrious family, because they lived after the Western Jin's 西晉 (265–317) conquest of Wu, the brothers were not able to pursue political careers in Wu. The biographical account of Lu Ji states that he was twenty when the Wu state was destroyed and that he retired to his old neighborhood to immerse himself in study for about a decade (年二十而吳滅，退居舊里，閉門勤學，積有十年).[65] Some suggest that Lu Yun also retired at

---

145. The *fu* on "Ascending the Terrace" that Lu Yun said Cui also composed is no longer extant.

63 Find the text of this letter in Lu Yun, *Lu Yun ji*, 140. Cf. Wu Sujane, "Clarity, Brevity, and Naturalness," 212–213. A portion of this letter is also translated by Tian Xiaofei, see her "Fan Writing," 53–54.

64 Lu, *Lu Yun ji*, 146.

65 Fang, *Jin shu*, 54.1467.

YE THE DYNASTIC CAPITAL

this time with his brother.[66] At the end of the Taikang 太康 reign (280–289), the Lu brothers both went to Luoyang, the capital at the time.[67] From then on, Lu Yun began his short political career under the Western Jin.

Lu Yun held a number of official positions in Jin and was at one time posted in Ye. In his biography in the *Jin shu*, it states that Lu Yun had official titles such as Secretarial Court Gentleman (*shangshu lang* 尚書郎), Attendant Censor (*shi yushi* 侍御史), Secretary of the Heir Apparent (*taizi zhong sheren* 太子中舍人), Attendant Gentleman of the Secretariat (*zhongshu shilang* 中書侍郎), and Administrator of Qinghe (Qinghe *neishi* 清河內史) (near modern day Xingtai 邢台, Hebei).[68] In the spring of 302, soon after the Prince of Chengdu 成都王, Sima Ying 司馬穎 (279–306), recommended Lu Yun for the Qinghe post, Lu Yun accompanied Sima Ying to Ye.[69]

While there are no historical records detailing Lu Yun's time spent in Ye, we can safely conclude that Lu Yun worked and resided in Ye during the last two years of his life. From the prefaces to some of his *fu*-poems and letters, we can also sense that this was an emotional time for him. In the preface attached to his "*Fu* on the Twilight of the Year" ("Suimu fu" 歲暮賦), Lu Yun mentions his position in Qinghe and the job he took when he accompanied Sima Ying 司馬穎 to Ye. He also explains the emotions behind creating this *fu*:

> It seems forever since I took a job in the capital. In the spring of the second year of Yongning (302), I had the honor to be favored in the northern commandery.[70] That summer I was then transferred to be the Right Defender-in-chief to the General-in-chief in Ye. It has been six years since I left home, and aunts and sisters are still left behind. I have carried this pain for ten thousand *li* and the sorrowful thoughts have hurt me like a poison. Days and months pass away so quickly, and the year is hurrying to its end. I am moved by that fact that everything has already changed. Looking forward at the heaven and earth, my heart aches. Thereupon, I composed a *fu* to express my feelings through it.

---

66   "Lu Ji and Lu Yun retired to the family estate in Huating 華亭 (near modern Shanghai). In 289 Lu Jin and Lu Yun, probably in response to a special summons from the Jin emperor, went to Luoyang, where they began a career with the Western Jin." See David Knechtges' chapter, "From the Eastern Han through the Western Jin (AD 25–317)," in *The Cambridge History of Chinese Literature*, vol.1, ed. Kang-I Sun Chang and Stephen Owen, 116–198 (Cambridge: Cambridge University Press, 2010), 188.

67   Fang, *Jin shu*, 54.1472 and 54.1481.

68   Fang, *Jin shu*, 54.1484.

69   Jiang Fang 蔣方, "Lu Ji, Lu Yun shi Jin huanji kao" 陸機、陸雲仕晉宦迹考, *Hubei daxue xuebao* 湖北大學學報, no. 3 (1995): 77.

70   Wu Sujane suggests this is the post Lu held in Qinghe. See Wu's "Clarity, Brevity, and Naturalness," 174,n38.

余祇役京邑載離永久。永寧二年春，忝寵北郡。其夏又轉大將軍右司馬於鄴都。自去故鄉荏苒六年，惟姑與姊仍見背棄。銜痛萬里，哀思傷毒。而日月逝速，歲聿云暮。感萬物之既改，瞻天地而傷懷，乃作賦以言情焉.[71]

From this preface alone, we can see that simply being in Ye during this phase of his personal life created some emotional torment. When he "ascends the Golden Tiger Terrace and paces in Wenchang Palace Hall" (Lines sixty-three and sixty-four of the "*Fu* on Ascending the Terraces"), what Lu Yun sees are the magnificent buildings that were constructed by Cao Cao now occupied by the Sima family. The change in dynasties and the transformation from one political family to another may have triggered the pain he felt for family members' life changes and deaths during these tumultuous years. Another *fu*-piece that Lu Yun most likely also composed in Ye is the "*Fu* on Sorrowing over Ceaseless Rain" ("Choulin fu" 愁霖賦). Its preface demonstrates a much lighter mood than the one above. The preface reads:

> In the summer, the sixth month of the second year of Yongning [July 13–August 10, 302],[72] the city of Ye had a downpour that lasted more than ten days straight. Farms were submerged, and people were sorrowful and haggard. At the time, men of elegant letters superbly composed [on this new topic] together. Commanded by my colleagues, I therefore composed this *fu* and it reads thus.
>
> 永寧二年夏六月，鄴都大霖，旬有奇日。稼穡沈湮，生民愁瘁。時文雅之士煥然並作，同僚見命，乃作賦曰.[73]

In another preface, to the "*Fu* on the Delight of Clearing Skies" ("Xiji fu" 喜霽賦), Lu Yun expressed an emotional connection with the earlier writers in Ye. He states in the preface that, "In the past, the scholars of letters in the Wei also composed *fu* on the delight of clearing skies. For now, I am picking up on the thread of these writers to compose this *fu*" (昔魏之文士又作喜霽賦。聊廁作

---

71   Lu, *Lu Yun ji*, 6.

72   Huang Kui notes that the "second year" was originally written "third year." Since Emperor Hui of Jin 晉惠帝 (r. 290–307) changed the reign title to Yongning 永寧 in the fourth month of the second year of Yongkang 永康, and he again changed it to be Taian 泰安 in the twelfth month of the second year [of Yongning]; there is no third year. The *Chuxue ji* 初學記 has it as the "second year," so he changed it accordingly. See Lu Yun, *Lu Yun ji*, 11.

73   Lu, *Lu Yun ji*, 9–10.

YE THE DYNASTIC CAPITAL

者之末而作是賦焉).[74] Lu Yun's emotional connection to Ye was not limited to the time when he was physically there; through reading the works of earlier poets of Ye, he was also linked to earlier times by descriptions of recurring natural cycles of weather there.

The two poems of Lu Chen and Lu Yun, cited at length above, are both anchored to the same central theme—ascending on high (*denggao* 登高). This popular tradition of expressing one's aspiration and ambition when climbing heights is textually affixed to the line, "A gentleman must express [his aspiration and/or ambition] when he ascends high" (君子登高必賦), believed to have been uttered by Confucius himself when he once roamed on a high mountain with three of his disciples.[75]

Poets of the Jin era, like those of the Three Kingdoms, were survivors of the chaos and death that accompanied the constant shifting of power. But, in contrast to Lu Chen's uncompromisingly forthright remark on the changes of Ye in the poem above, Lu Yun's "*Fu* on Ascending the Terrace" praised not only the current rulers—the Sima family who had previously served in the court of Cao Wei—but also the Cao family for recognizing the transfer of the Mandate of Heaven and relinquishing the throne.

While the theme of Lu Yun's work seems to echo Cao Zhi's piece on ascending the terrace, written nearly one hundred years earlier to praise the ruler, there are some differences. In the case of Cao Zhi, the ruler—his father—was the intended and, as patriarch, the inevitable audience. Moreover, Cao Zhi's poem is contextualized by the act of celebrations, as explained in his biography from the *San guo zhi*: "When Bronze Bird Terrace in Ye was newly completed, Cao Cao ascended it with all of his sons and ordered them each to compose a rhapsody. Cao Zhi took up his brush and was done in an instant. It was spectacular and Cao Cao marveled at him" (時鄴銅爵臺新成，太祖悉將諸子登臺，使各為賦。植援筆立成，可觀，太祖甚異之).[76] This description of the poet's raw talent that allowed him to compose an excellent poem when he was put on the spot provides a dramatic contrast to Lu Yun's experience as a writer.

74　Both Cao Pi and Cao Zhi had supposedly composed *fu* works on "Worrying about the Ceaseless Rain" ("Choulin fu" 愁霖賦) and "Pleased by the Clearing up" ("Xiji fu" 喜霽賦). See *Quan San guo wen* 全三國文, 4.1a-b and 13.1a-b, in *Quan shanggu sandai Qin Han San guo Liu chao wen* 全上古三代秦漢三國六朝文, comp. Yan Kejun 嚴可均 (1762–1843) (Beijing: Zhonghua shuju, 1991).

75　See Lai Yanyuan 賴炎元, ed. and trans., *Han Shi waizhuan jinzhu jinyi* 韓詩外傳今註今譯 (Taipei: Taiwan shangwu yinshu guan, 1972), 7.311.

76　See Robert Joe Cutter, "Cao Zhi (192–232) and his Poetry" (PhD diss., University of Washington, 1983), 481; and Chen Shou 陳壽 (233–297), *San guo zhi* 三國志 (Beijing: Zhonghua shuju, 1959), 19.557.

As Lu's letters to his brother demonstrate, he revised his piece repeatedly and even asked Lu Ji for help to polish it. Lu Yun's *fu* is much longer and more detailed than that of Cao Zhi, but the difference in length belies the basic treble structure—the reason for the ascent of the terrace, the scenery seen from atop the terrace, and a concluding section that praises the ruler. Moreover, the tone of the two poems is completely different. Cao Zhi's work is an optimistic description of what he chose to describe: the comparison of the grand and lofty buildings and the unrestrained growth of the natural world that all celebrated the accomplishments of his father. Lu Yun's *fu*, on the other hand, is more lamentative, longing for both physical artifacts and human activity that had disappeared from the city of Ye. Still at the end, though, Lu Yun rouses himself from his grief over the ephemerality of human life to praise the current ruler and the present condition of Ye.

Since Lu was a survivor from Wu who had to negotiate through life during the power shift from Cao Wei to Jin, the reader has no way of determining the sincerity of the concluding passages of the poem. Like Cao Zhi, maybe Lu Yun knew this poem would be read and assessed by those in power. Such historical circumstance always problematizes the question of authenticity. And, authorial intention can never be completely understood, even if articulated by the writer himself. As in other acts of communication, there is always an audience that is a determinative factor in poetic expression. While we might sort through Lu Yun's other writing, as we did with his letters to Lu Ji, and find insights into the practices of composition and into the poet's state of mind, in the latter case it is difficult to measure "real" feeling against the traditional pose of the composer as a person beset by sorrow. What one can see from this *fu*, however, is the beginning of the marriage of the trope of ascending the terraces of Ye to an expression of sorrow over the foibles and ephemerality of the human condition. The mood had changed forever: Cao Zhi wrote a celebratory piece to vaunt the glories of the past; from the Jin onward those same physical settings would now be a site of historical remembrance and lamentation over the brevity of human life and endeavor.

2   The Transformation of Ye in the Southern and Northern Dynasties

The fortunes of Ye continued to rise and fall in an age of civil wars and political disarray throughout most of the fourth and fifth centuries. The city was burned down and rebuilt repeatedly by those who came to occupy it. For example, Emperor Taiwu 太武帝 (r. 423–452) of the Northern Wei 北魏 (499–515)—Tuoba Dao 拓拔燾 (408–452)—burned the ruins of Shi Hu's palaces because he had been told about complaints from Ye that the locals were about to take over the city and rebel.[77] This happened between the years of 449 and 450; then almost fifty years later when Tuoba Dao's great-great grandson, Tuoba Hong 拓拔宏 (467–499)—Emperor Xiaowen 孝文帝 (r. 471–499)—relocated the Northern Wei capital from Pingcheng 平城 (modern day Datong 大同, Shanxi 山西) to Luoyang in 494, he also rebuilt the palace halls in Ye. He later visited Ye numerous times and held court banquets in his palaces there. On one lunar New Year's Day, the *dingwei* 丁未 day of the first month of the eighteenth year of the Taihe 太和 reign [January 24, 494], for example, Emperor Xiaowen received his court officials in audience at the Chengluan 澄鸞 Hall of the Ye palace.[78]

One anecdote well exemplifies the viewpoint of some officials in court about the city of Ye and the reason that it was not chosen to be the capital city during this troubled time. A narrative quoted from the no longer extant *Hou Wei shu* 後魏書 in the Song compilation *Taiping yulan* 太平御覽 states:

In the eighteenth year of the Taihe reign [January 24, 494–February 11, 495], Emperor [Xiao] Wen divined on relocating the capital. [He] passed through Ye and ascended the Bronze Bird Terrace. His Censor-in-chief Cui Guang (449–522) and others suggested, "the city of Ye has a thousand *li* of plains and the canal transportation reaches in all directions. It has the old traces of Ximen [Bao] and Shi Qi. [Ye] can endow [us] with rich abundance. It is a place of virtue, not of danger. [We] request to site the capital here." Emperor Xiaowen said, "You only know one, not the other. Ye is not a place in which one can endure long. Shi Hu failed here first and Murong was destroyed here later. When a state is rich and the ruler extravagant, violence comes full and failure comes fast. Besides, Injustice Mountain is in the west,[79] Lieren district [near modern day Feixiang

---

77   See Shen Yue 沈約 (441–513), comp., *Song shu* 宋書 (Beijing: Zhonghua shuju, 1974), 74.1923.

78   Wei Shou 魏收 (507–572), comp., *Wei shu* 魏書 (Beijing: Zhonghua shuju, 1974), 7b.173. New Year's Day in the twenty-third year of Taihe 太和 [January 29, 499], he hosted another court banquet in Ye. This was also the last New Year's Day banquet he hosted before his death in the early summer that year. See Li Yanshou 李延壽 (fl. 627–649), comp., *Bei shi* 北史 (Beijing: Zhonghua shuju, 1974), 3.119–120.

79   Injustice Mountain (Wangren *shan* 枉人山) (near modern day Jun county 浚縣, Henan) got its name from a folk tale saying that it was this mountain where the loyal official, Bi'gan 比干 (ca. 1092–1029 BCE), was killed by the cruel ruler, Zhou 紂 (ca. 1105–1046 BCE). See Li Fang 李昉 (925–996), comp., *Taiping yulan* 太平御覽 (Beijing: Zhonghua shuju, 1985), 45.1b.

102 CHAPTER 3

county 肥鄉縣, Hebei] in the east,[80] and Cypress Man City in the north.[81] A gentleman does not drink from Robber's Spring because he despises its name."[82] Thereupon, [the idea of placing the capital in Ye] stopped.

文帝太和十八年，卜遷都。經鄴，登銅雀臺。御史崔光等曰：「鄴城平原千里，漕運四通。有西門、使起舊跡，可以饒富。在德不在險，請都之。」孝文曰：「君知其一未知其二。鄴城非長久之地。石虎傾於前，慕容滅於後。國富主奢，暴成速敗。且，西有枉人山，東有列人縣，北有柏人城。君子不飲盜泉，惡其名也。」遂止.[83]

While this passage shows a pro-sinicization emperor modeling himself on Confucian values, it simultaneously demonstrates how people see a city: not just as a geographical space or topographical site, but also as a place that has layers of accumulated history and social activity.

From the perspective of cultural importance, one finds that, in popular mentality and in text, the city of Ye would remain tightly connected with its founder, Cao Cao, even though he was not the sole, or even the longest, occupant of Ye. During the Southern and Northern Dynasties, the city was expanded and the new southern city of Ye 鄴南城 was constructed under the Eastern Wei in 534. Fascination with Cao Cao and his Bronze Bird Terrace lingered on as a topic of either praise or blame. The theme of Cao Cao's terrace and the female entertainers grieving over him became a favorite *yuefu* topic in this

---

80 The words *lieren* 列人 and "low quality people" (*lieren* 劣人) are homophonous.

81 As for the Cypress Man City (Boren *cheng* 柏人城) (in modern day Tangshan city 唐山市, Hebei), it is said that:
In the eighth year of Han [October 25, 199–November 12, 198 BCE], Emperor Gaozu 高祖 (r. 202–195 BCE) returned from Dongyuan (near modern day Shijiazhuang 石家莊, Hebei) through the state of Zhao 趙. The prime minister of Zhao, Guan Gao 貫高 (d. 198 BCE) and others hid people in the walls in the town of Boren. This is to remain hidden [in order to ambush the emperor]. When the emperor passed by [the town] and wished to stay overnight, he had a gut feeling so asked, "What is the name of this town?" "Cypress Man," his attendants answered. Emperor Gaozu said, " 'Cypress Man' [*boren*] sounds like 'to force people' [*poren*]." The emperor then left right away without staying overnight.
漢八年，上從東垣還，過趙。貫高等乃壁人柏人，要之置廁。上過欲宿，心動，問曰：「縣名為何？」曰：「柏人。」「柏人者，迫於人也！」不宿而去。
See Sima Qian, *Shi ji*, 89.2583–2584.

82 Robber's Spring (Dao *quan* 盜泉), in modern day Sishui 泗水, Shandong. The legend has it that once Confucius (551–479 BCE) passed by the spring, although he was thirsty, he did not drink from it due to its name.

83 The text of this passage is in Li, *Taiping yulan*, 161.3b. A similar passage is also listed in the section of capital cities, 156.4b.

YE THE DYNASTIC CAPITAL

103

period and later.[84] The Three Terraces were the most iconic structures left from Cao Cao's constructions in Ye and were utilized either as a locus that symbolized his rapacious desire and overreaching ambition or as a resolute symbol of his heroic exploits. Even after Ye was burned to the ground by Yang Jian 楊堅 (541–604) in 580 and had been further eroded by flooding, the ruins of the terraces remained to become a site of commemoration or lamentation. And, as we will see in the literature that continued on throughout history, in a more general way it became a place that could evoke the futility of human endeavor against the ravages of history and time, a literary haven in which one was driven to lament traumatic events of dynastic change.

While the motif of Bronze Bird Terrace and its performers remained a recurring trope, interest gradually shifted away from the dying hero and toward the women who continued to pay homage to him through their performances atop Bronze Bird.[85] As earlier works focused more on Cao Cao and his achievements, the poems in this era create what we might call a "terrace-scape," in which many of the poems are written from the female persona's point of view. The imagery and lexicon turn more feminine and delicate as the poems shift from a celebration of the Terrace as an iconic reference to Cao Cao's glory and achievement to a symbol of the personal tragedies of the performers whose lives are imprisoned in service to his memory—merely one of the historical legacies of the great man. An excellent example of this "terrace-scape" is the following piece entitled "Performers of the Bronze Bird" ("Tongque ji" 銅雀妓) and attributed to He Xun 何遜 (d. ca. 518).

	秋風木葉落	In the autumn wind, tree leaves fall away,
2	蕭瑟管弦清	Bleak and sad, the pipes and strings are clear.
	望陵歌對酒	Gazing toward the tumulus, they sing "Facing ale,"
4	向帳舞空城	Turning toward the [mourning] tent, they dance atop the empty city wall.[86]
	寂寂簷宇曠	Quiet, so quiet, the roofs and eaves are broad,
6	飄飄帷幔輕	Fluttering, flapping, the curtains are so light.

---

84   Owen, *An Anthology of Chinese Literature*, 325.

85   A version of this particular section has been published by the author as "The Creation of the Bronze Bird Terrace-scape in the Northern and Southern Dynasties Period," in *Early Medieval China* 23 (2017): 89–104.

86   Since the word "city-wall" (*cheng* 城) is also used for the walled city itself, the ambiguity of this phrase also emphasizes the loss of Cao Cao from the city of Ye; this line, in fact, is also read by some as "the performers danced in the empty city." For example, see Liu Chang's 劉暢 annotation in Liu Chang and Liu Guojun 劉國珺, *He Xun ji zhu Yin Keng ji zhu* 何遜集注陰鏗集注 (Tianjing: Tiangjing guji chuban she, 1988), 12n5.

曲終相顧起	The song ends, they look at each other and rise;	
8	日暮松柏聲	The sun sets amid the sounds of cypress and pine.[87]

The poem does not speak directly in a first person voice of the female performers, as others below will; rather, it gives the observing eye to a third person who describes the physical movements of the performers: they gaze (*wang* 望) toward the gravemound and sing a line, "Facing ale" (see below), from one of Cao Cao's most famous compositions, "Short Song" ("Duange xing" 短歌行); they turn toward (*xiang* 向) the mourning screen and dance (*wu* 舞) on the city wall where their patron no longer stands; and finally the ladies rise (*qi* 起) from their performing space and look at each other (*xianggu* 相顧). The poet creates an imaginary drama staging the movements of actors in a ritual play within a setting of autumn. While Stephen Owen has noticed He Xun's attention to sounds,[88] what is also interesting are acts of looking: the performers pay their distant respects to Cao Cao's tumulus then turn toward the mourning tent, where one supposes the spirit tablet is kept. The deserted space, now empty of Cao's presence, is disturbed first by a faint wind as their dance seems to elicit a slight spiritual response from within the grave. The second act of looking, between the performers at the end, is pregnant with ambiguity. Are they signaling to each other that the performance is over? Or are they looking at each other in the quiet loneliness of longing? Or is it something else? While the performance has the desired effect—the returning resonance from the gravesite as a response to their dance and song—the effect on the women remains unspoken and unguessable. The simple fact that they are called to perform on a stipulated regular basis questions the authenticity of their feelings as they carry out their actions: are they really moved or just eager to leave?

Xie Tiao 謝脁 (464–499) uses the same terrace-scape in a poem written to accompany that of his paternal nephew, Xie Jing 謝璟 (n.d.), "A Companion work for Councilor Xie's 'Singing for the Bronze Bird Terrace'" ("Tong Xie ziyi yong Tongjue tai" 同謝諮議詠銅爵臺). But he utilizes first person voice:

	縜幄飄井榦	The muslin mourning-tent curtains flap on the terrace,
2	樽酒若平生	A goblet of wine—just like when he was alive.
	鬱鬱西陵樹	Thick, so thick—trees on the Western Tumulus,
4	詎聞歌吹聲	Can he really hear the sound of singing and pipes?
	芳襟染淚迹	Fragrant lapels are dyed with traces of tears,

---

87 Lu, *Xian Qin Han Wei Jin Nanbeichao shi*, 2:1679; and Guo, *Yuefu shiji*, 2:31.457. Cf. Owen, *An Anthology of Chinese Literature*, 325–326.

88 "The play of sounds in He Xun's version of the 'Terrace of the Bronze Sparrow' shows a controlled mastery of presentation that few earlier poets could have achieved." Owen, *An Anthology of Chinese Literature*, 325.

YE THE DYNASTIC CAPITAL   105

6 嬋娟空復情   As the beauties vainly repeat their sentiments.
   玉座猶寂寞   The jade seat is still desolate and lonely;[89]
8 況乃妾身輕   How much more, this insignificant person that I am.[90]

As the commentary in the *Wen xuan* suggests, the trees on Cao Cao's burial mound in line three are a literary euphemism for him because the poet dares not speak Cao's name directly ("[He] dares not directly address his name, therefore he uses the tree as a way to speak of him." 不敢指斥故以樹言之也).[91] In the first two couplets, the poet identifies the topic of this poem without actually mentioning the site. He uses a generalized term for a terrace—*jinggan* 井幹; and as in He Xun's verse above, instead of directly naming Cao Cao, uses the synecdoche of a goblet of wine to allude to Cao Cao through the opening couplets of his famous ballad "Short Song."[92] By doing so, the poet not only indicates the person under discussion, but also brings the ultimate question of human existence broached in the "Short Song" to the surface. This gesture toward the ephemeral nature of human life is made concrete by introducing the Western Tumulus where Cao Cao was supposed to have been buried. The gaze extends outward from the terrace, but also down, deep into the realm of the dead. The rhetorical question word, *ju* 詎, brings the reader back to the reality that comes after the hero's death. This question, which expects the dramatic response, "No, the dead cannot hear," is the point at which the poem switches to the sentiment of the living—the woman who is still singing and dancing. It simultaneously introduces the persona and accentuates the futility of her actions. This self-reflexive move subtly asks the question, "Why do we need to address the needs of the dead?" This question is answered in one way in the remainder of the poem, in terms of the effect on the living. But its challenge to culture is much greater. Remembering the dead is part of the culture of ancestor worship and also a major trope in Chinese poetry; the poem subtly asks about the propriety of what they are doing.

---

89 The jade-seat refers to the throne.

90 Lu, *Xian Qin Han Wei Jin Nanbeichao shi*, 2:1418. Cf. Owen, *An Anthology of Chinese Literature*, 326. The text of this poem is also in *Wen xuan*, which has the variants *chanyuan* 嬋媛 for *chanjuan* 嬋娟 in line six and the interchangeable characters *zun* 罇 for *zun* 樽 in line two and *nai* 迺 for *nai* 乃 in line eight. See Xiao, *Wen xuan*, 23.23b.

91 See Xiao, *Wen xuan*, 23.23b.

92 "Facing ale, one shall sing, / How long is a man's life? / It is like the morning dew, / I find it painful so many days are gone" (對酒當歌，人生幾何。譬如朝露，去日苦多). See the text of this verse in Lu, *Xian Qin Han Wei Jin Nan Be ichao shi*, 1:1.349. Cf. Paul W. Kroll, "Portraits of Ts'ao Ts'ao" (PhD diss., University of Michigan, 1976), 87–88; Stephen Owen, *The Making of Early Chinese Classical Poetry* (Cambridge, MA and London: Harvard University Asia Center, 2006), 197 and his *An Anthology of Chinese Literature*, 280–281; and Ding Xiang Warner, *A Wild Deer Amid Soaring Phoenixes: The Opposition Poetics of Wang Ji* (Honolulu: University of Hawai'i Press, 2003), 93.

106　　　　　　　　　　　　　　　　　　　　　　　　　　　　CHAPTER 3

In line six, the terms *chanjuan* or *chanyuan* introduce a beautiful woman who must perform this seemingly futile act. In lines five and six, we are confronted with tear-stained lapels (the use of "traces" or "stains" [*ji* 迹] of tears seems to indicate that it was a habitual action) and the deep sense of futility in uselessly voicing, over and over, the same sentiments. We can conclude, moreover, that these sentiments grow less and less authentic with each performance. The senselessness of it all comes home in the last couplet where she asks, "If the grand and noble lie in their tombs unhearing, what about us, we ignoble commoners?" Here, with the sudden introduction of the female first person pronoun *qie* 妾, the poet has shifted the focus of the poem from the missing, but still central figure of the grand hero, and makes this last line about the women performer(s) alone. But, at the finale, the poem resonates with complexity about the value of sacrifice and the possibility that performance (this includes both the singing and dancing, and the poet's production of the poem) can diminish authentic feeling through formal repetition. We can also see this question as a self-reflexive moment for the poet. Like the women who follow their set routine, the unavoidable use of a set combination of tropes also questions the authenticity of the poet's sense of empathy, which here is used to manipulate the feelings of the reader. The last two couplets not only ask how much we owe the dead when we all will die too soon in the end, but also ask the reader to consider the value of commemoration—either through stipulated sacrifice or through the act of writing.

Following is another poem in the female voice, "Performers of the Bronze Bird" ("Tongque ji" 銅雀妓), attributed to Liu Xiaochuo 劉孝綽 (481–539):

	雀臺三五日	On [Bronze] Bird Terrace, on the fifteenth [of the month],
2	絃吹似佳期	Strings and pipes are just like happy times.
	況復西陵晚	And more, from the Western Tumulus at night,
4	松風吹縑幰	Pine winds blow on the muslin mourning tent.
	危絃斷復續	Urgent strings—broken and restrung,
6	妾心傷此時	My heart is pained by this specific time.
	誰言留客袂	Who talks about "sleeves that make patrons linger?"[93]
8	還掩望陵悲	Instead they conceal the sorrow of gazing at the mound.[94]

93　In "The Great Summons" ("Dazhao" 大招) of *Chuci*, two couplets say, "With powdered face and brows of kohl, / And wearing fragrant oil; / Her long sleeves caress the faces: / She was good at making patrons stay" (粉白黛黑，施芳澤只。長袂拂面，善留客只). See Hong, *Chuci buzhu*, 222.

94　Lu, *Xian Qin Han Wei Jin Nanbeichao shi*, 3:1824. Also see annotations of this poem in Tian Yuxing 田宇星, "Liu Xiaochuo ji jiaozhu" 劉孝綽集校注 (MA thesis, Sichuan daxue 四川大學, 2006), 21–22; and Cao Dongdong 曹冬棟, "Liu Xiaochuo ji jiaozhu" 劉孝綽集校

YE THE DYNASTIC CAPITAL

107

In contrast to Xie Tiao's more subtle approach, Liu directly names the terrace in the opening couplet and also points out the precise schedule of performance mentioned in Cao Cao's "Testamentary Command." The statement that the sounds of the music are like those of happy times once again brings the issue of authenticity to the fore. This ritual was performed on the fifteenth or sixteenth night, the full moon, of every lunar month and became, therefore, expected. The comparison of the music to that of a marriage ceremony (referred to by the "happy time" *jiaqi* 佳期), a tryst, or the fine times of a reunion with friends or family suggests that the original ritual importance of the performance has been hollowed out so that the performance of music becomes more important than the authenticity of feeling it was supposed to evoke. This is countered in the second couplet, where the poet uses the wind generated from the pine trees on Cao Cao's burial mound to suggest a spiritual resonance with the music performed atop of the terrace and provides a transition for the following couplets. Liu's poem is much more about the grief over Cao Cao's death. The persona believes that the resonant winds from the pines are a response from the grave, evoked by the affective power of her performance. Both Liu Xiaochuo's and Xie Tiao's poems are written with a sorrowful tone, but Liu's poem, with its unremitting expression of sorrow over loss, lacks Xie's engagement of larger questions about the unpredictability and ephemerality of human life. It may not have the self-reflexive ending of Xie Tiao's poem, but by introducing the idea that the performance itself is seen by outsiders only as a musical entertainment like those of happy ceremonies, it accentuates the authentic grief of the performer. But both poems point to the affective nature of performance by expressing its power over the emotions of the performer and centering the focus of interest on the effect of Cao's death on the living, albeit in quite different ways.

Xun Zhongju's 荀仲舉 (d. ca. 550) "Bronze Bird Terrace" ("Tongque tai" 銅雀臺) is example of the theme of Bronze Bird in a female voice.

	高臺秋色晚	The tall terrace, in the twilight of autumn's aspect,
2	直望已悽然	A direct gaze already makes one miserably sad.[95]
	況復歸風便	How much worse when the wind returns with such ease,
4	松聲入斷弦	As the sound of pines enter the snapped strings.

注 (MA thesis, Dongbei shifan daxue 東北師範大學, 2006), 43–44. *Yuefu shiji* has a number of variants, see, Guo, *Yuefu shiji*, 2:31.457.

95 In the *Wenyuan yinghua* 文苑英華, this line is "The Bronze Bird is already miserably sad enough" (銅雀已悽然). See Li Fang 李昉 (925–996), comp., *Wenyuan yinghua* (Beijing: Zhonghua shuju, 1966), 2:204.1013.

108   CHAPTER 3

	淚逐梁塵下	My tears chase "dust from the roofbeams,"[96]
6	心隨團扇捐	As my heart is abandoned along with the "round fan."[97]
	誰堪三五夜	Who can endure the night of the fifteenth,
8	空對月光圓	And face in vain the full round of the moon?[98]

Again, the terrace-scape opens with the tall terrace and the end of autumn. The full moon of the fifteenth of the month makes a direct gaze at the cold world unbearably sad, and the woman (unnamed in the poem) is startled by the easy way in which the wind from the pines melds with the sounds of performance—so sorrowful that it breaks the strings of the zither. This returning wind is no less than a resonance sent from the soul of the dead Cao Cao, her appreciative audience in the underworld. This moment of the broken strings is when Cao Cao is with her again, entering literally into the instrument she plays. "Snapped strings" is a stock metaphor for a love irretrievably lost and unreclaimable. The ease (*bian* 便) with which the wind returns is echoed then by the casual way (*sui* 隨) in which she was cast aside by his death. The music, so powerful it shakes the dust from the roofbeams, is no longer a threnody for Cao Cao; rather, it is a lament for her own loss and desolation. The ideas of completion and union are expressed in the word "round" (*tuan* 團) in the

---

96 This refers to a tale of a certain master Yu 虞公 of the Lu 魯 during the Han period. It is said that master Yu was a skillful singer and his voice could shake the dust off the rafters or beams. The term "beam dust"(*liangchen* 梁塵), therefore, alludes to superb singing. See Li Fang, *Taiping yulan*, 572.2a.

97 This refers to the *yuefu* poem, "Song of Reproach" ("Yuange xing" 怨歌行), that is attributed to Lady Ban 班婕妤 (ca. 48–6 BCE):

	新裂齊紈素	I newly cut a piece of pure white fine silk from Qi,
2	鮮潔如霜雪	It is fresh and clean as frost and snow.
	裁為合歡扇	I sew it into a fan with symmetrical patterns,
4	團團似明月	Round—so round like the bright moon.
	出入君懷袖	It goes in and out of your bosom,
6	動搖微風發	When you wave it, soft breeze starts.
	常恐秋節至	I am often afraid when autumn arrives,
8	涼飆奪炎熱	A cool whirlwind will snatch the heat away.
	棄捐篋笥中	You will abandon [the fan] in its bamboo box,
10	恩情中道絕	And all grace and sentiments will be cut off midway.

In this verse, the poet uses a fan with symmetrical patterns—often used to refer to the union of a couple—to illustrate the persona's worrying that her lover or husband would one day abandon her like the fan that is not needed once the autumn arrives. This poem also generated a set phrase "autumn fans are thrown away" (*qiushan jianjuan* 秋扇見捐) used in reference to abandoned women. Cf. Stephen Owen's translation and reading of the poem in his *The Making of Early Chinese Classical Poetry*, 223–225.

98 Lu, *Xian Qin Han Wei Jin Nanbeichao shi*, 3:2267–2268; and Guo, *Yuefu shiji*, 2:31.455.

YE THE DYNASTIC CAPITAL

round fans (line six) and "fullness" (*yuan* 圓) in the full orb of the moon (line eight). These are conjoined to denote the singer's desire to be united (*tuan-yuan* 團圓) once again with the listener, who is now buried beneath the earth. The poem casts the performer in the role of a woman who has been rejected by her lover and pines for him on a moonlit night. But we also understand that the motif of a beautiful lover beseeching her patron has, since the time of the *Chu-ci*, been a common metaphor for a minister and his lord. Thus, the poem lies on the periphery of two major tropes, the political and the romantic/sexual. In the overlap of these two themes it is able to express a loss that is both personal—a lover, and political—a great leader who has passed away.

These poems in female voice and the use of the terrace-scape intrigue readers. Are the poems given a female voice because the poets utilize a trope made available by the testament of Cao Cao? Or did the poets find it a uniquely adaptable persona that allowed them to distance themselves from emotional attachment to a political leader like Cao Cao or to disassociate themselves completely from him? In any case, one thing they make clear is that death and tragedy exist only among the living. The resonance from the tumulus, sighing in the pines, becomes not only a point of contact with the person gone but also a reminder that such resonance is only produced through acts of the living. That same memory is a constant reminder of the brevity of one's own life.

In addition to the *yuefu* piece written in response to Xie Jing read above, there is a quatrain of "Sorrow the Bronze Bird" ("Tongque bei" 銅雀悲) also attributed to Xie Tiao.

落日高城上	In the setting sun on the tall city wall,
2　餘光入繐帷	The last rays enter the muslin mourning tent.
寂寂深松晚	Quiet, so quiet, this evening in the deep pines,[99]
4　寧知琴瑟悲	How can he know the sorrow of the zithers?[100]

99　In his preface of the *Xie Xuancheng ji jiaozhu* 謝宣城集校注, Cao Rongnan 曹融南 states that, as for poetry, Xie Tiao mostly used tropes of analogy and evocativeness (*bixing* 比興); he then points to this line as an example that Xie Tiao "uses the deep pines to name [Emperor] Wu of Wei" (託深松以指斥魏武). See Xie Tiao, *Xie Xuancheng ji jiaozhu*, ed. Cao Rongnan (Shanghai: Shanghai guji chuban she, 1991), 11. While it is true that the pines are an allegory of Cao Cao in this poem, the use of this metaphor was not limited to Xie Tiao alone. Since pines were often planted at graves to indicate life continuing as an evergreen; it was common to use pines as a metaphor for burial sites or the deceased.

100　See Lu, *Xian Qin Han Wei Jin Nanbeichao shi*, 2:1420. This poem is entitled "Performers of the Bronze Bird" ("Tongque ji" 銅雀妓) in Guo, *Yuefu shiji*, 2:31.456–457.

This quatrain, unlike the poems above, has no overt sound. The poet instead focuses the reader's attention on the last bit of the light from the setting sun, the terrace, and the mourning tent. Against the dimming twilight, the last rays of sunset bring the mourning tent into relief. The binome "quiet-quiet" (*jiji* 寂寂) in line three accentuates the stillness and soundlessness of the scene, and continues the mood into the night as the site shifts from the city wall and the mourning tent to the grave mound. After locating the poem at two points in space, the terrace with the performer and the tumulus with the dead hero, the poet then plays on the double meanings of the word *qinse* 琴瑟, zither, which is also a common metaphor for conjugal harmony.[101] By first dividing the physical scene into two sites, terrace and tumulus, one populated by a performer and the other a listener, the force of the metaphor the poet employs in the last line creates an ambiguity in the poem. It is both the performer's longing for her lost love and the sad and evocative ritual music played for the dead. This poem is short and straightforward. By forsaking the typical description of the performers' singing and dancing or their teary gazes into the distance, this lack of sound and movement gives the reader an eerie feeling that is almost stronger than any that could be delivered by the description of the sounds of their instruments. At the end, it is unclear who is stating the rhetorical question of whether or not the dead could actually have ever felt the sorrow (*bei* 悲) of either the musical instruments or the player. And, the lack of specificity about who asks, as well as the question itself, leave the reader in a state of anxiety over a question that is ultimately unanswerable.

While the poems of the terrace theme of this era share many similarities, there are a few that demonstrate slight variations in composition. The following is one entitled "The Bronze Bird Terrace" ("Tongque tai" 銅雀臺) or "Performers of the Bronze Bird" ("Tongque ji" 銅雀妓) attributed to Zhang Zhengjian 張正見 (527–575).

	淒涼銅雀晚	Bleak and cold, night at the Bronze Bird,
2	搖落墓田通	[Leaves] shaken down on the path to the graveyard.
	雲慘當歌日	Clouds grieve for the days of "one should sing,"
4	松吟欲舞風	Pines moan in the wind of wanting to dance.[102]
	人疏瑤席冷	People scatter and the jasper mat grows cold,
6	曲罷縹幃空	The song ends and the mourning tent is empty.

---

101   For instance, "The good union with wife and children, / Is like playing *qin* and *se*" (妻子好合，如鼓琴瑟). Cf. *Mao shi*, 164.

102   Line three is an allusion to Cao Cao's ballad "Short Song," however, I have not been able to identify whether "wanting to dance" in line four is an allusion.

YE THE DYNASTIC CAPITAL

可惜年將淚　It is a pity, the tears shed year after year,
8　俱盡望陵中　All spent gazing at his mound.[103]

A similar terrace-scape to other Bronze Bird poems, this verse begins by describing the performance space. Zhang uses the descriptive verbs "bleak and cold" and "shaken down" to sketch out the desolate scene and the sad mood evoked by the terrace and the path that provides a physical link to the grave-mound. The gaze of the poem moves from the specific and concrete sites of Cao Cao's grave and spirit way to the very clouds of the sky that grieve for the days when Cao was alive to sing his own lament over the brevity of life: "Facing ale, one should sing, / Human life, how long can it be?" The use of the pathetic fallacy, and the attribution of human feeling and voice to the clouds and human action to the pines, turns the response from perception (the condition of the path and terrace) to larger than life emotions, as nature itself joins in the grief over the loss of this hero. This, then, is followed by a returning gaze to the concrete sites of the mourning tent and the jasper mat, and to verbs of action as humans vacate the scene. In this empty world remain only the singer, who is suspended between feelings of sadness and futility. Her tears, she suggests, will be shed forever for Cao Cao and for her own life, one spent doing nothing more than a meaningless performance. The grief is recentered from sacrifice to performer and makes the actual performance of remembrance seem more distant and less important than personal sadness. The presence of Cao Cao is understated and tangible only from ambiguous natural signs. What ends the poem is a feeling of futility about the waste of life. This forces the reader to consider not only the lamentations of the mighty and heroic ("I sing") but also that of the performer, thereby bringing into question the futility of any human endeavor.

A last and slightly different composition of "Performers of the Bronze Bird" ("Tongjue ji" 銅爵妓) is one that is attributed to Jiang Yan 江淹 (444–506)).

武皇去金閣　The martial sovereign has left the golden gallery,[104]
2　英威長寂寞　His heroic mightiness has been long in silence.

103　Lu, *Xian Qin Han Wei Jin Nanbeichao shi*, 3:2480–2481; and Guo, *Yuefu shiji*, 2:31.454–455. In *Wenyuan yinghua*, the text of this poem shows variants of *huangliang* 荒涼 for *qiliang* 淒涼 in line one and *niannian* 年年 for *nianjiang* 年將 in line seven. See Li Fang, *Wenyuan yinghua*, 2:204.1013.

104　See similar usage of the word *wuhuang* 武皇 in the opening couplet of Cao Zhi's "Poem on Criticizing Myself" ("Zegong shi" 責躬詩): "Oh, amazing our late father, / This is the only valiant sovereign" (於穆顯考，時惟武皇). See Xiao, *Wen xuan*, 20.4a. Here the term refers to Cao Cao.

	雄劍頓無光	The precious sword suddenly has no radiance,[105]
4	雜佩亦銷爍	Pendants of assorted jades have also lost their luster.
	秋至明月圓	Autumn arrives, and the bright moon is full,
6	風傷白露落	The wind wounds, and the white dew falls.[106]
	清夜何湛湛	How heavy the dew on this clear night,
8	孤燭映蘭幕	As a lonely candle reflects on the orchid screen.
	撫影愴無從	We stroke the shadows, our pain absent of direction,
10	惟懷憂不薄	It is precisely our inner feelings where the unease lies full.
	瑤色行應罷	The movements of jasper-like beauties should be halted—
12	紅芳幾為樂	How long can rouged fragrance make one happy?
	徒登歌舞臺	Pointlessly we ascend this terrace to sing and dance,
14	終成螻蟻郭	For at the end, [the tomb] turns into a hill of mole crickets and ants.[107]

This poem is cast differently than those above. It does not begin with the terrace-scape or the activity of the ritual, and Bronze Bird Terrace itself is not pointed out until the last couplet. Instead, it points obliquely to the terrace by using a common generalized description as a "golden gallery" in the opening line. The poet begins with the void and silence left by Cao Cao's departure and the absence, really, of any human except the disembodied perceiver. We can construe that we are entering the world of the poem through the eyes of the performers. In the first two couplets the poet creates a striking contrast between the conditions before and after death by placing Cao's heroic might against silence and situating presence against memory. He then follows by focusing on the dullness and lack of luster of the personal symbols of Cao's might and majesty; material remains that are, like the space of the testament's commanded ritual, also marked by absence and lack. These comparisons not only give the reader a sense of Cao Cao's power to give life to objects around him, but also suggest that the enforced performance of the ritual is paired with the

---

105   Here I do not read the word *xiongjian* 雄劍 as the male sword of a pair that the legendary sword maker Ganjiang 干將 and his wife Moye 莫邪 of the Chunqiu 春秋 (770–ca. 476 BCE) period supposedly made. Rather it refers to its more common use as a synonym of *baodao* 寶刀, although the martial element of *xiong* should also not be overlooked.

106   Qiuzhi 秋至 (Autumn Arrives), also known as *qiufen* 秋分, is the autumn equinox, the beginning of the sixteenth of the twenty-four solar terms. *Bailu* 白露 (White Dew) is the beginning of the fifteenth of the twenty-four solar terms. For further discussion of the twenty-four solar terms see, for example, Derk Bodde, *Festivals in Classical China: New Year and Other Annual Observances During the Han Dynasty, 206 BC–AD 200* (Princeton: Princeton University Press, 1975).

107   Lu, *Xian Qin Han Wei Jin Nanbeichao shi*, 2:1555; and Guo, *Yuefu shiji*, 2:31.457–458. In *Yuefu shiji*, the text of this poem shows *huan* 圜 for *yuan* 圓 in line five.

YE THE DYNASTIC CAPITAL

113

growing dullness of the objects to measure a memory quickly fading and kept only dimly alive. This intensifies the lamentative mood of the poem and leads perfectly to the first word—autumn—of the next section. From its narrowed focus on the two personal objects, the gaze moves outward to the natural season: the first full moon of autumn. While the two terms "autumn arrives" and "white dew" make reference to the fifteenth and sixteenth of the twenty-four solar segments of the solar year (*qiufen* 秋分 and *bailu* 白露), the slight variation in using the term *qiuzhi* 秋至 allows us to read these terms in their simple meaning of the heavy dew that falls on the night of the first full moon of the autumn.[108] The clustering of these significant moments of the year, which would include the lunar date of the moon festival (fifteenth day of the eighth lunar month) evokes all its cultural meaning: gathering with friends and family to celebrate the mid-Autumn Festival and sharing social moments of shared cups of wine and the exchange of poems.

In the final section, against the lambent world of mid-Autumn, the poet sets a lone candle burning within the mourning tent. As the dancers brush their gazes over the shadows of their performance, reflected on the walls of the tent, they realize that the shadows they cast will have no more permanence than the grave mound, in which lies their purported listener. Like the drab and lackluster sword and pendants, these performers are artifacts that are left behind, soon to disappear like the man in his grave, nothing but food for ants and mole crickets. The pointlessness of their lives, the futility of the ritual, and the gradual reduction of their being to mere shadows combine in the last couplet to reduce everything to painful reflection.

As the reader can see, most of these pieces above have uniform elements that together make the distinctive "terrace-scape" of Bronze Bird Terrace. Of the repeated performances of the fifteenth of each month, the night of the full moon, the poems all use the months of autumn. A time of ending when, as Ouyang Xiu 歐陽修 (1007–1072) remarked years later, "Once things are past their prime they should be slain" (*wu guosheng er dangsha* 物過盛而當殺) by the cruel power of death that autumn brings.[109] In the poetic tradition, poets employ the imagery of autumn to deliver emotions of sorrow, low morale, and one's anticipation of an ending.[110] Often, the feeling of foreseeing the end is far

---

108   A reference from the "Zhanlu" 湛露 of the *Shijing*: "Clear and heavy dew—, / If not for the sun, it would not dry" (湛湛露斯，匪陽不晞). Cf. *Mao shi* 174.

109   See Stephen H. West, "Autumn Sounds: Music to the Ears, Ouyang Xiu's '*Fu* on Autumn's Sounds,'" *Early Medieval China* 10–11.2 (2005): 83.

110   A good example of this imagery of autumn in early poetry is a couplet from the "Siyue" 四月 of the *Shijing*: "Autumn days are cold and sad, / The flowers all wither away" (秋日 淒淒，百卉具腓). Cf. *Mao shi* 204.

114   CHAPTER 3

worse than the end itself. There are also associated images to set the background—the setting sun, the full moon, the cold wind, the pines, and the burial mound. Furthermore, the reader often finds a limited choice of words repeated for these emotional states, such as "sorrow" (*bei* 悲), "tears" (*lei* 淚), "empty" (*kong* 空), "desolate" (*jimo* 寂寞), "cold" (*leng* 冷), "pitiful or sorrowful" (*can* 慘 and *qi* 悽), and "lonely" (*gudu* 孤獨). Beyond the power of nature, human objects deepen the emotional mood and tie it to the larger question of the meaning of life: objects such as the mourning-tent curtains flapping in quietness, the tear-stained lapels of the women, the empty jade seat, or the colorless sword and jade pendants that used to belong to the deceased. The music always has a spiritual and emotional impact: it summons forth the sound of the winds from the gravesite pines, and the strings themselves are often broken by the lamentative sorrow—either that of the performer, the sad winds, or both together. This shared storehouse of words and images suggests more of a literary tradition than real acts of perception. Whereas Lu Yun actually was in Ye, later poets, mostly from the south, saw the place only through text and in their imagination. This is because poets of this time often shared their poems with one another and also answered or matched the works they received.[111] After the Three Kingdoms period ended, Ye and its terraces had become a common trope for the fall of great heroes, the impossible shortness of life, and the sad lives of women impressed into service to carry out the ritual stipulated in Cao Cao's testament. What the poets felt about the place was taken from texts. In the matching poems that they shared, they made Ye a common trope. Yet as the verses demonstrate, it was a powerful symbol of the sadness and frustration over one's own life that moved beyond any imagined scene that they inscribed in their works and evoked a more universal emotional value. In these terrace poems, the deft deployment of language and the image of Bronze Bird Terrace let the reader visualize and embody the internal feelings of the poets or the personas they described. This more than compensates for what these poems lack in individuality and originality.

These poems provide the first example of how Cao Cao and his city of Ye "lived" long after his death. Judging by the dates of these poets, the works above were written before the mid-sixth century. And most of the credited poets are from the south—despite the fact that Ye was a capital in the north. Ye had been

---

111   For detailed discussion on this subject and the poetic relationships among poets like Xie Tiao, Jiang Yan, He Xun, and Liu Xiaochuo see Ping Wang, *The Age of Courtly Writing: Wen Xuan Compiler Xiao Tong (501–531) and His Circle* (Leiden: Brill, 2012). Also see the subject of poetic exchange during the fourth and fifth centuries in Wendy Swartz, "Trading Literary Competence: Exchange Poetry in the Eastern Jin" in Paul W. Kroll, ed., 6–35, *Reading Medieval Chinese Poetry: Text, Context, and Culture* (Leiden: Brill, 2015).

YE THE DYNASTIC CAPITAL

destroyed and rebuilt many times after Cao Cao's death and the fall of the
Three Kingdoms era. The Eastern Wei built a new city at the old southern wall
when they made their capital in Ye. These occupants, and their successor, the
Northern Qi, continuously renovated and rebuilt the northern and southern
cities of Ye. Emperor Wenxuan 文宣帝 (r. 550–559) of the Northern Qi sent
more than three hundred thousand labor workers and craftsmen to renovate
the Three Terraces. In the eighth month of the ninth year of the Tianbao 天保
reign [September 1, 558–September 29, 558], he renamed the Three Terraces
when the construction was completed.[112] Yet the old names remained in literature, because Cao Cao and Bronze Bird Terrace could not be erased from poets'
hearts and minds. Even the emperors who ascended the newly rebuilt and
newly renamed terraces still composed poetry there, perhaps even using the
anachronistic cultural marker of the Bronze Bird.[113] Pan Ling 潘泠 delivers a
pointed explanation of the enduring use of these names:

> What poets were concerned with was not the city of Ye in their time. Men
> of the Southern Dynasties, who placed themselves in the legitimate suc-
> cession of the Jin, were not emotionally connected to a Northern political
> capital. What they paid attention to was the city of Ye of the Cao Wei
> era—a place that had more historical and cultural connection to the
> Southern Dynasties.... The meaning of Ye, newly developed by the Qi and
> Liang of the Southern Dynasties, had distilled into a set classic trope. Ye
> was not a city that was occupied by the non-Han power, but a twilight
> city no longer occupied by its hero. It was a city in which complicated
> feelings that intertwined the real and the historical could be lodged along
> with deep contemplation of the past.

詩人關注的不是當時的鄴都，承晉正統自居的南朝人，在感情上對一
個北方政權的都城，並不覺親切；他們關注的是與本朝有更多歷史與
文化關聯的曹魏時的鄴城。... ... 齊梁新出的鄴城之意已經逐漸凝聚成

---

112 The Bronze Bird was renamed the Golden Phoenix (Jinfeng 金鳳), the Golden Tiger—
which was renamed to be the Golden Beast (Jinshou 金獸) earlier to avoid the taboo
name of Shi Hu—was again renamed to be the Sage Conformity (Shengying 聖應), and
the Ice Well became the Lofty Light (Chongguang 崇光). See Li Baiyao 李百藥 (565–648)
comp., Bei Qi shu 北齊書 (Beijing: Zhonghua shuju, 1972), 4.65.

113 Take Emperor Wenxuan, for example: on the *jiawu* day of the eleventh month of the Tianbao reign [December 2, 558], he arrived in [Ye] from Jinyang 晉陽 (modern day Taiyuan
太原, Shanxi) to ascend the Three Terraces. He stayed in the Qianxiang Palace-hall and
hosted a court banquet for his officials and he ordered them to compose poetry [for
the occasion] (十一月甲午，帝至自晉陽，登三臺。御乾象殿，朝讌群臣，並命
賦詩). Li, *Bei Qi shu*, 4.65.

一個固定的經典意象。鄴城不是異族統治下的城市，它只是一個英雄不在的暮光之城，是一個寄托幽思，交織歷史與現實複雜情懷的城市。[114]

And this tradition only grew stronger with time. The poems we have considered here about the Bronze Bird Terrace deliver a quite different mood than those of the Jian'an period. No longer were they celebration and praise for Cao Cao's life and achievements; they became instead symbols and reminders of sorrowful lamentation for the past hero, for those he left behind in his service, and for unanswerable questions about human existence. What had once symbolized aspiration, desire, and the possibility of human achievement, in the end only evoked the futility of such human endeavor against the ravages of history and time.[115]

---

114 Pan Ling 潘泠, "Shilun 'Yuefu shiji' zhong Nanbei shiren dui Yecheng lishi wenhua de butong shuxie" 試論《樂府詩集》中南北詩人對鄴城歷史文化的不同書寫 *Lishi jiaoxue wenti* 歷史教學問題, no. 1 (2014): 104.

115 At the time of writing the concluding paragraph of this chapter, I came across Yuan Aixia's 袁愛俠 three-page article in which Yuan mentions Edward W. Said's "Traveling Theory" and Stephen Owen's reading on the terraces in her summary of the development of the terraces as a literary theme in the form of cultural travel. See her "Tongque wenhua de luxing: yi wenhua luxing de shidian kan cong Wei dao Nan Bei chao de tongque wenhua" 銅雀文化的旅行：以文化旅行的視點看從魏到南北朝的銅雀文化, *Sichuan wenhua chanyan zhiyan xueyuan xuebao* 四川文化產業職業學院學報, no. 3 (2008): 36–38.

CHAPTER 4

Ye in the Mind of Poets from the Seventh Century and Beyond

At the end of the Southern and Northern dynasties 南北朝 (420–598) period, the chancellor of Northern Zhou 北周 (557–581), Yang Jian 楊堅 (541–604), burned and destroyed Ye when his forces took over the Northern Qi 北齊 (550–577) regime and then its capital in 580. An entry in the *Jiu Tang shu* 舊唐書 provides a brief but clear introduction to what was going on with Ye after Yang Jian's action.

> Ye was a county during the Han and belonged to the commandery of Wei. Later, the [Northern] Wei established Xiang Prefecture here, and the Eastern Wei changed it to Si Prefecture. [When] the [Northern] Zhou overcame the [Northern] Qi, once again they changed it back to Xiang Prefecture. In the second year of the Daxiang reign [February 4, 580–January 22, 581] of Zhou, when [the later Emperor] Wen of Sui "assisted in governance," the Xiang Prefectural Inspector, Yuchi Jiong (d. 580), raised an army in resistance. Yang Jian ordered Wei Xiaokuan (509–580) to attack Yuchi Jiong. After suppressing Jiong, Yang Jian then burned the city of Ye and relocated its residents, moving them forty-five *li* to the south. The city of Anyang [modern day Anyang, Henan] was made the official government office location of Xiang Prefecture, and Ye again became Ye County. At the beginning of Emperor Yang's reign (r. 604–618), he established the Ye County offices in the Daci Temple in the old capital city of Ye. The small city that is the current government office was first built in the eighth year of the Zhenguan reign [February 7, 634–January 26, 635].

> 鄴漢縣，屬魏郡。後魏於此置相州，東魏改為司州。周平齊，復為相州。周大象二年，隋文輔政，相州刺史尉遲迥舉兵不順，楊堅令韋孝寬討迥。平之，乃焚燒鄴城，徙其居人，南遷四十五里。以安陽城為相州理所，仍為鄴縣。煬帝初，於鄴故都大慈寺置鄴城。貞觀八年，始築今治所小城。[1]

---

1 Liu Xu 劉昫 (887–947), comp., *Jiu Tang shu* 舊唐書 (Beijing: Zhonghua shuju, 1957), 39.1492.

© KONINKLIJKE BRILL NV, LEIDEN, 2020 | DOI:10.1163/9789004420144_006

118 CHAPTER 4

After the Sui 隋 (581–619) brought unity after such a long period of diverse and contentious dynastic change, what remained of Ye began to be presented as a problematic area in historical records. No longer a grand seat of political and literary accomplishments, Ye was described as a place "shabby in custom" (*subo* 俗薄), a term applied to an area in which long-standing fine customs had deteriorated. In the *Sui shu* 隋書, many entries mention that Ye was difficult to regulate, though rulers consistently picked the most able officials to try to govern it. The biography of Zhangsun Ping 長孫平 (d. ca. 601) remarks:

> Customs of the city of Ye became shabby and from old it had been called a place "difficult to regulate." None of the previous regional inspectors had been up to job. The court considered that [Zhangsun] Ping had been praised at his [other] posts and transferred him to be the regional inspector of Xiang Prefecture [which included Ye at the time]. Zhangsun Ping was very well known for being competent.

> 鄴都俗薄舊號難治。前後刺史多不稱職。朝廷以平所在善稱，轉相州刺史。甚有能名.[2]

Another official, Fan Shulue 樊叔略 (535–594), was also transferred to be regional inspector of Xiang after he earned a very high reputation for good work in Bian Prefecture卞州 (modern day Kaifeng 開封, Henan). His biography states:

> Customs of the city of Ye grew shabby and it was noted as a place "difficult to morally transform." Because Shulue had been up to his tasks no matter at which place [he served], the court transferred him to be the Regional Inspector of Xiang Prefecture. His administration was the best in that time.

> 鄴都俗薄號曰難化。朝廷以叔略所在著稱，遷相州刺史，政為當時第一.[3]

A similar account appears in the biography of Linghu Xi 令狐熙 (fl. 581–588). When Yang Jian heard that Linghu Xi had successfully governed Bian, he

---

2 Wei Zheng 魏徵 (580–643), comp., *Sui shu* 隋書 (Beijing: Zhonghua shuju, 1973), 46.1255.

3 Wei, *Sui shu*, 73.1677.

YE IN THE MIND OF POETS FROM THE SEVENTH CENTURY AND BEYOND

commanded the Regional Inspector of Xiang at the time, Doulu Tong 豆盧通 (538–597), to model himself on the achievements of Linghu Xi because "the city of Ye is the place most difficult to put in order in the empire" (鄴都天下難理處也).[4] Another well-known regional inspector who had a hard time regulating Ye during this period was Liang Yanguang 梁彥光 (fl. 585). Liang first held a post in Qi Prefecture 岐州 (near modern day Fengyang 鳳陽 Shaanxi 陝西). Describing his administration in Qi, he states that its customs were quite substantial so he used "quietness" to command it (其俗頗質，以靜鎮之). Later after he was transferred, he tried to use the same policy in Xiang that he had used in Qi. It turned out that "the city of Ye had mixed customs and people were often deceitful. [He] composed a song about it, stating it could not be put in order or transformed morally" (鄴都雜俗，人多變詐。為之作歌，稱其不能理化).[5] Particularly compelling in these accounts are the words that Liang Yanguang uses to describe Ye. In his word choices we can understand the possible reason behind Ye's reputation of being difficult for administrators in the early Sui period: in particular, he uses the word "mixed" (*za* 雜). For instance, we should perhaps take Liang's quote here in the context of his earlier use of *su* 俗, customs, in his quote about Qi prefecture. Of course, Ye was a mixture of ethnic northerners and foreigners (non-Han Chinese), but here he may be referring to the fact that local customs were so mixed that there was in fact no local set of normative values for people to follow. This is implied in the discussion about customs in the *Zizhi tongjian* 資治通鑑, where it remarks:

> In Ye, from the time that the [Northern] Qi perished, higher class gentry mostly moved [out and] into the area within the passes [i.e., Shaanxi], and only craftsmen, merchants, and entertainers moved [in] to fill the prefectural city and its environs. Their customs were repugnant and deviant, and they loved to give rise to rumors and lawsuits. They regarded [Liang] Yanguang as "a cap-wearing sweet rice-ball."

> 鄴自齊亡，衣冠士人多遷入關，唯工商樂戶移實州郭，風俗險詖，好興謠訟，目彥光為「著帽餳」.[6]

---

4 Wei, *Sui shu*, 56.1386.

5 Wei, *Sui shu*, 73.1675.

6 Sima Guang 司馬光 (1019–1086), comp., *Xinjiao Zizhi tongjian zhu* 新校資治通鑑注 (Taipei: Shijie shuju, 1974), 175.5447.

References to Ye as a disorderly place, however, may also be coded language to describe the large number of non-Han Chinese that lived there as a result of more than three hundred years of constant dynastic change in Ye. Zhu Heping 朱和平 suggests that during the early medieval period the reputation of a place having "diverse" or "mixed" customs may be due to the combination of a high concentration of population, differing policies of various regimes, and ethnic conflict.[7]

Ye was a governance problem for the Sui; as such, it is represented in historical texts even after the physical city was destroyed. The image of Ye in literary texts, however, continued to be as a place of literary remembrance and production. The theme of the Bronze Bird Terrace survived; later, as a marker of the past, it became accompanied by poems on the material remains of Ye.

1   Continuation of the Bronze Bird Trope

As mentioned in the previous chapter, Cao Cao's Bronze Bird Terrace and the apocryphal story of Cao ordering palace women to mark his death with performances on the terrace had quickly become a recurrent trope in literati writing about Ye. But the terrace itself was no longer a physical place and the women were only imaginary. Now, the terrace would become a figurative metaphor that could be adopted into later poems about abandoned women generally, such as those exemplified in the tradition of palace women laments (*gongyuan shi*宮怨詩). As such, the metaphorical topology of the terrace became only one of those of a number of popular transposed historical sites, including the laments of Changmen Palace (*Changmen yuan* 長門怨), the empress' laments on Changxin Palace (*Changxin yuan* 長信怨), and poems about Wang Zhaojun 王昭君.[8] In his thesis on Tang palace-resentment poetry, Cao Jingui 曹金貴 makes the following statement:

---

7 "Suichao Yecheng nanzhi shixi" 隋朝鄴城難治試析, *Zhongzhou xuekan* 中州學刊, no. 6 (1998): 136–138. Also see Sun Jimin's 孫繼民 discussion on the economic issues of the Ye area in his "Yexia subo de shangye wenhua xingzhi" 鄴下俗薄的商業文化性質, *Zhongguo jingji shi yanjiu* 中國經濟史研究, no. 2 (2004): 95–98.

8 For further discussion of the palace-resentment tradition, see Wang Juan 王娟, "Tangdai gongyuan shi yanjiu" 唐代宮怨詩研究 (MA thesis, Nanchang daxue 南昌大學, 2007); Cao Jingui曹金貴, "Tangdai gongyuan shi shige yishu yanjiu" 唐代宮怨詩詩歌藝術研究 (MA thesis, Nanjing shifan daxue 南京師範大學, 2004); Wu Xueling 吳雪伶, "Tangdai Tongque

In addition, Bronze Bird Terrace is also an image that often appears in the palace-resentment poems of the Tang. The terrace was originally the place where Cao Cao, Emperor Wu of Wei, held feasts and entertainments. Cao Cao left a testament that ordered his concubines and female performers to dwell in the terrace in order to perform ritual ceremonies, music, and present food. This, in fact, did away with any possibility for these concubines to have a good life for the rest of their lives and forced them to become "live" burial goods. Because of this, [the image of the] Bronze Bird Terrace became a metal cage in which to bury the youth and life of these ladies. It also became another outward manifestation of the resentful emotions and sorrowful feelings for Tang palace women.

另外，銅雀台亦是唐代宮怨詩中經常出現的意象。它原是魏武帝曹操宴飲歌舞之地，曹操曾留遺令命侍妾女伎居於銅雀台中，以設祭奏樂上食，這實際上就斷送了姬妾們後半生美好生活的可能性而不得不充當活的陪葬品。由此，銅雀台便成了埋葬侍妾青春和生命的鐵籠，也成為唐宮女怨緒愁情的又一表徵物.[9]

This statement illustrates how the terrace was transformed from a physical place into a metaphorical site for representing emotional turmoil over the loss of one's youth and beauty. This movement from physical space to an emotional or mental domain has also been deemed a "poetic trace" (*shiji* 詩跡) in Liao Yifang's 廖宜方 excellent description, which elegantly ties poetry and history together:

Simply put, poetic traces are poems that limn the customs and environments of local regions that are passed along for a long time because they are welcomed and popular, even to the point that the sights and scenes described in poems are exactly like those trace-patterns derived from [earlier] texts; therefore, they are called "poetic traces." That is to say, the marks left by historical events in any space are called "historical traces." Against the background of a natural environment that constantly evolves and is always being produced and obliterated, certain scenes and objects of places are remembered by people because of literary works; and these [literary works] are then unearthed and commemorated anew by later

---

tai shi de shuangchong huiyi moshi yu gongyuan zhuti" 唐代銅雀台詩的雙重回憶模式與宮怨主題, *Hubei shehui kexue* 湖北社會科學, no. 8 (2006): 105–107.

9 Cao Jingui, "Tangdai gongyuan shi shige yishu yanjiu," 44.

people. This is the same as a "historical trace" but because the source lies in poetry, they are called "poetic traces."

簡單來說，詩跡即詩人描繪地方風土的詩歌因為備受歡迎而流傳久遠，以致於詩歌所描述的景觀和風物宛如文本派生的痕跡，故稱「詩跡」。也就是說，歷史上發生的事件在空間中留下的痕跡，成為「史跡」；在自然環境不斷變遷與生滅的背景之下，地方上若干景觀與風物因為文學作品而為人所記憶，從而不斷被後人重新挖掘與紀念，猶如史跡一般，但因其根源來自詩歌，故稱「詩跡」.[10]

Liao also cites with approval Kakutani Satoshi's 角谷聰 idea that even though the Bronze Bird Terrace is a space where performers pay tribute to Cao Cao's tomb after his death, these works of later medieval literati "are moved to deep emotion over the sorrow of the performers and are not an appraisal of Cao Cao's worth" (感慨歌妓的悲哀，而非評價曹操).[11]

There are many poems, for example, in the *Quan Tang shi* 全唐詩 that mention Bronze Bird; including the following (See Table 1):

---

10   Liao Yifang 廖宜方, *Tang dai de lishi jiyi* 唐代的歷史記憶 (Taipei: Guoli Taiwan daxue chuban she, 2011), 47. It should be noted that this term is not a modern conception. For instance, Mei Yaochen 梅堯臣 (1002–1060) wrote in the, "Ballad of Yezhong" ("Yezhong xing" 鄴中行), a poem indirectly critical of Renzong's 仁宗 (r. 1022–1063) dismissal of Su Shunqin 蘇舜欽 (1009–1049) and others from court, employing the guise of writing about the fate of the "Seven Masters of Jian'an." In this poem he wrote about their posthumous writings and the ending couplets say:

      鳥烏聲樂臺轉高 The sound of birds and crows is delightful, the terrace turns upwards,

   2 各自畢逋誇臺尾 Each of them caught in the end, boasting of being "encumbered by their tails."*

      而今撫卷跡已陳 But now I stroke the fascicles, their traces already displayed,

   4 唯有漳河舊流水 All there is, as of old, is water flowing in the Zhang River.

    *This refers to a "children's ditty" from the late Han that criticized the greed of the upper classes. See the song in Fan Ye 范曄 (398–445), comp., *Hou Han shu* 後漢書, Li Xian 李賢 (654–684), ed. (Beijing: Zhonghua shuju, 1965), *zhi* 13.3281–3282; and for an analysis of this song, *ibid.*, 8.320n3. Also, from the *Shijing* "Wolf's Tail" ("Lang ba" 狼跋), "A wolf is encumbered by its tail, /And trips over its beard" (狼跋其胡，載疐其尾), which is glossed by Kong Yingda as "A wolf going forward treads on its beard, going back it trips over its tail—it is hard to advance or retreat" (老狼有胡，進則躐其胡，退則跲其尾。進退有難), Cf. *Mao shi*, 160. See Zhu Dongrun 朱東潤, *Mei Yaochen ji biannian jiaozhu* 梅堯臣集編年校注 (Shanghai: Shanghai guji chuban she, 2006), 1: 14.255; and *Mei Yaochen shixuan* 梅堯臣詩選 (Beijing: Renmin wenxue chuban she, 1980), 66–67.

11   Liao, *Tang dai de lishi jiyi*, 47–48.

YE IN THE MIND OF POETS FROM THE SEVENTH CENTURY AND BEYOND 123

TABLE 1   Poems on Bronze Bird Terrace in *Quan Tang shi*

Poet	Title of poem	Location
Cheng Changwen 程長文 (n.d.)	"Bronze Bird Terrace Resentment"	*Quan Tang shi*, 799.8997
Jia Zhi 賈至 (718–772)	"Bronze Bird Terrace"	*Quan Tang shi*, 235.2594–2595
Li He 李賀 (ca. 791–817)	"Matching the Pieces of 'Bronze Bird Performers' by He and Xie" ("Zhuihe He Xie 'Tongque ji'" 追和何謝銅雀妓)	*Quan Tang shi*, 392.4412
Li Xianyong 李咸用 (fl. 873)	"Bronze Bird Terrace"	*Quan Tang shi*, 644.7383
Liang Qiong 梁瓊 (n.d.)	"Bronze Bird Terrace"	*Quan Tang shi*, 801.9009
Liu Zhangqing 劉長卿 (709–780)	"Bronze Bird Terrace"a	*Quan Tang shi*, 151.1578
Liu Tingyi 劉庭琦 (ca. 720)	"Bronze Bird Terrace"	*Quan Tang shi*, 110.1132
Luo Yin 羅隱 (833–910)	"Bronze Bird Terrace"	*Quan Tang shi*, 656.7545
Wang Bo 王勃 (fl. ca. 650–676)	"Bronze Bird Performers" [2 verses]	*Quan Tang shi* 19.219–220 and 56.678
Wang Zun 汪遵 (fl. 877)	"Bronze Bird Terrace"	*Quan Tang shi*, 602.6958–6959
Wang Wujing 王無兢 (652–706)	"Bronze Bird Terrace"	*Quan Tang shi*, 67.761
Xue Neng 薛能 (ca. 817–880)	"Bronze Bird Terrace"	*Quan Tang shi*, 561.6514
Song Zhiwen 宋之問 (ca. 656–712)	"Bronze Bird Terrace"b	*Quan Tang shi*, 52.644–645.

a   This piece is also credited to Wang Jian 王建 (fl. 797), see Quan Tang shi, 298.3387.
b   Also attributed to Shen Quanqi 沈佺期 (ca. 656–715) in Quan Tang shi, 96.1031.

In the Southern Song 南宋 (1127–1279), Ge Lifang 葛立方 (fl. 1138) wrote a retrospective on the Bronze Bird Performer poems in *Yunyu yangqiu* 韻語陽秋, noting what were considered the best poems of the day:

Many of the ancients wrote poetry about female performers on Bronze Bird. Zheng Yin (d. 710) wrote, "After the dance, they lean against the

124 CHAPTER 4

[mourning] tent and weep, / The song finished, they look toward the tumulus." Zhang Zhengjian (527–575) wrote, "Clouds grieve for the days of 'one should sing,' / Pines moan in the wind of wanting to dance." Jia Zhi (d. 772) wrote, "To the spirit table they approached with morning sacrifice of wine, / On the empty bed they rolled up the night clothes." Wang Bo (ca. 650–676) wrote, "I was originally a performer from the deepest palace, / The layered walls enclosed nine concentric layers; /The love of my lord the king has ended, / By whom will my singing and dancing be countenanced?" Shen Quanqi (656–715) wrote, "In olden years a third of a divided land, / Today behold the terrace and tumulus; / In one morning the plan of the hero finished, / His thousand-year-posthumous order was launched." These are all fine lines.

Luo Yin (833–909) wrote, "Forced to sing, forced to dance, in the end hard to succeed, / Flowers fell, flowers opened, tears covered the gauze; / In that year she should have followed her lord in death, / And avoided being made to look, haggard and gaunt, off to the western tumulus." This seems to be a little different than others.

King Wu of Wei was malicious and dangerous. He stole the spiritual implements of state in order to claim a name as a hero. But on the day he approached his death, he gave an order to his various sons not to forget him at the place his bones were buried, and he ordered the performers to dance and sing to his soul—this can truly be called stupid. [Su] Dongpo once said, "When Cao was dying of illness, in front of all his sons and grandsons, whimpering and weeping, loath to leave his wives and concubines, [he told them to] divide the incense, sell shoes, and take care of his clothes. In his whole life he was treacherous and deceitful, and when he died his real nature was revealed." These are truly famous words!

銅雀伎古人賦詠多矣。鄭愔云「舞餘依帳泣，歌罷向陵看。」張正見云「雲慘當歌日，松吟欲舞風。」賈至云「靈几臨朝奠，空牀卷夜衣。」王勃云「妾本深宮妓，曾 [層] 城閉九重；君王歡愛盡，歌舞為誰容。」沈佺期云「昔年分鼎地，今日望陵臺；一旦雄圖盡，千秋遺令開。」皆佳句也。

羅隱云「强歌强舞竟難勝，花落花開淚蒲繒；秖合當年伴君死，免教憔悴望西陵。」似比諸人差有意也。

魏武陰賊險很 [狠]，盜有神器實竊英雄之名，而臨死之日乃遺令諸子，不忘於葬骨之地，又使伎人著銅雀墓上以歌舞其魂，亦可謂愚矣。東坡云「操以病亡，子孫滿前而呷嚶，涕泣留連，姜婦分香賣履，區處衣物。平生姦偽，死見真性。」真名言哉。[12]

---

12   Ge Lifang, *Yunyu yangqiu* (rpt. Shanghai: Guji chuban she, 1984), 19.7a–b.

YE IN THE MIND OF POETS FROM THE SEVENTH CENTURY AND BEYOND   125

In addition to those mentioned above, there are many other writers who turned their hand to Bronze Bird; at least it is clear that, by the Southern Song, writers considered Bronze Bird Terrace a poetic trace that had begun in the Tang. One of the features of the poems in the Tang and later is the movement of the familiar terrace-scape diction and setting out of its attachment to a specific place to be used as generalized metaphors and contexts to represent abandoned women. For instance, Gao Shi's 高適 (ca. 700–765) "Bronze Bird Performers" ("Tongque ji" 銅雀妓).

	日暮銅雀迥	The day grows late, Bronze Bird recedes,
2	秋深玉座清	Autumn deepens, the jade throne is quiet.
	蕭森松柏望	Soughing and sighing, the pines and cypress still watch,
4	委鬱綺羅情	Sad and depressed, the sentiments of those in exquisite gauze.
	君恩不再得	My lord's grace cannot be gotten one more time,
6	妾舞為誰輕	So for whom do I dance so lightly?[13]

In this poem, Gao Shi has evoked the original feel of the terrace-scape: the gloomy tumulus, the depressed sentiments of the performer who has lost her lord and now questions why she still performs. But the poet has done so in a remarkable way. The use of the adjectival verb *jiong* 迥 is interesting: normally it means a distant place or somewhere that grows ever more distant, but it can also mean "tall" or "high," probably in the sense of something far above and out of reach. Likewise *qing* 清 here carries the sense of "still" or "quiet," but it can also mean "cold." The two contrasting binomes *xiaosen* 蕭森 and *weiyu* 委鬱 are both terms that have several, even opposite meanings. *Xiaosen* can be used as an onomatopoeic word for the sound of rustling trees, but it can also mean thick and dense vegetation or the appearance of plants that are withering and dying. Moreover, *weiyu* can mean both thick and luxurious vegetation as well as overwhelming feelings of sad depression. The claustrophobic feeling elicited by these two binomes of lines three and four complicate the last couplet, as the end of the day, the end of the year, and the end of youth draws near for the poet. The implication in these two lines is that the dancing must have a point: an audience or a reason to perform.

From the perspective of the performer, it is not a question of performing proper sacrifices; for her the point of performing while alive—to obtain the grace that comes from pleasing the lord—is now gone; the dance (to the performer) seems senseless and lacks all meaning. Gao ends the poem on the word *qing* 輕, which seems to imply at least two levels of understanding. First, of course, the adjectival verb can simply refer to the "lightness" and seemingly

---

13   *Quan Tang shi*, 211.2189.

126 CHAPTER 4

effortlessness of the dance, but it can also mean "to treat lightly," to consider frivolous or unimportant. The meaning of the performance, for the performer, is gone, never to be used to access her lord's favor. Instead, it becomes a duty that has no aim, a senseless and completely unimportant act. But we, the readers, also have a sense that the feelings have become more universalized and now somewhat separate from the actual terrace; they are the poetic traces left of a place that can be used as a metaphor for much more general circumstances—now, for any woman who has been rejected or abandoned.

For some poets, the historical and physical traces of Ye merged with the poetic. Particularly illustrative is a piece attributed to Cen Shen's 岑參 (715–770), "Ascending Ancient Ye City Walls" ("Deng gu Yecheng" 登古鄴城).

	下馬登鄴城	I dismount and ascend the Ye city wall,
2	城空復何見	The city is empty, what will be seen again?
	東風吹野火	The east wind feeds the fire in the wilds,[14]
4	暮入飛雲殿	Dusk enters the Flying Cloud Hall.[15]
	城隅南對望陵臺	The corner of the city wall on the south, faces the tumulus-gazing terrace,[16]
6	漳水東流不復回	The Zhang River flows eastwards never to return.
	武帝宮中人去盡	People in the palaces of the Emperor Wu are all gone,
8	年年春色為誰來	For whom will the annual colors of spring come now?[17]

---

14 The east wind is also known as the spring breeze (*chunfeng* 春風). The fire in the wilds here refers to the will-o-the-wisp, also known as "ghost fire" (*guihuo* 鬼火 or *linhuo* 燐火).

15 Gao Guangfu 高光復 states that this could be one of the palace-halls in Ye, and Liu Kaiyang 劉開揚 states that there was a Flying Cloud Hall in Luoyang 洛陽. *Quan Tang shi*, however, shows a variant line, "The gathering dusk sets the clouds and lightning flying" (入暮飛雲電), which makes more semantic and syntactic sense in parallelism with line three. See Gao Guangfu, *Gao Shi Cen Shen shi yishi* 高適岑參詩譯釋 (Harbin: Heilongjiang renmin chuban she, 1984), 148–150; Liu Kaiyang, *Cen Shen shiji biannian jianzhu* 岑參詩集編年箋註 (Chengdu: Ba Shu shushe, 1995), 40–42; and *Quan Tang shi*, 199.2061.

16 The term "the corner of the city walls" (*chengyu* 城隅) could also mean the battlements on the walls. The Three Terraces of Ye were located just south of the northwest corner of the city on the western wall. The tumulus-gazing terrace is Bronze Bird Terrace.

17 The text of this poem is in *Quan Tang shi*, 199.2061. Gao Guangfu dates this piece to between February 17, 739 and February 5, 740, the twenty-seventh year of the Kaiyuan 開元 reign (713–742), when Cen Shen traveled to the area on the north side of the Yellow River (*heshuo* 河朔). See Gao's work, *Gao Shi Cen Shen shi yishi*, 148–150. Even though Liu Kaiyang agrees that this piece was written during the poet's trip to the north side of the Yellow River, he dates the trip to the twenty-ninth year of the Kaiyuan reign, between January 26, 741 and February 13, 742, using more compelling evidence. See Liu, *Cen Shen shiji biannian jianzhu*, 40–42.

YE IN THE MIND OF POETS FROM THE SEVENTH CENTURY AND BEYOND   127

Here Cen Shen uses the emptiness of the lost city to express the contrast between natural and human (historical) time. The poet is obviously viewing the remains of a city destroyed by Yang Jian two hundred years earlier, with nothing really remaining except, as he remarks in a couplet of another poem on Ye, "All that can be seen in the city of Ye are the mounds of yesteryear, / Still the Zhang River flows as of old" (鄴都唯見古時丘，漳水還如舊日流).[18]

The second line of the couplet opens two possibilities: "that the city will never be seen again," but also "when will it appear again." But the stillness of the empty city expressed in line two is also the stillness of human habitation: Cao Cao's people are gone, the city now no more than piles of rubble. Against the stillness of the human world we (both the poet and the reader) find the relentless recurrence of nature: the spring winds, the setting sun, the flowing water. A connection is drawn between the world of man and that of nature: the fire in the wilds, the phosphors or will-o-the-wisps, which are actually the residue of human blood. As the *Liezi* 列子 remarks, "The livers of goats transform into the fat of the earth; the blood of horses turns into phosphors; and the blood of humans becomes fire in the wilds" (羊肝化為地皋，馬血之為轉鄰也，人血之為野火也).[19] The remnants of war, the blood spilled in battle, will be renewed by the spring winds that fan the flames of a new dynastic ascension and bring more bloodshed. Thus, the lines imagine Ye as a site of recurring conflict, but now it is displaced as a "trace" of both history and poetry, a metaphor for the generalized anxieties about warfare that accompanies the rise and fall of dynasties. The question asked above, "when will it be seen again" is reintroduced in the final line, as a new emperor comes to replace Cao Cao or any last ruler, whose old court is as empty now as the city. Against this cycle of inevitable historical change, Cen Shen places the recurring and predictable flow of the Zhang River and the re-emergence of spring. The poem is also a striking foreshadowing of Du Fu's famous lines, "The state is sundered, only the mountains and rivers endure, / Trees and grass deepen in the springtime city" (國破山河在，城春草木深).[20]

---

18   See Cen Shen's "Comment After Visiting a Building in the Southern County Submitted to Magistrate Di in the Inn by the Yellow River" ("Linghe keshe cheng Di mingfu xiong liuti xiannan lou" 臨河客舍呈狄明府兄留題縣南樓) in *Quan Tang shi*, 199.2050. Du Fu has a poem entitled "Magistrate Di" ("Di mingfu" 狄明府), the opening line of which introduces the person to whom it is presented as "The great-grand-son of Duke Liang and my maternal cousin" (梁公曾孫我姨弟). Duke Liang (Liang *guo gong* 梁國公) was one of Di Renjie's 狄仁傑 (630–700) posthumous titles, therefore, Magistrate Di should be Cen Shen and Du Fu's contemporary, Di Boji 狄博濟 (n.d.).

19   Following the emendations and readings suggested in Yang Bojun 楊伯峻, *Liezi ji shi* 列子集釋 (Beijing: Zhonghua shuju, 1979), 1.14–15.

20   This is Du Fu's "Spring Gaze" ("Chun wang" 春望). See the full text of this poem in *Quan Tang shi*, 224.2404.

128 CHAPTER 4

While Cao Cao was alive, Ye had been a place where writers celebrated the greatness of his achievements and happiness over even the most trivial moments of life, all despite the political and military turmoil and unexpected life changes (for example, the pandemic of 217). After Cao Cao's death in 220, the city—especially Bronze Bird Terrace, where his performers paid postmortem tribute to him—became a local space where writers who visited the city expressed their lamentations. Whereas this second phase of poetry that was inspired by place and focused on the political achievements of the dead Cao Cao or on his performers, we can see by the early Tang that Ye clearly has become an imagined site. The city, its terraces, and the Zhang River eventually grew to be a fluid poetic motif transferrable as a metaphorical space to any place in which short-lived glory and the uselessness of power could be celebrated. Consider, for instance, "Resentment at the Bronze Bird Terrace" ("Quetai yuan" 雀臺怨), attributed to Ma Dai 馬戴 (d. ca. 869).

	魏宮歌舞地	At the site of singing and dancing in the Wei palace,
2	蝶戲鳥還鳴	Butterflies play and birds sing as they return.
	玉座人難到	The jade seat—hard for the man to reach,
4	銅臺雨滴平	Bronze Terrace—leveled by drops of rain.
	西陵樹不見	On the Western Tumulus trees are no longer seen,
6	漳浦草空生	And grass along the banks of the Zhang pointlessly sprouts.
	萬恨盡埋此	Ten thousand resentments are all buried here,
8	徒懸千載名	Just to continue in vain a name to last a thousand years.[21]

This poem beautifully captures the "resentment" of the title. We have no idea when Ma Dai wrote this poem, but there is little reason to assume that he was actually at the ruins of Ye. Rather, he uses the poetic traces of the place to write a bitter lament over the price that one man's power demands of others. The human activity of the terrace-top "singing and dancing" reverts to a natural scene where now butterflies dance and the birds sing on their nightly return to roost. This not only captures the ephemerality of Cao Cao's legacy, but more generally the futility of human endeavor in the face of nature. The image of the returning birds leads to the second couplet, in which is expressed the idea that any man who would take the throne must struggle against human and natural odds to reach it. The matching line of the couplet makes use of the ambiguity inherent in the word *ping* 平. Normally, we would understand the term to mean an "even" spread of the rain on the terrace; but the parallel active verb *dao* 到, "to reach to," calls for a reading of *ping* as equally active: to level or erode. Even as human aspiration leads one to try and claim the throne, nature is already reducing the remnants of past attempts (the tower was made of

---

21 *Quan Tang shi*, 555.6432.

rammed earth construction) through erosion. Since raindrops are also a standard metaphor for tears, the line also evokes an image of the tower being reduced to a hillock by the tears of those made to suffer atop the terrace after Cao had died, victims of his power that reaches beyond the grave. The last couplet is a perfect return to the anchor of place in the first line, *di* 地, as it becomes a figurative burial ground for all of the pain and misery of those who have suffered so one man can leave his name in history.

In verse, a poet's intention and message are not always clear. Nonetheless, the reader's ability to understand and appreciate the work is equally as important as the poet's ability to compose it. In many cases a metaphor or an allusion is the linchpin of the poet's message. Following is one example, Li Jiayou's 李嘉祐 (fl. 748) "Feelings Inspired by the Ancient" ("Guxing" 古興):

十五小家女	A fifteen year old girl from a humble family,
2 雙鬟人不如	With double hair buns, more beautiful than all.
蛾眉暫一見	A single glance from her moth-wing brows,
4 可直千金餘	Can be worth a thousand gold and more.

自從得向蓬萊裏	Ever since she went into the midst of Penglai,[22]
6 出入金輿乘玉趾	Exiting and entering, the golden carriage conveys her little toes of jade.

梧桐樹上春鴉鳴	In *wutong* trees, spring crows are cawing,[23]
8 曉伴君王猶未起	In the morning, companion to the lord, she has yet to arise.

莫道君恩長不休	Don't say, "The lord's kindness goes on without end,"
10 婕妤團扇苦悲秋	That Lady's "round fan" bitterly grieved over autumn.
君看魏帝鄴都裏	Look sirs, inside of the capital Ye of Emperor Wei,
12 惟有銅臺漳水流	Only the Bronze Terrace and the flow of the River Zhang remain.[24]

22　This is the Penglai Palace, built (construction started) on the *xinsi* 辛巳 day of the fourth month in the second year of the Longshuo 龍朔 reign [May 18, 662] of Gaozong of Tang 唐高宗 (r. 649–683). See Ouyang Xiu 歐陽修 (1007–1072) and Song Qi 宋祁 (998–1061) comps., *Xin Tang shu* 新唐書 (Beijing: Zhonghua shuju,1975), 3.62. The *Jiu Tang shu* indicates the construction of the Penglai Palace was completed on the *xinsi* day and Gaozong moved in (辛巳，造蓬萊宮成，徙居之), See Liu, *Jiu Tang shu*, 4.83.

23　*Wutong* tree is *firmiana simplex*, also known as Chinese parasol tree. As for the "spring ducks," while there are fulvous whistling ducks that are known for nesting in low trees or bushes near water, in this line these ducks might be lifelong pair bonding birds, the legendary "Phoenix birds" (*fenghuang* 鳳凰) or the "Mandarin ducks" (*yuanyang* 鴛鴦) since *wutong* tree is often connected to these birds in Chinese texts.

24　*Quan Tang shi*, 206.2145.

130 CHAPTER 4

The verse is reminiscent of a *yuefu* poem, and even though only twelve lines, is broken into three discrete parts by rhyme: [MC *–yo*], [MC *–iX*], and [MC *–juw*].[25] The first section begins with a light mood and focuses on the beauty of a young girl from a humble household who, having barely reached maturity, still wears her childhood hairdo. The second section describes her life after she is taken into the imperial palaces. While this may be a direct reference to the Penglai Palace constructed by Tang Gaozong in Luoyang, the very mention of Penglai indicates the transcendent abode of beautiful women. She is highly favored, is transported everywhere by an imperial carriage, and sleeps late with the emperor. There is a note of remonstrance here, since the emperor should arise for morning court before sunrise. Another note of discord is introduced into the poem in the second couplet of the section (lines seven and eight). The *wutong* tree normally symbolizes the intimate feeling between lovers and is particularly known as the nesting place for phoenix pairs. The noise of cawing crows here probably refers to other women in the imperial harem voicing complaints over being overlooked. Coupled with the emperor's neglect of his duties, the couplet hints at an unsustainable situation. As expected in lines nine and ten, the poet begins to directly address the inevitable outcome. He uses an early *yuefu* poem supposedly written by Lady Ban that describes a fan that is stored away when the heat of summer is replaced by the cold winds of autumn to give vent to her feelings of anxiety, "I am often afraid when autumn arrives, / A cool whirlwind will snatch the heat away; / You will abandon [the fan] in its bamboo box, / And all grace and sentiments will be cut off midway" (常恐秋節至，涼飆奪炎熱；棄捐莢笏中，恩情中道絕) (see Ch. 3). The final couplet addresses the reader directly, summoning the concrete image of the ruined terrace and river's flow, to make the point about the demands and cost of the exercise of imperial prerogative.

2 The Tiles of Ye as Material Synecdoche

The last material vestige of Ye to have a significant presence in both literati consciousness and literature are its tiles (Ye *wa* 鄴瓦) that were uncovered over the years. Many of these—or their fakes—became inkstones that allowed, as Han Qi 韓琦 (1008–1075) wrote, "… generations of men to write about 'rise and fall'" (see below). They also became significant tokens of exchange between writers and scholars. Their gifting not only resulted in a number of inscriptions

---

25 For Middle Chinese reading, see Paul W. Kroll, *A Student's Dictionary of Classical and Medieval Chinese* (Leiden: Brill, 2015).

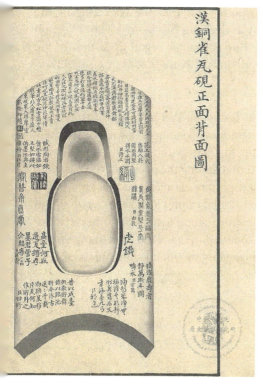 

FIGURES 6 AND 7   Prints of a Bronze Bird tile inkstone, recto and verso, from *Xiqing yan pu* 西清硯譜.
COURTESY OF ACADEMIA SINICA.

for the inkstones but also sparked controversy about the issue of authenticity and about what they signified as a memento of Cao Cao's rule and power.[26] These inkstones (see figs. 6 and 7) were known by various names, including: "old Ye titles" (Ye *guwa* 鄴古瓦), "tiles from Xiang Prefecture" (Xiangzhou *wa* 相州瓦), and the most valued of all, the "Bronze Bird Inkstone" (Tongque *yan* 銅雀硯). Just as the Bronze Bird Terrace had been the single site in Ye that had captured the imagination of writers, similarly the tiles thought to have come from the terrace occupied a pre-eminent place in the ranking of old inkstones from Ye.

---

26 Bronze Bird tile inkstones were only one of many objects that medieval literati collected. For further discussion on the subject of inkstones see, for example, Yang Xiaoshan, *Metamorphosis of the Private Sphere: Gardens and Objects in Tang-Song Poetry* (Cambridge, MA: Harvard University Asia Center, 2003); and Yang Zhiyi, *The Dialectics of Spontaneity: The Aesthetics and Ethics of Su Shi (1037–1101)* (Leiden: Brill, 2015), particularly the chapter entitled "Eloquent Stones," 86–118.

132   CHAPTER 4

Wang Shizhen 王士禛 (1634–1711) points out that the collecting of the Bronze Bird inkstones is noted as early as the Tang (see below). The collection of and discourse about these Bronze Bird inkstones began in earnest in the Song. The earliest reliable record is found in Su Yijian's 蘇易簡 (958–996) *Wenfang sipu* 文房四譜:

> From the ruin of the Bronze Bird Terrace of Wei [era], people often unearthed its old tiles and carved them into inkstones. They were extremely well made and could hold water for days without drying up. A story passed along for generations said that among the people of the past who built this terrace, tile makers and potters clarified mud by straining it through fine hemp sieves and then added walnut oil before kneading and shaping the clay. These tiles, therefore, stood apart from others. Nowadays, in places like Daming (in modern day Shandong) and Xiang Prefecture, there are many locals who make forgeries of inkstones in the style of the old tiles to sell.

> 魏銅雀臺遺址，人多發其古瓦，琢之爲硯，甚工，而貯水數日不燥。世傳云，昔人製此臺，其瓦俾陶人澄泥以絺濾過，加胡桃油方埏埴之，故與眾瓦有異焉。　即今之大名相州等處，土人有假作古瓦之狀硯，以市于人者甚眾.[27]

This piece persuasively represents the dual views of these tiles that men from the tenth century onward also held. Many of them did indeed cherish the inkstones, even though they knew that they were probably fakes. Shortly after Su Yijian, Yang Yi 楊億 (974–1020) noted a story about a fake stone that had been given to Xu Xuan 徐鉉 (916–991):

> Xu Xuan was skilled in the seal script and was fond of brushes and inkstones. When returning to court, he heard that people who plowed in Ye often obtained old tiles from the Bronze Bird Terrace. [The tiles] were smoothed into inkstones that were extremely good. Just at that time, someone he was close to was transferred to be the acting magistrate in Ye, so he gave him the task. After a number of years, [he] found two old tiles. They were extremely thick and large. [He] ordered a craftsman to make two inkstones and brought them back, personally giving them to Xuan. When Xuan got them, he was delighted and right away poured some water in. When he was about to test the ink the tile, being buried in the ground for so long, was extremely dry and absorbed all the water. He poured more in; right away it dried up. And, it had a muffled moist sound,

---

27   *Wenfang sipu* (SKQS ed.), 3.4b.

YE IN THE MIND OF POETS FROM THE SEVENTH CENTURY AND BEYOND 133

sounding like *zek-zek*. Xuan laughed and said, "Could it be the thirst of the bronze bird?" In the end, they could not be used and were no different from any other tiles or shards.

徐鉉工篆隸，好筆硯。歸朝，聞鄴中耕人，時有得銅雀臺古瓦，琢為硯，甚佳。會所親調補鄴令，囑之，凡經年，尋得古瓦二，絕厚大，命工為二硯持歸，面以授鉉。鉉得之，喜，即注水，將試墨，瓦瘗土中，枯燥甚，得水即滲盡。又注之，隨竭，浯浯有聲嘖嘖焉。鉉笑曰：『豈銅雀之渴乎？』終不可用，與常瓦礫無異.28

Around 1085, Yang Tingling 楊廷齡 (ca. 1060–1090) would even add a nickname for these fakes:

The [tiles] that people obtain now often are fake. Even though their shape and making are good, water disappears as soon as it is put in. And [the inkstones] are very coarse and unusable, so people call them [by the Buddhist term] "tonsuring the brush."29

今人所得往往皆偽者，形製雖佳，置水則立盡。疎盉不可用，人謂之「筆普度」.30

Wang Anshi 王安石 (1021–1086) likewise held a strong opinion about the authenticity of these tiles. In a short poem, "An Inkstone from the Old Tile of Xiang Prefecture" ("Xiangzhou guyan wa" 相州古硯瓦), he wrote:

	吹盡西陵歌舞塵	All the dust from singing and dancing for the Western Tumulus must be blown away,
2	當時屋瓦始稱珍	Before the building tiles of those days can be claimed as precious.
	甄陶往往成今手	Their molding is often accomplished by modern hands,
4	尚託聲名動世人	But they still bank on the reputation of the name to move those of this generation.31

---

28 Yang Yi [oral transmission] transcribed by Huang Jian 黃鑑 (fl. 1027), *Yang Wen gong tanyuan* 楊文公談苑, ed. Song Xiang 宋庠 (996–1066) in *Yang Wen gong tanyuan; Juanyou zalu*, 倦遊雜錄, ed. Li Yumin 李裕民 (Shanghai: Guji chuban she, 1993), 159.

29 Stephen Bokenkamp suggests that since *pudu* means "universal crossing to the other side," it might refer to the unsparing destruction of every brush used on it, so that the brushes need no longer labor in this world.

30 *Yanggong bilu* 楊公筆錄 (*SKQS* ed.), 9a.

31 *Wang Jinggong shi zhu* 王荊公詩注, ed. Li Bi 李壁 (ca. 1157–1222) (*SKQS* ed.), 46.8. This verse is entitled "Bronze Bird Inkstone" ("Tongque yan" 銅雀硯) in *Henan tongzhi* 河南通志 (*SKQS* ed.), 74.77.

The issue of authenticity may at first seem secondary to the discussion on the remnants of Ye, but it is necessary to understand that discussions of old objects are generally governed by debates in the contemporary environment. In some senses, the attitude about the issue of authenticity can be used to make a sharp divide between true literati or "men of worth" (*shi* 士) and those who were simply dilettantes—("enthusiasts" *haoshi zhe* 好事者 or "lovers of the interesting" *hao qishi zhe* 好奇事者)—those interested in the value of the inkstones only for purposes of ownership, a way to display their supposed sensibility or wealth. As the following will show, this divide provoked a considerable response from men of worth about how dilettantes' love of these inkstones came at the cost of suppressing historical memory. The discussion of the authenticity of Ye tiles did not end in the Song. For instance, Wang Shizhen in his citation of a passage from the *Zhangde fuzhi* 彰德府志, compiled by Cui Xian 崔銑 (1478–1541), considered the provenance of such tiles.

Cui Houqu's *Zhangde fuzhi* discriminates inkstones thusly:

> It has been passed down through generations that the old tile inkstones from the city of Ye all say "Bronze Bird brick inkstones from the Cao Wei" or "Ice Well [Terrace]." Perhaps [people] just went by the name but did not verify their authenticity. The palaces of Wei were all destroyed by conflagrations during the cataclasm of dynastic change. And after the [Later] Zhao and [Former] Yan, other dynasties rose and fell, so what was there left in terms of tiles?

[Wang Shizhen adds,] the *Yezhong ji* states,

> When the Northern Qi arose in Ye, the tiles of the new southern city were all infused with walnut oil, so that they shone and did not allow moss to grow. Semi-circular tiles that were used front [concave]-side down got oiled on their backs, and the flat tiles, used front-side up, were oiled on their faces. Semi-circular tiles were about two *chi* long and one *chi* wide. Flat tiles were the same length but twice as wide. If one now obtains an authentic piece, there are fine patterns in the places they were oiled, and these were conventionally called 'zither patterns.' If there are floral designs, they are called 'pewter blossoms.' Oral tradition says that [people] mixed orpiment, cinnabar, lead, and pewter into clay; and after many years the pewter blossoms would appear. The larger of these old bricks were four-*chi* square. On the surface were patterns of twining flowers, birds and animal, as well as the words "A Thousand Autumns" and "Ten Thousand Years." As for the reign titles, they were either Tianbao [June 11, 550–November 27, 559] or Xinghe [December 11, 539–January 22, 543], so

YE IN THE MIND OF POETS FROM THE SEVENTH CENTURY AND BEYOND

perhaps they were from the Northern Qi and Eastern Wei.[32] There were also brick semi-circular tiles, which had the same patterns and reign titles. They were rounded on the inside and square on the outside, and they were used as rain gutters along the eaves. These could also be used to make inkstones."

During the Yuanfeng [January 23, 1078–January 23, 1086] era, Regional Chief Li Cong (fl. 1079–1090) once acquired an old Ye inkstone from Shao Buyi (fl. 1080) of Danyang that had been kept in the family of Yuan Jie 元結, Cishan (723–772), of the Tang. On the back were flower patterns and the word "Ten thousand Years," which accords with the *Yezhong ji*. It also had written on it, "Made in the second year of the Xinghe [January 27, 540–February 12, 541] reign of the Great Wei." Therefore, even the ones that the Tang worthies loved all came from the southern [addition to the old] city.

崔後渠《彰德府志》辨硯云：「世傳鄴城古瓦硯，皆曰曹魏銅雀塼硯，皆曰冰井，蓋狥名而未審其實。魏之宮室，焚蕩於汲桑之亂，趙燕而後，迭興代毀，何有於瓦礫乎？」《鄴中記》云：「北齊起鄴，南城屋瓦皆以胡桃油油之，光明不蘚。筒瓦用在覆，故油其背。版瓦用在仰，故油其面。筒瓦長二尺，闊一尺。版瓦之長如之，而其闊倍。今或得其真者，當油處必有細紋，俗曰琴紋。有花曰錫花，傳言當時以黃丹鉛錫和泥，積歲久而錫花乃見。古塼大者方四尺，上有盤花鳥獸紋，千秋萬歲字，其紀年非天保則興和，蓋東魏、北齊也。又有塼筒者，花紋年號如塼，內圓外方，用承簷溜，亦可為硯。」宋刺史李琮，元豐中於丹陽邵不疑家得唐元次山家藏鄴城古塼硯，背有花紋及萬歲字，與《鄴中記》合。又曰「大魏興和二年造」，則唐賢所珍，已出於南城矣.[33]

While Wang Shizhen makes no personal evaluation of authenticity, by citing a comment that people perhaps did not verify the authenticity of tiles, a passage that describes the constituents of a genuine tile, and an example from the Song, he points to a continuing issue regarding establishing the undisputed origin of such tiles. He remains content with simply providing historical opinion, the tools for assessing the genuine article, and a historical incident that

---

32 Tianbao was the reign title of Emperor Wenxuan 文宣帝 (r. 550–559) of Northern Qi and then Prince Jinan 濟南王, Gao Yin 高殷 (545–561) kept using it until February 13, 560. Xinghe was one of the reign titles of Emperor Xiaojing 孝靜帝 (r. 534–550) of Eastern Wei.

33 Wang Shizhen, *Chibei outan* 池北偶談, ed. Jin Siran 靳斯仁 (Beijing: Zhonghua shuju, 1997), 16.398–399.

136 CHAPTER 4

demonstrates the value of possessing a real tile. One must also consider the possibility that Wang, by emphasizing the provenance of treasured inkstones as the later southern addition, distances himself from Cao Cao, the Bronze Bird Terrace, and historical arguments of both.

Ouyang Xiu 歐陽修 (1007–1072) had a different take on the question of authenticity, one that underscores the view of literati. He wrote in his short essay "A Register of Inkstones" ("Yanpu" 硯譜):

> The old tiles of Xiang Prefecture are truly fine, but very few of them are genuine. It was probably because the real tiles were decayed and useless, yet ordinary men of the world still esteem their reputation. Modern people make tiles with clarified mud in the shape of the old tiles and bury them in the ground. After a while, they chisel them into inkstones. [The inkstones], however, do not necessarily have to be real [Xiang Prefecture] tiles, because all ordinary tiles produce thick and glossy ink and are better than stone.

> 相州古瓦誠佳，然少真者。蓋真瓦朽腐不可用，世俗尚其名爾。今人乃以澄泥如古瓦狀作瓦埋土中，久而鑿以為硯。然不必真古瓦，自是凡瓦皆發墨，優於石爾。[34]

Ouyang Xiu was interested less in authenticity; he was willing to accept a fake if it was useful and had some value besides the question of being a "true" Xiang Prefecture tile. As he wrote in a poem, "Old Tile Inkstones" ("Gu wa yan" 古瓦硯):

	磚瓦賤微物	Bricks and tiles are cheap, insignificant things,
2	得廁筆墨間	But they get to be tucked alongside brush and ink.
	於物用有宜	For things, use is what one considers as appropriate,
4	不計醜與妍	There is no reckoning of ugly or beautiful.
	金非不為寶	It is not that gold is not treasured,
6	玉豈不為堅	Or that jade is surely not solid;
	用之以發墨	But use them in order to produce [thick and lustrous] ink,
8	不及瓦礫頑	And they will not reach the toughness of shards of tile.
	乃知物雖賤	So [we] come to know that although something is cheap,
10	當用價難攀	It is hard to grasp its value when needed for use.

---

34 Li Zhiliang 李之亮, ed., *Ouyang Xiu ji biannian jianzhu* 歐陽修集編年箋注 (Chengdu: Ba Shu shushe, 2007), 4: 369.

YE IN THE MIND OF POETS FROM THE SEVENTH CENTURY AND BEYOND 137

	豈惟瓦礫爾	How could it only be about shards of tile?
12	用人從古難	From old times on, using a person has been just as hard.[35]

For Ouyang Xiu, the question of value was directly related to the object's potential use. Even in cases where the stones seemed to the person to be authentic, the necessary point of possession did not seem to be the value of the tile on the market, but rather that they had personal point of contact with the writer as an instrument of memory or utility. For instance, in his "Bronze Bird [Inkstones] and Guan Inkstones" ("Tongque, Guan yan" 銅雀、灌硯), Hong Mai 洪邁 (1123–1202) notes:

> Xiang Prefecture is the ancient capital of Ye, and the Bronze Bird Terrace of the Grand Progenitor of Wei is located there. Presently it seems as if the old site still exists. The tiles are enormous. Wang Wenshu [n.d.] of Aicheng [possibly near modern day Yongxiu 永修, Jiangxi 江西] obtained one of them and made it into an inkstone, which he gave as a gift to Huang Luzhi [Huang Tingjian 黃庭堅 (1045–1105)]. This is the one for which Dongpo [Su Shi 蘇軾 (1037–1101)] wrote an inscription. Later on, it was returned to the Wang family. The tile was almost three *chi* long, and its width was half that. My late father also got two such inkstones when he returned from the area of Yan [in modern day Hebei]. The larger one was one *chi* and a half *cun* long and eight *cun* wide. In the middle, it was the shape of a gourd, and on the back in relief were six characters in clerical script. They were clear and strong and read, "Made in the fifteenth year of Jian'an [February 12, 210–January 31, 211]." The Progenitor of Wei [Cao Cao] became the Regional Governor of Ji Prefecture and governed Ye in the ninth year of Jian'an [February 18, 204–February 6, 205] and first began to construct this terrace. In terms of standard norms, the smaller one was inferior [to the larger], but there were also six characters in clerical seal script in its mid-section that read, "Made in the years of Xinghe of the Great Wei [December 11, 539–January 22, 543];" in the middle there were small clusters of flowers. Xinghe is the reign period of Emperor Xiaojing (r. 534–550) of the Eastern Wei, and at this time he had his capital in Ye. It was some three hundred years from the Jian'an era, and it is also six hundred years from then to now. Both [inkstones] are stored in the residence of my great nephew Hong Xian 洪侚 (fl. 1220–1235). I wrote an inscription for the Jian'an piece that reads:

---

35 Find the text of this poem in Ouyang's "Jushi waiji yi" 居士外集一 in *Ouyang Xiu quanji* 歐陽修全集 (Taipei: Heluo tushu chuban she, 1975), 2.194.

138   CHAPTER 4

The way that the Ye tile is molded,
Ah, is it a true one?
Nine hundred years later,
It comes back with [another] raft of the Han.[36]
Moisten your brush tip,
And set free its powerful beauty.
Xian truly does value this,
And so, illumines our family.

I also wrote an inscription for the Xinghe piece that reads:

When the Yuan clan's Wei turned to the Eastern [Wei],
"Dog's Paw" was in Ye.[37]
It appears that his tile has survived,
Through successions of a thousand *kalpas*.
Like a goose taken in Shanglin Park,[38]
Gathered in and stored, then brought it home in a basket.

---

36   His father had come back from a long trip to the steppes. The reference to the raft is to a
     legendary myth about the historical and great explorer Zhang Qian 張騫 (d. 113 BCE) who
     floated a raft to the headwaters of the Yellow River, and then out onto the Milky Way,
     where he encountered the Weaving Maiden.

37   Emperor Xiaojing was called "Dog's Paw." See, Liu Xuetiao 劉學銚, *Lidai Huzu wangchao
     zhi minzu zhengce* 歷代胡族王朝之民族政策 (Taipei: Zhishufang chuban jituan, 2005),
     59.

38   Refers to the story of Su Wu 蘇武 (ca. 140–60 BCE), who spent twenty years as a captive of
     the Xiongnu before returning home. According to the *Han shu* 漢書,
     Several years [after Emperor Zhao] ascended the throne, the Xiongnu made peace [by
     forming marriage alliance] with the Han. Han sought after Wu and others, but the Xion-
     gnu lied, saying that Wu was dead. Later an envoy from Han went again to the Xiongnu.
     Chang Hui (d. 64 BCE) requested the people who guarded him together to [visit the en-
     voy] and got to see the Han envoy at night. He told the envoy what happened and in-
     structed him to tell the Chanyu [ruler of Xiongnu] that the Han emperor had been
     hunting in Shanglin Park, and felled a goose, to the leg of which was attached a letter
     written on silk, which said that Wu and others were in such-and-such a marsh. The envoy
     was delighted and spoke as Hui had instructed, chastising the Chanyu. Chanyu looked his
     attendants left and right, he was surprised by this and then apologized to the Han envoy
     and said, "Wu and others are indeed here."
     即位。數年，匈奴與漢和親。漢求武等，匈奴詭言武死。後漢使復至匈
     奴，常惠請其守者與俱，得夜見漢使，具自陳道。教使者謂單于，言天
     子射上林中，得雁，足有係帛書，言武等在某澤中。使者大喜，如惠語
     以讓單于。單于視左右而驚，謝漢使曰「武等實在。」
     See Ban Gu 班固 (32–92), *Han shu* (Beijing: Zhonghua shuju, 1962), 54.2466. Here, this
     phrase refers to his father coming home from the northlands.

YE IN THE MIND OF POETS FROM THE SEVENTH CENTURY AND BEYOND

I put this inscription on it playfully,
But tears of old age perch on my lashes.

相州，古鄴都，魏太祖銅雀臺在其處。今遺址彷彿尚存。瓦絕大，艾城王文叔得其一，以為硯，餉黃魯直，東坡所為作銘者也。其後復歸王氏。硯之長幾三尺，闊半之。先公自燕還，亦得二硯。大者長尺半寸，闊八寸，中為瓢形，背有隱起六隸字甚清勁曰「建安十五年造」。魏祖以建安九年領冀州牧治鄴，始作此臺云。小者規範全不逮，而其腹亦有六篆字曰「大魏興和年造」，中皆作小簇花團。興和乃東魏孝敬帝紀年，是時正都鄴，與建安相距三百年，其至於今，亦六百餘年矣。二者皆藏姪孫偁處。予為銘建安者曰「鄴瓦所范，嘻其是邪？幾九百年，來隨漢槎。淬爾筆鋒，肆其滂葩。偁實寶此，以昌我家。」銘興和者曰「魏元之東，狗腳于鄴。呈其瓦存，亦禪千劫。上林得雁，獲儲歸笈。玩而銘之，衰淚棲睫」.[39]

Here, the difference between the dilettante and the men of worth certainly complicates the simple feeling that was found earlier in Lu Yun's "*Fu* on Ascending the Terrace," where he wrote, "I am affected by the presence of all the old things—, / And lament over the death of that one from long ago" (感舊物之咸存兮，悲昔人之云亡) (see Ch. 3). For Lu Yun, the material vestiges of Cao Cao evoked a strong sense of grief over his passing. This is a mode of early poetry, where a poet's emotion is often aroused by an object that was tied to a certain person or an event in the past. Like the halberd (*ji* 戟) in Du Mu's "The Red Cliff" (see Ch. 2), the object does not represent the past; rather, it "... links present to past and leads us toward a lost fullness."[40] This sense was still present in the Northern Song 北宋 (960–1127), for instance in a quatrain by the noted chancellor of that time, Han Qi,[41] "Bronze Bird Inkstone" ("Tongque yan" 銅雀硯):

	鄴城宮殿已荒涼	The Ye palace halls are already overgrown and desolate,
2	依舊山河半夕陽	Leaning against the old mountains and rivers, half in the setting sun.
	故瓦鑿成今日硯	Old tiles are carved to become inkstones of today,
4	待教人世寫興亡	Just to let generations of men write about "rise and fall."[42]

---

39 See the text and Cao Daoheng's 曹道衡 reading of this entry in Hong Mai, *Rongzhai suibi quanshu leibian yizhu* 容齋隨筆全書類編譯注, ed. Xu Yimin 許逸民 (Changchun: Shidai wenyi chuban she, 1993), 2: 640–642.

40 Stephen Owen, *Remembrances: The Experience of the Past in Classical Chinese Literature* (Cambridge, MA: Harvard University Press, 1986), 2.

41 Han Qi was chancellor from 1058 to around 1067.

42 See the text of this poem in *Henan tongzhi* (SKQS ed.), 74.77a.

The first couplet of this quatrain again contrasts human landscape, "palace halls" (*gongdian* 宮殿), with the realm of nature "mountains and rivers" (*shanhe* 山河). The overgrown and deserted palace halls of Ye lean against the mountains and rivers in sunset; this is a typical representation both of the end of historical life, and the renewal of nature—the mountains and rivers are old and enduring, remaining to see the sunshine again the next day. Against this vision of the end of the day and the end of life, the old tiles emerge ironically to give the city a new life, both in the form of their materiality, but also as the very instrument that makes it possible for people to write about the rise and fall of human history and of Ye itself. It is as if the city retains the material power to participate in a self-reflexive discourse on its fall. This is what *yongwu* 詠物 poems often do: they provide a concrete object that leads the writer back to a reconstituted realm over which the poet can reflect on the historical and ethical reasons that led to its demise or extinction.

But the issue was not as simple as that. Historical remembrance became only part of the literary life of inkstones, where the act of receiving and giving gifts and appreciation of friends' fine inkstones resulted in a plethora of poems, essays, and inscriptions. All of these poems, like Hong Mai's essay and inscriptions, have a deep personal sense to them that often overshadows the historical. For instance, Ouyang Xiu's "A Song in Responding to Xie Jingshan's [Xie Bojing 謝伯景] (998–1054) Gift of an Ancient Tile Inkstone" ("Da Xie Jingshan yi gu wayan ge" 答謝景山遺古瓦硯歌) is an excellent example:

	火數四百炎靈銷	Fire's number reached to four hundred, and the noumenon of heat dissipated,[43]
2	誰其代者當塗高	And, who was to replace it, but "the tall one on the road;"[44]
	窮姦極酷不易取	But, when the depth of his perfidy and height of cruelty could not be accepted,

---

43   "Fire's number" refers to the four hundred years of the Han 漢 (206 BCE–220) dynasty. A note in the *Han shu* indicates that Yan Shigu 顏師古 (581–645) accepted Official Zan's 臣瓚 (n.d.) commentary saying that "Han received the pedigree of Yao to be the virtue of fire" (漢承堯緒，為火德), Ban, *Han shu,* 1b.83.

44   A famous oracle from the *Chunqiu chen* 春秋讖 that is most often interpreted as a reference to the Cao Wei reads, "The one who replaces the Han is the tall one on the road" (代漢者當塗高). The *dang tu gao* refers to *wei* as a watchtower, and by homophone to the Wei dynasty. In his *The Talent of Shu: Qiao Zhou and the Intellectual World of Early Medieval* Sichuan (Albany: State University of New York Press, 2007), p. 20; however, J. Michael Farmer reads *wei* in the verbal sense of being "lofty." Also see the notes to a passage in Fan Ye's biography of Yuan Shu 袁術 (d. 179), where Yuan Shu willfully distorts the meaning of the phrase to refer to himself. See, Fan, *Hou Han shu,* 75.2439.

4	始知文景基扃牢	They began to know the foundations of Wen and Jing were firm.[45]
	坐揮長喙啄天下	Sitting and waving his long beak, one "pecked" away at the empire,[46]
6	豪傑競起如蝟毛	As the brave and mighty vied, rising like bristles on a hedgehog;
	董呂催汜相繼死	Dong, Lü, Jue, and Si died one after the other,[47]
8	紹術權備爭咆咻	Shao, Shu, Quan, and Bei contested with fierce bellows.[48]
	力彊者勝怯者敗	Those whose power was strong won and those who were weak lost,
10	豈較才德為功勞	How can we compare talent and virtue to determine their merit?
	然猶到手不敢取	Still, when landed in hand he did not dare to take it,
12	而使蟒蝗生蝮蜪	And, so caused the locusts to bear more larvae.
	子丕當初不自恥	His son, Cao Pi, in the beginning had no shame,
14	敢謂舜禹傳之堯	Daring to say that he, like Shun and Yu, received it from Yao.[49]
	得之以此失亦此	Once so-gotten, it was so-lost,
16	誰知三馬食一槽	Who could have known three "horses" would eat at a single "trough."[50]
	當其盛時爭意氣	When at the height, they vied in ambition and spirit,
18	叱吒雷雹生風飆	Pealing and pelting, thunder and hail birthed violent storms.

---

45   These are Emperor Wen 漢文帝 (r. 180–157 BCE) and Emperor Jing 漢景帝 (r. 157–141 BCE) of Han.

46   The word "to peck" (*zhuo* 啄) and the given name of Dong Zhuo 董卓 (141–192) are homophones. Dong Zhuo unseated Emperor Ling's 漢靈帝 (r. 168–189) heir Liu Bian 劉辯 (176–190) and installed Liu Bian's half-brother, Liu Xie 劉協 (181–243) on the throne, known to posterity as Emperor Xian 獻帝 (r. 189–220). Fan, *Hou Han shu*, 72.2324.

47   These are Dong Zhuo, Lü Bu 呂布 (d. 199), Li Jue 李催 (d. 198), and Guo Si 郭汜 (d. 197).

48   Yuan Shao 袁紹 (153–202), Yuan Shu, Sun Quan 孫權 (182–252), and Liu Bei 劉備 (161–223).

49   This refers to Cao Pi's patent of enfeoffment (*ce* 冊) when he made the Han emperor abdicate the throne. The opening lines say, "In the past, the thearch Yao abdicated his throne to Shun of Yu. Shun also did the same and mandated Yu. The mandate of Heaven is not given to the ordinary, it only tends toward the one who has virtue" (昔者帝堯禪位於虞舜，舜亦以命禹，天命不于常，惟歸有德). See Chen Shou 陳壽 (233–297), *San guo zhi* 三國志 (Beijing: Zhonghua shuju, 1959), 2.62.

50   The three horses (*ma* 馬) are Sima Yi 司馬懿 (179–251) and his sons Shi 師 (208–255) and Zhao 昭 (211–265). Sima Yi was an important general who served under members of the Cao family including Cao Cao, Cao Pi, and Cao Rui (d. 239)—Emperor Ming 明帝 (r. 226–239). The power and military authority Sima Yi was given over the years led to the coup when he was the regent of Cao Fang 曹芳 (232–274). The word "trough" (*cao* 槽) and surname Cao are homophones.

	干戈戰罷數功閱	When battles of buckler and spear came to an end, they counted up their merit,
20	周蔑方召堯無皋	Like a Zhou with no Fang or Shao, or a Yao without a Gao.[51]
	英雄致酒奉高會	Heroes brought forth wine to serve their great feasts,
22	巍然銅雀高岑岑	Rising steeply, Bronze Bird was surpassingly tall.
	圓歌宛轉激清徵	Full songs twined and wound, stirring a clear *zhi* note,
24	妙舞左右回纖腰	Marvelous dances turned left and right, making twirl delicate waists.
	一朝西陵看拱木	[But] one morning on the Western Tumulus they looked at trees an arm-span round,
26	寂寞總帳空蕭蕭	Lonely and deserted, the muslin mourning tent was empty and still.
	當時淒涼已可歎	The desolate loneliness of that time can be lamented for sure,
28	而況後世悲前朝	And how much more for later generations that grieve for former dynasties?
	高臺已傾漸平地	The tall terrace already decrepit, turned gradually to level ground.
30	此瓦一墜埋蓬蒿	This tile, once fallen, was buried among brushy weeds.
	苔文半滅荒土蝕	Their patterns of moss half extinguished, swallowed up by the wilderness earth,
32	戰血曾經野火燒	Where blood of battles once spilled, phosphor fires now burn.
	敗皮弊網各有用	Worn skin and broken nets each has its use [for making paper]—
34	誰使鐫鑱成凸凹	Who caused its carving to form relief and intaglio?
	景山筆力若牛弩	The power of Jingshan's brush is like a crossbow of horn,
36	句遒語老能揮毫	Sentences are powerful and words are seasoned, he can wield the brush.
	嗟予奪得何所用	Ah, now that I have it, how shall I use it?
38	簿領朱墨徒紛淆	Red and black in my official journal are simply a chaotic mess.
	走官南北未嘗捨	Running from office to office, north to south, I have never set it aside,
40	緹襲三四勤緘包	A package in red silk, bound tightly with three or four cords.

---

51   These are Fangshu 方叔 and Shaohu 召虎, both worthy officials of King Xuan 周宣王 (r. 828–783 BCE) of Zhou. In his "Memorial Seeking a Chance to Prove Myself" (Qiu zi shi biao" 求自試表) to Emperor Ming, Cao Zhi writes, "[You my lord] used officials that are like Fangshu and Shaohu to pacify and control all within four borders, being the claws and teeth of the state, they can be called proper" (以方叔召虎之臣鎮御四境，為國爪牙者可謂當矣). Chen, *San guo zhi*, 19.566. For another translation see Cutter, "Cao Zhi (192–232) and his Poetry," 20–21.

	有時屬思欲飛灑	There are times when I organize my thinking and wish to let it fly and pour out,
42	意緒軋軋難抽繰	But, threads of my thought stick tight, hard to pull from their cocoon.
	舟行屢備水神奪	Traveling by boat, constantly on guard, lest it be snatched by water spirits,
44	往往冥晦遭風濤	For I have often encountered windblown waves in the dark.
	質頑物久有精怪	Insensate substance, as the thing grows older, it has a demonic [force],
46	常恐變化成靈妖	And I constantly fear it will transform and turn into a spiritual demon.
	名都所至必傳玩	In every major city I reach, I must pass it around [for others] to enjoy,
48	愛之不換魯寶刀	Yet, cherish it so much I would not exchange it for the precious sword of Lu.[52]
	長歌送我怪且偉	The long song you sent me is unique and great,
50	欲報慚愧無瓊瑤	I wish to repay you but am ashamed to have no precious jades.[53]

This poem represents a delicate balance between history and the personal. Ouyang Xiu's recounting of history of the Three Kingdoms and his criticisms of the Cao Wei are couched in a body of allusions that represent ethical contrasts between legitimate rule and that which was founded by the Cao family, whose inability to carry out their hereditary role of being proper ministers of the Han, and who shamelessly compared themselves to the Sage Kings without any sense of irony or guilt, mark them as inferior. But this tone is modulated at the end of the long verse by the act of friendship, and the place that the inkstone occupied in the personal life of Ouyang Xiu. Whatever the inkstone might have symbolized historically, its usefulness and the personal bond of friendship created a certain kind of purposeful historical amnesia about its provenance.

Other voices, however, were less muted at this time, and the reader sees from the eleventh century onward an increasing stridency in the writing about

---

52 This refers to the legendary Menglao 孟勞 sword. See Fan Ning 范甯 (ca. 339–401) and Yang Shixun 楊士勳 (fl. 627–649), comm. and ann., *Chunqiu guliang zhuan zhushu* 春秋 穀梁傳注疏, in *Shisan jing zhushu fu jiaokan ji* 十三經注疏附校勘記, ed. Ruan Yuan 阮 元 (1764–1849), 8 vols., (Taipei: Yiwen yingshu guan, 1982), 7: 7.3b.

53 In the "Mugua" 木瓜 of the *Shijing* it reads, "When given a large peach, / I return it with precious jades. / This is not repaying, / But rather lasting friendship" (投我以木桃，報 之以瓊瑤。匪報也，永以為好也). Cf. *Mao shi* 64. Ouyang Xiu's poem is found in "Jushi waiji yi" in *Ouyang Xiu quanji*, 2.193–194.

144 CHAPTER 4

Cao Cao. A good example is found in He Wei's 何薳 (1077–1145) brief note and poem on a tile from the Bronze Bird Terrace in his *Chunzhu jiwen* 春渚紀聞.

> Xiang Prefecture is the old capital of Emperor Wu of Wei. The tiles from the Bronze Bird Terrace that he had constructed were originally pounded [clay] mixed with lead, cinnabar, and walnut oil and then fired, because this would mean they would not absorb moisture. Once the rain had passed, they were dry. Later people would unearth these tiles at its old foundations and cut them into inkstones. Although it was easy to produce ink in them, in the end [the ink] lacked a full glossiness. Dilettantes were only interested in the fact that they were of high antiquity. Those that had pewter patterns were considered to be authentic. When each inkstone was finished, [the makers] were worried that the place where the water would be poured would be clogged up by sand, so they removed the sand and created "sand-eyes," to the point that it was hard to get an even and lustrous surface. Probably, the tiles were originally not meant to be inkstones, so they did not clarify the clay with a sieve, as in the process of making Lü inkstones later. When Zhang Xuchen (n.d.) got hold of this, he asked me to write a poem for it to be engraved on the back. It states:

> 相州，魏武故都。所築銅雀臺，其瓦初用鉛丹雜胡桃油搗治火之，取其不滲，雨過即乾耳。後人於其故基，掘地得之，鑱以為研，雖易得墨而終乏溫潤，好事者但取其高古也。下有金錫文為真。每研成，受水處常恐為沙粒所隔，去之則便成沙眼，至難得平瑩者。蓋初無意為研，而不加澄濾，如後來呂研所製也。章序臣得之，屬余為詩，將刻其後，云：

He Wei's poem, which has circulated under the title "Tile from Bronze Bird Terrace" ("Tongque tai wa" 銅雀臺瓦) reads:

	阿瞞恃姦雄	A-man relied on his treacherous usurpation,[54]
2	挾漢令天下	To hold the Han hostage and command the empire.
	惜時無英豪	I lament there were no real heroes in that age,
4	磔裂異肩踝	To rip him apart with chariots so his shoulders and ankles would be in different places.
	終令盜抔土	In the end, he commanded [workers] to snatch handfuls of earth,
6	埏作三臺瓦	And mold it into tiles for the Three Terraces.
	雖云當塗高	Although [his empire] was called "the tall one on the road,"

---

54 Cao Cao's childhood name, "Little Deceiver."

8	會有食槽馬	There were still "horses that ate at the trough."
	人愚瓦何罪	People are stupid, but what faults do the tiles have?
10	淪蟄翳梧檟	They sank into hibernation, hiding [a fine quality like] the *wutong* and catalpa.
	錫花封雨苔	Flowers of pewter were sealed over by the moss from rain,
12	鴛彩晦雲罅	Colors of mandarin duck darkened by [light from] the fissures in the clouds.
	當時丹油法	The way of mixing cinnabar with oils from those days,
14	實非謀諸野	Really was not something that planned for them to be in the wild.
	因之好奇士	Because of this, lovers of the rare [or marvelous],
16	探琢助揮寫	Sought them, ground them, so aiding the wielding of a brush to write.
	歸參端歙材	They come back to compare them in quality with [those] from Duan and She,
18	堅澤未渠亞	Their hardness and luster were not inferior.
	章侯捐百金	Master Zhang spent a hundred gold,
20	訪獲從吾詫	His visit [to show me his] acquisition was followed by my astonishment.
	興亡何復論	Why again discuss the "rise and fall?"
22	徒足增忿罵	That would only be enough to increase our anger and cursing.
	但嗟瓦礫微	I simply sigh that a tile so insignificant,
24	亦以材用捨	Can be used or set aside on the basis of its quality.
	徒令瓴甓餘	It is not worth letting this little piece of leftover brick,
26	當擅瓊瑰價	Command the price of precious stones.
	士患德不修	A man of worth should worry only that his virtue is not cultivated,
28	不憂老田舍	And not fret about his old fields and farmstead.[55]

As opposed to the playful irony of Han Qi's poem, and the carefully modulated think-piece poem by Ouyang Xiu, this piece can barely conceal its contempt for Cao Cao and for the dilettantes. He Wei's retrospective criticism of the Three Kingdoms in general and of Cao Cao in particular (lines one to eight) is caught quite directly in his comment that people are stupid, but the tiles are faultless. In the middle section, He Wei discusses the "faultless tiles" but returns to people again in the last part of the poem, condemning the dilettantes, whose aim is not to make good inkstones, but find an item that has a certain market value. So, the stupidity runs both backward and forward in this poem:

---

55 He Wei, *Chunzhu jiwen*, ed. Zhang Minghua 張明華 (Beijing: Zhonghua shuju, 1997), 136–137.

146   CHAPTER 4

back to the actors in the rise of Cao Wei (beyond discussion and only a prompt to anger) and forward to the collector of precious things, whose interest in material value (cost) outweighs historical significance or use. As He Wei writes at the end, a real *shi* should be concerned about moral development, not about property.

The unhappiness with Cao Cao continued in the Song and Yuan 元 (1259–1368), seemingly growing more severe as time passed. And it took an interesting turn, for instance, in the writing of Zhao Wen 趙文 (1239–1315), a native of Luling 盧陵 (near modern day Ji'an 吉安, Jiangxi 江西). Zhao who had sought refuge with Wen Tianxiang 文天祥 (1236–1283) after the collapse of Southern Song, wrote a poem, "Bronze Bird Tile" ("Tongque wa" 銅雀瓦), that presents a view of Cao Cao that turns the sentimental trope of the terrace-scape and of Cao's deathbed wishes on its head. And while this poem comes from the Southern Song, as the reader shall see, it draws primarily on the earlier opinion of Cao Cao voiced in the Northern Song by one of its literary giants. The poem reads:

	曹公築銅臺	The revered Cao built the Bronze [Bird] Terrace,
2	氣力雄九有	His energy and strength powered through the "Nine Divisions."
	咿嚶到香履	But from the "whimpering" to the "incense and shoes,"[56]
4	千古開笑口	He opened laughing mouths for a thousand antiquities.
	猶餘當時瓦	Still, there are leftover tiles from that time,
6	作硯傳不朽	To be made into inkstones and passed along without decay.
	涪翁所珍惜	That which had been cherished by Codger Fu,[57]
8	又復落吾手	Once again fell into my hands.
	鬼奪與客偷	Ghosts grab and guests filch;
10	任運不汝守	[They are] left to fate's movement, never as protected as Ru ware.[58]

---

56   The "incense and shoes" refers to the quote from Cao Cao's testament: "the leftover incense can be split among my ladies. If they have nothing to do in their chambers, they can learn to make decorative lacings for shoes and sell them" (餘香可分與諸夫人。諸舍中無所為，學作履組賣也) in Lu Ji's 陸機 (261–303) "Lamenting the Death of Emperor Wu of Wei" ("Diao Wei Wudi wen" 弔魏武帝文). See Ch. 2.

57   "Codger Fu" ("Fuweng" 涪翁), the old man by the Fu River, is Huang Tingjian 黃庭堅 (1045–1105). Huang had written a short inscription for a Bronze Bird inkstone. See "Bronze Bird Terrace Inkstone" ("Tongque tai yan" 銅雀臺硯) in his *Shangu ji* 山谷集 (SKQS ed.), 2.4b. Su Shi 蘇軾 (1037–1101) also wrote an inscription on said inkstone, see "Inscription on Huang Luzhi's Bronze Bird Inkstone" ("Huang Luzhi Tongque yan ming" 黃魯直銅雀硯銘) in, for example, *Su Shi wenji* 蘇軾文集, ed. Kong Fanli 孔凡禮 (Beijing: Zhonghua shuju, 1986), 2:19.552.

58   The Ru Kiln (Ruyao 汝窯) was one of several famous kilns during the Northern Song era. It was located near modern day Linru county 臨汝縣 in Henan.

| 可憐臺上人 | How sad that those people atop the terrace, |
| 12 不如此瓦壽 | Could not live as long as these tiles.[59] |

The opening couplet expresses the might of Cao Cao, whose power spread through the nine realms, whose ambitions were visible in his construction of Ye based on an imperial model, and particularly in his construction of the Bronze Bird Terrace. The second couplet owes its source to Su Shi's "Encomium to Kong Beihai with Preface" ("Kong Beihai zan bingxu" 孔北海贊並序),[60] which introduces the image of Cao's progeny weeping at his death bed, "whimpering" and crying:

> With a substance of heroic stature that capped the world, Wenju was a model teacher for all within the seas. All under heaven followed that which he chose or discarded—he was a dragon among men. Cao Cao, on the other hand, was malicious and dangerous, and he was a mighty person who brought others low by devious and otherworldly methods. The power of these two could not possibly exist alongside each other; if the noble [Kong] were not going to execute Cao, then Cao would harm him— this is a constancy of principle. Yet the former histories say of the noble [Kong], "he was extremely willful, and although his ambition was in settling the difficulties, his talent was too weak and his ideas too broad to realize that ambition, so he never had any success."[61] These are certainly words written by some little person, a slave of those times. That the noble [Kong] had no success was due to Heaven. If Heaven had not wanted to destroy the Han, the noble one would have executed Cao in the same way as killing a fox or hare—no need to talk of that further. A man of power, so declaimed in any era, has either higher or lower gifts, but no [men of power] show fear when approaching a difficult time—laughing and chatting, they go to their deaths as heroes. But when Cao was dying of illness, in front of all his sons and grandsons, whimpering and weeping, loath to leave his wives and concubines, [he told them to] split the incense, sell shoes, and take care of his clothes. In his whole life he was treacherous and deceitful, and when he died his real nature was revealed! The world evaluates personalities on whether they are "successful" or not, so Cao gets to be listed as a hero and that the noble [Kong Rong] as "talent was too weak and his ideas too broad." Isn't that just sad!

---

59 See the text of this poem in *Qingshan ji* (SKQS ed.), 7.12b.

60 This is an encomium to Kong Rong 孔融 (153–208), also known as Wenju 文舉, who was executed by Cao Cao.

61 Fan, *Hou Han shu*, 70.2264.

文舉以英偉冠世之資，師表海內，意所予奪，天下從之，此人中龍
也。而曹操陰賊險狠，特鬼蜮之雄者耳。其勢決不兩立，非公誅操，
則操害公，此理之常。而前史乃謂公「負其高氣，志在靖難，而才疎
意廣，迄無成功。」此蓋當時奴婢小人論公之語。公之無成，天也。
使天未欲亡漢，公誅操如殺狐兔，何足道哉！世之稱人豪者，才氣各
有高庳，然皆以臨難不懼，談笑就死為雄。操以病亡，子孫滿前而咿
嚶涕泣，留連姜婦，分香賣履，區處衣物，平生姦偽，死見真性。世
以成敗論人物，故操得在英雄之列。而公見謂才疎意廣，豈不悲哉!62

As noted above in Ge Lifang's earlier citation of this passage, by the Southern
Song, these "famous words" of Su Shi had become a view about Cao Cao and
his accomplishments that held great sway among the literati. Cao Cao's weak-
willed softness at his death along with the collapse of his ambition and vision
of empire to the small circle of his family and women are contrasted with the
brutality he caused in his life; and as Su Shi suggests, what emerges is not a
great hero who goes to his death "laughing and chatting," but one who is loath
to part with his beautiful women. Instead of worrying about the empire, an act
that would be commensurate with his ambitions while alive, at the end Cao
Cao was concerned about no more than the small group at his deathbed and
the material possessions he had gathered. As Zhao Wen remarks here, a century or more after Su Shi, Cao Cao's testament simply provokes laughter. Zhao
Wen makes use of that general opinion by shifting the view of the reader from
the grand accomplishment of the Bronze Bird Terrace in the beginning of the
poem, reducing it to the "incense and shoes" in line three. All of the past has
been lost or eroded: both the majesty and folly of Cao Cao have disappeared
and his last wishes have been savaged by time. Only tiles from that time remain
(line five), objects that can be held and reshaped at will. In lines seven through
ten, the poet describes how a piece of inkstone made of a tile from Cao Cao's
Bronze Bird Terrace came into his possession through various hands. He then
reflects on the vicissitudes of such treasured items, purloined by ghosts and
filched by guests in his house, and then his reluctance, in the face of fate, to
protect them as valuable items.[63]

---

62   Kong, *Su Shi wenji*, 2:21.601.

63   In a preface and postscript (*tiba* 題跋) titled "Writing on the Inkstone of the Man of the
Way, Lü" ("Shu Lü daoren yan" 書呂道人硯). A "man of the Way" in Song times can refer
either to a Daoist or Buddhist person, although one should not overlook the possibility of
reference to Lü Dongbin 呂洞賓 (796–1016), a famous figure of the Daoist tradition. Su
Shi described how he "stole" a precious inkstone from an acquaintance who did not know
of its value: Most inkstones made of submerged mud by the Man of the Way, Lü of Ze
Prefecture [near modern day Jincheng 晉城, Shanxi 山西] have the form of a pitch-pot.
The top has a character, *lü*, and it is neither carved nor painted. [The inkstone] is durable
yet delicate and can be tested by metal. The man of the Way has passed on and his inkstones are hard to obtain. On the seventh day of the third month in the fifth year of

YE IN THE MIND OF POETS FROM THE SEVENTH CENTURY AND BEYOND 149

The poet then laments that the lifespan of those who used to be atop this marvelous terrace could not last as long as a piece of insensate tile. Zhao Wen does not say who these people are. It is left to the reader to determine if the poet meant the performers or if he meant Cao Cao and his sons who famously ascended the terrace to compose their poems. The poet could also be suggesting that the inkstones are a concrete synecdoche for certain historical and poetic moments as well as for what those moments spawned in poetry and literature. He makes a link through the inkstone to a poetic history, moving from the object itself and what it denotes, to the last line where he brings not only the inkstone, but those atop the terrace back to life in a repetition of the poetic trace.

This disdain for Cao Cao is articulated again in a poem written by Zhao Wen's contemporary, Ai Xingfu 艾性夫 (fl. 1279), lengthily titled:

Sundry masters have composed [verses] to extremely praise brother Dongyuan's Bronze Bird Inkstone. I, alone, do not think this way. But, Master Su's [Su Shi] poem-inscription and the Criminal Administrative Mei's [Mei Yaochen] long verse, in each and every case, treat it as so. For instance, words like, 'All the world competes to extol the durability of Ye tiles, / A single piece cannot be exchanged for a distribution of a hundred in gold;'[64] '[It] does not do the flight of mandarin ducks, / Yet it has the sentiment of tadpole [characters];' and 'To take it in for use it must certainly be precious, / And to discourse on its antiquities, there is no other'[65] are all this type. [I] dare to join in and compose one that is opposite.

Yuanfeng reign [April 13, 1082], by chance I arrived at Mr. Huang's house in Shahu [possible near modern day Huhan 武漢] and saw one [of these inkstones]. Mr. Huang never knew that was valuable, so [I] took it into my possession. 澤州呂道人沈泥硯，多作投壺樣。其首有呂字，非刻非畫，堅緻可以試金。道人已死，硯漸難得。元豐五年三月七日，偶至沙湖黃氏家，見一枚，黃氏初不知貴，乃取而有之。Kong, *Su Shi wenji*, 5: 70.2238.

64 This couplet is from Su Shi's "Matching in Order the Rhymes of Ziyou's [Original Poem] on Wanting to Obtain a Piece of Chengni Inkstone from Mount Li" ("Ciyun he Ziyou yude Lishan chengni yan" 次韻和子由欲得驪山澄泥硯). Zeng Zaozhuang 曾棗莊 comp., *Su Shi huiping* 蘇詩彙評 (Chengdu: Sichuan wenyi chuban she, 2000), 107; Wang Wengao 王文誥 (b. 1764), ed., *Su Dongpo shiji* 蘇東坡詩集, proofread by Tang Yunzhi 唐云志 (Beijing: Zhuhai chubanshe, 1996), 185–186; and Wang Wengao, ed., *Su Shi shiji* 蘇軾詩集, proofread by Kong Fanli 孔凡禮 (Beijing: Zhonghua shuju, 1982), 5. 211–212.

65 These lines are from Mei Yaochen's "Bronze Bird Inkstone." Roughly the lines mean, "The tile is not decorated with patterns of mandarin ducks in flight, but its seal-script character [words] have all the sentiment that is needed." See Zhu, *Mei Yaochen ji biannian jiaozhu*, 3: 26.906.

150   CHAPTER 4

諸公賦東園兄銅雀硯甚夸，余獨不然。然蘇長公詩銘，梅都官長句皆
爾。如謂「舉世爭稱鄴瓦堅，一枚不換百金頒。」「不及鴛鴦飛，乃
有科斗情。」「入用固爲貴，論古難與并。」之類是已。敢併爲之反
騷。

The poem reads:

	臨洮健兒衷甲衣	The sturdy lad of Lintao wore his armor underneath,[66]
2	曹家養兒乘禍機	And the adopted son of the Cao exploited a moment of crisis.[67]
	匹夫妄作九錫夢	A common man wildly dreamed of Nine Bestowments,[68]
4	鬼蜮敢學神龍飛	Ghostly monsters dared to imitate the flight of the spirit dragon.
	負鼎而趁不遄死	He hastened to "carry a tripod on his back" but did not die quickly,[69]
6	築臺尚欲儲歌舞	And constructed a terrace still desiring to make a place for songs and dances.
	但知銅雀望西陵	He only knew that the Bronze Bird gazed toward the Western Tumulus,
8	不覺妖狐叫墟墓	And was unaware that demons and foxes would yelp in his ruined grave.

---

66   Refers to Dong Zhuo 董卓 (141–192), a native of Lintao (in modern day Gansu 甘肅). The use of *zhong* 衷, to wear undergarments or under-layers of clothing is interesting, since it suggests that he kept his desire to conquer the empire publicly hidden but, one assumes, still visible under his court robes.

67   Refers to Cao Cao's father Cao Song 曹嵩 (d. 193), who was an adopted son of the eunuch Cao Teng 曹藤 (100–159). Chen, *San guo zhi*, 1.1.

68   The Nine Bestowments include: chariot and horse (*chema* 車馬), clothing (*yifu* 衣服), musical instruments (*yueqi* 樂器), vermillion gates (*zhuhu* 朱戶), ceremonial stairway (*nabi* 納陛), one hundred brave warriors and men of worth (*huben shi bairen* 虎賁士百人), axe and broad-axe (*fuyue* 斧鉞), bow and arrow (*gongshi* 弓矢), and ceremonial fragrant wine brewed from black millet (*juchang* 秬鬯); were the highest honors given to officials by a ruler. On the *bingshen* day of the fifth month, summer of the eighteenth year of Jian'an reign [June 16, 213], Cao Cao set himself up as the Duke of Wei and added the Nine Bestowments" (夏五月丙申，曹操自立為魏公，加九錫). Fan, *Hou Han shu*, 9.387.

69   This refers to the saying that the mythical Minister Yi 伊尹 once "carried a tripod vessel on his back to encourage Tang (r. 1675–1646 BCE) to become the king" (... ... 負鼎而勉湯以王). Sima Qian, *Shi ji*, 74.2345. "To not die quickly" refers to the often quoted line from the poem, "Xiangshu" 相鼠, "To be a human and without a sense of propriety, / Why do you not die quickly?" (人而無禮，胡不遄死), i.e. Cao Cao rushed to the aid of the Emperor, but he should have died because he was without a sense of propriety. Cf. *Mao shi*, 52.

	分香賣履吁可憐	"Splitting the incense" and "selling shoes," ah, so pitiful,
10	所志止在兒女前	Everything he aimed for ceased in the presence of his sons and daughters.
	竟令山陽奉稚子	In the end, he ordered Shanyang to support his young child,[70]
12	出爾反爾寧無天	But what goes around comes around—would you rather no heavenly principle?
	陳留作賓向司馬	Chenliu was a "guest" and sided with the Sima,[71]
14	包羞更出山陽下	And in the shame he suffered, he was worse off than Shanyang.
	國亡臺廢天厭之	The state lost, the terrace destroyed, Heaven had enough of it,
16	何事人猶拾殘瓦	So why do people still gather together these remnants of tiles?
	古來觀物當觀人	From ancient times to now, when observing an object, we should also observe the person,
18	虞琴周鼎絕世珍	The zithers of Yu and the tripods of Zhou are truly one of a kind treasures for the ages.[72]
	區區陶甓出漢賊	These tiny little pottery tiles come from a traitor to Han,
20	矧可使與斯文親	And more, how can they be made part of our culture?
	歙溪龍尾誇子石	The "Dragon-tails" from Shexi are boasted of as "seeds of stone,"
22	端州鴝眼真蒼璧	And the "Magpie-eyes" from Duanzhou are known for the true green jade discs.[73]

---

70 Cao Cao forced Emperor Xian of Han 漢獻帝 (r. 189–220) to unseat his empress, Fu Shou 伏壽 (d. 214), and then Cao married his own daughter Cao Jie 曹節 to the emperor. After Cao Cao died, Cao Pi became Emperor Wen of Wei 魏文帝 (r. 220–226) and the dethroned Emperor Xian was given the title of Duke of Shanyang 山陽公 on the *yimao* 乙卯 day of the tenth month, winter of the twenty-fifth year of Jian'an [November 25, 220]. Fan, *Hou Han shu*, 10b.455 and 9.390.Cao Cao had sent several of his daughters to Emperor Xian to become concubines and consorts; some were not yet age appropriate, and they remained in Ye with the Cao family, until they reached the proper age. See Ch. 2.

71 Chenliu was the hereditary fief of the Caos. After the cessation of Wei and founding of Jin 晉 (266–420), Sima Yan 司馬炎 (236–290) granted Wei's last emperor, Cao Huan 曹奐 (246–302), an inheritable title—Prince of Chenliu (Chenliu *wang* 陳留王) and had him reside at the old palace complex of Ye: "capital" of the Chenliu state 陳留國. See more details in Fang Xuanling 房玄齡 (579–648) and others, *Jin shu* 晉書 (Beijing: Zhonghua shuju, 1974), 3.51–53.

72 I.e., the zither marked the age of the Sage King Shun 舜, and the tripods of Zhou signified the moral worth of Zhou's reign.

73 The Dragon Tails and Magpie Eyes both are famous inkstones. Magpie eyes are where the sand was washed away, leaving pockets in the stone that were smoothed and made into receptacles for ink and water.

	好奇不惜買千金	The dilettantes do not begrudge buying them for a thousand gold,
24	首惡寧容汙寸墨	But the prime fault is to allow them to soil even just a smidgeon from the inkstick.
	書生落筆驅風雷	I, a person of letters, use my brush to drive away wind and thunder,
26	要學魯史誅姦回	And want to imitate the scribe of Lu to punish the evil and recalcitrant.[74]
	請君唾去勿復用	I request you sir, spit on it, throw it out, and never use it again,
28	銅雀猶在吾當摧	If the Bronze Bird [Terrace] still stood, I would destroy it.[75]

This is a very straightforward poem in its disdain of Cao Cao, a mere commoner who could never possess the mandate and who, in the end thought only of the comfort of his family and of his possessions. The poet asks why people would be so obsessed with a material object closely associated with someone whose tumulus is haunted by ghosts and foxes and who was punished by Heaven. The object, he points out, is never free of its association with a person and his acts. To possess such an inkstone was to turn one's back on historical judgment and the will of Heaven.

The controversy over Cao Cao continued on into the Yuan period. For instance in the preface to a *fu* on the Bronze Bird Terrace ("Tongque tai youxu" 銅雀臺有序), Liu Shen 劉詵 (1268–1350) wrote:

In the fifteenth year of Jian'an [February 12, 210–January 31, 211], Cao Cao constructed two terraces in Ye that were so high they reached to the Milky Way. On one he cast and erected a bronze phoenix there and called it the Bronze Bird. When Cao died in the first year of the Huangchu [December 11, 220–February 9, 221] reign, the terraces had been erected for fewer than ten years. If we consider how often he was at war, how many days could he have roamed there in pleasure? In his testamentary command he ordered his beauties and palace women to make sacrifices in the mornings and evenings, and to have female musicians perform on the first and fifteenth of the [lunar] month. Because Cao was unable to separate himself from his concubines and wives, because of his order to "split the incense" and "sell shoes," and because of his obsessive planning of household affairs, generations of people have considered him impaired by minutiae. Actually, only in his death, after a life of treacherous lying

---

74 The scribe of Lu authored the *Springs and Autumns* 春秋, a chronology of historical events noted for its precise vocabulary parceling out of praise and blame.

75 *Shengyu* 剩語 (*SKQS* ed.), 1.4b–5a.

were his true sentiments—the very basest quality of his mind—displayed.

Some do not consider it so, taking it to be that Cao's testament concealed his greatest desires, which were simply transferred to household matters and showed the profound hidden intention of Cao. The facts were that he was a traitor to the Han yet himself enjoyed the rank of minister of the Han—this is sufficient enough to give a glimpse of the heart of this treacherous usurper. Thus, I humbly consider it this way: Cao's insolence had been plainly shown to the world for a long time. He sought the Nine Bestowments and prepared a ceremonial entourage. He mocked Chen Qun (d. 237) and Dong Zhao (ca. 157–236) for trying to persuade [him] to advance,[76] just because [Cao] procrastinated and dragged it along into later years simply because public voice and the climate of opinion were still rampant; we cannot say that he did not finally get his way.[77] Returning from the area of Long and Han,[78] he died before making it to Luoyang,[79] so his lifelong ambitions could not be carried out after all. Therefore, he wept uncontrollably, and cast his covetousness upon his small children and young consorts. And when we observe his desire to have constant female performers arranged, and his having people constantly gaze to his Western Tumulus; his inability to cut off the riches and nobility he had while alive to this extent—are we willing to say that these were carried out on behalf of his overarching virtue? Lu Shiheng [Lu Ji] got it right when he said, "In long range calculations he was thwarted by the short number of his days, / In [imagined] far reaching traces of move-

---

76   Chen Qun and Dong Zhao both were important officials of Cao Cao. Dong once advised Cao Cao to place his rank among the five liege-lord ranks of the Zhou era, which would have placed him among the ennobled. Cao Cao initially declined, saying that those who established ranks were sages and how could he—merely an official—be capable of shouldering such task. But after Dong's lengthy statement of Cao's merits. Cao Cao, as a result, "accepted" the titles of "Duke of Wei" and "King of Wei." See Chen, *San guo zhi*, 14.439–440.

77   Cf. The commentary, quoting *Weilue* 魏略 and *Weishi Chunqiu* 魏氏春秋, in the *San guo zhi* says that Sun Quan presented a letter to Cao Cao and addressed Cao with the mandate of heaven. Cao Cao then showed this letter to others. Chen Qun and Huan Jie 桓階 (d. ca. 221) presented a memorial to Cao Cao to persuade him to take the throne. Xiahou Dun 夏侯惇 (d. 220) also requested Cao Cao to put an end to the Han, but Cao refused and said "If the mandate of heaven is on me, I would be King Wen of Zhou" (若天命在吾，吾為周文王矣。). King Wen of Zhou (1152–1056 BCE) did not take the throne from Shang 商 (ca. 1600–1046 BCE); rather his son King Wu 武王 (r. ca. 1050–1043 BCE) did and became the first king of Zhou. Chen, *San guo zhi*, 1.52–53n2.

78   According to Li Xian's 李賢 (654–684) commentary, this area is also known as Hanyang 漢陽. Fan, *Hou Han shu*, 60a.1973n1.

79   Cao Cao died in Luoyang. Chen, *San guo zhi*, 1.53.

154   CHAPTER 4

ment he was halted by a short road."[80] If he had not died, he would have
been incapable of even waiting for his own son [to take the throne], so
how could [his ambition] have been taken away from him by the political
counsel of Kong Beihai [Kong Rong] or Xun Wenruo [Xun Yu 荀彧] (163–
212)]?[81]

建安十五年，曹操作二臺於鄴，高入雲漢。其一冶銅為鳳凰置焉，因
名銅雀。黃初元年操死，臺成未十年。計其馳騁兵間，觀游之日，復
幾何哉？遺令婕好美人，朝晡上脯糒，朔望作妓樂。世以操留連妾
婦，分香賣履，區畫家事，傷於纖悉。乃平生姦偽，死見真情，為其
心之陋也。
　或者謂不然，以為遺令藏其所大欲，而徒及家事，乃操之微意。實
為漢賊，而身享漢臣之名，此固足以窺姦雄之心。然愚以為，操之不
遜，顯白於世久矣。求九錫，備儀扈，諷陳羣、董昭以勸進，特以清
議未泯，遲之歲月間耳，不謂不得逞。於隴漢歸未及洛而沒，蓋平生
心事竟不得遂。故流涕不自制，而寄愛於幼子少妾焉。觀其欲嘗設妓
樂，及使人嘗望西陵，不能割生前富貴如此，而肯為盛德事乎？陸士
衡以為，長算屈於短日，遠跡頓於促路，斯言得之矣。使其未死，彼
固不能忍以待其子也。又豈孔北海、荀文若之清議所能劫哉.[82]

Certainly, there was not a unified vision of what Cao Cao was like as a man, or
what the Cao Wei Dynasty signified in the flow of Chinese history. By the Yuan
era, of course, the pejorative view of Cao had been strengthened by his portrayal in various burgeoning forms of colloquial literature. But Liu Shen's essay
hints at a complicated matrix of opinion. The reader should also consider that
the inkstones left from Ye were not solely valued simply on their own merit. In
the Song dynasty there is a rather long discourse on the quality and kind of
inkstones. Most people felt that the "clarified clay" (chengni 澄泥) inkstones
cast by a man of the Way, Lü of Ze Prefecture, were of superior quality. They
were, as Chen Yuyi 陳與義 (1090–1138) expresses in the first three couplets of a

---

80   This is in Lu Ji's "Lamenting the Death of Emperor Wu of Wei." See Ch. 2.

81   Both Kong Rong and Xun Yu were known for voicing unfiltered criticism and candid ad-
      vice about court policies and at the one who was in power. In the end, Cao Cao had Kong
      Rong executed in the marketplace and his body was left there for the public to witness.
      Kong Rong's wife and children, except for his seven-year-old daughter and nine-year-old
      son, were all executed as well. Xun Yu was believed by historians to have committed
      suicide at age fifty. See Kong Rong's and Xun Yu's biographical accounts in Fan, *Hou Han
      shu*, 70.2261–2297.

82   Found under this title in Liu Shen's collected works, *Guiyin wenji* 桂隱文集 (SKQS ed.),
      1.13b–14b and in Li Xiusheng 李修生, ed. *Quan Yuan wen* 全元文 vol. 22, Liu Shen 1, (Nan-
      jing: Jiangsu guji chuban she, 2001), 681.10.

YE IN THE MIND OF POETS FROM THE SEVENTH CENTURY AND BEYOND   155

poem, superior to the Bronze Bird tiles for many reasons—not the least of
which was that they did not carry the stench of Cao Cao:

君不見	Don't you see, sir—
銅雀臺邊多事土	There by Bronze Bird Terrace, the earth where so much happened,
2 走上觚稜蔭歌舞	And the [tiles] flew up to rooftop corners to shade songs and dances.
餘香分盡垢不除	The leftover incense was completely split yet the filth was never dissipated,
4 卻寄書林汙縑楮	Sent instead to the grove of letters to soil paper and brush.
豈如此瓦凝青膏	How can they be equal to the congealed dark paste of this tile,
6 冷面不識姦雄曹	Its cold face recognizes no treacherous usurper Cao.[83]

We have seen that the inkstones from Bronze Bird Terrace were not uniformly
described in terms of quality. Some were said to have been made of clarified
clay method; others appear rough and unable to keep a reservoir of water. In-
terestingly, the issue of quality does not seem to be a criterion in determining
authenticity, since both kinds were open to accusations of being fake, or appreciation for being real. These are questions that lie outside of purview of this
chapter but are there for future research.

But the early modern [Song through Yuan] discourse on Cao Cao and Ye
completes in some ways a full circle: from the construction of Ye and the celebration of the Cao family as its occupants it came down to a small fragment, a
handheld remnant from a troubling and complex past. By the end of the Yuan,
in the mid-fourteenth century, the major literary tropes associated with Ye had
been more or less set: it was a place of celebration, of loss, of sorrow, and of
ambiguous worth, both materially and historically. This is a fitting place to end,
with the last material fragments of that grand city.

---

83   See the poem "Instructor Qian Dongzhi Gave Me an Inkstone by Man of the Way, Lü of Ze
Prefecture; I Wrote a Long Poem for this" ("Qian Dongzhi jiaoshou hui Zezhou Lü daoren
yan wei fu changju" 錢東之教授惠澤州呂道人硯為賦長句) in Zheng Qian 鄭騫, ed.
Chen Jianzhai shiji hejiao huizhu 陳簡齋詩集合校彙注 (Taipei: Lianjing chuban shiye
gongsi, 1975), 74–75.

Conclusion

Framed against a background of the archeological and historical evidence, we have followed the shifting representation of the city of Ye and its iconic structures—particularly that of Bronze Bird Terrace—from the earliest records to the end of the Song-Yuan era. Like almost all place-based investigations, the archeology of texts also shows that the same spaces of Ye can be open to multiple interpretations, depending on time and activity. We have moved from the creation of the city as a monument to Cao Cao's political achievements to the last remaining material shards of the city—its tiles. Throughout, we have seen that nearly all of the writing about Ye is focused on Cao Cao—either as a real historical figure or as an imagined hero, traitor, or a man who lacked the resolve to carry out his destiny. But no matter how these representations of the city and of Cao Cao have changed over time, no amount of chronological distance from the founding of the city can break the inextricable link between that man and this place. Whether being praised or condemned, Cao Cao remained the vanishing point of writing about Ye—whether clearly denoted or half-hidden in the circumlocution of textual aesthetics. He may have constructed the city, but it was writers through the centuries who constantly created and recreated "the Ye of Cao Cao." Their ongoing work kept the imagined city alive, even until modern times.

Literary writing about Ye begins with poems on two of the most iconic sites—terraces and gardens—particularly the Bronze Bird Terrace. The city was founded in an era of constant warfare, but the early poems about Ye are mostly celebratory in nature, vaunting the achievement of Cao Cao in founding what was essentially a planned "imperial" city.

There are rhymed works (including *shi* and *fu*) written on command at visits to the terrace, where the audience of the poems was of course Cao Cao himself. Other poems celebrate the enjoyable moments of literati gatherings or outings to the suburban gardens, where poets celebrate the pleasures of life. Like all poems on such pleasure and friendship, there is also a deeper level of sorrow and an awareness of just how short those moments of pleasure are. The early poetry makes very effective use of situating place as a site of enjoyment within the passage of time and situating Cao Cao's achievement within the flow of history.

The next stage brought under discussion was the period after the fall of the Cao Wei and the changing political scene in Ye. In the immediate aftermath of the demise of Cao Wei, poets like the Jin official (and immigrant southerner), Lu Yun, roamed Ye. Still a functional city, although no longer a capital, its built

© KONINKLIJKE BRILL NV, LEIDEN, 2020 | DOI:10.1163/9789004420144_007

CONCLUSION

structures led him to ruminate on the forces that led to the rise and fall of the Wei and of subsequent dynasties. The grandeur of the gardens, walls, terraces, and palaces were a perfect physical and durable contrast to the rupture of dynastic changes and uncertainty of life.

But, perhaps the most important event during this period, from the literary point of view, was Cao Cao's "Testamentary Command" that Lu Ji read. As the dying warlord's vision of empire fell away and he was reduced to the adulation of the small circle of his family and his female companions, he divided up his personal property and had women perform daily tasks in his memory. Twice a day in the morning and evening, they had to make offerings to his spirit tablet in a mourning tent on top of the Bronze Bird Terrace, and twice a month they had to face his tumulus in the west and perform songs and dances atop the terrace for his deceased soul. What had been a place of celebration now became a site of lamentation for the dead. As the process dragged on (it had no specified end date), it modulated from lamentation for Cao Cao to a focus on the sorrow and grief of the performers. Several poems questioned whether or not the dead could actually hear anything in the human world.[1] These deeper questions about the possibility of postmortem consciousness inevitably led to a sense of futility over the performances and the toll they took on the lives of the living. Poets now began to consider the subjective lives of the performers, whose daily and bi-monthly execution of ever more hollow rituals led to a sense of their imprisonment in sorrow. There were many such poems, and they developed a standard set of vocabulary and images that were tied tightly to the Bronze Bird Terrace, creating what I have termed a "terrace-scape" that set a body of standard tropes. Like the performances themselves, the poems become more and more clichéd until the whole scene—its language, images, and sites—became a convertible and common metaphor that could be used allusively in any setting to denote the sorrows of an abandoned woman. From this time on, one only needed to evoke the phrase "Bronze Bird" in the right context, and it brought to the fore a whole complex of sentiments about a woman abandoned after service to her lord.

Finally, there were the shards of tile from Ye—most importantly those from the Bronze Bird Terrace—that were carved into inkstones. The considerable body of text on these inkstones can be seen to fall into at least two major categories. The first group is concerned with the authenticity of the pieces. There

---

1   Stephen Bokenkamp points out that these doubts began with the Cao family itself. See his discussion on Cao family's support of "austere burials" in Stephen R. Bokenkamp, *Ancestors and Anxiety: Daosim and the Birth of Rebirth in China* (Berkeley: University of California Press, 2007), 54–56.

are also two different takes on this issue. According to the first, "men of ink" (*moke* 墨客) were not as interested in the inkstones as artifacts so much as they appreciated the inkstone's ability to produce a dense and lustrous ink (*famo* 發墨); their primary concern was the utility of these objects, although they were interested in their history as well. They were of course happy to possess the tiles, but their evaluation was driven by a larger argument about the quality of tiles (including both Ye tiles and the clarified clay tiles of Shanxi) and their superiority to stone for use as inkstones. A subset of this group, as exemplified by Su Shi, saw in Cao Cao's "Testamentary Command" the complete failure of will, a retreat to his family in weakness that belied his bravado. As Su remarked, a great hero will go to his death laughing, but Cao Cao went meekly to his, caring in the end only about his immediate family and his women. He showed his real character "only at his death."

The second group that is interested in authenticity is comprised of those literati writers sometimes disparagingly called "dilettantes," who were more interested in the monetary value of the artifact and the social capital that derived from owning it than in its use. This group came under fire particularly because their desire to possess the inkstone fostered a kind of historical amnesia, in which the cruelty of its creator, Cao Cao, was suppressed or pushed out of memory.

Certainly, by this period, there was a highly ambivalent attitude about Cao Cao. Everyone seems to have agreed on his denotation as a treacherous pretender or treacherous usurper (*jianxiong* 姦雄), but some felt he was completely open about his ambition. For the most part, though, he was a target of vituperation, someone who some writers wanted to rip apart so that, as He Wei remarked above, "his shoulders and ankles would be in different places." To covet these tiles at the expense of forgetting the lessons of history was unforgivable.

Postscript: Beyond the Song-Yuan Era

Interest in the city of Ye and its tiles certainly did not stop with the discussions of the Song-Yuan era. There are many poems beyond the scope of this book that continue in the same vein: for instance, the prominent Qing poet Chen Weisong's 陳維崧 (1625–1682) "*Fu* on the Tongque Tile" ("Tongque wa fu" 銅雀瓦賦).

	魏帳未懸	When the Wei [mourning] tent was not yet hung,
2	鄴臺初築	The Ye terraces were first constructed.
	複道袤延	The double-deck walkways stretched on and on,
4	綺窻交屬	Windows screened with silk were crosshatched with stiles.
	雕甍繡棟	The carved ridgepoles and embroidered ridge beams,
6	矗十里之粧樓	Seraglio that towered ten *li* high.
	金埒銅溝	The "golden walls" and bronze moats,[1]
8	響六宮之脂盝	Echoed sounds of makeup boxes from the six palaces.[2]
	庭棲比翼之禽	In the courtyard perched birds that flew wing to wing,[3]
10	戶種相思之木	At the gates, they planted lovelorn trees.[4]

---

1   It is said in Liu Yiqing's 劉義慶 (403–444) *Shishuo xinyu* 世說新語 that the Western Jin 西晉 (265–317) dynasty general, Wang Ji 王濟 (n.d.), enjoyed horseback riding and archery. When he resided at Mount Beimang 北邙山 (near modern day Luoyang), he built enclosed fences with braids of coins to keep his horses. Locals called these fences "golden walls" (*jinlie* 金埒) or "golden moats" (*jingou* 金溝). See the story in Yang Yong 楊勇, *Shishuo xinyu jiaojian* 世說新語校箋 (Taipei: Letian chuban she, 1973), 30.662.

2   These were the palace-halls that housed court ladies. For example in Bai Juyi's 白居易 "The Song of Everlasting Sorrow" ("Changhen ge" 長恨歌), it reads, "One smile from her turning glance, a hundred enchantments are born, / All the powder and kohl of six palaces become colorless" (回眸一笑百媚生，六宮粉黛無顏色). See the text of this poem in *Quan Tang shi* 全唐詩, 435.4816–4820. Here the "echoed sound" is from the makeup boxes opened and closed.

3   *Erya* 爾雅 explains the birds that fly wing to wing (or linked-wing birds) as "The southern quadrant has linked-wing birds. If they are not conjoined, they do not fly. Their names are called *jianjian*" (南方有比翼鳥焉，不比不飛，其名謂之鶼鶼). See Guo Pu 郭璞 (276–324) and Xing Bing 邢昺 (932–1010), comm. and ann., *Erya zhushu* 爾雅注疏, in *Shisan jing zhushu fu jiaokan ji* 十三經注疏附校勘記, ed. Ruan Yuan 阮元 (1764–1849), 8 vols., (Taipei: Yiwen yingshu guan, 1982), 8: 7.5b. Also, Cao Zhi has a couplet "I want to become linked-wing birds, / Stretching our quills, rising and soaring high" (願爲比翼鳥，施翮起高翔). See this couplet in Cao Zhi's "Seeing off the Yings" ("Song Yingshi" 送應氏) in Robert Joe Cutter, "Cao Zhi (192–232) and His Poetry" (PhD diss., University of Washington, 1983), 223.

4   It is said that Lord Kang of Song 宋康王 (r. 318–286 BCE) forcefully appropriated the wife of his retainer Han Ping 韓憑 (n.d.) as his concubine. Han Ping and his wife committed suicide one after another. Angered, Lord Kang ordered them buried apart so that they would be separated for all eternity. But, overnight, a catalpa began to sprout on the top of each tomb. Within ten days, the roots and branches of the two trees became intertwined. People felt sorry for the

	駊娑前殿	Sasuo, the front hall [of the Han],[5]
12	遜彼清陰	Yielded to the clear shade [of the Bronze Bird].
	柏梁舊寢	Boliang, the old sleeping chamber,[6]
14	啞其局蹙	Laughed at its [own] small space [in comparison].
	無何而	In no time at all then—
	墓田渺渺	The burial field is remote and indistinct,
16	風雨離離	And wind and rain came together.
	泣三千之粉黛	To weep for the three thousand who were powdered and rouged,[7]
18	傷二八之蛾眉	And feel pain for those moth brows of sixteen years of age.
	雖有	Although [he] had—
	彈棊愛子	A beloved son who played chess,[8]
20	傅粉佳兒	A fine boy who powdered [his face],[9]
	分香妙伎	Alluring entertainers to split the incense,
22	賣履妖姬	And enchanting concubines to sell shoes;
	與夫	Together with those—

---

couple and called the two trees "lovelorn trees" (*xiangsi shu* 相思樹). See the story in Gan Bao 干寶 (ca. 286–336), *Sou shen ji* 搜神記 (Beijing: Zhonghua shuju, 1979), 11.141–142.

5   This is the Sasuo Palace mentioned in the "*Fu* on the Western Capital" ("Xidu fu" 西都賦) of Ban Gu's 班固 (32–92) "*Fu* on the Two Capitals" ("Liangdu fu" 兩都賦)—"One could cross Relaxation Hall and come out at Rapid Gallop, / Or enter Linden Hall to reach Celestial Beams" (經駘盪而出駊娑，洞枌詣以與天梁). David R. Knechtges, *Wen xuan, Or Selections of Refined Literature*, vol. 1, *Rhapsodies on Metropolises and Capitals* (Princeton: Princeton University Press, 1996), 1:133.

6   This is the Boliang Terrace 柏樑臺. It was built in the spring of the second year of Yuanding 元鼎 [October 26, 115–November 13, 114 BCE] reign of Emperor Wu of the Western Han 西漢 武帝 (r. 140–86 BCE). Ban Gu 班固 (32–92), *Han shu* 漢書 (Beijing: Zhonghua shuju, 1962), 6.182.

7   Three thousand is a general number to describe the large number of women in the imperial harem.

8   This is Cao Pi 曹丕 (187–226). A commentary regarding board games in the *Shishuo xinyu* quoted Cao Pi's preface in his *Standard Treatises* (*Dianlun* 典論) where he said, "I am seldom pleased with gaming and playing, it is only in playing chess that I have exhausted some its marvelousness" (戲弄之事少所喜，惟彈棋略盡其妙). See Yang Yong, *Shishuo xinyu jiao-jian*, 21.537n2.

9   This is He Yan 何晏 (d. 249). Cao Cao adopted He Yan when he took in He's widowed mother. It was said that "He Yan's nature is narcissistic, [a container of] finishing powder never left his hands wherever he went, and he always checked out his shadow whenever he was walking" (晏性自喜，動靜粉白不去手，行步顧影). See Chen Shou 陳壽 (233–297), *San guo zhi* 三國志 (Beijing: Zhonghua shuju, 1959), 9.292n1.

POSTSCRIPT: BEYOND THE SONG-YUAN ERA

楊林之羅襪	The "gauze slippers" from the "poplar groves,"[10]
24 西陵之玉肌	The jade-like skin at the Western Tumulus.
無不	All of it—
煙消灰滅	Disappeared like smoke and died away like ash,
26 矢激星移	As fast as arrows fly and stars move.
何暇問	What leisure was there to ask about,
黃初之軼事	The gathered anecdotes of Huangchu reign,[11]
28 銅雀之荒基也哉	Or the overgrown foundations of the Bronze Bird?
春草黃復綠	Spring grass turns yellow and then green again,
30 漳流去不還	Zhang River waters flow away never to return.
只有千年遺瓦在	All that is left are leftover tiles from a thousand years ago,
32 曾向高臺覆玉顏	That once faced the tall terrace and sheltered those jade-like faces.[12]

Certainly, this is a more neutral poem than those written in the Song. But again, it stresses how nature's power constantly overwhelms human endeavor, as the regenerative power of vegetative growth reclaims the grandest of man's structures. But when Chen Weisong turns to a discussion of how the march of time turned all of Ye and its inhabitants to dust and ash, he also implies that the flow of history—the course of which can never be reversed—swallowed the Cao Wei so quickly that there was no time to gather information or ask questions about its own founding. Founded in turmoil and soon replaced, there was no "leisure," no rest to gather stories about it—all that is left is the mute witness of the tiles. Here the linkage to the past is much more sentimental. It is also much more in the mode of traditional *yongwu* poems where an object, while it retains its linkage to a specific era and a specific site, calls to mind a more generalized feeling about the erasure of the past. In this meditation on the object, the issue of text is brought to the fore as a deficiency in the case of the Cao Wei. Without the proper historical materials to create its own place in history, the dynasty will remain only in the "overgrown foundations" of the Bronze Bird Terrace and in the

---

10 This refers to Cao Zhi's *Fu on the Luo River Goddess* ("Luo shen fu" 洛神賦). In it Cao Zhi writes, "Ambling about the poplar groves, / I wander my gaze over the Luo River" (容與乎楊林，流眄乎洛川) and "Crossing the billows, she walks with dainty steps, / Her gauze slippers stirring up dust" (陵波微步，羅襪生塵). The English translation of these two couplets is from David R. Knechtges, trans., *Wen xuan, Or Selections of Refined Literature*, vol. 3, *Rhapsodies on Natural Phenomena, Birds and Animals, Aspirations and Feelings, Sorrowful Laments, Literature, Music, and Passions* (Princeton: Princeton University Press, 1996), 3:357 and 363.

11 Huangchu was Emperor Wen of Wei 魏文帝 (r. 220–226), Cao Pi's, reign title. It ran from December 11, 220 to June 28, 226.

12 The text of this *fu*-poem is in *Chen Jiantao siliu* 陳檢討四六 (*SKQS* ed.), 1.22a–23b.

162   POSTSCRIPT: BEYOND THE SONG-YUAN ERA

occasional tile that comes into the hands of a poet. The poet, living in an age that was conscious of a number of long-lived dynasties and an abundance of historical source materials, wonders not only about how much more there was to know about the Cao Wei but also about other dynasties as well in the near four hundred years of chaos and contention Ye witnessed until the founding of the Sui.

During later dynasties, there are also works by poets who visited the ruined city and were moved to meditate on the past. These trips may have been the result of a designated route or a chance opportunity to pass by the ruins on a journey to somewhere else. One should always hold out the possibility too that some of these might have been imagined journeys stimulated by reading other then-current works on the city of Ye or the poetic traces of the past. The number of these works is very substantial. Moreover, it seems that the availability increases with the actual chronological distance from the lived city. Whether an actual physical or mental journey to Ye, the city becomes what we might call a "place metaphor." That is, it provided a space in which poets see in the city an analogy to their own circumstances; alternatively, it was concrete place to begin a contemplation of the past. In works that utilize a place metaphor, as David Knechtges puts is, a poet "reflects on the scene and is moved by the thought that what had once been a place of glory and prosperity has now become a site of decay and destruction. The poet more importantly reflects on the past and sees in it a lesson or mirror to the present."[13] Just as the reception history of poets over time is fertile ground for the study of poetics, the city as a site is amenable to such an approach since it becomes in each later instance a cultural memory that can be deployed in situations contemporary to the writer in order to make a powerful point about his own present. While there is not space here to touch on many of these poets, I would like to present a few here as excellent examples of the afterlife of Ye. For the first poem, we must go back in time to Duan Junyan 段君彥 (fl. 581–619), who wrote, "A Poem on Stopping by the Former Ye" ("Guo gu Ye shi" 過故鄴詩).

玉馬芝蘭北	To the north of the "Jade Horse" and the "Iris and Orchid,"[14]
金鳳鼓山東	To the east of the "Golden Phoenix" and the "Mount Drum."[15]

2

---

13   "Ruin and Remembrance in Classical Chinese Literature: The '*Fu* on the Ruined City' by Bao zhao," in *Reading Medieval Chinese Poetry: Text, Context, and Culture*, ed. Paul W. Kroll (Leiden: Brill, 2015), 55.

14   Sima Teng 司馬騰 (d. 307) once dug up a jade horse in the snow in Zhending 真定 (near modern day Shijiazhuang) on his way to his new post in Ye. Fang Xuanling 房玄齡 (579–648) and others, *Jin shu* 晉書 (Beijing: Zhonghua shuju, 1974), 28.854.

15   The Bronze Bird Terrace, along with other two terraces in Ye, was renovated and renamed as the "Golden Phoenix" by Emperor Wenxuan 文宣帝 (550–559) of the Northern Qi in the eighth month of the ninth year of the Tianbao 天保 reign [September 11, 557–October 10, 557]. See Li Baiyao 李百藥 (565–648), comp., *Bei Qi shu* 北齊書 (Beijing: Zhonghua shuju, 1972), 4.65. Also there is statement saying that Shi Hu renamed the Golden Tiger Terrace to be Golden Phoenix, see Lu Hui 陸翽 (fl. 317), *Yezhong ji* 鄴中記 (*SKQS* ed.), 3a.

POSTSCRIPT: BEYOND THE SONG-YUAN ERA

	舊國千門廢	A "thousand gates" of the old city are [all] abandoned,
4	荒壘四郊通	The decrepit ramparts are open to all four outskirts.
	深潭直有菊	A once deep pool now has only chrysanthemums,
6	涸井半生桐	At a dried up well, a half-alive paulownia tree.
	粉落粧樓毀	Powder fallen away, seraglio destroyed,
8	塵飛歌殿空	Dust flies, the singing hall is empty.[16]
	雖臨玄武觀	Although I approach the Xuanwu watchtower,
10	不識紫微宮	I cannot recognize the Ziwei Palace.[17]
	年代俄成昔	Those eras have turned suddenly into the ancient past—
12	唯餘風月同	And only the wind and moon are still the same.[18]

This poem was probably written after the city had been destroyed by Yang Jian, and we may see this as a lament for the city itself. Its old walls and gates, known now only through text, are crumbled, the ponds of the gardens and moat of the city are dried up, growing chrysanthemum instead of lotus or water lilies, and the dry well holds nothing but a half-alive paulownia tree. Ye was not yet an ancient ruin, but the poet remarks how the physical destruction now moves knowledge of the city back into time, since the only thing remaining now are the imagined incidents of the past. The phrase "years and generations," which I have translated above as "era," is the term *niandai* 年代. This term is often used to refer to a particular historical period, "those years in the past" (as in modern *neige niandai* 那個年代), which are no longer current in a physical or material form, but have now receded into the antiquity of book learning.

In his commentary to the Mount Bear 熊山 cave in the Central Mountains section (*Zhongshan jing* 中山經) of the *Shanhai jing* 山海經, Guo Pu's 郭璞 (276–324) states there was a Mount Drum to the northwest of Ye. In the foothills, there was a likeness of a stone drum hanging on the side of the mountain. When it made a sound, military affairs happened (今鄴西北有鼓山。下有石鼓象懸著山旁，鳴則有軍事). See Guo Pu, ed., *Shanhai jing*, (rpt. Shanghai: Shanghai guji chuban she, 1991), 5.24b.

16   This is a muted reference to the common phrase in antiquity used to describe clear and beautiful singing, "to shake the dust from the roofbeams" (*dong liang chen* 動梁塵) or "make the dust on the roofbeams fly" (*liang chen fei* 梁塵飛). See Ch. 3.

17   Guo Jiqiao states that this line reveals the mystery about where the palace complex of Ye was placed in a position in which "palace complex of Ye 'reflected the image of Heaven and Earth and simulated the Ziwei constellation so that Heaven and Human are united as one'" (鄴城宮城「象法天地，模擬紫微宮，天人合一」). See Guo's "Yecheng—Sanguo gudi liuchao gudu" 鄴城—三國故地六朝古都, *Hebei ribao* 河北日報, March 15, 2013, <http://theory.people.com.cn/BIG5/n/2013/0315/c40531-20801980.html> (accessed July 11, 2015). Also see Edward H. Schafer's discussion on the idea of "concrete objects or whole scenes are transformed into visions of their astral or celestial 'counterparts'" in his, "Hallucinations and Epiphanies in T'ang Poetry," *Journal of the American Oriental Society*, 104, no. 4 (Oct.–Dec., 1984): 757–760.

18   Lu Qinli 逯欽立, ed., *Xian Qin Han Wei Jin Nan Bei chao shi* 先秦漢魏晉南北朝詩 (Beijing: Zhonghua shuju chuban she, 1983), 3: 2732.

A nice comparison to this poem by the mostly unknown Duan Junyan is a set of two *ci* lyrics, written by Yuan Haowen 元好問 (1190–1257), probably in the year 1253, nearly twenty years after the fall of the Jin 金 (1115–1234) capital to the Mongols. Yuan had lived through the siege of Kaifeng, a bitter and traumatic experience. He is best known for his contributions to Jin historiography and his poems on the Mongol conquest, called "poems on loss and chaos" (*sangluan shi* 喪亂詩). The *ci*-poem, written to the lyric pattern *Mulan hua man* 木蘭花慢, is entitled, "Roaming the Three Terraces" ("You santai" 遊三臺).

	擁岩岩雙闕	Embracing the two pylons far off in the distance,
2	龍虎氣	Is the aura of dragon and tiger,
	鬱崢嶸	Engulfing them, rising steeply aloft.[19]
4	想暮雨珠簾	I think about the "evening rain," the "beaded curtain,"
	秋香桂樹	"Autumn's fragrance" and the "osmanthus tree,"
6	指顧臺城	And point and glance at the old capital.
	臺城	The old capital—
8	為誰西望	For whom do they gaze westward?
	但哀弦	Simply grieve over the strings—
10	淒斷似平生	That break desolately, just as they do in one's own life.
	只道江山如畫	Simply say, "The [Yangzi] River and mountains are like a painting,"
12	爭教天地無情	And thus struggle to make heaven and earth be without feelings.[20]
	風雲奔走十年兵	In tumult of wind and cloud he rushed about in ten years of battle,[21]
14	慘澹入經營	"Struggled" when entering the phase of "planning and execution" [of the city].[22]

19　The aura of dragon and tiger is a metaphor for the aura of the Son of Heaven. Fan Zeng 范增 (277–204 BCE) once tried to exhort Xiang Yu 項羽 (232–202 BCE) to consider the dangers posed by Liu Bang 劉邦 (256–195 BCE). Fan said, "I had someone examine his aura. It is all dragons and tigers and completes the five colors. This is the aura of the Son of Heaven" (吾令人望其氣，皆為龍虎成五采，此天子氣也). See Sima Qian 司馬遷 (145–ca. 86 BCE), *Shi ji* 史記 (Beijing: Zhonghua shuju, 1959), 7.311.

20　Cf. "In the end heaven and earth have no feelings at all" (天地終無情) in Du Fu's 杜甫 (712–770) "The Clerk of Xin'an" ("Xin'an li" 新安吏). *Quan Tang shi*, 217.2282–2283.

21　Cao Cao captured Ye in 204 and was enfeoffed as "King of Wei" (Wei *wang* 魏王) in 213. In Ye, he established ancestral temples for rulers of Wei as well as state sacrificial altars. In this ten year period, Ye grew to be his seat of power—a "kingly city" (*wangcheng* 王城).

22　The words *candan jingying* 慘淡經營 are from the line, "Brooding art-thoughts struggled there, between plan and execution" (意匠慘淡經營中), of Du Fu's poem "Song of a Painting" ("Danqing yin: Zeng Cao jiangjun Ba" 丹青引贈曹將軍霸). The translation of

POSTSCRIPT: BEYOND THE SONG-YUAN ERA

	問對酒當歌	I ask, "If 'facing the ale one should sing,'
16	曹侯墓上	Then, on the tomb of Marquis Cao,[23]
	何用虛名	Why use an empty title?"
18	青青故都喬木	Green, so green, the lofty trees in this ancient capital—
	恨西陵	Disappointed there in the Western Tumulus,
20	遺恨幾時平	When will his lingering regret be soothed?
	安得參軍健筆	Where can I get the strong pen of the Adjutant,[24]
22	為君重賦蕪城	To compose a *fu*-poem on the "Weed-covered city" for you, sir.

The first lyric begins with a distant view of the old capital over which the aura of the Son of Heaven still rises, obscuring the imagined site of ancient capital. Drawing on the age-old belief that the geomantic nature of a particular place makes it particularly suitable for an emperor to be resident there, Yuan Haowen creates here an imaginary vision of a once powerful place. But, his perception and the memory it stirs are soon replaced by his imagination; the poet conjures in his mind not a vision of the old capital but earlier texts on men of power and their fall. For instance, his references to the "evening rain" (*muyu* 暮雨) and "beaded curtain" (*zhulian* 珠簾) in line four draw directly on Wang Bo's 王勃 (649–675) poem, "Gallery of Prince Teng" ("Teng wang ge" 滕王閣), which is prefaced by a longer prose passage, itself written in heavily metrical parallel prose. Wang's piece describes a gallery built by Tang Taizong's 唐太宗 (r. 626– 649) younger brother, Prince Teng (Li Yuanying 李元嬰 [d.684]), to house his gatherings and celebrations after he was assigned to Hong Prefecture 洪州 (near modern day Nanchang 南昌, Jiangxi 江西). The poem itself reads:

---

    this line is from Stephen Owen, *An Anthology of Chinese Literature*, 429–31. *Quan Tang shi*, 220.2322–2323.

23   Cao Cao was enfeoffed as "Marquis of Wuping" (Wuping *hou* 武平侯) in the first year of Jian'an reign (196). See Chen, *San guo zhi*, 1.13.

24   Here the Adjutant is Bao Zhao 鮑照 (ca. 415–466) and the "weed-covered city" in the following line refers to his "*Fu* on the Weed-covered City" ("Wu cheng fu" 蕪城賦). Bao Zhao, styled Mingyuan 明遠, a native of Donghai 東海 (modern day Lianshui 漣水 in Jiangsu 江蘇). He held position of adjutant (*canjun* 參軍) when Liu Zixu 劉子頊 (d. 466) governed Jingzhou 荊州 (could be in modern day Hubei 湖北). "*Fu* on the Weed-covered City" is one of Bao's most widely known works. The weed-covered city, Guangling 廣陵 (modern day Jiangdu 江都 Jiangsu), was established as a major city by feudal lord Wu of Former Han 西漢吳王, Liu Pi 劉濞 (215–154 BCE). A few centuries later, the city was ruined by war-fires. In his work Bao Zhao illustrates the strong contrast between the glamour of the city during its builder's lifetime and the later ruins. The title of this work is also translated as "Rhapsody on the Ruined City." See David R. Knechtges, trans., *Wen xuan, Or Selections of Refined Literature*, vol. 2, *Rhapsodies on Sacrifices, Hunting, Travel, Sightseeing, Palaces and Halls, Rivers and Seas* (Princeton: Princeton University Press, 1987), 253– 262; and also see his "Ruin and Remembrance in Classical Chinese Literature," 55–89.

滕王高閣臨江渚	Prince Teng's high gallery overlooks the Gan riverside,
2　佩玉鳴鸞罷歌舞	Pendant jades and "chirping *luan*-bird" bells stop singing and dancing.
畫棟朝飛南浦雲	Morning comes, the painted beams seem to fly toward the clouds on the south shore,
4　珠簾暮捲西山雨	And in the evening, the beaded curtains roll up the rain of the west mountain.
閑雲潭影日悠悠	Lazy clouds cast shadows on the lake—the day stretches on and on,[25]
6　物換星移幾度秋	Objects change and stars shift in their course—how many autumns has it been?
閣中帝子今何在	And the son of the emperor that was in the gallery—where is he now?
8　檻外長江空自流	Beyond the balustrade, a long river flows aimlessly alone.[26]

What Yuan captures in his gesture to Wang Bo is the way the earlier poet used metaphors of ending (the late evening) and tears (falling rain and the beads) to shift the reader's perception from the objective, a description of place, to a subjective state of mind, a sense of sorrow over ceaseless change and lamentation for things lost in the past. This is an excellent example of the process of "poetic traces" that was discussed above and of how adaptation of those traces allows a seamless interweaving of three moments in time. That is, the sense of ending and grief felt in Wang Bo's lines can be read as a later poetic trace from earlier writing about lamentation over Cao Cao's capital. Moreover, Wang's poem (and its poetic traces from the past) echo in Yuan's own thoughts about the end of the Jin. An imagined place—the Gallery in Nanchang, the old capital of Ye, and the lost Jin capital of Kaifeng—are all devoid of the powerful princes and rulers that once had inhabited them.[27]

In line five, Yuan Haowen continues to find in text parallels for dynastic fall and for landscapes of capitals in decay. This time it is to a famous poem by Li He 李賀 (790–816) "A Song on Golden Bronze Transcendent Taking Leave of the Han" ("Jintong xianren ci Han ge" 金銅仙人辭漢歌). Yuan uses allusions to this song twice, once here and once below in the second lyric. Like the poem he used in line four, this one is about loss. In the preface to the poem Li He wrote:

> In the eighth month of the first year of the Qinglong reign [September 22–October 20, 233], Emperor Ming [of the Wei] ordered his palace officials to send a cart westward to take the [statue of] "Immortal Holding the Dew Plate" because he

---

25　There is a nice double-meaning to this line, which can also be understood, as "those days are far away now."

26　*Quan Tang shi*, 55.672–673.

27　Cf. Timothy Wai-Keung Chan, "Dedication and Identification in Wang Bo's Compositions on the Gallery of Prince Teng," *Monumenta Serica*, vol. 50 (2002), pp. 215–255; and Stephen Owen, *The Late Tang: Chinese Poetry of the Mid-Ninth Century (827–860)* (Cambridge, MA: Harvard University Asia Center, 2006), 192–193.

POSTSCRIPT: BEYOND THE SONG-YUAN ERA

wanted to erect it at [his own] front palace hall.[28] Once the palace officials had snapped off the plate, and the immortal was about to be loaded onto the cart, it wept copiously. Descendant of the Tang royal house, I, Li Changji, compose "A Song on Golden Bronze Transcendent Taking Leave of the Han."[29]

明帝青龍元年八月，詔宮官牽車西取漢孝武捧露盤仙人，欲立置前殿。宮官既拆盤，仙人臨載乃潸然淚下。唐諸王孫李長吉遂作《金銅仙人辭漢歌》.

Li He's poem itself is a masterpiece of sentiment about the rise and fall of dynasties and the sense of displacement, of moving from one place to another under a new ruler.

	茂陵劉郎秋風客	Master Liu of Tumulus Mao, a traveler on the autumn wind,[30]
2	夜聞馬嘶曉無跡	At night, I hear his horse whinny, in the dawn there is no trace.
	畫欄桂樹懸秋香	At the painted railing an osmanthus suspends its autumn fragrance,
4	三十六宮土花碧	In all thirty-six palaces the "flowers on the ground" are bluish-green.[31]
	魏官牽車指千里	A Wei official took a cart, and pointed to a thousand *li* away,[32]
6	東關酸風射眸子	The biting wind at the Eastern Pass penetrated the eyes.
	空將漢月出宮門	For nothing did they bear the moon of Han out of the palace gate,[33]

---

28   Emperor Ming of Wei is Cao Rui 曹叡 (206–239), who was Cao Cao's grandson and reigned from 226 to 239. The statue itself was ordered constructed by Emperor Wu of Han 漢武帝 (r. 141–87 BCE) and placed in front of the Jianzhang Palace 建章宮.

29   For another translation, see A.C. Graham, *Poems of the Late Tang* (New York: New York Review of Books, 1965), 106–108.

30   This is the tumulus of Emperor Wu of the Han, the poet of "Lyrics on the Autumn Wind." (see Ch. 2).

31   While the term has a Daoist image from the Shangqing 上清 scriptures, in this context, "thirty-six palaces" is a generic counter for palace buildings, particularly those filled with the emperor's women.

32   This is the distance from Chang'an to Luoyang, where the statue was being moved.

33   This is the bronze dew-catching plate. Along with the statue itself, it proved too difficult to be moved and both were abandoned at the eastern gate of Chang'an. According to Pei Songzhi's 裴松之 (372–451) commentary [quoting the *Wei lue* 魏略], in the process of removing it from the palace, the plate snapped and the attached bronze transcendent statue was too heavy to be moved; consequently, it was left behind at the east city gate— Bacheng Gate 霸城—of Chang'an. Here Li He imagines the journey. See Pei's commentary in Chen, *San guo zhi*, 3.110.

8	憶君清淚如鉛水	Thinking of its lord, its fresh tears were like molten lead.
	衰蘭送客咸陽道	Withered orchids send the traveler off on the Xianyang road,[34]
10	天若有情天亦老	If heaven had feelings, heaven would also grow old.
	攜盤獨出月荒涼	Carrying the plate out alone, the moon is bleak and chill,
12	渭城已遠波聲小	The city by the River Wei [Chang'an] already distant, the sounds of the waves decay.[35]

Li He's poem is woven like a slender thread through the tapestry of Yuan's piece. By simply evoking one line from Li's poem (line three), Yuan brings the entirety of that piece to the reader's mind. The way that the Tang poem relates the disappearance of iconic features from Chang'an of the Han dynasty, the useless vanity of human desire, and the belief in the endlessness of one's creations (whether material or activity) anticipates Yuan's discussion of the Bronze Bird Terrace. Li He's line ten can also be read against lines eight through ten of Yuan Haowen's poem, where Yuan acknowledges that the landscape itself not just a place or a site, but something that has absorbed and contains within it the feeling and sentiment of those who have lived within its spaces.

Lines six through ten of Yuan's poem then evoke Cao Cao's testamentary command and the sadness of the performers atop the terrace. Yuan probably uses the term *taicheng* 臺城 in the first instance in its then-contemporary meaning of "a capital city," although it certainly alludes to the city wall, where the performers gazed off to the west on Bronze Bird Terrace. There is a wonderful ambiguity about these lines: is it the persona in the poem or the performer who is gazing? In either case, as readers have seen above, there is a definite understanding that there really is no person left to see. The next line about the broken strings, which the reader will remember from the terrace-scape poems, marvelously wraps past and present together. In the first instance, we may understand a reference to the strings of the instruments used by Cao's performers that snapped in cold desolation as he was lost; however, the phrase "just as in one's own life" (*si pingsheng* 似平生), is perhaps also a reference to the poetic persona's present. The term certainly reflects the common use of the metaphor of a snapped string of a musical instrument that can never, no matter how hard one tries, be made whole again. Here again, is an ambiguity: who grieves over the snapped strings: Cao Cao, the performers, or the poet? Yuan Haowen perhaps is reading this poem here retrospectively from his own feelings—what is normally read as a cliché metaphor for one's personal feelings of heartbreak can be renewed by reading back to the sorrow of that historical moment through the experiences of one's own life. This makes the contact

---

34 This refers to the name of the road, not the direction in which they were traveling.

35 *Quan Tang shi*, 391.4403.

between past and present real: an understanding that not only do we remember the past, but our personal experiences allow us to reread the past in such a way that we can emotionally connect with it.

In the final two lines of the first stanza, Yuan cites lines from Su Shi's 蘇軾 (1037–1101) famous meditation on the Red Cliff.[36] The word for word quote in line eleven invariably evokes the unspoken matching line of the original poem about the disappearance of heroes, "The [Yangzi] River and mountains like a painting, / How many heroes were there in that time?" (江山如畫，一時多少豪傑). Here, Yuan uses it in a more direct way to refer specifically to Cao Cao. The imperative "just say" (*zhidao* 只道), however carries forward the meaning of the first half of Su Shi's line. If one only says that mountains and rivers are like a painting, one objectifies the natural world and robs the landscape of any sense of the human feelings and sentiments that its spaces now possess as a part of their historical meaning. In Su's original, his matching line to "River and mountains like a painting"—"How many heroes were there in that time"—brings sorrow back into the equation. Landscape, natural or built, becomes not simply an objective background to human activity but also a fertile site of history and sentiment. Yuan is aware that place is not just a site that disappears under nature's reclamation, but also a space in which activity creates significant moments of remembrance and historical meaning that neither nature nor time can erase.

The second stanza returns to the immediate history of Ye, recounting Cao Cao's ten years occupation of the city before he was granted his title as King of Wei. As the poet did in the first stanza ("I think" [*xiang* 想] in line four), Yuan Haowen breaks the third person description of the first lines by introducing a direct question, "I ask" (*wen* 問) in line fifteen. There, the poet asks primarily two questions. First, he asks, "If one believes human life should be lived in enjoyment in the face of death, why were you [Cao Cao] obsessed with making your name?" And a second, "Why did you turn your back on the Han?" To make his point, Yuan cites two famous pieces from Cao Cao, the first is Cao's ballad "Short Song" ("Duange xing" 短歌行) and the second from a command in which Cao states his personal ambition. The first two stanzas of the "Short Song" read:

對酒當歌	Facing ale, one should sing,
人生幾何	How long is a man's life?
譬如朝露	It is like the morning dew,
去日苦多	I find it painful so many days are gone.
慨當以慷	These strong feelings should be fervent,

36 This is from Su's "The Charms of Nian-nu: Meditation on the Past at Red Cliff" ("Nian-nu jiao: Chi bi huaigu" 念奴嬌赤壁懷古). Cf. Stephen Owen's translation of this verse in his, *An Anthology of Chinese Literature: Beginnings to 1911* (New York: W. W. Norton & Company, Inc., 1996), 579–80.

6	憂思難忘	For anxious thoughts are hard to lay aside.
	何以解憂	What shall I use to release my anxiety?
8	唯有杜康	There is only [the ale of] Du Kang![37]

Yuan immediately contrasts the message addressed in these lines with another quote from Cao Cao's own statement about his personal ambition.

> Later I was enlisted as Chief Commandant and promoted to become a Commandant of Control Army. My intention accordingly changed to desire to capture traitors and establish merit for the state and clan [of Han]. I desired to be enfeoffed with a feudal rank and be made the General of the Army that Campaigns Westward, so that later my grave could be inscribed "The Tomb of Marquis Cao, Former General of the Army that Campaigns Westward of the Han." This was my ambition.

> 後徵為都尉，遷典軍校尉，意遂更欲為國家討賊立功，欲望封侯作徵西將軍，然後題墓道言「漢故徵西將軍曹侯之墓」此其志也.[38]

So, Yuan faults Cao Cao by using these citations, asking why he did not continue to make his career as a great general of the Han, earning a place in history that would have carried his name through the ages as a hero, rather than a dishonorable traitor. Yuan follows this in line eighteen by describing the trees on Cao's tumulus, now grown to mighty height. There is also an implicit criticism here as well. The term "lofty trees" (*qiaomu* 喬木), inextricably tied to Mencius who pointed out to King Xuan of Qi 齊宣王 (ca. 350–301 BCE) that he had no loyal ministers, "That which is called 'a state of long endurance' is not called that way because it has lofty trees, it is called that because there are hereditary ministers in it" (所謂故國者，非謂有喬木之謂也，有世臣之謂也).[39] Here of course, it is used with irony. Cao's short-lived dynasty left tall trees on

---

37   See the text of this verse in Lu, *Xian Qin Han Wei Jin Nan Bei chao shi*, 1:1.349. For Stephen Owen's translation see his *The Making of Early Chinese Classical Poetry* (Cambridge, MA: Harvard University Asia Center, 2006), 197 and *An Anthology of Chinese Literature*, 280–281. Cf. Paul W. Kroll, "Portraits of Ts'ao Ts'ao" (PhD diss., University of Michigan, 1976), 87–88; and Ding Xiang Warner, *A Wild Deer Amid Soaring Phoenixes: The Opposition Poetics of Wang Ji* (Honolulu: University of Hawai'i Press, 2003), 93.

38   This text is found, cited by Pei Songzhi in his commentary to the *Wei shu* 魏書, in *Wei Wu gushi* 魏武故事, which states that Cao Cao issued this command on the *jihai* 己亥 day of the twelfth month in the fifteenth year of Jian'an [January 3–31, 211. *There was no *jihai* in this particular month]. See Chen, *San guo zhi*, 1.32n1. Cf. Paul Kroll's translation of the complete text and dating of this command in his dissertation, "Portraits of Ts'ao Ts'ao," 9–14 and 36, n47. This text is also known as "Written from Rang County, Clarifying My Own Ambitions" ("Rangxian ziming benzhi ling" 讓縣自明本志令). See Cao Cao, *Cao Cao ji* 曹操集 (Beijing: Zhonghua shuju, 1959), 2.41–43.

39   *Mencius* 孟子, I.B.7.

POSTSCRIPT: BEYOND THE SONG-YUAN ERA

his grave, but not a line of strong progeny to carry on the state. And Cao Cao lies disappointed in his tumulus, there to eternally embrace his lingering regret. In typically classical Chinese way, by asking "when" (*jishi* 幾時) rhetorically, Yuan turns the sentence "When will his lingering regret be soothed?" (遺恨幾時平) into a strong statement implying a negative answer—never. Yuan Haowen hopes to soothe Cao Cao by writing a poem for him that would be the equal of the famous "*Fu* on the Weed-covered City" by Bao Zhao, thus both soothing Cao Cao and also assuring Yuan himself an equal place in literary history.

In this first lyric of two, the reader sees something that occurs in many later poems about Ye. Yuan Haowen seemingly is talking about Ye, but he is also searching for a way to embed his poem and his thoughts within a larger literary tradition. In this piece, Yuan has marshaled lines from several of the best-known works on reminiscence of bygone dynasties and laments over their demise. When he introduces the word "think" in the first stanza, the poet is not thinking about the sight before his eyes but is recalling texts written about similar moments and similar spaces in the past. In line six, where he makes a very muted gesture toward Li He's line about palace officials "pointing a thousand *li* away," Yuan is not looking far away to some imagined place to which he would be displaced, but directly at the old capital of Ye—where he sees the same artifacts of loss carried forward from the past. He finds there a replication of his own life; he, like the statue of the immortal, has been set adrift by historical circumstances. In using these poetic traces, Yuan sees Bronze Bird Terrace as both created by and surrounded by other texts that talk about prosperous sites of the past: the gallery of Prince Teng, the bronze dew-catching plate of Emperor Wu of Han, and the ever more famous landscape feature of the Red Cliffs. In some ways, Yuan's contextualization of Ye within a larger framework moves the poem from a meditation on the city of Ye to one on historical cycles of dynastic rise and fall; it also transforms it into a "topography" of pain that is inscribed into the very landscape. One cannot say that it is "without feeling." Each of the allusions is to a different place, and the poet is mapping the failure of human desire across the physical and cultural landscape of his "travels."

The second lyric to "Visiting the Three Terraces" reads:

	渺漳流東下	The endless Zhang flowing down toward the east,
2	流不盡	Cannot carry away,
	古今情	All of the feelings from past to present.
4	記海上三山	Remember—Three mountains in the sea,[40]
	雲間雙闕	Two pylons amid the clouds.[41]

---

40 These three mountains refer to the three divine islands: Fangzhang 方丈, Penglai 蓬萊, and Yingzhou 瀛洲. See Sima Qian, *Shi ji*, 6.247.

41 See the couplet, "Constructing the craggy heights of the lofty palace hall, / They floated twin pylons in the great clarity" (建高殿之嵯峨兮，浮雙闕乎太清。), in Cao Zhi's "*Fu* on Ascending the Terrace." See Ch. 2.

6	當日南城	The southern city of those days.
	黃星	And that yellow star,[42]
8	幾年飛去	How many years since it flew away?
	澹春陰	On this bland overcast spring day—
10	平野草青青	On the flat plain, the grass is green, so green.
	冰井猶殘石甃	The Ice Well still has its well wall of broken-stone,
12	露槃已失金莖	But the dew-catching plate has already lost its golden stem.[43]
	風流千古短歌行	An air and style for all antiquity is the "Ballad of the Short Song,"
14	慷慨缺壺聲	Full of brave emotion are the sounds from the "chipped spittoon."[44]
	想釃酒臨江	I think about "Pouring wine and standing over the river,"[45]
16	賦詩鞍馬	Composing poems as he saddled up the horses,
	詞氣縱橫	And his rhetorical force covering everything—
	飄零	All tossed to nothing now.
18	舊家王粲	A Wang Can of long ago,[46]
	似南飛	Just like south flying.
20	烏鵲月三更	Crows and magpies at the third watch of the night.
	笑煞西園賦客	Poetic guests in the West Garden laugh heartily at me, the poeticizing traveler,[47]
22	壯懷無復平生	My strength and breadth of vision never to be as before.[48]

42　It is believed that yellow stars are the sign of auspiciousness.

43　See above on Li He's "A Song on Golden Bronze Transcendent Taking Leave of the Han."

44　This refers to an anecdote in the "Forthright" (*Haoshuang* 豪爽) section of *the Shishuo xinyu* that describes that every time Wang Dun 王敦 (266–324) drank, he would always recite the lines of Cao Cao. When he sang, he beat out the rhythm on the mouth of his spittoon with his *ruyi*, completely chipping the lip. See Yang Yong, *Shishuo xinyu jiaojian*, 13.455.

45　This quotation is from Su Shi's first "*Fu* on the Red Cliff" ("Chibi *fu*" 赤壁賦).

46　Wang Can 王粲 (177–217), style name Zhongxuan 仲宣, was a native of Gaoping 高平 (in modern day Shandong). He was considered by many the most talented of the Seven Masters of Jian'an. Wang came from a high-ranking bureaucrat family. For Yuan Haowen's constant use of the term *jiujia* 舊家 to mean "former," see Zhao Yongyuan, *Yishan yuefu jiaozhu*, 172.

47　This line seems to carry a hidden message that the poet feels his poetry can never be as good as the works done by the poets from Jian'an time. The Cao family often hosted gatherings for literati in West Garden. In his "Lord's Feast" ("Gongyan shi" 公燕詩), Cao Zhi describes gathering hosted by his brother: "The young lord honors and loves his guests, / The whole feast long he does not tire. / In the clear night we tour West Garden, / Our flying canopies follow one another" (公子敬愛客，終宴不知疲。清夜游西園，飛蓋相追隨). Cf. Robert Joe Cutter, "Cao Zhi's (192–232) Symposium Poems," *Chinese literature: Essays, Articles, Reviews* (*CLEAR*) 6, no. 1/2 (1984): 9.

48　The text of these two verses is in Yao Dianzhong 姚奠中, comp., *Yuan Haowen quanji* 元好問全集, vol. 2, (Taiyuan, Shanxi: Shanxi renmin chubanshe, 1990), 226–227. Also see

POSTSCRIPT: BEYOND THE SONG-YUAN ERA

This lyric opens with a vista of the Zhang River flowing eastward, unable to carry away the sentiments of past and present. Like the water, such feelings flow by in history, yet are always new and present. As above, Yuan Haowen interrupts the flow of the first section of the stanza and interjects a direct statement, "remember" (*ji* 記), an imperative that moves the reader from perception to remembrance—to remember the mythical three mountains in the sea, which might be a muted reference to the Three Terraces that Cao Cao himself had constructed, and the two pylons amid the clouds that Cao Zhi described in his own poem as, "Constructing the craggy heights of the lofty palace hall, / They floated twin pylons in the great clarity." But these lines are used anachronistically to evoke the image of the southern addition of Ye constructed by Gao Huan in the Eastern Wei. Standing against the background of the southern city of Ye is the absent yellow star. Here in lines seven and eight, Yuan turns to the prognostication about Cao Cao's rise found in the *San guo zhi*:

At first, during the time of Emperor Huan (r. 146–167), there was a yellow star that appeared in the sky right above where Chu and Song's border divides.[49] A certain Yin Kui from Liaodong was skilled in astronomy. He predicted that fifty years later there would be a perfected one that would arise from the area between Liang and Pei, and that his impetus could not be blocked. As it reached this year [fifth of Jian'an, February 2, 200–February 20, 201] it was fifty years and the noble [Cao] had defeated Yuan Shao, and his match could not be found under heaven.

初桓帝時有黃星見於楚宋之分。遼東殷馗善天文。言後五十歲當有真人起於梁沛之間。其鋒不可當。至是凡五十年，而公破紹，天下莫敵矣。[50]

The legendary construction of Cao Cao is gone, and the southern addition of the city no longer retains the astral connection that early city held. In fact, all that is left in the eye of the poet is a scene of nature's constant renewal, the greening grass of spring. Li He's poem recurs in this stanza as a symbol of loss, the bronze pillar that held the dew-catching plate itself now gone as well.

Zhao Yongyuan's 趙永源 notes in his *Yishan ci yanjiu* 遺山詞研究 (Shanghai: Shanghai guji chuban she, 2007), 119–121; and *Yishan yuefu jiaozhu* 遺山樂府校註 (Nanjing: Fenghuang chuban she, 2006), 79–87. On the dating of the poem, see *Yishan yuefu jiaozhu*, 80n1.

An English translation of this poem is published as "Yuan Haowen—Written to the Lyric Pattern Mulan Hua Man: Two Poems of the 'Roaming the Three Terraces'" in *Metamorphoses* 26 (Spring/Fall, 2018): 54–58.

49   Referring to the *fenye* 分野 system in Chinese astral-geography, in which certain stars and constellations adumbrate a portion of the earth to govern, and which are associated with the states that govern those places.

50   See Chen, *San guo zhi*, 1.22.

174 POSTSCRIPT: BEYOND THE SONG-YUAN ERA

Yuan's first three lines in the second lyric, "The endless Zhang flowing down toward the east, / Cannot carry away, / All of the sentiments from past to present" are again a muted echo of Su Shi's meditation on the Red Cliff, "The great River goes eastward, / Waves washing away, / Figures who had the air and style of a thousand antiquities" (大江東去，浪淘盡，千古風流人物) discussed above. Here the poet moves from object to person, remarking on how Su Shi's poem, along with the chipped-pot singing of Wang Dun, have been immortalized in text as paeans to great heroes. The song that Wang Dun had sung was actually from Cao Cao's, "Ballad of Walking Out of Xia Gate" ("Buchu Xiamen xing" 步出夏門行): "An old thoroughbred horse may droop its head in the stable, / But its ambition is still to gallop a thousand *li*. / A martyr might be in his evening years, / But his lofty aspirations never end" (老驥伏櫪，志在千里。烈士暮年，壯心不已).[51] In lines fifteen to seventeen, Yuan acknowledges the power of Cao's poetry. But he immediately counters this, again introducing the word "think" in line fifteen, bringing his poem back from admiration over the power of Cao's writing to consider its relationship to the actions of the man. All of that rhetorical power in Cao Cao's poetry was never matched by the completion of his ambition. The criticism is implicit in Yuan's use of lines from Su Shi's work, this time from the "*Fu* on the Red Cliff."

	方其破荊州	[Cao Cao] had just smashed Jing Prefecture,
2	下江陵	And came down to Jiangling,
	順流而東也	Following the current to the east.
4	舳艫千里旌旗蔽空	On boats prow to stern for a thousand *li*, battle flags obscured the sky.
	釃酒臨江	He poured a libation of ale as he approached the River,
6	橫槊賦詩	Laid his spear crosswise and composed that poem.
	固一世之雄也	Certainly a hero for the whole age,
8	而今安在哉	But where is he now?[52]

"That poem" referred to in line six of Su Shi's *fu*, which Yuan also cites in lines nineteen and twenty, makes reference to another couplet in Cao Cao's "Short Song," "The moon is bright, stars few, / Crows and magpies fly south" (月明星稀，烏鵲南飛). For Yuan, Cao Cao's poems echo through history for their powerful bravado and forthright feeling, but they are all that are left of a man who had failed to live up to his words or his stated ambitions. The bravado of the poems in these two couplets has been destabilized by the careful positioning of muted references to both images of Cao Cao: the one who dreamed of glory in his statement of ambition, and the other the pitiful figure of

---

51   See the text of this poem in Lu Qinli, *Xian Qin Han Wei Jin Nan Bei chao shi*, 1.353–354.

52   See the text of this *fu* in Kong Fanli, *Su Shi wenji*, 1:1.5–6. Cf. Stephen Owen's translation in his *An Anthology of Chinese Literature*, 293.

POSTSCRIPT: BEYOND THE SONG-YUAN ERA

his testamentary command. Finally, using Wang Can as an alter ego, Yuan wonders what will be left of his own legacy. Faced with such a magnificent failure of ambition in Cao, Yuan can only be asking, "What of my own ambitions in life?" Like Wang Can, perhaps the finest of the Jian'an writers, Yuan was set adrift after the Mongols defeated the Jin, and he also fled south like the crows and magpies. Yuan's fear that his poetry can never be as good as poets from the Jian'an era is accentuated in the final couplet where, as an unwanted intruder in the famous West Garden, the site of so many gatherings in Ye, he would be laughed at for his failures as a poet. Having failed as an official, captured and held by the Mongols, set adrift in the world and deeply engaged in chronicling the history and literary legacy of the Jin, he abruptly faced with the prospect of his failure as a writer, leaving behind no vestiges of his own time.

Ye would go on as a site for thinking about the past and the self, even into very late nineteenth century. In supposedly the only *ci* lyric left by Zhang Zhidong 張之洞 (1837–1909), "Meditation on the Past in the City of Ye" ("Yecheng huaigu" 鄴城懷古), Zhang was moved to write the following to the *ci* pattern, Moyu'er 摸魚兒.

	控中原北方門戶	It controls the northern entrance to the central plain,
2	袁曹舊日疆土	And was the territory of Yuan and Cao in the old days.
	死胡敢囓生天子	A dead barbarian dares bite a living Son of Heaven,[53]
4	袞袞都如囈語	Rolled out like a torrent, all like absurd words of a dream.
	誰足數	But who is worthy of being chastised?
	強道是	Truly it is said—
6	慕容拓跋如龍虎	The Murongs and Tuobas were like dragons and tigers[54]
	戰爭辛苦	Wearied in battle.
8	讓佺傯追歡	Then, forgetting about crucial matters in his chase after joy,
	無愁高緯	The carefree Gao Wei,
10	消受閑歌舞	Wasted his time in senseless singing and dancing.
	荒台下	Below the ruined terraces,
	立馬蒼茫吊古	I draw my horse to a stop in the boundless haze to mourn the past.
12	一條漳水如故	The Zhang River is like before,
	銀槍鐵錯銷沈盡	The silver spears and iron rasps all melted down and sunk away,
14	春草連天風雨	Spring grass links to heaven in the wind and rain.
	堪激楚	Here one can be stirred to grieve indignantly,
16	可恨是	What is regrettable is that—
	英雄不共山川住	Heroes do not remain fixed with mountains and rivers,
18	霸才無主	"The best of talents [are] without a proper master."

---

53 This refers to Murong Jun's 慕容儁 (319–360) dream mentioned in the *Jin shu* (see Ch. 1).

54 Dragons and tigers have double meanings here: they represent the prosperous and strong but also are a metaphor for the aura of the Son of Heaven.

剩定韵才人	All that is left is a place where a talented one who sets rhymes,
賦詩公子	A young master who composes poetry,
20 想像留題處	Can have the imagination to inscribe lines to mark the occasion.[55]

Here it comes to closure, in a poem where Ye has become a "place" (*chu* 處) that held within its spaces certain assumptions about expected actions—what Edward Casey has defined as the *habitus* of place. For a literatus, who comes into this space where earlier writers have generated text about the place, the very sedimentation of these texts creates for any writer who enters it the necessity of participating in that textual production. A writer in Ye is *supposed* to and is *expected* to write poetry on its traditional themes. At the same time, *habitus* demands something new and creative within a set of expected behaviors. Thus, the poem or the text is generated by the place and is in conversation with earlier texts in that same place; at the same time, it also creates something new or related to the subject who is the creator of the text.[56] Zhang begins with a historical summary in the first stanza, scarcely mentioning Cao Cao the great hero, and his rival, Yuan Shao. Rather he moves on to the Murongs of Former Yan and the Tuobas of Eastern Wei, dynasties that do not figure much in earlier poems on Ye. The story in lines three and four about Murong Jun's dream of Shi Hu biting him are coupled with a reference to the weak ruler Gao Wei 高緯 (556–577), known as the Last Ruler of Northern Qi 北齊後主 (r. 565–577), in lines eight through ten. Together, these paint a picture of violence and weakness typical of rulership that plagued the physical space of Ye. Gao Wei was overly fond of music, particularly that from the steppes and the western regions, and he had even enfeoffed singers with the status of royal princes.[57] These moments force the persona in the poem to halt his travels below the ruins and ruminate not so much on the past history of Ye, but really on the *place* of Ye.

---

55   The text of this lyric is in Yuan Shuyi 苑書義 and others, comp., *Zhang Zhidong quanji* 張之洞全集 (Shijiazhuang, Hebei: Hebei renmin chuban she, 1998), 12: 297.10596. In Xia Jingguan's 夏敬觀 (1875–1953) collection, "Rengu lou cihua" 忍古樓詞話, this *ci*-poem is titled as "Yincheng huaigu" 鄞城懷古. This is likely a misprinted or wrongly written character of Ye 鄴 since both characters share the same *yi* 邑 radical and the left parts of the graph are very similar. Yincheng is located near modern day Fenghua 奉化 of Zhejiang 浙江, which is not anywhere near the "northern entrance of the central plain"; moreover, it was never the territory of the Yuan family and Cao Cao. See "Yincheng huaigu" in Tang Guizhang 唐圭璋, ed., *Cihua congbian* 詞話叢編, vol. 5 (Beijing: Zhonghua shuju, 1986), 4817.

56   I am using the term *habitus* as defined by Edward S. Casey in "Body, Self, and Landscape," in *Textures of Place: Exploring Humanist Geographies*, ed. Paul Adams and others (Minneapolis: University of Minnesota Press, 2001), 410–413; as the place that mediates "between lived place and the geographical self," in which the self is active and productive in a space that has "customary ways of being."

57   See, for instance, the conversation between Taizong of Tang and Wei Zheng 魏徵 (580–643) in Sima Guang's 司馬光 (1019–1086), *Zizhi tongjian* 資治通鑑, 194.6110 and

POSTSCRIPT: BEYOND THE SONG-YUAN ERA

The second stanza begins in meditation on the landscape; these three lines (twelve through fourteen) are predictable: the ruins are gone, the weapons melted down and sunk out of sight; nothing is visible except nature's bandage for the scars of history: the green spreading grass of another year's renewal. But rather than calming the poet, the sight brings to the fore a sense of indignation mixed with grief. He laments the lack of heroes in his own age (a very troubling period of internal uprisings and foreign incursions), since they disappear, as Su Shi said, like the flowing water of time. They do not remain fixed like the mountains and hills.

Zhang Zhidong then brings the act of writing to the foreground with an allusion to a poem by Wen Tingyun 溫庭筠 (798–ca. 868), "Stopping by the Grave of Chen Lin" ("Guo Chen Lin mu" 過陳琳墓).

	曾於青史見遺文	I once saw your texts left in the green books of history,
2	今日飄蓬過古墳	And today, a floating tumbleweed, I pass this ancient grave.
	詞客有靈應識我	If you, noted writer, have a soul, you should recognize me,
4	霸才無主始憐君	As a real talent without a master, I begin to feel for you.
	石麟埋沒藏春草	The stone unicorn buried away, held by the spring grass,
6	銅雀荒涼對暮雲	Bronze Bird desolate and bleak, facing the evening clouds.
	莫怪臨風倍惆悵	Do not find it strange that welcoming the wind doubles melancholy,
8	欲將書劍學從軍	I desire to take both book and sword and learn to follow the army.[58]

This poem, read in many ways by critics through the ages,[59] is not so much about Chen Lin (d. 217), who served both Yuan Shao and Cao Cao, as about the persona of the poem. Even Chen Lin, after having written a long brief from Yuan Shao to Liu Bei enumerating the faults of Cao Cao—"On Behalf of Yuan Shao Writing a Call-to-arms for Yu Prefecture" ("Wei Yuan Shao xi Yuzhou wen" 為袁紹檄豫州文)—was still given a high position in the military bureaucracy by Cao.[60] In contrast, the persona of the poem

---

particularly Sima Guang's citation of the *Sui zhi* 隋志 in his notes to a passage in the records of Emperor Yang of Sui 隋煬帝 (r. 604–618):

The Last Ruler of [Northern] Qi enjoyed music of the Hu and the Rong, infatuated with it without end. Therefore, fancy playing and indulgent sounds all bringing out resentment between those who sought to struggle for the new. Therefore [favorite entertainers] like Cao Miaoda (n.d.) and An Maju (n.d.) were even enfeoffed as princes and head magistrates.

齊後主賞胡戎樂，耽愛無已。於是繁手淫聲，爭新哀怨。故曹妙達、安馬駒之徒，至有封王、開府。

See, Sima Guang, *Xinjiao Zizhi tongjian zhu* 新校資治通鑑注 (Taipei: Shijie shuju, 1974), 180.5627.

58   *Quan Tang shi*, 578.6723.

59   See Liu Xuekai 劉學鍇, *Wen Tingyun quanji jiaozhu* 溫庭筠全集校注 (Beijing: Zhonghua shuju, 2007), 1:4.387.

60   See Chen Lin's text in *Quan Hou Han wen* 全後漢文, 92.5b–8a, in *Quan shanggu sandai*

finds himself with talent worthy of admiration but with no master to follow. It implies of course, that the poet is rejected by his age, but also that there is no one in power of the same stature as Cao Cao who, despite his other faults, can still be recognized as worthy.

Zhang Zhidong also uses this citation from Wen Tingyun to turn inward to his own life. Just as Chen Lin's lonely and deserted grave spurred Wen to consider joining the army, Zhang finds in Ye a moment when he adopts the persona of a man misunderstood in a world in which there are no real leaders, no resistance to the forces that were weakening China, no person for him to attach himself to so he can display his own talents. But the final part of Zhang's poem lacks Wen Tingyun's resolve, as the poet acknowledges there is nothing to do but to scribble his resentment and leave it as one more signature on Ye, a souvenir of a place now fully synonymous with both futility and the act of writing.

It is a treat for us, readers of the twenty-first century, to immerse ourselves in literary works on the city of Ye written throughout the past seventeen hundred years. These spaces are deeply sedimented repositories of history that have the power to create a sympathetic and emotional bond with the reader. The modern obsession with finding out where precisely Cao Cao's tomb is, or to map, preserve, and explain the site itself shares this mode of thinking, whether powered by sentiment, nationalistic fervor, or academic desire. What I hoped to have done in this book is perform a parallel textual archeology of the meanings attached to that site and to show how the city lived on not only physically but in the cultural memory of authors who were moved to write about their encounters. In a curious paradox, while the physical remains deteriorated over time, writing about that place continued to grow in size and complexity. As readers, we are not only privileged to look back in order to see how memory and place worked together to fuel historical consciousness and deep sympathetic emotions, but the act of reading and interpreting the past places us in a continuum where we probe past meanings but also wonder about what our own places, our own sentiments, and our own built landscapes will signify in the times and spaces that lie before us.

Qin Han San guo Liu chao wen 全上古三代秦漢三國六朝文, comp. Yan Kejun 嚴可均 (1762–1843) (Beijing: Zhonghua shuju, 1991).

Works Cited

Allan, Sarah. "Sons of Suns: Myth and Totemism in Early China." *Bulletin of the School of Oriental and African Studies*, University of London, vol. 44, no. 2 (1981): 290–326.

Bao Yuanhang 鮑遠航. "Jin Lu Xui 'Yezhong ji' kaolun: 'Shuijing zhu' zhengyin wenxian kao zhiyi" 晉陸翽《鄴中記》考論—《水經注》徵引文獻考之一. *Huabei shuili shuidian daxue xuebao* 華北水利水電大學學報 30, no. 3 (Jun. 2014): 1–4.

Bei Qi shu 北齊書. Beijing: Zhonghua shuju, 1972.

Bei shi 北史. Beijing: Zhonghua shuju, 1974.

Beijing tushu guan 北京圖書館, ed. Huabei juan 華北卷. Vol. 35, *Difang zhi renwu zhuanji ziliao congkan* 地方志人物傳記資料叢刊. Beijing: Beijing tushu guan, 2002.

Bodde, Derk. *Festivals in Classical China: New Year and Other Annual Observances During the Han Dynasty, 206 BC–AD 200*. Princeton: Princeton University Press, 1975.

Bokenkamp, Stephen R. *Ancestors and Anxiety: Daoism and the Birth of Rebirth in China*. Berkeley: University of California Press, 2007.

Cai Yanxin. *Chinese Architecture*. Cambridge: Cambridge University Press, 2011.

Cai Zong-Qi, ed. *How to Read Chinese Poetry: A Guided Anthology*. New York: Columbia University Press, 2008.

Cao Cao 曹操 (155–220). *Cao Cao ji* 曹操集. Beijing: Zhonghua shuju, 1959.

Campbell, Duncan. "Transplanted Peculiarity: The Garden of the Master of the Fishing Nets." *New Zealand Journal of Asian Studies* 9, no. 1 (June, 2007): 9–25.

Cao Dongdong 曹冬棟. "Liu Xiaochuo ji jiaozhu" 劉孝綽集校注. MA thesis, Dongbei shifan daxue 東北師範大學, 2006.

Cao Jingui 曹金貴. "Tangdai gongyuan shi shige yishu yanjiu" 唐代宮怨詩詩歌藝術研究. MA thesis, Nanjing shifan daxue 南京師範大學, 2004.

Casey, Edward S. "Body, Self, and Landscape." In *Textures of Place: Exploring Humanist Geographies*, edited by Paul Adams and others, 403–425. Minneapolis: University of Minnesota Press, 2001.

Chan, Timothy Wai-Keung. "Dedication and Identification in Wang Bo's Compositions on the Gallery of Prince Teng." *Monumenta Serica*, vol. 50 (2002): 215–255.

Chang Conghui 常聰慧. "Tongque yifeng" 銅雀遺風. *Qinghaihu wenxue yuekan* 青海湖文學月刊, no. 8 (2013): 61–63.

Chang, Kwang-chih. "Towns and Cities in Ancient China." In *Early Chinese Civilization: Anthropological Perspectives*, 61–71. Cambridge, MA: Harvard University Press, 1976.

Chang Kang-I Sun, and Stephen Owen, eds. *The Cambridge History of Chinese Literature*. Cambridge: Cambridge University Press, 2010.

Chen Hongtian 陳宏天, and Gao Xiufang 高秀芳, eds. *Su Che quanji* 蘇轍全集. Beijing: Zhonghua shuju, 1990.

Chen, Jack W. "The Writing of Imperial Poetry in Medieval China." *Harvard Journal of Asiatic Studies*, vol. 65, no. 1 (June, 2005): 57–98.

Chen Jian 陳劍. "Ye cheng yizhi de kantan fajue yu yanjiu: Xu Guangji yanjiu yuan xueshu baogao hui jiyao" 鄴城遺址的勘探發掘與研究：徐光冀研究員學術報告會紀要. *Sichuan wenwu* 四川文物, no. 1 (2005): 87–89.

Chen Jinquan 陳金全. "Wei Jin Nan Bei chao shiqi Yecheng de diwei jiqi yingxiang yinsu yanjiu" 魏晉南北朝時期鄴城的地位及其影響因素研究. MA thesis, Lanzhou daxue 蘭州大學, 2012.

Chen Liao 陳遼. "Zhongguo gudai sanwen zhong de jianzhu xuxie" 中國古代散文中的建築敘寫. *Xuzhou shifan daxue xuebao* 徐州師範大學學報 35, no. 3 (2009): 12–15.

Chen Qiaoyi 陳橋驛, ed. *Zhongguo qi da gudu* 中國七大古都. Beijing: Zhongguo qing-nian chuban she, 1991.

Chen Weisong 陳維崧 (1625–1682). *Chen Weisong ji* 陳維崧集. Shanghai: Guji chuban she, 2010.

Cheng Sen 程森, and Li Junfeng 李俊鋒. "Lun Cao Wei Ye cheng ji qi zhoubian ziran jingguan he wenhua jingguan" 論曹魏鄴城及其周邊自然景觀和文化景觀. *Sanmen-xia zhiye jishu xueyuan xuebao* 三門峽職業技術學院學報 7, no. 3 (September, 2008): 42–45.

Cheng Yi 程義. "Shilun Ye beicheng de sheji sixiang, buju yu yingxiang" 試論鄴北城的設計思想、佈局與影響. *Xibei daxue xuebao* 西北大學學報 31, no. 1 (2001): 106–111.

Cheng Zhangcan 程章灿. *Wei Jin Nanbei chao fu shi* 魏晉南北朝賦史. Nanjing: Jiangsu guji chuban she, 2001.

Chi Jitang 郗吉堂. "Yecheng, Liuchao gudu yu duanming wangchao" 鄴城、六朝古都與短命王朝. *Dangdai ren* 當代人, no. 6 (2010): 70–73.

Chunqiu guliang zhuan zhushu 春秋穀梁傳注疏. Annotated by Fan Ning 范甯 (ca. 339–401) and Yang Shixun 楊士勳 (fl. 627–649). In *Shisan jing zhushu fu jiaokan ji* 十三經注疏附校勘記, edited by Ruan Yuan 阮元 (1764–1849), 8 vols. Taipei: Yiwen yingshu guan, 1982.

Chuxue ji 初學記. Taipei: Dingwen shuju, 1972.

Clark, Peter, ed. *The Oxford Handbook of Cities in World History*. Oxford: Oxford University Press, 2013.

Cohen, Alvin P. "Coercing the Rain Deities in Ancient China." *History of Religions* 17, no. 3/4 (May, 1978): 244–265.

Cotterell, Arthur. *The Imperial Capitals of China: An Inside View of the Celestial Empire*. London: Pimlico, 2007.

Cui Yanhua 崔彥華. "'Ye-Jinyang' liangdu tizhi yu Dong Wei Bei Qi zhengzhi" 『鄴―晉陽』兩都體制與東魏北齊政治. *Shehui kexue zhanxian* 社會科學戰線, no. 7 (2010): 242–245.

Cook, Johannah. "Works of Gold and Jade—Cao zhi (192–232 CE): The Man and His Poetry." MA. Thesis, University of Otago, 2010.

Cutter, Robert Joe. "Cao Zhi (192–232) and His Poetry." Ph.D. Diss., University of Washington, 1983.

WORKS CITED 181

Cutter, Robert Joe. "Cao Zhi's (192–232) Symposium Poems." *Chinese Literature: Essays, Articles, Reviews (CLEAR)* 6, no. 1/2 (1984): 1–32.

Cutter, Robert Joe. "Letters and Memorials in the Early Third Century: The Case of Cao Zhi." In *A History of Chinese Letters and Epistolary Culture*, edited by Antje Richter, 307–330. Leiden and Boston: Brill, 2015.

Cutter, Robert Joe. "Poetry From 200 BCE To 600 CE." In *The Columbia History of Chinese Literature*, edited by Victor H. Mair, 248–273. New York: Columbia University Press, 2001.

Cutter, Robert Joe. "Three Rhapsodies on Flying Creatures by Cao Zhi." *Chinese literature* (Summer, 1999): 114–118.

Cutter, Robert Joe, and William Gordon Crowell. *Empresses and Consorts: Selections from Chen Shou's Records of the Three States with Pei Songzhi's Commentary.* Honolulu: University of Hawai'i Press, 1999.

Deng Fushun 鄧福舜, and Li Decheng 李德成. "Yexia wenren jihui yu Yexia shifeng" 鄴下文人集會與鄴下詩風. *Daqing gaodeng zhuanke xuexiao xuebao* 大慶高等專科學校學報 16, no. 3 (1996): 30–34

Deng Zhongtang 鄧中堂. *Yedu chunqiu* 鄴都春秋. Beijing: Zhongguo wenshi chuban she, 1999.

Dien, Albert E. *Six Dynasties Civilization*. New Haven: Yale University Press, 2007.

Ding Haibin 丁海斌. *Zhongguo gudai peidu shi* 中國古代陪都史. Beijing: Zhongguo shehui kexue chuban she, 2012.

Du Yanyan 杜艷艷. "Shilun gudai ducheng de jingshen yule xiaofei bianqian: yi bei Wei Luoyang, Tang chao Chang'an, Song dai Kaifeng ji Hangzhou weili" 試論古代都城的精神娛樂消費變遷：以北魏洛陽、唐朝長安、宋代開封及杭州為例. *Cangsang* 滄桑, no. 4 (2006): 9–10.

Egan, Charles. "Recent-Style Shi Poetry: Quatrains (Jueju)." In *How to Read Chinese Poetry: A Guided Anthology*, edited by Zong-Qi Cai, 199–225. New York: Columbia University Press, 2008.

Erya zhushu 爾雅注疏. Annotated by Guo Pu 郭璞 (276–324) and Xing Bing 邢昺 (932–1010). In *Shisan jing zhushu fu jiaokan ji* 十三經注疏附校勘記. Edited by Ruan Yuan 阮元 (1764–1849), 8 vols. Taipei: Yiwen yingshu guan, 1982.

Fang Dai. "Drinking, Thinking, and Writing: Ruan Ji and the Culture of his Era." PhD diss., University of Michigan, 1994.

Farmer, J. Michael. *The Talent of Shu: Qiao Zhou and the Intellectual World of Early Medieval Sichuan*. Albany: The State University of New York Press, 2007.

Feng Junshi 馮君實. "Yezhong ji jibu" 《鄴中記》輯補. *Guji zhengli yanjiu xuekan* 古籍整理研究學刊, no. 2 (1985): 5–13 and 17.

Fu Chunxi 傅春喜. "Yecheng suochu lidai taowen jianshu" 鄴城所出歷代陶文簡述. *Dongfang yishu* 東方藝術, no. 12 (2009): 102–21.

Fu Dingyu 付定裕. "'Pi Zhi zhengchu' yu Yexia wenshi zhi guanxi kaolun" 『丕植爭儲』與鄴下文士之關係考論. *Xingtai xueyuan xuebao* 邢台學院學報 25, no.2 (2012): 49–51.

Fu Gang 傅剛. *Han Wei Liuchao wenxue yu wenxian lungao* 漢魏六朝文學與文獻論稿. Beijing: Shangwu yinshuguan, 2005.

Fu Gang 傅剛. "'Jianlong qianmei, zuofan houlai' de Jian'an shige" 『兼籠前奏，作範後來』的建安詩歌. In *Zhongguo shige shi luncong shu* 中國詩歌史論叢書, 1–41. Jilin: Jilin jiaoyu chuban she, 1995.

Fu Gang 傅剛. "'Wen gui qing sheng' shuo de shidai yiyi: luetan Lu Yun 'Yu xiong Pingyuan shu'" 『文貴清省』說的時代意義：略談陸雲《與兄平原書》. *Wenyi lilun yanjiu* 文藝理論研究, no.2 (1984): 93–99.

Gan Bao 干寶 (ca. 286–336). *Sou shen ji* 搜神記. Beijing: Zhonghua shuju, 1979.

Gao Guangfu 高光復. *Gao Shi Cen Shen shi yishi* 高適岑參詩譯釋. Harbin: Heilongjiang renmin chuban she, 1984.

Gao Guihui 高桂惠. "Zuo Si shengping jiqi Sandu fu zhi yanjiu" 左思生平及其三都賦之研究. MA thesis, Guoli Zhengzhi daxue, 1981.

Gao Min 高敏. "Luelun Yecheng de lishi diwei yu fengjian geju de guanxi" 略論鄴城的歷史地位與封建割據的關係. *Zhongzhou xuekan* 中州學刊, no. 3 (1989): 111–115.

Gao Mingqian 高明乾, Tong Yuhua 佟玉華, and Liu Kun 劉坤. *Shijing dongwu shigu* 詩經動物釋詁. Beijing: Zhonghua shuju, 2005.

Gong Kechang 龔克昌, Su Jui-Lung 蘇瑞隆, and Zhou Guanghuang 周廣璜, eds. *Quan Sanguo fu pingzhu* 全三國賦評註. Ji'nan: Qi Lu chuban she, 2013.

Ge Lifang 葛立方. *Yunyu yangqiu* 韻語陽秋. Rpt. Shanghai: Guji chuban she, 1984.

Graham, A.C. *Poems of the Late Tang*. New York: New York Review of Books, 1965.

Gu Naiwu 顧乃武, and Pan Yanrui 潘艷蕊. "Dong Wei, Bei Qi shiqi Yedi muzhi wenxue guankui" 東魏、北齊時期鄴地墓誌文學管窺. *Qianyan* 前沿 298, no. 20 (2011): 174–76.

Gu Sili 顧嗣立 (1669–1722), comp. *Yuan shi xuan* 元詩選, vol. 3. Beijing: Zhonghua shuju, 1987.

Gu Yanwu 顧炎武 (1613–1682). *Lidai [diwang] zhai jing ji* 歷代［帝王］宅京記. Beijing: Zhonghua shuju, 1984.

Guo Jiqiao 郭濟橋. "Beichao shiqi Ye nancheng buju chutan" 北朝時期鄴南城佈局初探. *Wenwu chunqiu* 文物春秋, no. 2 (2002): 16–26.

Guo Jiqiao 郭濟橋. "Cao Wei Ye heng zhongyang guanshu buju chushi" 曹魏鄴城中央官署佈局初釋. *Yindu xuekan* 殷都學刊, no. 2 (2002): 34–38.

Guo Jiqiao 郭濟橋. "Dong Wei Bei Qi Yejing chengxiang jianzhi" 東魏、北齊鄴京城鄉建制. *Yindu xuekan* 殷都學刊, no. 4 (2012): 38–43.

Guo Jiqiao 郭濟橋. "Ye nancheng de gongcheng xingzhi" 鄴南城的宮城形制. *Yindu xuekan* 殷都學刊, no. 2 (2013): 34–37.

WORKS CITED

Guo Jiqiao 郭濟橋. "Yecheng: Sanguo gudi liuchao gudu" 鄴城—三國故地六朝古都. *Hebei ribao* 河北日報, March 15, 2013, <http://theory.people.com.cn/BIG5/n/2013/0315/c40531-20801980.html> (accessed July 11, 2015).

Guo Jiqiao 郭濟橋. "Yecheng fengyu: Ningsuo sibai nian de huihuang" 鄴城風雨—凝縮四百年的輝煌. *Wenhua wenwu* 文化文物, no. 5 (2014): 31–37.

Guo Shengqiang 郭勝強, and Xu Hu 許滸. "Cao Wei Ye du de yingjian ji yingxiang" 曹魏鄴都的營建及影響. *Sanmenxia zhiye jishu xueyuan xuebao* 三門峽職業技術學院學報 10, no. 2 (June, 2011): 34–37.

Han Fei zi jijie 韓非子集解. Compiled by Wang Xianshen 王先慎 (fl. ca. 1897). In *Xinbian zhuzi jicheng* 新編諸子集成, vol. 5, 1–368. Taipei: Shijie shuju, 1979.

Han Geping 韓格平 and others. *Quan Wei Jin fu jiaozhu* 全魏晉賦校注. Changchun: Jilin wenshi chuban she, 2008.

Han shu 漢書. Beijing: Zhonghua shuju, 1962.

He Hongyan 何紅艷. "Lun Jian'an gongyan shi de jiazhi xuanze" 論建安公宴詩的價值選擇. *Nei Menggu shehui kexue* 內蒙古社會科學 24, no. 6 (2003): 77–80.

He Wei 何薳 (1077–1145). *Chunzhu jiwen* 春渚紀聞. Edited by Zhang Minghua 張明華. Beijing: Zhonghua shuju, 1997.

He Yun'ao 賀雲翱, and Shan Weihua 單衛華, comps. *Cao Cao mu shijian quan jilu* 曹操墓事件全記錄. Ji'nan: Shandong huabao chuban she, 2010.

Hebei sheng wenwu yanjiu suo 河北省文物研究所, comp. *Hebei kaogu zhongyao faxian* 河北考古重要發現 (1949–2009). Beijing: Kexue chuban she, 2009.

Henan sheng wenwu kaogu yanjiu suo 河南省文物考古研究所, comp. *Cao Cao gaoling kaogu faxian yu yanjiu* 曹操高陵考古發現與研究. Beijing: Wenwu chuban she, 2010.

Heng Chye Kiang 王才強. *Cities of Aristocrats and Bureaucrats: The Development of Medieval Chinese Cityscapes*. Honolulu: University of Hawai'i Press, 1999.

Ho Cheung Wing 何祥榮. *Han Wei Liuchao Yedu shifu xilun* 漢魏六朝鄴都詩賦析論. Hong Kong: The Jao Tsung-I Petite Ecole, 2009.

Holzman, Donald. "Literary Criticism in China in the Early Third Century AD" *Asiatische studien* 28.2 (1974): 113–149.

Hong Kong Zhongwen daxue Zhongguo yuyan wenxue xi 香港中文大學中國語言文學系, ed. *Wei Jin Nanbeichao wenxue lunji* 魏晉南北朝文學論集. Taipei: Wenshizhe chubanshe, 1994.

Hong Mai 洪邁 (1123–1202). *Rongzhai suibi quanshu leibian yizhu* 容齋隨筆全書類編譯注. Edited by Xu Yimin 許逸民. Changchun: Shidai wenyi chuban she, 1993.

Hong Xingzu 洪興祖 (1090–1155). *Chuci buzhu* 楚辭補注. Edited by Bai Huawen 白化文 and others. Beijing: Zhonghua shuju, 1983.

Hou Han shu 後漢書. Beijing: Zhonghua shuju, 1965.

Hou Tingsheng 侯廷生. "Meiyou weizhi de gudu: Ye cheng de lishi yu wenhua diwei kaocha" 沒有位置的古都：鄴城的歷史與文化地位考察. *Handan zhiye jishu xueyuan xuebao* 邯鄲職業技術學院學報 16, no. 4 (December, 2003): 12–16.

Hou Tingsheng 侯廷生. *Yecheng lishi gushi* 鄴城歷史故事. Beijing: Guoji wenhua chuban gongsi, 1996.

Hu Shengyuan 胡勝源. "'Renxin si Wei' yu Wei Qi shandai" 『人心思魏』與魏齊禪代. *Taida lishi xuebao* 臺大歷史學報, no. 42 (2008): 1–43.

Hu Ying 胡鶯, and Du Jian 杜健. "Wudai shiqi de 'Yedu' jinzhi kao" 五代時期的『鄴都』今址考. *Liaoning shizhuan xuebao* 遼寧師專學報 68, no. 2 (2010): 132–33.

Huang Huixian 黃惠賢. "Jijiao Yezhong ji" 輯校《鄴中記》. In *Yecheng ji Beichao shi yanjiu* 鄴城暨北朝史研究, edited by Liu Xinchang 劉心長 and Ma Zhongli 馬忠理, 368–377. Shijiazhuang, Hebei: Hebei Renmin chuban she, 1991.

Huang Jie 黃節. *Cao Zijian shi zhu [wai sanzhong]; Ruan bubing yonghuai shi zhu* 曹子建詩注（外三種）；阮步兵詠懷詩注. Beijing: Zhonghua shuju, 2008.

Huang Rensheng 黃仁生, ed. *Xinyi Wu Yue chunqiu* 新譯吳越春秋. Taipei: Sanmin shuju, 1996.

Huang Shoucheng 黃守誠. *Cao Zijian xintan* 曹子建新探. Taipei: Zhi shufang chuban jituan, 1998.

Huang Yazhuo 黃亞卓. *Han Wei Liuchao gongyan shi yanjiu* 漢魏六朝公宴詩研究. Shanghai: Huadong shifan daxue chubanshe, 2007.

Huang Yazhuo 黃亞卓. "Lun Jian'an gongyan shi jiqi dianfan yiyi" 論建安公宴詩及其典範意義. *Guangxi shifan xueyuan xuebao* 廣西師範學院學報 23, no. 2 (2002): 59–63.

Hucker, Charles O. *A Dictionary of Official Titles in Imperial China*. Taipei: SMC Publishing Inc., 1995.

Hughes, E. R. *The Art of Letters: Lu Chi's "Wen fu" AD 302*. New York: Pantheon Books, 1951.

Idema, Wilt L., and Stephen H. West. *Records of the Three Kingdoms in Plain Language*. Indianapolis: Hackett Publishing Company, 2016.

Jia Xiaohong 賈曉紅. "Yexia wenxue jituan shimo kaoshu" 鄴下文學集團始末考述. *Zhongguo xiaowai jiaoyu zazhi* 中國校外教育雜誌, no. 8 (2008): 53–54.

Jiajing Zhangde fu zhi 嘉靖彰德府志. Compiled by Cui Xian 崔銑 (1478–1541). Rpt. Shanghai: Guji shudian, 1982.

Jiang Dahuang 江達煌. "Yecheng liudai jiandu shulue: fulun Cao Cao du Ye yuanyin" 鄴城六代建都述略：附論曹操都鄴原因. *Wenwu chunqiu* 文物春秋 S1 (1992): 87–97.

Jiang Fang 蔣方. "Lu Ji, Lu Yun shi Jin huanji kao" 陸機、陸雲仕晉宦迹考. *Hubei daxue xuebao* 湖北大學學報, no. 3 (1995): 76–80, 86.

Jiang Guanwu 姜觀吾. "Yedu zai Zhongguo gudai shi shang de diwei" 鄴都在中國古代史上的地位. *Yancheng shizhuan xuebao* 鹽城師專學報, no. 2 (1994): 65–67.

Jiang Shaohua 蔣少華. "Cao Wei wudu kaolun" 曹魏五都考論. *Xiangfan xueyuan xuebao* 襄樊學院學報 31, no. 12 (December, 2010): 5–10.

Jiao Zhiqin 焦智勤. "Ye cheng wadang fenqi yanjiu" 鄴城瓦當分期研究. *Yindu xuekan* 殷都學刊, no. 2 (2007): 43–54.

Jin shu 晉書. Beijing: Zhonghua shuju, 1974.

WORKS CITED

Jiu Tang shu 舊唐書. Beijing: Zhonghua shuju, 1957.

Ke Qiandi 柯遷娣. "Lun Yexia wenren youyan de wenhua yiyi" 論鄴下文人游宴的文化意義. *Xiandai yuwen* 現代語文, no. 12 (2010): 38–40.

Kleeman, Terry F. "Land Contracts and Related Documents." In *Makio Ryōkai Hakas Shōju Kinen Ronshū: Chūgoku no Shūkuō, Shisō, to Kagaku*, 1–34. Tokyo: Kokusho kankōkai, 1984.

Knechtges, David R. "Court Culture in the Late Eastern Han: The Case of the Hongdu Gate School." In *Interpretation and Literature in Early Medieval China*, edited by Alan K. L. Chan and Yuet-Keung Lo, 9–39. Albany: State University of New York Press, 2010.

Knechtges, David R. "From the Eastern Han through the Western Jin (AD 25–317)." In *The Cambridge History of Chinese Literature*, vol.1, edited by Kang-I Sun Chang and Stephen Owen, 116–198. Cambridge: Cambridge University Press, 2010.

Knechtges, David R. "Jingu and Lanting: Two (or Three?) Jin Dynasty Gardens." In *Studies in Chinese Language and Culture: Festschrift in Honor of Christoph Harbsmeier on the Occasion of His 60th Birthday*, 399–403. Oslo: Hermes Academic Publishng, 2006.

Knechtges, David R. "Letters in the Wen xuan." In *A History of Chinese Letters and Epistolary Culture*, edited by Antje Richter, 189–238. Leiden: Brill, 2015.

Knechtges, David R. "Liu Kun, Lu Chen, and Their Writings in the Transition to the Eastern Jin." *Chinese Literature: Essays, Articles, Reviews (CLEAR)* 28 (December, 2006): 1–66.

Knechtges, David R. "Ruin and Remembrance in Classical Chinese Literature: The 'Fu on the Ruined City' by Bao zhao." In *Reading Medieval Chinese Poetry: Text, Context, and Culture*, edited by Paul W. Kroll, 55–89. Leiden: Brill, 2015.

Knechtges, David R., trans. *Wen xuan, Or Selections of Refined Literature*, vol. 1, *Rhapsodies on Metropolises and Capitals*. Princeton: Princeton University Press, 1996.

Knechtges, David R. *Wen xuan, Or Selections of Refined Literature*, vol. 2, *Rhapsodies on Sacrifices, Hunting, Travel, Sightseeing, Palaces and Halls, Rivers and Seas*. Princeton: Princeton University Press, 1996.

Knechtges, David R. *Wen xuan, Or Selections of Refined Literature*, vol. 3, *Rhapsodies on Natural Phenomena, Birds and Animals, Aspirations and Feelings, Sorrowful Laments, Literature, Music, and Passions*. Princeton: Princeton University Press, 1996.

Knechtges, David R., and Taiping Chang, eds. *Ancient and Early Medieval Chinese Literature: A Reference Guide, Part 1*. Leiden: Brill, 2010.

Kong Anguo 孔安國 (ca. 156–74 BCE), and Kong Yingda 孔穎達 (574–648), comm. and ann. *Shang shu zhengyi* 尚書正義. In *Shisan jing zhushu fu jiaokan ji* 十三經注疏附校勘記. Edited by Ruan Yuan 阮元 (1764–1849) 8 vols. Taipei: Yiwen yingshu guan, 1982.

Kong Fanli 孔凡禮, ed. *Su Shi wenji* 蘇軾文集. 6 Vols. Beijing: Zhonghua shuju, 1986.

Kroll, Paul W. *A Student's Dictionary of Classical and Medieval Chinese*. Leiden: Brill, 2015.

Kroll, Paul W. "Portraits of Ts'ao Ts'ao: Literary Studies on the Man and the Myth." PhD diss., University of Michigan, 1976.

Kroll, Paul W. "Seven Rhapsodies of Ts'ao Chih." *Journal of the American Oriental Society* 120, no. 1 (Jan.–Mar. 2000): 1–12.

Kroll, Paul W., ed. *Reading Medieval Chinese Poetry: Text, Context, and Culture*. Leiden: Brill, 2015.

Lai, Whalen. "Looking for Mr. Ho Po: Unmasking the River God of Ancient China." *History of Religions* 29, no. 4 (1990): 335–350.

Lai Yanyuan 賴炎元, ed. and trans. *Han Shi waizhuan jinzhu jinyi* 韓詩外傳今註今譯. Taipei: Taiwan shangwu yinshu guan, 1972.

Lang Xiaobin 郎曉斌. "Yexia wenren xintai" 鄴下文人心態. *Xiandai yuwen* 現代語文, no. 11 (2007): 8–9.

Laozi jinzhu jinyi 老子今註今譯. Edited and translated by Chen Guying 陳鼓應. Taipei: Taiwan shangwu yinshu guan, 1970.

Laozi jinzhu jinyi ji pingjie 老子今註今譯及評介. Edited and translated by Chen Yinggu 陳應鼓. Taipei: Taiwan Shangwu yinshu guan, 1970.

Lavallee, Thomas. "Formality and the Pursuit of Pleasure in Early Medieval Chinese Banquet Poetry." PhD. Diss., Washington University, Saint Louis, Mo., 2004.

Leban, Carl. "Ts'ao Ts'ao and the Rise of Wei: The Early Years." PhD diss., Columbia University, 1971.

Legge, James, trans. *The Chinese Classics with a Translation, Critical and Exegetical Notes, Prolegomena, and Copious Indexes: The She King or the Book of Poetry*. 2nd ed. Vol. 4.; Hong Kong: Lane, Crawford & Co; London: Trubner & Co., 1871; rpt. Taipei: Wenshizhe chuban she, 1971.

Lei Jianhong 雷建紅, comp. "Wei Jin Bei chao kaogu zongshu" 魏晉北朝考古綜述. In *Hebei kaogu zhongyao faxian (1949–2009)*, edited by Hebei sheng wenwu yanjiu suo, 204–211. Beijing: Kexue chuban she, 2009.

Leng Weiguo 冷衛國. "Lu Ji Lu Yun de fuxue piping" 陸機陸雲的賦學批評. *Qilu xuekan* 齊魯學刊, no. 5 (2005): 69–73.

Lewis, Mark Edward. *China between Empires: The Northern and Southern Dynasties*. Cambridge, MA: Harvard University Press, 2009.

Li Daoyuan 酈道元 (d. 527). *Shuijing zhu* 水經注. Edited by Chen Qiaoyi 陳橋驛. Shanghai: Shanghai guji chuban she, 1990.

Li Haibo 李海波 and Meng Qingke 孟慶科. "Yecheng yizhi: Chenshui qiannian de li-uchao gudu" 鄴城遺址：沈睡千年的六朝古都. *Hebei ribao* 河北日報, May 25, 2015 <http://hebei.hebnews.cn/2015-05/25/content_4793945.htm> (accessed October 3, 2019).

WORKS CITED

Li Jing 李菁. "Yecheng zhi wei yu Du Fu de Yecheng shi shulun" 鄴城之圍與杜甫的鄴城詩述論. *Guyuan shizhuan xuebao* 固原師專學報 22, no. 2 (2001): 11–14.

Li Meitian 李梅田. "Bei Qi muzang wenhua yinsu fenxi: Yi Ye cheng, Jinyang wei zhongxin" 北齊墓葬文化因素分析：以鄴城、晉陽為中心. *Zhongyuan wenwu* 中原文物, no. 4 (2004): 59–65.

Li Meitian 李梅田. "Cong Luoyang dao Ye cheng: Beichao mushi huaxiang ji xiangzheng yiyi de zhuanbian" 從洛陽到鄴城：北朝墓室畫像及象徵意義的轉變. *Kaogu yu wenwu* 考古與文物, no. 2 (2006): 65–72.

Li Min 李旻. "Lu Qian muzhi de lishi jiedu: Jian bo zaowei lun" 魯潛墓誌的歷史解讀：兼駁造偽論. *Fudan daxue chutu wenxian yu guwenzi yanjiu zhongxin* 復旦大學出土文獻與古文字研究中心, August 30, 2010. www.gwz.fudan.edu.cn/SrcShow.asp?Src_ID=1246 (accessed September 18, 2014).

Li Wencai 李文才. "Wei Jin Nanbei chao shiqi de Hualin yuan: Yi Luoyang, Jiankang liangdi wei zhongxin lunshu" 魏晉南北朝時期的華林園：以洛陽、建康兩地為中心論述. In *Wei Jin Nanbei chao Sui Tang zhengzhi yu wenhua lungao* 魏晉南北朝隋唐政治與文化論稿, 126–166. Beijing: Shijie zhishi chuban she, 2006.

Li Yumin 李裕民, ed. *Yang Wen gong tanyuan Juanyou zalu* 楊文公談苑 倦遊雜錄. Shanghai: Guji chuban she, 1993.

Li Zhiliang 李之亮, ed. *Ouyang Xiu ji biannian jianzhu* 歐陽修集編年箋注. 8 Vols. Chengdu: Ba Shu shushe, 2007.

Li Zhiliang 李之亮, and Xu Zhengying 徐正英, eds. *Anyang ji biannian jianzhu* 安陽集編年箋注. Chengdu: Ba Shu shushe, 2000.

Liang Jianjiang 梁鑒江. *Chen Weisong ci xuanzhu* 陳維崧詞選注. Shanghai: Guji chuban she, 1990.

Liang shu 梁書. Beijing: Zhonghua shuju, 1973.

Liao Yifang 廖宜方. *Tang dai de lishi jiyi* 唐代的歷史記憶. Taipei: Guoli Taiwan daxue chuban she, 2011.

Liezi ji shi 列子集釋. Annotated by Yang Bojun 楊伯峻. Beijing: Zhonghua shuju, 1979.

Liji zhengyi 禮記正義. Annotated by Zheng Xuan 鄭玄 (127–200) and Kong Yingda 孔穎達 (574–648). In *Shisan jing zhushu fu jiaokan ji* 十三經注疏附校勘記, edited by Ruan Yuan 阮元 (1764–1849), 8 vols. Taipei: Yiwen yingshu guan, 1982.

Liu An 劉安 (179–122 BCE). *The Huainanzi: A Guide to the Theory and Practice of Government in Early Han China*. Translated by John S. Major and others. New York: Columbia University Press, 2010.

Liu Chang 劉暢, and Liu Guojun 劉國珺. *He Xun ji zhu Yin Keng ji zhu* 何遜集注陰鏗集注. Tianjing: Tiangjing guji chuban she, 1988.

Liu Huairong 劉懷榮. "Lun Yexia houqi yanji huodong dui Jian'an shige de yingxiang" 論鄴下後期宴集活動對建安詩歌的影響. In *Zhongguo zhonggu wenxue yanjiu* 中國中古文學研究, edited by Zhao Minli 趙敏俐 and Satō Toshiyuki 佐藤利行, 511–520. Beijing: Xueyuan chuban she, 2005.

Liu Jia 劉佳. "Wei Jin Nan Bei chao shiqi Yecheng chengshi jianshe yu gengxin fazhan gouchen" 魏晉南北朝時期鄴城城市建設與更新發展鈎沈. MA thesis, Hebei gongye daxue, 2007.

Liu Kaiyang 劉開揚. *Cen Shen shiji biannian jianzhu* 岑參詩集編年箋註. Chengdu: Ba Shu shushe, 1995.

Liu Mingwei 劉銘緯, and Lai Guangbang 賴光邦. "Zhongguo gudai chengguo dushi xingtai jianlun: Fangshi geming yiqian Huaxia ducheng xingtai de juhe, fenhua yu qi zhidu hua chengxu" 中國古代城郭都市形態簡論：坊市革命以前華夏都城型態的聚合、分化與其制度化程序. *Guoli Taiwan daxue jianzhu yu chengxiang yanjiu xuebao* 國立臺灣大學建築與城鄉研究學報, no. 16 (December, 2010): 79–119.

Liu Qingzhu 劉慶柱. "Cong Cao Wei ducheng jianshe yu beifang yunhe kaizao kan Cao Cao de lishi gongji" 從曹魏都城建設與北方運河開鑿看曹操的歷史功績. *Anhui shixue* 安徽史學, no. 2 (2011): 28–34.

Liu Weiqi 劉瑋琦. "Dong Wei Bei Qi Yecheng he Jinyang taoyong yanjiu" 東魏北齊鄴城和晉陽陶俑研究. MA thesis. Dongwu University, 2008.

Liu Wu-chi, and Irving Yucheng Lo, eds. *Sunflower Splendor: Three Thousand Years of Chinese Poetry*. New York: Anchor Press, 1975.

Liu Wuquan 劉武泉. "Wei Wen hou duye bian" 魏文侯都鄴辨. *Zhongnan minzu xueyuan xuebao* 中南民族學院學報, no. 4 (1982): 54.

Liu Xinchang 劉心長 and Ma Zhongli 馬忠理, eds. *Yecheng ji Beichao shi yanjiu* 鄴城暨北朝史研究. Shijiazhuang, Hebei: Hebei Renmin chuban she, 1991.

Liu Xuekai 劉學鍇. *Wen Tingyun quanji jiaozhu* 溫庭筠全集校注. Beijing: Zhonghua shuju, 2007.

Liu Xuetiao 劉學銚. *Lidai huzu wangchao zhi minzu zhengce* 歷代胡族王朝之民族政策. Taipei: Zhishufang chuban jituan, 2005.

Liu Yaojin 劉躍進. " 'Er Lu' de beiqing yu chuangzuo" 『二陸』的悲情與創作. *Beijing Lianhe daxue xuebao* 北京聯合大學學報, no. 3 (2012): 12–17.

Liu Zhiling 劉志玲. "Zonglun Wei Jin Bei chao Ye cheng de zhongxin diwei" 縱論魏晉北朝鄴城的中心地位. *Handan xueyuan xuebao* 邯鄲學院學報 18, no. 4 (2008): 27–32.

Lü Chunsheng 呂春盛. "Bei Qi zhengzhi shi yanjiu: Bei Qi shuaiwang yuanyin zhi kaocha" 北齊政治史研究：北齊衰亡原因之考察. MA thesis. Guoli Taiwan daxue, 1986.

Lu Hui 陸翽 (fl. 317). *Yezhong ji* 鄴中記. (Extant fragments). See Shafer and Zhou Yiliang.

Lu Ji 陸機 (261–303). *Lu Shiheng wenji jiaozhu* 陸士衡文集校注. Edited by Liu Yunhao 劉運好. 2 Vols. Nanjing: Fenghuang chuban she, 2007.

Lu Qinli 逯欽立, ed. *Xian Qin Han Wei Jin Nan Bei chao shi* 先秦漢魏晉南北朝詩. 3 Vols. Beijing: Zhonghua shuju chuban she, 1983.

Lu Yun 陸雲 (262–303). *Lu Yun ji* 陸雲集. Huang Kui 黃葵, ed. Beijing: Zhonghua shuji, 1988.

WORKS CITED

Lu Zheng 盧楨, and Wu Congcong 吳聰聰. "Zhongguo gudai chengshi shige zonglun" 中國古代城市詩歌綜論. *Hebei shifan daxue xuebao* 河北師範大學學報 31, no. 3 (2008): 100–05.

Luan Guichuan 欒貴川. "San~liu shiji Yecheng yu Luoyang wenhua guanxi chutan" 三 ～六世紀鄴城與洛陽文化關係初探. *Yindu xuekan* 殷都學刊, no. 3 (1991): 31–35.

Lunyu yizhu 論語譯注. Annotated by Yang Bojun 楊伯峻. Beijing: Zhonghua shuju, 1958.

Ma Aimin 馬愛民. "Yexia foxue zhisheng he Beichao, Sui Tang de Anyang fosi wuseng wuyi" 鄴下佛學之盛和北朝、隋、唐的安陽佛寺武僧武藝. *Anyang shifan xueyuan xuebao* 安陽師範學院學報, no. 5 (2009): 22–29.

Ma Aimin 馬愛民, and others. "Lun Yedu lishi shang shangwu fengxi yu minzu wushu wenhua de ronghe" 論鄴都歷史上尚武風習與民族武術文化的融合. *Xi'an tiyu xueyuan xuebao* 西安體育學院學報18, no. 2 (2001): 15–18.

Ma Maoyuan 馬茂元, and others., *Chuci zhushi* 楚辭註釋. Hubei: Renmin chuban she, 1985.

Mair, Victor H, ed. *The Columbia History of Chinese Literature*. New York: Columbia University Press, 2001.

Mair, Victor H, and others, eds. *Hawai'i Reader in Traditional Chinese Culture*. Honolulu: University of Hawai'i Press, 2004.

Maoshi zhengyi 毛詩正義. In *Shisan jing zhushu fu jiaokan ji* 十三經注疏附校勘記, edited by Ruan Yuan 阮元 (1764–1849), 8 vols. Taipei: Yiwen yingshu guan, 1982.

Marney, John. "Cities in Chinese Literature." *Michigan Academician* 10, no. 2 (Fall, 1977): 225–238.

Mei Yaochen 梅堯臣 (1002–1060). *Mei Yaochen ji biannian jiaozhu* 梅堯臣集編年校注. Edited by Zhu Dongrun 朱東潤. Shanghai: Shanghai guji chubanshe, 2006.

Miao, Ronald C. "Literary Criticism at the End of the Eastern Han." *Literature East and West* 16 (1972): 1016–1026.

Miyazaki Ichisada 宮崎市定. "Kandai no risei to Tōdai no bōsei" 漢代の里制と唐代の 坊制. In *Miyazaki Ichisada zenshū* 宮崎市定全集, vol. 7. Tokyo: Iwanami Shoten, 1962.

Miyazaki Ichisada 宮崎市定. "Les villes en Chine à l'époque des Han." T'oung Pao 通報 48, no. 4/5 (1960): 376–392.

Müller, Shing. "Yezhong ji" 鄴中記. In *Early Medieval Chinese Texts: A Bibliographical Guide*, 442–449, edited by Cynthia L. Chennault and others. Berkeley: Institute of East Asian Studies, University of California, Berkeley, 2015.

Müller, Shing. *Yezhongji: Eine Quelle zur materiellen Kultur in der Stadt Ye im 4. Jahrhundert*. Stuttgart: Franz Steiner Verlag, 1993.

Niu Runzhen 牛潤珍. "Dong Wei Bei Qi Yejing lifang zhidu kao" 東魏北齊鄴京里坊制 度考. *Jinyang xuekan* 晉陽學刊, no. 6 (2009): 81–85.

Niu Runzhen 牛潤珍. "Hou Zhao Ye ducheng zhi jianzhu kao: Zhong shiji dongya ducheng zhidu tanyuan zhi er" 後趙鄴都城制建築考： 中世紀東亞都城制度探源之二. *Hebei xuekan* 河北學刊 28, no. 3 (2008): 84–90.

Niu Runzhen 牛潤珍. "Qin Han Yecheng gouchen" 秦漢鄴城鈎沈. *Jinyang xuekan* 晉陽學刊, no. 6 (2011): 111–115.

Niu Runzhen 牛潤珍. "Ruhe zhuiqiu lishi zhenshi: you gudu Yecheng yanjiu suo tihui daode" 如何追求歷史真實： 由古都鄴城研究所體會到的. *Xuexi yu tansuo* 學習與探索, no. 2 (2009): 213–15.

Niu Runzhen 牛潤珍. "Xigaoxue damu shifou wei Cao Cao mu" 西高穴大墓是否為曹操墓. *Zhongguo Renmin daxue xuebao* 中國人民大學學報 4, no. 3 (2010): 127–133.

Niu Runzhen 牛潤珍. "Ye yu zhongshiji dongya ducheng chengzhi xitong" 鄴與中世紀東亞都城城制系統. *Hebei xuekan* 河北學刊 26, no. 5 (2006): 105–114.

Niu Runzhen 牛潤珍. "Yecheng chengzhi dui gudai Chaoxian, Riben ducheng zhidu de yingxiang" 鄴城城制對古代朝鮮、日本都城制度的影響. In *Hanguo yanjiu luncong* (Di shiwu ji) 韓國研究論叢 (第十五輯), edited by Shi Yuanhua 石源華, 271–289. Beijing: Shijie zhishi chuban she, 2007.

Niu Runzhen 牛潤珍. "Yecheng: Zhongguo, yazhou yu shijie chengshi shi yanjiu zhong de yige mi" 鄴城： 中國、亞洲與世界城市史研究中的一個迷. *Shilin* 史林, no. 3 (2009): 12–20.

Ōji Oka 岡大路. *Zhongguo gongyuan yuanlin shi kao* 中國宮苑園林史考. Translated by Chang Yingsheng 常瀛生. Beijing: Xueyuan chuban she, 2008.

Quan Yuan wen 全元文. Nanjing: Jiangsu guji chuban she, 2001.

Ouyang Xiu 歐陽修 (1007–1072). *Ouyang Xiu quanji* 歐陽修全集. Taipei: Heluo tushu chuban she, 1975.

Owen, Stephen. *An Anthology of Chinese Literature: Beginnings to 1911*. New York: W. W. Norton & Company, Inc., 1996.

Owen, Stephen. "A Discourse on Literature." In *Readings in Chinese Literary Thought*, 57–72. Cambridge: Council on East Asian Studies Harvard University, 1992.

Owen, Stephen. *Remembrances: The Experience of the Past in Classical Chinese Literature*. Cambridge, MA: Harvard University Press, 1986.

Owen, Stephen. *The Late Tang Chinese Poetry of the Mid-Ninth Century (827–860)*. Cambridge, MA: Harvard University Asia Center, 2006.

Owen, Stephen. *The Making of Early Chinese Classical Poetry*. Cambridge, MA: Harvard University Asia Center, 2006

Pak T'ae-dök 朴泰德. "Jian'an shidai Ye xia wenshi de yanjiu" 建安時代鄴下文士的研究. MA thesis, Taiwan University, 1990.

Pan Fujun 潘富俊. *Tangshi zhiwu tujian* 唐詩植物圖鑑. Taipei: Maotouying chuban she, 2001.

Pan Ling 潘泠. "Shilun 'Yuefu shiji' zhong Nanbei shiren dui Yecheng lishi wenhua de butong shuxie" 試論《樂府詩集》中南北詩人對鄴城歷史文化的不同書寫. *Lishi jiaoxue wenti* 歷史教學問題, no. 1 (2014): 101–106.

WORKS CITED

Pan Xiaolong 潘嘯龍. "Yexia shehui he Jian'an zhu zi de chuangzuo fengmao" 鄴下社會和建安諸子的創作風貌. *Anhui shida xuebao* 安徽師大學報 21, no. 4 (1993): 419–27.

Peng Hongcheng 彭鴻程. "Shilun Lu Yun de wenxue chuangzuo" 試論陸雲的文學創作. *Hubei shehui kexue* 湖北社會科學, no. 1 (2008): 142–144.

Pollard, David. "Ch'i in Chinese Literary Theory." In *Chinese Approaches to Literature from Confucius to Liang Ch'i-ch'ao*, edited by Adele Rickett, 43–66. Princeton: Princeton University Press, 1978.

Pregadio, Fabrizio. *Great Clarity: Daoism and Alchemy in Early Medieval China*. Stanford: Stanford University Press, 2005.

Qin Peiheng 秦佩珩. "Yecheng kao" 鄴城考. *Henan wenbo tongxun* 河南文博通訊, no. 1 (1979): 37–42 and 44.

Qin Peiheng 秦佩珩. "Yedu zhuosuo" 鄴都掇瑣. *Zhengzhou daxue xuebao* 鄭州大學學報, no. 4 (1978): 95–106.

Quan Jiayu 權家玉. "Han mo Xuchang diwei de bianqian" 漢末許昌地位的變遷. *Xinyang shifan xueyuan xuebao* 信陽師範學院學報 28, no. 6 (2008): 152–56.

Quan Tang shi 全唐詩. 25 Vols. Beijing: Zhonghua shuju, 1960.

Reed, Bernard E., comp. *Chinese Medicinal Plants from the Pen Ts'ao Kang Mu* 本草綱目 *A.D. 1596 of a Botanical, Chemical and Pharmacological Reference List* (the reprint of 1936 Shanghai edition). Taipei: Nantian shuju, 1977.

Ren Huifang 任慧芳. "Tangdai Ye di shiren shige chutan: jianlun Ye wenhua de xingcheng he shanbian" 唐代鄴地詩人詩歌初探：兼論鄴文化的形成何嬗變. *Gansu linye zhiye jishu xueyuan xuebao* 甘肅林業職業技術學院學報, no. 7 (2006): 100–03.

Richter, Antje, ed. *A History of Chinese Letters and Epistolary Culture*. Leiden: Brill, 2015.

Rickett, Adele, ed. *Chinese Approaches to Literature from Confucius to Liang Ch'i-ch'ao*. Princeton: Princeton University Press, 1978.

Roberts, Moss. *Three Kingdoms: A Historical Novel*. Beijing: Foreign Languages Press and Berkeley: University of California Press, 1994.

San guo zhi 三國志. Beijing: Zhonghua shuju, 1959.

Schaberg, David. "Travel, Geography, and the Imperial Imagination in Fifth-Century Athens and Han China" *Comparative Literature* 51, no. 2 (Spring, 1999): 152–191.

Schafer, Edward H. "Hallucinations and Epiphanies in T'ang Poetry." *Journal of the American Oriental Society*, 104, no. 4 (October–December, 1984): 757–760.

Schafer, Edward H. *Pacing the Void: T'ang Approaches to the Stars*. Berkeley: University of California Press, 1977.

Schafer, Edward H. "The Yeh Chung Chi" *T'oung Pao* 通報, no. 76 (1990): 147–207.

Sedo, Timothy R. "Linzhang County and the Culturally Central Periphery in Mid-Ming China." PhD diss., University of British Columbia, 2010.

Shanhai jing 山海經. Edited by Guo Pu 郭璞 (276–324). Rpt. Shanghai: Shanghai guji chuban she, 1991.

Shen Jianshi 沈兼士. *Guangyun shengxi* 廣韻聲系. Taipei: Dahua shuju, 1984.

Shen Kun 沈琨. "Zhanghe anpan fang Yecheng" 漳河岸畔訪鄴城. *Xungen* 尋根, no. 5 (2004): 50–57.

Shen Youshun 申有順. "Ye cheng—woguo gudai chengshi fazhan shi shang de licheng bei" 鄴城：我國古代城市發展史上的里程碑. *Handan zhiye jishu xueyuan xuebao* 邯鄲職業技術學院學報 20, no. 2 (2007): 4–9.

Shi Changyou 史昌友. *Yecheng-Ye wenhua-Cao Cao* 鄴城－鄴文化－曹操. Zhengzhou, Henan: Zhongzhou guji chuban she, 2012.

Shi Hejin 施和金, comp. *Bei Qi dili zhi* 北齊地理志. In *Ershisi shi yanjiu ziliao congkan* 二十四史研究資料叢刊. Beijing: Zhonghua shuju, 2008.

Shi Hejin 施和金, comp. *Zhongguo lishi dili yanjiu (xuji)* 中國歷史地理研究 (續集). Beijing: Zhonghua shuju, 2009.

Shi ji 史記. Beijing: Zhonghua shuju, 1959.

Shi Nianhai 史念海. "Huangtu gaoyuan zhuyao heliu liuliang bianqian" 黃土高原主要河流流量變遷. *Zhongguo lishi dili luncong* 中國歷史地理論叢, no. 2 (1992): 1–36.

Shi Yuanhua 石源華, ed. *Hanguo yanjiu luncong (Di shiwu ji)* 韓國研究論叢 (第十五輯). Beijing: Shijie zhishi chuban she, 2007.

Shih, Hsiang-Lin. "Jian'an Literature Revisited: Poetic Dialogues in the Last Three Decades of the Han Dynasty." PhD diss., University of Washington, 2013.

Shuowen jiezi zhu 說文解字注. Annotated by 段玉裁 (1735–1815). Qing edition 1873 photo-reprinted. Shanghai: Shanghai guji chuban she, 1981.

Song shu 宋書. Beijing: Zhonghua shuju, 1974.

Song Yanpeng 宋燕鵬. "Ximen Bao xinyang: Zhonggu Yexia jumin de yige shenghuo neirong" 西門豹信仰：中古鄴下居民的一個生活內容. *Handan zhiye jishu xueyuan xuebao* 邯鄲職業技術學院學報 20, no. 4 (December, 2007): 7–11.

Song Yanpeng 宋燕鵬, and Sun Jimin 孫繼民. "Lun liu shiji Yecheng wenxue zai Bei chao wenxue shishang de diwei" 論六世紀鄴城文學在北朝文學史上的地位. *Handan xueyuan xuebao* 邯鄲學院學報 18, no. 4 (2008): 21–26, 40.

Stuart G. A. *Chinese Materia Medica: Vegetable Kingdom* (The reprint of 1911 Shanghai edition). Taipei: Nantian shuju, 1979.

Steinhardt, Nancy Shatzman. "China." In *The Oxford Handbook of Cities in World History*, edited by Peter Clark, 105–124. Oxford: Oxford University Press, 2013.

Steinhardt, Nancy Shatzman. *Chinese Imperial City Planning*. Honolulu: University of Hawai'i Press, 1990.

Steinhardt, Nancy Shatzman, and Fu Xinian. *Chinese Architecture*. New Haven: Yale University Press, 2002.

Su Jui-Lung 蘇瑞隆. "The Patterns and Changes of Literary Patronage in the Han and Wei." In *Interpretation and Literature in Early Medieval China*, edited by Alan K. L. Chan and Yuet-Keung Lo, 41–61. Albany: State University of New York Press, 2010.

Su Xiaohua 蘇小華. "Bei Wei Xiaowu di yu Dong Xi Wei fenlie" 北魏孝武帝與東西魏分裂. *Huaiyin shifan xueyuan xuebao* 淮陰師範學院學報 31, no. 4 (2009): 490–94.

WORKS CITED

Su Xiaohua蘇小華. "Dong Wei Bei Qi zhongbei qingnan de yuanyin ji qi yingxiang" 東魏、北齊重北輕南的原因及其影響. *Shehui kexue pinglun* 社會科學評論, no. 4 (2009): 80–87.

Sui shu 隋書. Beijing: Zhonghua shuju, 1973.

Sun Jimin 孫繼民. "Yexia subo de shangye wenhua xingzhi" 鄴下俗薄的商業文化性質. *Zhongguo jingji shi yanjiu* 中國經濟史研究, no. 2 (2004): 95–98.

Sun Lian 孫煉. "Dazhe zhao tiandi zhi biao xizhe ru haoqian zhi nei: Han dai yuanlin shi yanjiu" 大者罩天地之表細者入毫纖之內：漢代園林史研究. MA thesis, Tianjin daxue 天津大學, 2003.

Sun Mingjun 孫明君. "Di san zhong shili: zhengzhi shijiao zhong de Hongdu men xue" 第三種勢力：政治視角中的鴻都門學. *Xuexi yu tansuo* 學習與探索 142, no. 5 (2002): 124–29.

Sun Mingjun 孫明君. "Xie Lingyun 'Ni Wei taizi Yezhong ji shi bashou' zhong de Yexia zhi you" 謝靈運《擬魏太子鄴中集詩八首》中的鄴下之游. *Shaanxi shifan daxue xuebao* 陝西師範大學學報 35, no. 1 (2006): 24–28.

Sun Mingjun 孫明君. "Zhongguo gudai yonghuai shi de jiben leixing" 中國古代詠懷詩的基本類型. *Shaanxi shifan daxue jixu jiaoyu xuebao* 陝西師範大學繼續教育學報 19, no. 1 (2002): 53–56.

Swartz, Wendy. "Revisiting the Scene of the Party: A Study of the Lanting Collection." *Journal of the American Oriental Society* 132, no. 2 (2012): 275–300.

Swartz, Wendy. "Trading Literary Competence: Exchange Poetry in the Eastern Jin." In *Reading Medieval Chinese Poetry: Text, Context, and Culture*, edited by Paul W. Kroll, 6–35. Leiden: Brill, 2015.

Taiping yulan 太平御覽. Beijing: Zhonghua shuju, 1985.

Tang Guizhang 唐圭璋, ed. *Cihua congbian* 詞話叢編. 5 Vols. Beijing: Zhonghua shuju, 1986.

Tian, Xiaofei. "A Preliminary Comparison of the Two Recensions of 'Jinpingmei.'" *Harvard Journal of Asiatic Studies* 62, no. 2 (December, 2002): 347–388.

Tian, Xiaofei. "Cao Pi, 'A Discourse on Literature.'" In *Hawai'i Reader in Traditional Chinese Culture*, edited by Victor H. Mair, and others, 231–233. Honolulu: University of Hawai'i Press, 2004.

Tian, Xiaofei. "Fan Writing: Lu Ji, Lu Yun and the Cultural Transactions between North and South." In *Southern Identity and Southern Estrangement in Medieval Chinese Poetry*, edited by Ping Wang and Nicholas Morrow Williams, 43–78. Hong Kong: Hong Kong University Press, 2015.

Tian Yuxing 田宇星. "Liu Xiaochuo ji jiaozhu" 劉孝綽集校注. MA thesis, Sichuan daxue 四川大學, 2006.

Tsao, Joanne. "The Creation of the Bronze Bird Terrace-scape in the Northern and Southern Dynasties Period." *Early Medieval China* 23 (2017): 89–104.

Tsao, Joanne. "Yuan Haowen—Written to the Lyric Pattern Mulan Hua Man: Two Poems of the 'Roaming the Three Terraces.'" *Metamorphoses* 26 (Spring/Fall, 2018): 54–58.

Wan Shengnan 萬繩楠. *Wei Jin Nanbei chao wenhua shi* 魏晉南北朝文化史. Taipei: Zhishufang chuban jituan, 1995.

Wang Dehua 王德華. "Zuo Si 'Sandu fu' Yedu de xuanze yu miaoxie: Jianlun 'Luoyang zhigui' de lishi yu zhengzhi Beijing" 左思《三都賦》鄴都的選擇與描寫—兼論「洛陽紙貴」的歷史與政治背景. *Zhejiang daxue xuebao* 浙江大學學報 43, no. 4 (July 2013): 146–156.

Wang Huanbiao 王煥鑣, ed. *Han Fei zi xuan* 韓非子選. Shanghai: Renmin chuban she, 1974.

Wang Jiajun 王家俊. "Watou lingluo liu canming: Yecheng tongque wayan kaobian" 瓦頭零落留殘銘：鄴城銅雀瓦硯考辨. *Yindu xuekan* 殷都學刊, no. 4 (1989): 32–34.

Wang Jing 王靜, and Shen Ruiwen 沈睿文. "Yige gushi chuanshuo de jiajie: Dong Wei Yecheng xingzhi yanjiu" 一個古史傳說的嫁接：東魏鄴城形制研究. *Beijing daxue xuebao* 北京大學學報, no. 3 (2006): 86–91.

Wang Juan 王娟. "Tangdai gongyuan shi yanjiu" 唐代宮怨詩研究. MA thesis, Nanchang daxue 南昌大學, 2007.

Wang Lin 王琳. "Zhongguo gudai zaoqi wangdu de jiben tezheng" 中國古代早期王都的基本特徵. *Zhongyuan wenwu* 中原文物, no, 4 (2006): 22–28.

Wang Liwei 王麗偉. "Tangdai Wudi shiren yanzhong de Ye yu Cao Cao" 唐代吳地詩人眼中的鄴與曹操. *Jiannan wenxue* 劍南文學, no. 3 (2011): 53–54.

Wang Ping. *The Age of Courtly Writing: Wen Xuan Compiler Xiao Tong (501–531) and His Circle*. Leiden: Brill, 2012.

Wang Ping, and Nicholas Morrow Williams, eds. *Southern Identity and Southern Estrangement in Medieval Chinese Poetry*. Hong Kong: Hong Kong University Press, 2015.

Wang Shizhen 王士禎 (1634–1711). *Chibei outan* 池北偶談. Edited by Jin Siran 靳斯仁. Beijing: Zhonghua shuju, 1997.

Wang Weiji 王偉濟, and Zhang Yumei 張玉梅, eds. *Zhongguo kaogu xue lunji* 中國考古學論集. Beijing: Kexue chubanshe, 1993.

Wang Wengao 王文誥 (b. 1764), ed. *Su Dongpo shiji* 蘇東坡詩, proofread by Tang Yunzhi 唐云志. Beijing: Zhuhai chubanshe, 1996.

Wang Wengao 王文誥 (b. 1764), ed. *Su Shi shiji* 蘇軾詩集. Proofread by Kong Fanli 孔凡禮. Beijing: Zhonghua shuju, 1982.

Wang Yichen 王怡辰. *Dong Wei Bei Qi de tongzhi jituan* 東魏北齊的統治集團. Taipei: Wenjing chuban she, 2006.

Warner, Ding Xiang. *A Wild Deer Amid Soaring Phoenixes: The Opposition Poetics of Wang Ji*. Honolulu: University of Hawai'i Press, 2003.

WORKS CITED

Wei Hongcan 魏宏燦. "Caoshi fuzi yu Yexia wenshi de wenxue jiaoyou" 曹氏父子與鄴下文士的文學交游. *Fuyang shifan xueyuan xuebao* 阜陽師範學院學報 100, no. 4 (2004): 39–42.

Wei Hongcan 魏宏燦. "Yexia wenxue jituan de guizu hua tezheng" 鄴下文學集團的貴族化特徵. *Huainan shifan xueyuan xuebao* 淮南師範學院學報 12, no. 4 (2010): 21–23.

Wei Shu 魏書. Beijing: Zhonghua shuju, 1974.

Wenyuan yinghua 文苑英華. Beijing: Zhonghua shuju, 1966.

West, Stephen H. "Autumn Sounds: Music to the Ears, Ouyang Xiu's 'Fu on Autumn's Sounds.'" *Early Medieval China*, 10–11.2 (2005): 73–99.

Wu Fusheng 吳伏生. "I Rambled and Roamed Together with You: Liu Zhen's (d. 217) Four Poems to Cao Pi." *Journal of the American Oriental Society* 129, no. 4 (Oct.–Dec. 2009): 619–633.

Wu Fusheng 吳伏生. "Wang Can 'Congjun shi' xilun: jiantan gudai de songshi" 王粲《從軍詩》析論—兼談古代的誦詩. *Zhongguo shixue* 中國詩學, no. 10 (2004): 75–81.

Wu Sujane. "Clarity, Brevity, and Naturalness: Lu Yun and his Works." PhD diss., University of Wisconsin-Madison, 2001.

Wu Xueling 吳雪伶. "Tangdai Tongque tai shi de shuangchong huiyi moshi yu gongyuan zhuti" 唐代銅雀台詩的雙重回憶模式與宮怨主題. *Hubei shehui kexue* 湖北社會科學, no. 8 (2006): 105–107.

Xiao Tong 蕭統 (501–531). *Wen xuan* 文選. Beijing: Zhonghua shuju, 1977.

Xie Chengren 謝承仁, comp. *Yang Shoujing ji* 楊守敬集, vol. 5. Wuhan: Hubei renmin chuban she, 1988.

Xie Tiao 謝朓 (464–499). *Xie Xuancheng ji jiaozhu* 謝宣城集校注. Annotated by Cao Rongnan 曹融南. Shanghai: Shanghai guji chuban she, 1991.

Xin Tang shu 新唐書. Beijing: Zhonghua shuju,1975.

Xinhua Daily Telegraph 新華每日電訊. "Xi gaoxue cun cunmin Xu Yuchao: Lu Qian muzhi shi wo juan de" 西高穴村村民徐玉超：魯潛墓誌是我捐的. September 3, 2010, sec. 4. <http://news.xinhuanet.com/mrdx/2010-09/03/content_14121770.htm> (accessed September 18, 2014).

Xinjiao Zizhi tongjian zhu 新校資治通鑑注. Compiled by Sima Guang 司馬光 (1019–1086). Taipei: Shijie shuju, 1974.

Xing Peishun 邢培順. "Lun Jian'an wenxue de qianqi tedian" 論建安文學的前期特點. *Liaocheng daxue xuebao* 聊城大學學報, no. 2 (2012): 51–57.

Xu Shuyi 徐樹儀. "Shi emeng zhi xiang haishi zuojia leyuan: luelun Yexia wentan de chuangzuo huanjing" 是噩夢之鄉還是作家樂園：略論鄴下文壇的創作環境. *Shanghai shifan daxue xuebao* 上海師範大學學報, no. 2 (1988): 42–48.

Xu Guangji 徐光冀. "Cao Wei Ye cheng de pingmian fuyuan yanjiu" 曹魏鄴城的平面復原研究. In *Zhongguo kaogu xue lunji* 中國考古學論集, edited by Wang Weiji 王偉濟, and Zhang Yumei 張玉梅, 422–428. Beijing: Kexue chubanshe, 1993.

Xu Zuomin 許作民, ed. *Yedu yizhi ji jiaozhu* 鄴都佚志輯校注. Zhengzhou, Henan: Zhongzhou guji chuban she, 1996.

Xu Zuosheng 徐作生. "Jianxiong sihou yi qiren: Cao Cao qishier yizhong tafang" 奸雄死後亦欺人：曹操七十二疑塚踏訪. In *Zhongwai zhongda lishi zhi mi tukao* 中外重大歷史之謎圖考, 191–239. Beijing: Zhongguo shehui kexue chuban she, 2006.

Yan Chongnian 閻崇年, comp. *Zhongguo lidai ducheng gongyuan* 中國歷代都城宮苑. Beijing: Zijin cheng chubanshe, 1987.

Yan Kejun 嚴可均 (1762–1843), comp. *Quan shanggu sandai Qin Han San guo Liu chao wen* 全上古三代秦漢三國六朝文. 4 Vols. Beijing: Zhonghua shuju, 1991.

Yang Fei 楊飛, Liu Yanjun 劉彥軍, and Li Guichang 李貴昌. "Yecheng, Anyang chen ji qi jiuge" 鄴城、安陽城及其糾葛. *Yindu xuekan* 殷都學刊, no. 3 (2004): 26–28.

Yang Hongquan 楊洪權. "Yecheng zai Wei Jin Nan Bei chao junshi shang de diwei" 鄴城在魏晉南北朝軍事上的地位. *Yantai shifan xueyuan xuebao* 煙臺師範學院學報, no. 2 (1991): 40–45 and 31.

Yang Hongquan 楊洪權. "Yecheng zai Wei Jin Nan Bei chao zhengzhi shang de diwei" 鄴城在魏晉南北朝政治上的地位. *Yantai shifan xueyuan xuebao* 煙臺師範學院學報, no. 1 (1993): 70–74.

Yang Kuan 楊寬. *Zhongguo gudai ducheng zhidu shi* 中國古代都城制度史. Shanghai: Renmin chuban she, 2006.

Yang Qian 楊倩. "Yexia gongyan shi: Xian Qin yanyin shi de jicheng he fazhan" 鄴下公宴詩：先秦宴飲詩的繼承和發展. *Shidai wenxue* 時代文學, no. 2 (2008): 70–71.

Yang Wenheng 楊文衡. "Turang dili" 土壤地理. In *Zhongguo gudai dili xue shi* 中國古代地理學史, edited by Zhongguo kexue yuan ziran kexue shi yanjiu suo dixueshi zu, 202–233. Beijing: Kexue chuban she, 1984.

Yang Wuquan 楊武泉. "Wei Wenhou du Ye bian" 魏文侯都鄴辨. *Zhongnan minzu xueyuan xuebao* 中南民族學院學報, no. 4 (1982): 54.

Yang Xiaoshan. *Metamorphosis of the Private Sphere: Gardens and Objects in Tang-Song Poetry*. Cambridge, MA: Harvard University Asia Center, 2003.

Yang Yang 楊陽. "Ye cheng chutu foxiang yi shi miefo yundong suo mai" 鄴城出土佛像疑是滅佛運動所埋. *Zhongguo shehui kexue bao* 中國社會科學報, March 21, 2012. <http://news.sina.com.cn/c/2012-03-21/163924152099.shtml> (accessed October 3, 2019).

Yang Yong 楊勇. *Shishuo xinyu jiaojian* 世說新語校箋. Taipei: Letian chuban she, 1973.

Yang Zhiyi. *The Dialectics of Spontaneity: The Aesthetics and Ethics of Su Shi (1037–1101)*. Leiden: Brill, 2015.

Yao Dianzhong 姚奠中, comp. *Yuan Haowen quanji* 元好問全集. 2 Vols. Taiyuan, Shanxi: Shanxi renmin chubanshe, 1990.

Ye Xiaojun 葉驍軍. *Zhongguo ducheng fazhan shi* 中國都城發展史. Xi'an: Shanxi remin chuban she, 1988.

WORKS CITED

Ye Xiaojun 葉驍軍. *Zhongguo ducheng lishi tulu* 中國都城歷史圖錄. 4 Vols. Lanzhou, Gansu: Lanzhou daxue chuban she, 1986.

Yi Jianxian 易健賢, ed. *Wei Wendi ji quanyi* 魏文帝集全譯. Guiyang: Guizhou renmin chuban she, 2009.

Yin zhizhang 尹知章 (ca. 669–718), ed. "Guanzi jiaozheng ershisi juan" 管子校正二十四卷. In *Xinbian Zhuzi jicheng* 新編諸子集成, vol. 5, 1–427. Taipei: Shijie shuju, 1979.

Yiwen leiju 藝文類聚. Taipei: Wenguang chuban she, 1974.

Yu Shaochu 俞紹初. *Jian'an qizi ji* 建安七子集. Beijing: Zhonghua shuju, 2005.

Yu Shiling 俞士玲. "Lu Yun 'Yu xiong Pingyuan shu' zhaji yize" 陸雲《與兄平原書》札記一則. *Guji zhengli yanjiu xuekan* 古籍整理研究學刊, no. 3 (1996): 47–48.

Yu Weichao 俞偉超. "Ye cheng diaocha ji" 鄴城調查記. *Kaogu* 考古, no. 1 (1963): 15–25.

Yuan Aixia 袁愛俠. "Tongque wenhua de luxing: yi wenhua luxing de shidian kan cong Wei dao Nan Bei chao de tongque wenhua" 銅雀文化的旅行：以文化旅行的視點看從魏到南北朝的銅雀文化. *Sichuan wenhua chanyan zhiyan xueyuan xuebao* 四川文化產業職業學院學報, no. 3 (2008): 36–38.

Yuan Shuyi 苑書義, and others, comps. *Zhang Zhidong quanji* 張之洞全集. 12 Vols. Shijiazhuang, Hebei: Hebei renmin chuban she, 1998.

Yuefu shiji 樂府詩集. Compiled by Guo Maoqian 郭茂倩 (1041–1099). Beijing: Zhonghua shuju, 1979.

Zeng Zaozhuang 曾棗莊, comp. *Su shi huiping* 蘇詩彙評. Chengdu: Sichuan wenyi chuban she, 2000.

Zhan Zongyou 詹宗祐. "Wei Jin Nan Bei chao shiqi de Yecheng" 魏晉南北朝時期的鄴城. MA thesis. Zhongguo Wenhua University, 1990.

Zhang Huizhi 張慧芝. "Gudu wenhua zai chengshi yu xiangcun wenhua ronghe fazhan zhong de zuoyou: Yedu wenhua yu Linzhang chengxian wenhua yiti hua de sikao" 古都文化在城市與鄉村文化融合發展中的作用：鄴都文化與臨漳城鄉文化一體化的思考. *Handan zhiye jishu xueyuan xuebao* 邯鄲職業技術學院學報 24, no. 4 (2011): 7–12.

Zhang Keli 張可禮. *San Cao nianpu* 三曹年譜. Ji'nan: Qilu shushe, 1983.

Zhang Junrui 張俊銳. "Huiwang Yecheng" 回望鄴城. *Sanwen baijia* 散文百家, no. 12 (2009): 19–20.

Zhang Lanhua 張蘭花. "Jian'an wenxue chuangzuo quyu de qianyi yu wenfeng shanbian kaolun: Yi Xuxia he Yexia wenren qunti wei zhongxin" 建安文學創作區域的遷移與文風嬗變考論：以許下和鄴下文人群體為中心. *Zhonghua wenhua luntan* 中華文化論壇, no. 4 (2007): 90–97.

Zhang Lianying 張蓮英. "Cao Cao zai Anyang" 曹操在安陽. *Jilin huabao* 吉林畫報, no. 2 (2011): 62–64.

Zhang Pingyi 張平一. "Cong wenxian kan gudu Yecheng de xingfei" 從文獻看古都鄴城的興廢. *Wenwu chunqiu* 文物春秋, no. 1 (1989): 92–102.

198   WORKS CITED

Zhang Pingyi 張平一. "Gudu Yecheng lueshu" 古都鄴城略述. *Hebei xuekan* 河北學刊, no. 1 (1983): 171–75.

Zhang Qinnan 張欽楠. *Zhongguo gudai jianzhu shi* 中國古代建築師. Beijing: Sanlian shudian, 2008.

Zhang Zhao 張照. "Cong 'Yu xiong Pingyuan shu' kan Lu Yun cifu" 從《與兄平原書》看陸雲辭賦. *Daxian shifan gaodeng zhuanke xuexiao xuebao* 達縣師範高等專科學校學報, no. 4 (2006): 41–43.

Zhang Zhenlong 張振龍. "Yexia wenren jituan neibu huodong dui wenren guannian de yingxiang" 鄴下文人集團內部活動對文人觀念的影響. *Nanyang shifan xueyuan xuebao* 南陽師範學院學報 4, no. 5 (2005): 71–77.

Zhang Zhenlong 張振龍. "Yexia wenxue jituan jiaoji huodong de wenxue tezheng" 鄴下文學集團交際活動的文學特徵. *Xi'an wenli xueyuan xuebao* 西安文理學院學報 8, no. 3 (2005): 5–8.

Zhang Zhenlong 張振龍. "Yexia wenxue jituan neibu huodong yu xing, guan, qun, yuan de wenxue guannian" 鄴下文學集團內部活動與興、觀、群、怨的文學觀念. *Nanyang shifan xueyuan xuebao* 南陽師範學院學報, 8 no. 1 (2009): 87–93.

Zhao Feng 趙豐. *Jincheng—Zhongguo sichou yu sichou zhi lu* 錦程：中國絲綢與絲綢之路. Hong Kong: City University of Hong Kong Press, 2012.

Zhao Minli 趙敏俐, and Satō Toshiyuki 佐藤利行, eds. *Zhongguo zhonggu wenxue yanjiu* 中國中古文學研究. Beijing: Xueyuan chuban she, 2005.

Zhao Runtian 趙潤田. "Cong Yecheng dao Beijing" 從鄴城到北京. *Gonghui bolan* 工會博覽, no. 4 (2012): 40–41.

Zhao Yaofeng 趙耀鋒. "Lun Yexia shiqi wenxue de zijue" 論鄴下時期文學的自覺. *Ningxia shifan xueyuan xuebao* 寧夏師範學院學報 29, no. 4 (2008): 25–29.

Zhao Yongyuan 趙永源. *Yishan ci yanjiu* 遺山詞研究. Shanghai: Shanghai guji chuban she, 2007.

Zhao Yongyuan 趙永源. *Yishan yuefu jiaozhu* 遺山樂府校註. Nanjing: Fenghuang chuban she, 2006.

Zhao Youwen 趙幼文. *Cao Zhi ji jiaozhu* 曹植集校注. Beijing: Renming wenxue chuban she, 1984.

Zheng Hui 鄭輝, and others. "Cao Wei shiqi Ye cheng yuanlin wenhua yanjiu" 曹魏時期鄴城園林文化研究. *Beijing linye daxue xuebao* 北京林業大學學報 11, no. 2 (June, 2012): 39–43.

Zheng Qian 鄭騫, ed. *Chen Jianzhai shiji hejiao huizhu* 陳簡齋詩集合校彙注. Taipei: Lianjing chuban shiye gongsi, 1975.

Zheng Liang-shu 鄭良樹. "Chuti fengzuo: Cao Wei jituan de fuzuo huodong" 出題奉作—曹魏集團的賦作活動. In *Wei Jin Nanbeichao wenxue lunji* 魏晉南北朝文學論集. Edited by Hong Kong Zhongwen daxue Zhongguo yuyan wenxue xi 香港中文大學中國語言文學系. Taipei: Wenshizhe chubanshe, 1994.

WORKS CITED

Zheng Wenqiao 鄭文僑. "Wei Jin yuanlin zhi shi wenhua yiyun" 魏晉園林之士文化意蘊. MA thesis, Chenggong daxue, 2004.

Zheng Hui 鄭輝, Li Geng 麗耕, and Li Fei 李飛. "Cao Wei shiqi Yecheng yuanlin wenhua yanjiu" 曹魏時期鄴城園林文化研究. *Beijing linye daxue xuebao* 北京林業大學學報 11, no. 2 (2010): 39–43.

Zheng Yu-yu 鄭毓瑜. "Shilun gongyan shi zhiyu Yexia wenren jituan de xiangzheng yiyi" 試論公讌詩之於鄴下文人集團的象徵意義. In *Liuchao qingjing meixue zonglun* 六朝情境美學綜論. Taipei: Taiwan Xuesheng shuju, 1996.

Zheng Yu-yu 鄭毓瑜. *Wenben fengjing: Ziwo yu kongjian de xianghu dingyi* 文本風景：自我與空間的相互定義. Taipei: Maitian chuban she, 2005.

Zhongguo daojiao da cidian 中國道教大辭典. Taizhong: Dongjiu qiye, 1996.

Zhongguo kexue yuan ziran kexue shi yanjiu suo dixueshi zu 中國科學院自然科學史研究所地學史組, ed. *Zhongguo gudai dili xue shi* 中國古代地理學史. Beijing: Kexue chuban she, 1984.

Zhou shu 周書. Beijing: Zhonghua shuju, 1971.

Zhou Weiquan 周維權. *Zhongguo gudian yuanlin shi* 中國古典園林史. Beijing: Qinghua daxue chuban she, 1999.

Zhou Yiliang 周一良. "Du Ye zhong ji" 讀《鄴中記》. In *Wei Jin Nan Bei chao shilun* 魏晉南北朝史論, 585–606. Shenyang, Liaoning: Liaoning jiaoyu chuban she, 1998.

Zhouli jinzhu jinyi 周禮今註今譯. Edited by Lin Yin 林尹. Taipei: Taiwan Shangwu yinshuguan, 1972.

Zhouli zhengyi 周禮正義. Annotated by Zheng Xuan 鄭玄 (127–200) and Jia Gongyan 賈公彥 (fl. 618–907). In *Shisan jing zhushu fu jiaokan ji* 十三經注疏附校勘記, edited by Ruan Yuan 阮元 (1764–1849), 8 vols. Taipei: Yiwen yingshu guan, 1982.

Zhu Dawei 朱大渭 and others. *Wei Jin Nan Bei chao shehui shenghuo shi* 魏晉南北朝社會生活史. Beijing: Zhongguo shehui kexue chuban she, 2005.

Zhu Dongrun 朱東潤. *Mei Yaochen ji biannian jiaozhu* 梅堯臣集編年校注. Shanghai: Shanghai guji chuban she, 2006.

Zhu Dongrun 朱東潤. *Mei Yaochen shixuan* 梅堯臣詩選. Beijing: Renmin wenxue chuban she, 1980.

Zhu Heping 朱和平. "Suichao Yecheng nanzhi shixi" 隋朝鄴城難治試析. *Zhongzhou xuekan* 中州學刊, no. 6 (1998): 136–138.

Zhu Shangshu 祝尚書. *Lu Sidao ji jiaozhu* 盧思道集校注. Chengdu: Ba Shu shushe, 2001.

Zhu Yanshi 朱岩石. "Ye cheng yizhi" 鄴城遺址 In *Hebei kaogu zhongyao faxian* 河北考古重要發現, edited by Hebei sheng wenwu yanjiu suo 河北省文物研究所. Beijing: Kexue chuban she, 2009.

Zhu Yanshi 朱岩石, and others. "Hebei Linzhang xian Ye cheng yizhi Bei Wuzhuang fojiao zaoxiang maicang keng de faxian yu fajue" 河北臨漳縣鄴城遺址北吳莊佛教造像埋藏坑的發現與發掘. *Kaogu* 考古, no. 4 (2012): 3–6.

Zhu Yanshi 朱岩石, and others. "Hebei Linzhang xian Ye cheng yizhi Dongwei Beiqi fosi taji de faxian yu fajue" 河北臨漳縣鄴城遺址東魏北齊佛寺塔基的發現與發掘. *Kaogu* 考古, no. 10 (2003): 3–6.

Zhu Yanshi 朱岩石, and others. "Hebei Linzhang xian Ye cheng yizhi Zhaopeng cheng Beichao fosi yizhi de kantan yu fajue" 河北臨漳縣鄴城遺址趙彭城北朝佛寺遺址的勘探與發掘. *Kaogu* 考古, no. 7 (2010): 31–42,102–105.

Zhuang Chengheng 莊程恆. "Bei Qi Jinyang: Ye cheng diqu mushi bihua de sangzang zhuti jiqi kongjian yingjian: Yi Bei Qi Xu Xianxiu mu wei zhongxin" 北齊晉陽: 鄴城地區墓室壁畫的喪葬主體及其空間營建: 以北齊徐顯秀墓為中心. *Meishu xuebao* 美術學報, no. 2 (2011): 23–32.

Zhuangzi ji shi 莊子集釋. Compiled by Guo Qingfan 郭慶藩 (1844–1896). Beijing: Zhonghua shuju, 1961.

Zou Yilin 鄒逸麟. "Shilun Yedu xingqi de lishi dili beijing jiqi zai gudu shi shang de diwei" 試論鄴都興起的歷史地理背景及其在古都史上的地位. *Zhongguo lishi dili luncong* 中國歷史地理論叢, no. 1 (1995): 77–89.

Zou Yilin 鄒逸麟. "Zhanguo shidai Yedu de xingqi" 戰國時代鄴都的興起. In *Zhongguo qi da gudu* 中國七大古都, edited by Chen Qiaoyi 陳橋驛, 131–134. Beijing: Zhongguo qingnian chuban she, 1991.

Index

Ai Xingfu 艾性夫 149–52

Allan, Sarah 76n103

Analects (*Lunyu* 論語) 90n47

ancestor worship 27n71, 105

Anyang 安陽 (Henan) 7, 117

"Arrowhead from the Battlefield of Changping" ("Changping jiantou ge" 長平箭頭歌; Li He) 56

"Ascending Ancient Ye City Walls" ("Deng gu Yecheng" 登古鄴城; Cen Shen) 126–27

Bai Juyi 白居易 159n2

"Ballad of Walking Out of Xia Gate" ("Buchu Xiamen xing" 步出夏門行; Cao Cao) 174

"Ballad of Yezhong" ("Yezhong xing" 鄴中行; Mei Yaochen) 122n10

Ban, Lady 班婕妤 108n97, 130

Ban Gu 班固 74n95, 160n5

Bao Zhao 鮑照 65n24, 171

barbarians 32, 35–36, 53n29, 119–20, 176. *See also* Yuan 元 dynasty

Bi'gan 比干 101n79

Bokenkamp, Stephen 133n29, 157n1

Bramble Terrace 荊臺 91n53

"Bronze Bird and Guan Inkstones" ("Tongque, Guan yan" 銅雀、灌硯; Hong Mai) 137–39

"Bronze Bird Inkstone" ("Tongque yan" 銅雀硯; Han Qi) 139–40

Bronze Bird Inkstones (Tongque yan 銅雀硯) 130–55; authenticity of, 131–37, 155, 157–58; and literati (*shi* 士) vs. dilettantes (*haoshi zhe* 好事者), 5–6, 134, 139, 144, 145–46, 158; utility of, 136–37, 144, 158

Bronze Bird Park (*Tongque yuan* 銅雀園; West Garden; *Xiyuan* 西園) 23, 57, 61, 65–66, 172n47, 175

"Bronze Bird Performers" ("Tongque ji" 銅雀妓; Gao Shi) 125–26

Bronze Bird Terrace (Tongque *tai* 銅雀臺) 2–5, 9, 26; Cao brothers on, 5, 46–49, 99; and Cao Cao, 17, 24, 45–56, 57, 99, 152; female performers on, 5, 103–7, 110–13, 120–26, 128–29, 142, 152, 153, 157, 168; in later poems, 161, 168, 171; and Murong Jun, 33; renaming of, 115n112, 162n15; and Shi Hu, 30, 32; in Southern and Northern dynasty poetry, 101–3, 115, 116; in Tang poetry, 120–30; tiles from, 4, 131, 136, 137, 144, 156

"Bronze Bird Terrace" ("Tongque tai" 銅雀臺; Xun Zhongju) 107–9

"Bronze Bird Terrace" ("Tongque tai" 銅雀臺; Zhang Zhengjian) 110–11

"Bronze Bird Tile" ("Tongque wa" 銅雀瓦; Wen Tianxiang) 146–47

Buddhism 9–10, 42

Campbell, Duncan 66n69

Cao Cao 曹操: and Bronze Bird Terrace 17, 24, 45–56, 57, 99, 152; capture of Ye by, 16, 164n21; criticism of, 5, 146, 149–52, 154–55, 158; female performers of, 5, 103–7, 110–13, 120–26, 128–29, 142, 152, 153, 157, 168; and Jian'an literature, 4–5, 34, 57, 58; in Jin poetry, 84, 98, 99–100; in later poetry, 124, 127, 128, 141n50, 146–48, 152–55, 158, 168, 169, 173, 177–78; poetry by, 104, 105, 110n102, 169–70, 172, 174; reconstruction of Ye by, 13, 16–26; and Shi Hu, 30, 32, 84; in Song poetry, 124, 146–48, 155, 158; in Southern and Northern dynasty poetry, 102, 103, 108, 112–13, 115, 116; "Testamentary Command" of, 54, 107, 109, 114, 146n56, 148, 153, 157, 158, 168, 175; and Three Terraces, 3, 16, 17, 19, 43; and tiles, 136, 144, 145; tomb of, 7–9, 104, 105, 109, 111, 157, 170, 171, 178; Ye's identification with, 1, 3–6, 44, 78, 156–58; in Yuan poetry, 146, 152–55

Cao Fang 曹芳 (Prince of Qi 齊王) 59, 60, 141n50

Cao Huan 曹奐 (Prince of Chenliu 陳留王) 151n71

Cao Jie 曹節 58n46, 151n70

Cao Jingui 曹金貴 120–21

Cao Pi 曹丕 (Emperor Wen of Wei 魏文帝) 36, 60, 141, 151n70, 160n8, 161n11; and Bronze Bird Terrace, 4–5, 46–47, 51; on literature, 45–46; in Luoyang, 26, 34, 59, 78;

202 INDEX

Cao Pi 曹丕 (cont.)
and parks, 58, 63–64, 67–68; poems by, 5,
53, 63–64, 67–73, 99n74
Cao Rongnan 曹融南 109n99
Cao Rui 曹叡 (Emperor Ming 明帝) 60,
141n50, 166–67, 167n28
Cao Song 曹嵩 150n67
Cao Teng 曹騰 150n67
Cao Wei 曹魏 dynasty 12, 27, 29, 140n44,
162; criticism of, 143, 146, 154; fall of, 5, 156,
161; and Jin dynasty, 85, 99; Luoyang as
capital of, 26, 34, 59, 78; and Northern Qi,
36; Ye under, 43, 115
Cao Zhi 曹志 (Cao Zhi 曹植's son) 95n62
Cao Zhi 曹植 5, 45, 95n62, 111n104, 142n51;
and Bronze Bird Terrace, 47–49, 51, 99; vs.
Lu Yun, 99–100; on parks, 59–60; poems
by, 50, 69, 159n3, 161n10, 172n47, 173
Casey, Edward 176
Cen Shen 岑參 126–27
Chang Hui 常惠 138n38
Chang'an 長安 (Xi'an 西安) 2, 26, 27n71, 51,
167nn32–33, 168; destruction of, 15, 16;
and Shi Hu 28, 61; vs. Ye 44
Changmen Palace laments (Changmen yuan
長門怨) 120
Changxin Palace laments (Changxin yuan
長信怨) 120
Chen Lin 陳琳 177–78
Chen Qun 153
Chen Weisong 陳維崧 159, 161
Chen Yuyi 陳與義 154–55
Cheng Changwen 程長文 123
Cheng Xuanying 成玄英 48n11, 69
Chuci 楚辭 53n30, 76n103, 89n43, 106n93,
109
Chunqiu chen 春秋讖 140n44
Chunzhu jiwen 春渚紀聞 (He Wei) 144
"Clerk of Xin'an" ("Xin'an li" 新安吏; Du
Fu) 164n20
"Companion work for Councilor Xie's 'Singing
for the Bronze Bird Terrace'" ("Tong Xie
ziyi yong Tongjue tai" 同謝諮議詠銅
爵臺; Xie Tiao) 104–5
Confucianism 68, 102
Cui Guang 崔光 101
Cui Junmiao 崔君苗 95, 96
Cui Xian 崔銑 23n57, 32, 134
Cutter, Robert Joe 50

Daoism 68. See also Laozi; Zhuangzi
dew-catching plate 承露盤 59–60, 167n33,
171, 172, 173
Di Boji 狄博濟 127n18
Di Renjie 狄仁杰 127n18
dilettantes (haoshi zhe 好事者) 5–6, 134,
139, 144, 145–46, 158
Disorder of the Eight Princes (bawang zhi
luan 八王之亂) 86
Disorder of Yongjia (Yongjia zhi luan 永嘉
之亂) 86
Ditches of Ximen (Ximen qu 西門渠) 12, 13
Dong Zhao 153
Dong Zhuo 董卓 15, 31n85, 141nn46–47,
150n66
Dongming Watchtower 東明觀 (Ye) 30
Doulu Tong 豆盧通 119
Du Fu 杜甫 127, 164n20, 164n22
Du Mu 杜牧 55–56, 139
Du Xi 杜襲 25
Duan Junyan 段君彦 162, 164
Duan Mobo 段末波 86
Duan Pidi 段匹磾 86

Eastern Wei 東魏 dynasty 36, 43, 78, 117,
176; and inkstones 135, 137, 138; and
southern city of Ye 1, 27, 39–40, 102, 115,
173
"Encomium to Kong Beihai with Preface"
("Kong Beihai zan bingxu" 孔北海贊
並序; Su Shi) 147–48
"Encountering Sorrow" ("Lisao" 離騷; Chuci
楚辭) 53n30, 76n103
ephemerality 2–3, 37–38, 56, 156; of
dynasties 127, 130, 139, 157, 167, 171; in Jin
poetry 94, 100; in later poetry 128, 140,
145, 161, 166; in Southern and Northern
dynasty poetry 105, 107, 114, 116; and Ye
gardens 57–77

Fan Shulue 樊叔略 118
Fan Zeng 范增 164n19
Fanglin Park 芳林園 (Hualin Park 華林園)
23n57, 57, 58, 59–60, 61, 89n44
Fangshu 方叔 142n51
"Feelings Inspired by the Ancient" ("Guxing"
古興; Li Jiayou) 129–30
Fei Chang 費昶 81n12
Feng Weina 馮惟訥 14n27

INDEX 203

five *du* 五都 cities 27n71

Five Hegemons of Spring and Autumn
(*chunqiu wuba* 春秋五霸）49n16

Five Phases 五行 84

"For Xu Gan" (*Zeng* Xu Gan 贈徐幹; Cao
Zhi) 48n12

Former Qin 前秦 dynasty 34

Former Yan 前燕 dynasty 1, 27, 33, 34, 78,
134, 176

Fu Jian 苻堅 31n85, 34

"*Fu* of Sir Vacuous" ("Zi Xu fu" 子虛賦; Sima
Xiangru) 67n71

"*Fu* on Ascending the Terrace" ("Deng tai fu"
登臺賦; Cao Zhi) 47–50, 52–53, 99–100

"*Fu* on Ascending the Terrace" ("Deng tai fu"
登臺賦; Cui Junmiao) 96

"*Fu* on Ascending the Terrace" ("Deng tai fu"
登臺賦; Lu Yun) 87–100, 139

"*Fu* on Ascending the Ye Terrace" ("Deng Yetai
fu" 登鄴臺賦; Lu Chen) 85–87, 99

"*Fu* on Pondering over the Abstruse" ("Sixuan
fu" 思玄賦; Zhang Heng) 90n46

"*Fu* on Regulating Roaming" ("Jieyou fu"
節遊賦; Cao Zhi) 73–77

"*Fu* on Sorrowing over Ceaseless Rain"
("Choulin fu" 愁霖賦; Lu Yun) 98

"Fu on the Delight of Clearing Skies" ("Xiji fu"
喜霽賦; Lu Yun) 98–99

"*Fu* on the East Capital" ("Dongjing fu"
東京賦; Zhang Heng) 60n51

"*Fu* on the Great Man" ("Daren fu" 大人賦;
Sima Xiangru) 90n49

"*Fu* on the Luo River Goddess" ("Luo shen fu"
洛神賦; Cao Zhi) 161n10

"*Fu* on the Red Cliff" ("Chibi fu" 赤壁賦; Su
Shi) 172n45, 174

"*Fu* on the Tongque Tile" ("Tongque wa fu"
銅雀瓦賦; Chen Weisong) 159–60

"Fu on the Twilight of the Year" ("Suimu fu"
歲暮賦; Lu Yun) 97–98

"*Fu* on the Weed-covered City" ("Wu cheng
fu" 蕪城賦; Bao Zhao) 165n24, 171

"*Fu* on the Wei Capital" ("Wei *du fu*" 魏都賦;
Cao Zhi) 48n12

"*Fu* on the Western Capital" ("Xidu fu"
西都賦; Ban Gu) 160n5

Fu Shou 伏壽 訥151n70

"Gallery of Prince Teng" ("Teng wang ge"
滕王閣; Wang Bo) 165–66

Ganjiang 干將 112n105

Gao Guangfu 高光復 126nn15–17

Gao Huan 高歡. *See* Xianwu, Emperor

Gao Longzhi 高隆之 39, 41n116

Gao Shi 高適 125

Gao Wei 高緯 175, 176

Gao Yang 高洋. *See* Wenxuan, Emperor

Gao Yin 高殷 (Prince Jinan 濟南王;
Northern Qi) 135n32

Gaozong, Emperor (Tang) 唐高宗 129n22,
130

Gaozu 高祖, Emperor (Liu Bang; Han)
102n81, 164n19

gardens 57–77, 156, 157, 163. *See also* parks

Ge Lifang 葛立方 123–24, 148

Golden Tiger Terrace (Jinhu *tai* 金虎臺) 9,
17, 19n43, 32, 98; renaming of 115n112,
162n15

Golden Valley Garden gathering (*Jingu zhi hui*
金谷之會) 66

Gong Kechang 龔克昌 48n9, 73n90, 75n100

Guan Gao 貫高 102n81

Guanzi 管子 11

Guo Jiqiao 郭濟橋 163n17

Guo Pu 郭璞 74n97, 163n15

Guo Si 郭汜 15, 141n47

Guo Xiang 郭象 69

Han Fu 韓馥 16

Han Ping 韓憑 159n4

Han Qi 韓琦 130, 139–40, 145

Han shu 漢書 31n85, 58n47, 138n38

Han 漢 dynasty 27n71, 31n85, 58n46, 168, 170

Hanfeizi 韓非子 72

Haojing 鎬京 37n105

He Wei 何蔇 144–46, 158

He Xun 何遜 103–4, 105

He Yan 何晏 160n9

Helü 闔閭 (Ji Guang 姬光) 80n9

Heng Chye Kiang 王才強 27n72

Heshu 和叔 75n103

Hezhong 和仲 75n103

Ho Cheung Wing 何祥榮 3–4

Hong Mai 洪邁 137–39, 140

Hong Xian 洪偘 137

Hou Han shu 後漢書 31n85, 122n10

INDEX

Hou Wei shu 後魏書   101
Huainanzi 淮南子 (Liu An)   71n83, 90n48
Hualin Park. *See* Fanglin Park
Huan, Duke of Qi 齊桓公   9, 11, 12, 49n16
Huan Jie 桓階   153n77
Huan Yi 桓齮   14
Huan 洹 River   17
Huang Gai 黃蓋   56
Huang Jian 黃鑑   133n28
Huang Kui 黃葵   93, 96, 98n72
Huang Shoucheng 黃守誠   57n40
Huang Tingjian 黃庭堅   137, 146n57
Huayang, Lady 華陽夫人   80n6
Huba 瓠巴   71n83
Hui, Emperor (Jin) 晉惠帝   98n72
hydraulic systems   12–14, 16–17, 26, 39

Ice Well Terrace (Bingjing *tai* 冰井臺)
   9, 19n43, 115n112, 134, 172
Imperial Forest Park (*Shanglinyuan* 上林苑)
   66n69
imperial streets (*yujie* 御街)   21, 23
"Inkstone from the Old Tile of Xiang
   Prefecture" ("Xiangzhou guyan wa" 相州
   古硯瓦; Wang Anshi)   133–34
inkstones. *See* Bronze Bird Inkstones
"Inscription of the Dew-Catching Plate"
   ("Chenglu pan ming" 承露盤銘; Cao
   Zhi)   59–60

Ji Liao 姬僚   80n9
Ji Qingji 姬慶忌 (King Wu of Wu 吳國
   武王)   80n9
Jia Xu 賈詡   48n11
Jia Zhi 賈至   123, 124
Jian'an literature (Jian'an *wenxue* 建安
   文學)   1–5, 45–77, 116, 172n47, 175; and
   Cao Cao   4–5, 34, 57, 58; gardens and
   parks in   57–77; Three Terraces
   in   45–56, 57
Jiang Shang 姜尚   37n105, 52n27
Jiang Yan 江淹   111–13
Jiangbiao zhuan 江表傳   55
Jiangwu City 講武城   9
Jiao Zhiqin 焦智勤   11
Jie 羯 people   28, 35
Jin shu 晉書   28, 29, 34–35, 60, 61, 85–86, 97

Jin 晉 dynasty   28, 115, 151n71; and Cao
   Wei   85; fall of   164, 166, 175;
   Western   97; Ye in literature of   5,
   79–100, 156–57
Jing, Emperor (Han) 漢景帝   141n45
Jiu Tang shu 舊唐書   117

Kaifeng 開封   2, 118, 164, 166
Kakutani Satoshi 角谷聰   122
Kang, Lord of Song 宋康王   159n4
Kaogong ji 考工記   21
Knechtges, David   1, 23n58, 60n51, 162
Kong Anguo 孔安國   75n103
Kong Rong 孔融   147–48, 154
Kong Yingda 孔穎達   71n85, 122n10
Kuang, Master 師曠   71n87, 72

"Lamenting the Death of Emperor Wu of
   Wei" ("Diao Wei Wudi wen" 弔魏武帝文;
   Lu Ji)   53–54
Lanting gathering (*Lanting zhihui* 蘭亭之會)
   66
Laozi 老子   85, 89n40, 90n47
Later Zhao 後趙 dynasty   1, 13, 27, 28, 34, 78,
   79, 82n13, 134
Legalism   27n72
Lei Jianhong 雷建紅   10
Li Cong 李琮   135
Li Daoyuan 酈道元   17, 25, 61, 62
Li Dian 李典   25
Li He 李賀   56, 123, 166–67, 168, 171, 173
Li Jiayou 李嘉祐   129–30
Li Jue 李傕   15, 141n47
Li Meitian 李梅田   10
Li Qi 李頎   79
Li Shangyin 李商隱   55n37, 78
Li Xian 李賢   91n53
Li Xianyong 李咸用   123
Li Yuanying 李元嬰 (Prince Teng 滕王)
   165, 171
li 里 and *fang* 坊 districts   27n72
Liang Qiong 梁瓊   123
Liang Xi 梁習   32
Liang Yanguang 梁彥光   119
Liang 梁 dynasty   115
Liao Yifang 廖宜方   121–22
Liezi 列子   127
Liji 禮記   37n103, 71n85, 76n106, 89n39

INDEX

205

Lin, Pauline 61n56
Ling, Duke of Wei 魏靈公 72
Ling, Emperor (Han) 漢靈帝 16, 141n46
Ling, King of Chu 楚靈王 91n53
Linghu Xi 令狐熙 118–19
Lingzhi Park 靈芝園 23n57, 57, 58
Lingzhi Reservoir 靈芝池 58
Linzhang 臨漳 1, 78n1
literary gatherings 65–66, 156, 172n47
Liu An 劉安 (Prince of Huainan 淮南王) 66n69, 90n48
Liu Bang 劉邦 (Emperor Gaozu) 102n81, 164n19
Liu Bei 劉備 51, 53, 56, 141n48, 177
Liu Bian 劉辯 141n46
Liu Biao 劉表 15n33
Liu Kaiyang 劉開揚 126nn15–17
Liu Kun 劉琨 85, 86
Liu Pi 劉濞 (Lord Wu of Former Han 西漢吳王) 165n24
Liu Qingzhu 劉慶柱 8–9
Liu Shen 劉詵 152–54
Liu Tingyi 劉庭琦 123
Liu Xiang 劉向 91n53
Liu Xiaochuo 劉孝綽 106–7
Liu Xie 劉協. See Xian, Emperor
Liu Yiqing 劉義慶 159n1
Liu Zhangqing 劉長卿 123
Liu Zixu 劉子頊 165n24
"Lord's Feast" ("Gongyan shi" 公燕詩; Cao Zhi) 172n47
Lord's Feast poems (Gongyan shi 公燕詩) 65–66, 70
Lü Bu 呂布 141n47
Lu Chen 盧諶 5, 85–87, 99
Lü Dongbin 呂洞賓 148n63
Lu Hui 陸翽 12, 79
Lu Ji 陸機 53–54, 95–96, 97n66, 100, 153, 157
Lu Kang 陸抗 96
Lu Qian 魯潛 7–8
Lu Qin 盧欽 86
Lu Xun 陸遜 96
Lu Yun 陸雲 5, 87–100, 114, 139, 156–57
Lu Zhi 盧志 86
Lu Zhi 盧植 86
Luo Guanzhong 羅貫中 50
Luo Yin 羅隱 123, 124

Luoyang 洛陽 2, 10, 36, 37, 42, 167n32; as capital, 26–27, 34, 59, 60, 78, 101; destruction of, 15, 16; and Shi Hu, 28, 31, 61, 84
Luoyi 雒邑 38n105
"Lyrics on the Autumn Wind" ("Qiufeng ci" 秋風辭; Emperor Wu of Han) 71n85, 167n30

Ma Dai 馬戴 128–29
Mandate of Heaven 24, 91n52, 92, 95, 99, 141n49, 152, 153n77
"Marvelous!" ("Shanzai xing" 善哉行; Cao Pi) 70–73
"Meditation on the Past in the City of Ye" ("Yecheng huaigu" 鄴城懷古; Zhang Zhidong) 175–76
Mei Yaochen 梅堯臣 122n10, 149
Mencius 170
Menglao 孟勞 sword 143n52
Min, Emperor (Jin) 晉愍帝 (Sima Ye 司馬鄴) 78n1
Ming, Emperor 明帝. See Cao Rui
Moye 莫邪 112n105
Mu, Duke of Qin 秦穆公 49n16
Murong Jun 慕容儁 1, 78, 101; dream of, 33–34, 175n53, 176
Murong Ping 慕容評 33
Murong Wei 慕容暐 (Emperor You 幽帝) 34

Naixian 乃賢 41n116
Niu Runzhen 牛潤珍 14, 44
Northern Dynasties 北朝 10. See also Southern and Northern dynasties
Northern Qi 北齊 dynasty 115, 117, 119, 176; and inkstones, 134, 135; Ye as capital of, 1, 27, 36, 40, 42, 43, 78
Northern Song 北宋 dynasty 139
Northern Wei 北魏 dynasty 36, 39, 100–102, 117
Northern Zhou 北周 dynasty 42, 43, 44, 117

Ōji Oka 岡大路 57n43
"Old Tile Inkstones" ("Gu wa yan" 古瓦硯; Ouyang Xiu) 136–37
"On Literature" (Cao Pi) 45–46
Ouyang Xiu 歐陽修 136–37, 140–43, 145

Owen, Stephen   55n37, 104, 116n115

palace women laments (*gongyuan shi* 宮怨詩; palace-resentment poetry) 120–21

parks   23, 57, 58–68, 75n100. *See also* Bronze Bird Park; Fanglin Park; gardens

Pei Songzhi 裴松之   55, 59, 60, 167n33, 170n38

Pei Yin 裴駰   74n97, 75n103

Penglai 蓬萊 Palace   129n22, 130

"Performers of the Bronze Bird" ("Tongjue ji" 銅爵妓; Jiang Yan)   111–13

"Performers of the Bronze Bird" ("Tongque ji" 銅雀妓; He Xun)   103–4

"Performers of the Bronze Bird" ("Tongque ji" 銅雀妓; Liu Xiaochuo)   106–7

"Performers of the Bronze Bird" ("Tongque ji" 銅雀妓; Zhang Zhengjian)   110–11

Ping, Duke of Jin 晉平公   72

Pingcheng 平城   101

place: *habitus* of   176; metaphors of, 3, 4, 5, 121, 125, 126, 128, 162, 178

"Pleased by the Clearing Up" ("Xiji fu" 喜霽賦; Cao Pi, Cao Zhi)   99n74

"Poem Composed on the Furong Pond" ("Furong chi zuo shi" 芙蓉作詩; Cao Pi)   67–69

"Poem Composed on the Xuanwu Bank" ("Yu Xuanwu bei zuo shi" 於玄武陂作詩; Cao Pi)   63–64

"Poem on Criticizing Myself" ("Zegong shi" 責躬詩; Cao Zhi)   111n104

"Poem on Furong Pond" ("Furong chi shi" 芙蓉池詩; Cao Zhi)   69

"Poem on Stopping by the Former Ye" ("Guo gu Ye shi" 過故鄴詩; Duan Junyan)   162–63

"Poem on the Bronze Bird Park" ("Tongque yuan shi" 銅雀園詩; Cao Pi)   70–73

poetic traces (*shiji* 詩跡)   125, 126, 128; and historical traces, 121–22, 127; and inkstones, 149; in later poems, 162, 166, 171

poetry: autumn theme in   104, 108, 112, 113–14, 125, 129, 130, 167; courtly feast (*Gongyan shi* 公燕詩), 23; eulogy (*songshi* 頌詩), 50; on gardens, 77, 156, 157; in Jian'an literature, 1–5, 45–77; Jin, 5, 79–100;

palace-resentment (*gongyuan shi* 宮怨詩), 120–21; post-Song/Yuan, 159–78; Southern and Northern-dynasty, 100–116; Tang, 120–30; on terraces, 46–56, 156, 157; "written at imperial command" (*yingzhao shi* 應詔詩), 50; *yongwu* 詠物, 140, 161; Yuan, 146, 152–55

"Preface to *fu* on the Bronze Bird Terrace" ("Tongque tai youxu" 銅雀臺有序; Liu Shen)   152–54

Qi 齊 dynasty   115

Qiao 橋 sisters   51–53, 55, 56

Qiao 譙 (city)   26, 27n71

Qidou Tower 齊斗樓 (Ye)   30

Qin, First Emperor of 秦始皇   14, 15, 27n72, 32

"Qin Prince Rolls Robes" ("Qin wang juanyi" 秦王卷衣)   80n6

Qin 秦, state of   14

Qing 清 dynasty   4, 159

Quan Tang shi 全唐詩   122–23

Rabbit Garden 兔園 (East Park 東苑)   66n69

Ran Min 冉閔 (Shi Min 石閔)   33, 35, 36, 82n14

Ran Wei 冉魏 dynasty   27, 33

Ran Zhan 冉瞻   82n14

"Record of Music" ("Yueji" 樂記; *Liji*)   71n85

"Red Cliff" ("Chibi" 赤壁; Du Mu)   55–56, 139

Red Cliffs, Battle of (Chibi *zhi zhan* 赤壁之戰)   53, 169, 171, 174

"Register of Inkstones" ("Yanpu" 硯譜; Ouyang Xiu)   136

Renzong 仁宗, Emperor (Tang)   122n10

"Resentment at the Bronze Bird Terrace" ("Quetai yuan" 雀臺怨; Ma Dai)   128–29

"Rhapsody on the Southern Capital" ("Nandu fu" 南都賦; Zhang Heng)   75n102

"Rhapsody on the Tall Gate Palace" ("Changmen fu" 長門賦; Sima Xiangru)   74n94

"Rhapsody on the Wei Capital" (*Wei du fu* 魏都賦; Zuo Si)   85n24

"Roaming the Three Terraces" ("Yu santai" 遊三臺; Yuan Haowen)   164–75

INDEX

Said, Edward W. 116n115

San guo zhi 25, 56, 57, 58; on Bronze Bird Terrace, 47, 52, 99; on Cao Cao, 55, 173

Sanfu jiushi 三輔舊事 31n85

Sanguo pinghua 三國平話 50, 51–52

Sanguo yanyi 三國演義 (Luo Guanzhong) 50–51, 52

Schafer, Edward H. 163n17

"Seeing off the Yings" ("Song Yingshi" 送應氏; Cao Zhi) 159n3

"Seven Inducements" ("Qi qi" 七啟; Cao Zhi) 73n91, 76n105

"Seven-fold Sorrows" ("Qi ai shi" 七哀詩; Wang Can) 15

Shang shu 尚書 42n120

Shang 商 dynasty 37n104, 92n54

Shanyang, Duke of 山陽公 58n46

Shao Buyi 邵不疑 135

Shaohu 召虎 142n51

Shen Quanqi 沈佺期 123, 124

Shi Hong 石弘 28

Shi Hu 石虎 13, 78, 100, 101, 115n112, 162n15; and Hualin Park, 60–61; and Luoyang, 28, 31, 61, 84; in Murong Jun's dream, 33–34, 176; and women, 79–85; Ye as capital of, 1, 5, 28–35

Shi ji 詩紀 14n27, 31n85, 74n97, 75n103

Shi Jian 石鑒 35

Shi Jilong 石季龍 31n85

Shi Le 石勒 7n2, 28, 32

Shi Min 石閔 (Ran Min 冉閔) 33, 35, 36, 82n14

Shi Qi 史起 12, 13, 17, 101

Shi Shi 石世 33

Shi Sui 石邃 83

Shi Zun 石遵 33, 83

Shijing 詩經 23n58, 43n122, 53n28, 75nn98–99, 122n10, 143n53; and Jin poetry, 92n54, 93n59; and Southern and Northern dynasty poetry, 113n108, 113n110

"Short Song" ("Duange xing" 短歌行; Cao Cao) 104, 105, 110n102, 169–70, 172, 174

Shu 蜀, state of 51

Shuijing zhu 水經注 (Xie Chengren, comp.) 13n23, 17, 18, 25, 26, 27n71, 46n4, 61; on Shi Hu 29, 30

Shuoyuan 說苑 (Liu Xiang) 91n53

Sima Shi 司馬師 141n50

Sima Teng 司馬騰, 162n14

Sima Xiangru 司馬相如 67n71, 74n94, 90n49

Sima Yan 司馬炎 151n71

Sima Yi 司馬懿 141n50

Sima Ying 司馬穎 (Prince of Chengdu 成都王) 86, 97

Sima Zhao 司馬昭 141n50

Sima Zhen 司馬貞 31n85

Sima Ziqi 司馬子綦 91n53

Sixteen States 五胡十六國 period 28

"Snapping the Willow" ("Zhe yangliu xing" 折楊柳行; Cao Pi) 68

"Song in Responding to Xie Jingshan's Gift of an Ancient Tile Inkstone" ("Da Xie Jingshan yi gu wayan ge" 答謝景山遺古瓦硯歌; Ouyang Xiu) 140–43

"Song of a Painting" ("Danqing yin: Zeng Cao jiangjun Ba" 丹青引贈曹將軍霸; Du Fu) 164n22

"Song of Cherry Zheng" ("Zheng Yingtao ge" 鄭櫻桃歌; Li Qi) 79–85

"Song of Everlasting Sorrow" ("Changhen ge" 長恨歌; Bai Juyi) 159n2

"Song of Reproach" ("Yuange xing" 怨歌行; Lady Ban) 108n97, 130

"Song of the Locals of Ye" ("Yemin ge" 鄴民歌) 14

"Song on Golden Bronze Transcendent Taking Leave of the Han" ("Jintong xianren ci Han ge" 金銅仙人辭漢歌; Li He) 166–68

Song Zhiwen 宋之問 123

Song 宋 dynasty: inkstones in 132, 134, 135, 154–55; Southern 南, 123–25, 148; views of Cao Cao in, 124, 146–48, 155, 158

"Sorrow the Bronze Bird" ("Tongque bei" 銅雀悲; Xie Tiao) 109–10

Southern and Northern dynasties 南北朝 3, 100–116, 117; Bronze Bird Terrace in, 101–3, 115, 116

"Spring Gaze" ("Chun wang" 春望; Du Fu) 127n20

Standard Treatises (Dianlun lunwen 典論・論文; Cao Pi) 45–46

Steinhardt, Nancy 20–21, 42

"Stopping by the Grave of Chen Lin" ("Guo Chen Lin mu" 過陳琳墓; Wen Tingyun) 177–78

208 INDEX

Su Che 蘇轍 11
Su Jui-lung 蘇瑞隆 48n9
Su Shi 蘇軾 (Su Dongpo 蘇東坡) 169,
    172n45, 174, 177; on Cao Cao, 124, 146n57,
    147–48, 158; and Ye tiles, 11, 137, 149
Su Shunqin 蘇舜欽 122n10
Su Wu 蘇武 138n38
Su Yijian 蘇易簡 132
Sui shu 隋書 79, 118
Sui 隋 dynasty 1, 117–20
Sun Ce 孫策 55
Sun Quan 孫權 51, 53, 56, 141n48, 153n77

Taiping yulan 太平御覽 101
Taiwu, Emperor 太武帝 (Tuoba Dao 拓拔燾;
    Northern Wei) 100–101
Taiwu Hall 太武殿 (Ye) 29–30, 34
Tang Taizong 唐太宗 165, 176n57
Tang 唐 dynasty 120–23, 125–27, 128, 132, 135
Teng, Prince 滕王 (Li Yuanying 李元嬰)
    165, 171
terrace-scapes 5, 103, 104, 108–13, 125, 157, 168
"Testamentary Command" ("Yiling" 遺令;
    Cao Cao) 54, 146n56, 148, 153, 158, 175; on
    Bronze Bird performers, 107, 109, 114, 121,
    157, 168
Three Kingdoms 三國 53, 78, 99, 114, 115,
    143, 145
Three Terraces 三臺 10, 126n16, 144; and
    Cao Cao, 3, 16, 17, 19, 43; changes to, 43–44;
    in Jian'an literature, 45–56, 57, 65, 73, 76,
    77; in Jin poetry, 87; in later poetry, 164–75;
    ruins of, 3, 56; and Shi Hu, 28, 31; in
    Southern and Northern dynasty poetry,
    103, 115. *See also* Bronze Bird Terrace;
    Golden Tiger Terrace; Ice Well Terrace
Tian Chou 田疇 25
"Tile from Bronze Bird Terrace" ("Tongque tai
    wa" 銅雀臺瓦; He Wei) 144–46
"Treatise of Astronomy" (*Tianwen zhi*
    天文志; *Jin shu*) 92nn57–58
Tuoba Dao 拓拔燾 (Emperor Taiwu
    太武帝) 100–101
Tuoba Hong 拓拔宏. *See* Xiaowen, Emperor
Twelve Weirs (*Shier qu* 十二堰; Weirs of
    Heaven's Well; Tianjing *yan* 天井堰) 12,
    13, 16

Wang Anshi 王安石 133–34
Wang Bo 王勃 123, 124, 165, 166
Wang Can 王粲 15–16, 50, 73n90, 172, 175
Wang Chen 王沈 58
Wang Dun 王敦 172n44, 174
Wang Ji 王濟 159n1
Wang Jian 王翦 14, 123
Wang Shihan 汪師韓 19
Wang Shizhen 王士禎 132, 134, 135–36
Wang Wenshu 王文叔 137
Wang Wujing 王無兢 123
Wang Zhaojun 王昭君 120
Wang Zun 汪遵 123
Wei, Duke of (Wei *gong* 魏公). *See* Cao Cao
"Wei Capital Rhapsody" 魏都賦 (Zuo Si) 1
Wei shu 魏書 (Wang Chen) 58, 170n38
Wei Xiaokuan 韋孝寬 117
Wei Zheng 魏徵 176n57
Wen, Duke of Jin 晉文公 49n16
Wen, Emperor (Han) 漢文帝 141n45
Wen, Emperor (Sui) 隋文帝 117
Wen, Emperor (Wei) 魏文帝. *See* Cao Pi
Wen, King of Zhou 周文王 52n27, 153n77
Wen, Marquis of Wei 魏文侯 12, 13, 17
Wen Tianxiang 文天祥 146
Wen Tingyun 溫庭筠 78, 177–78
Wen xuan 文選 23n58, 105
Wenchang Hall (Wenchang dian 文昌殿)
    23, 26, 29, 32, 48n12, 65, 85, 98
Wenfang sipu 文房四譜 (Su Yijian) 132
Wenxuan, Emperor 文宣帝 (Gao Yang 高洋;
    Northern Qi) 36, 78, 115, 135n32, 162n15
Wenxuan lixue quanyu 文選理學權輿 19
West Garden. *See* Bronze Bird Park
"Western Capital Rhapsody" ("Xijing fu" 西京
    賦; Ban Gu) 74n95
Western Park (*Xi yuan* 西園) 23
Western Wei 西魏 dynasty 39
women: abandoned 5, 120–21, 125, 126, 157;
    and Bronze Bird Terrace, 5, 51, 103–7,
    110–13, 120–26, 128–29, 142, 148, 152, 153,
    157, 168; Qiao 橋 sisters, 51–53, 55, 56; and
    Shi Hu, 79–85; in Southern and Northern
    dynasty poetry, 102, 103, 104, 114; voices of,
    103, 106–9, 111
"Worrying about the Ceaseless Rain"
    ("Choulin fu" 愁霖賦; Cao Pi, Cao Zhi)
    99n74

INDEX

"Written from Rang County, Clarifying My Own Ambitions" ("Rangxian ziming benzhi ling" 讓縣自明本志令; Cao Cao) 170
Wu, Emperor (Jin) 晉武帝 86
Wu, Emperor 武帝 (Northern Zhou) 42–43
Wu, Emperor (Han) 漢武帝 71n85, 167nn28–30; dew-catching plate of, 59–60, 167n33, 171, 172, 173
Wu, King of Wei. *See* Cao Cao
Wu, King of Zhou 周武王 153n77
Wu Fusheng 吳伏生 50
Wu 吳, state of 51, 96–97, 100
Wuyi Lane gathering (*Wuyi zhi you* 烏衣之游) 66

Xiahou Dun 夏侯惇 153n77
Xian, Emperor (Han) 漢獻帝 (Liu Xie 劉協) 15, 19, 58n46, 141n46, 151n70
Xianbei 鮮卑 people 33, 36
Xiang, Duke of Song 宋襄公 49n16
Xiang, King of Wei 魏襄王 12, 17
Xiang Yu 項羽 164n19
Xiangguo 襄國 (city) 28
Xianwu, Emperor 獻武帝 (Gao Huan; Northern Qi) 1, 36–37, 38, 41n116, 78, 173
Xiao, Prince of Liang 梁孝王 66n69
Xiaojing, Emperor 孝靜帝 (Yuan Shanjian 元善見; Eastern Wei) 1, 36, 78, 135n32, 137, 138n37
Xiaoming, Emperor 孝明帝 (Northern Wei) 38n107
Xiaowen, Emperor 孝文帝 (Tuoba Hong 拓拔宏; Northern Wei) 36, 38, 101–2
Xiaowu, Emperor 孝武帝 (Northern Wei) 36, 37
Xie Cheng 謝承 31n85
Xie Chengren 謝承仁 18
Xie Fei 解飛 31
Xie Jian 解建 8
Xie Jing 謝璟 104, 109
Xie Tiao 謝朓 104, 107, 109–10
Ximen Bao 西門豹 9, 12, 13, 17, 101
Xin Shu 辛術 39
Xin Tang shu 新唐書 79
Xingyang, Princess 滎陽公主 86
Xiongnu 匈奴 people 28n73, 138n38
Xishu 義叔 75n103

Xizhong 義仲 75n103
Xu Gan 徐幹 73n90
Xu Guangji 徐光冀 9
Xu Xuan 徐鉉 132–33
Xu Yi 許顗 (Hsü Yen-chou) 55n37
Xu Yuchao 徐玉超 7
Xuan, Emperor 宣帝 (Northern Zhou) 44
Xuan, King of Qi 齊宣王 170
Xuan, King of Zhou 周宣王 142n51
Xuanwu Park 玄武苑 57, 61–62, 63–65, 75n100
Xuanwu Reservoir (Xuanwu *chi* 玄武池) 16, 57, 61, 75n101
Xuchang 許昌 (city) 26, 27n71
Xue Neng 薛能 123
Xun Yu 荀彧 154
Xun Zhongju 荀仲舉 107–9

Yan Shigu 顏師古 58n47, 140n43
Yang, Emperor (Sui) 隋煬帝 117
Yang Duan 楊端 14
Yang Jian 楊堅 1, 5, 44, 103, 117, 118–19, 127, 163
Yang Tingling 楊廷齡 133
Yang Xiu 楊修 73n90
Yang Yi 楊億 132–33
Yang Yue 陽約 34
Yaoli 要離 80n9
Ye Xiaojun 葉驍軍 10, 20
Ye 鄴, city of (Linzhang 臨漳 Hebei 河北): administrative problems of 118–20; archeological finds from, 7–11, 45; Cao Cao's identification with, 44, 156–58; Cao Cao's reconstruction of ,16–26; celebration of, 4–5, 44, 56, 78, 99, 100, 103, 116, 128, 155, 156; and city planning, 1, 9, 10, 21–22, 45; cultural life in, 24; destruction of, 1, 42–44; as dynastic capital, 78–116; early history of, 1, 11–16; four quadrants of, 23, 26; gates of, 21, 23, 26, 35, 42n117, 81n11, 83, 85; lamentation for, 5, 44, 56, 77, 78, 100, 103, 116, 128, 155, 157, 163, 166, 171; later history of, 1, 26–45; moats around, 25, 42; name of, 1n1; palace complex in, 20–21, 26, 65, 73, 163n17; physical development of, 7–44; plans of, 18, 20, 40, 41; population of, 24, 25; southern city of (Ye *nancheng* 鄴南城), 1, 27, 39–40, 41n116, 134–36, 173;

210 INDEX

Ye 鄴, city of (cont.)
  studies of, 1–2; tiles (Ye *wa* 鄴瓦) from, 4,
    5–6, 11, 130–55, 157–58, 161, 162
Yellow River 黃河   12–14, 17, 31–32, 37, 126n17
Yezhong ji 鄴中記 (Lu Hui)   12–13, 41nn116,
  60, 79, 82n13, 134, 135; on Shi Hu, 29–30, 83,
  84, 85
Yin Kui 殷尰   173
Ying Zhu 嬴柱, King Xiaowen 孝文王   80n6
Ying Zichu 嬴子楚, King Zhuangxiang
  莊襄王   80n6
Yingqiu 營丘 (Linzi 臨淄)   37n105
Yiwen leiju 藝文類聚   48n8, 49n17, 71n88,
  93n60
You, Emperor 幽帝 (Murong Wei 慕容暐;
  Former Yan)   34
Yu, Master 虞公   108n96
Yu Fu 虞溥   55
Yu Weichao 俞偉超   10
Yuan Aixia 袁愛俠   116n115
Yuan Haowen 元好問   78, 164–66, 168–71,
  173–75
Yuan Jie 元結   135
Yuan Shang 袁尚   16, 25
Yuan Shanjian 元善見. *See* Xiaojing, Emperor
Yuan Shao 袁紹   16, 141n48, 173, 176, 177
Yuan Shu 袁術   140n44, 141n48
Yuan Tan 袁譚   16, 25
Yuan 元 dynasty: conquest by   164, 175;
  views of Cao Cao in, 146, 152–55
Yuanwu Park 元武苑 (Xuanwu Park)   57n43
Yuchi Jiong 尉遲迴   44, 117
Yunyu yangqiu 韻語陽秋 (Ge Lifang)   123–
  24

Zhang Heng 張衡   60n51, 75n102, 90n46

Zhang Mi 張彌   31
Zhang Qian 張騫   138n36
Zhang Qinnan 張欽楠   20
Zhang Qun 張群   61
Zhang River 漳水   12–15, 17; in later poems,
  171, 173, 174, 175; in Tang poetry, 122n10, 126,
  127, 128
Zhang Shoujie 張守節   31n85
Zhang Xuchen 章序臣   144
Zhang Zhengjian 張正見   110–11, 124
Zhang Zhidong 張之洞   175–76, 177, 178
Zhangde fu zhi 彰德府志   23n57, 28, 58, 60,
  134
Zhangsun Ping 長孫平   118
Zhao, King of Chu 楚昭王   91n53
Zhao Feng 趙豐   82n13
Zhao Wen 趙文   146, 148, 149
Zhao Youwen 趙幼文   48n12, 73n90,
  75nn100–101
Zhao 趙, state of   14
Zheng Xuan 鄭玄   76n106, 92n54
Zheng Yin 鄭愔   123–24
Zhou, King of Shang 商紂王   52n27, 101n79
Zhou Guanghuang 周廣璜   48n9
Zhou Weiquan 周維權   61n56
Zhou Yiliang 周一良   62
Zhou Yu 周瑜   51–52, 53, 55, 56
Zhou 周 dynasty   21, 52n27, 142n51, 153n77
Zhu Biliang 朱碧蓮   55n37
Zhu Heping 朱和平   120
Zhu Yanshi 朱岩石   9, 40n116
Zhuang, King of Chu 楚莊王   49n16
Zhuangzi 莊子   48n11, 68–69, 85
Zhuge Liang 諸葛亮   51–52, 53
Zizhi tongjian 資治通鑑   34n94, 119
Zuo Si 左思   1, 13, 61–62, 64, 85n24

Printed in the United States
By Bookmasters